W9-BSR-144

Taste of Home prize winning RECIPES

Executive Editor, Books: Heidi Reuter Lloyd
Senior Book Editor: Mark Hagen
Project Editor: Julie Schnittka
Art Director: Gretchen Trautman
Contributing Art Director: Nicole Trapp
Editorial Assistant: Barb Czysz
Proofreaders: Linne Bruskewitz, Jean Steiner
Associate Food Editors: Coleen Martin, Diane Werner
Senior Recipe Editor: Sue A. Jurack
Recipe Editor: Mary King
Test Kitchen Assistants: Rita Krajcir, Megan Taylor
Senior Food Photographer: Rob Hagen
Food Photographers: Dan Roberts, Jim Wieland
Associate Food Photographer: Lori Foy
Set Stylist: Jennifer Bradley Vent
Set Stylist Assistant: Melissa Haberman
Senior Food Stylist: Joylyn Trickel
Food Stylist: Sarah Thompson
Photo Studio Coordinator: Suzanne Kern
Contributing Food Stylists: Diane Armstrong,
Suzanne Beckenridge, Sue Draheim, Mary Franz,
Julie Herzfeldt, Jennifer Janz, Jim Rude
Contributing Set Stylists: Stephanie Marchese,
Julie Ferron, Nancy Seaman, Grace Natoli Sheldon,
Gail Engeldahl
Creative Director: Ardyth Cope
Senior Vice President, Editor in Chief: Catherine Cassidy
President: Barbara Newton
Founder: Roy Reiman

Pictured on the front cover: Tangy Beef Brisket (p. 5), Orange Avocado Salad (p. 181) and Frosty Lemon Pie (p. 276).
Pictured on the back cover: Pear Custard Bars (p. 245) and Pork and Pear Stir-Fry (p. 246).

Taste of Home Books
©2006 Reiman Media Group, Inc.
5400 S. 60th St., Greendale WI 53129
International Standard Book Number: 0-89821-550-1
Library of Congress Control Number: 2006931720
Printed in U.S.A.

your single source for
438 of our very best recipes!

WHEN we launched *Taste of Home* magazine—and its "sister" publications, *Country Woman* and *Simple & Delicious*—we wanted them to be better than any other food magazines on the market. We knew the best way to attract and keep readers was to focus on down-home foods that cooks across the country enjoyed in their *own* kitchens.

So that's what we did...and continue to do today. Each and every issue of those three cooking magazines is packed with fantastic, *family-approved* recipes.

But what makes these publications even more special is that in each issue we hold a national contest asking our readers to share their very best recipes. After sorting through *millions* of entries, testing in our kitchens and tasting by a panel of judges, a Grand Prize Winner as well as runners-up are selected for each contest. Only a select few from each contest earn the "prize winning" title...and now they're right at your fingertips.

With 438 winning recipes from dozens of our national contests, *Taste of Home's Prize Winning Recipes* will become a treasured cookbook in your kitchen for years to come.

Is your family tired of the same old chicken dishes? Turn to page 26 and check out the winners of our Choice Chicken Recipes contest, including Sweet Gingered Chicken Wings, Cheesy Chicken Chowder...and Grand Prize Winner Nutty Oven-Fried Chicken.

For a satisfying, stick-to-your-ribs dinner, reach for Beef Stew with Potato Dumplings. (This Grand Prize Winner of our Meat-and-Potato Combos can be found on page 53.)

Busy cooks will really appreciate the convenience of Slow-Cooked Specialties—with winner Tangy Pork Chops—and the 5-Ingredient Recipes contest, highlighting tasty Taco Puffs.

Chocolate Malted Cookies...Chunky Blonde Brownies...Sunshine Sherbet...Lemon Supreme Pie...Rich Truffle Wedges...Carrot Layer Cake. These winners from our six dessert contests (beginning on page 260) will ensure happy endings at any meal!

Hungry yet? That's just a small sample of the mouth-watering recipes featured in this timeless treasury. (Check out the complete listing of contests on the facing page.)

With 438 winning recipes—and a color photo of each and every dish—*Taste of Home's Prize Winning Recipes* will help make you a winner, too!

For additional copies of this book, write *Taste of Home* Books, P.O. Box 908, Greendale WI 53129. Or to order by credit card, call toll-free 1-800/344-2560 or visit our Web site at **www.reimanpub.com**.

p. 118 p. 89 p. 216 p. 85

Table of "Contests"

p. 80 p. 166 p. 293 p. 215

BEEFING IT UP

#1

TANGY BEEF BRISKET

tangy beef brisket

Chances are when you plan a meal, you first think of meat, and none whets an
appetite more than beef. So it's no surprise the "Steaks" were high in *Country Woman's* Beefing
It Up contest...and so were
the roasts, ribs, tenderloins
and briskets.

Whether roasted, broiled,
pan-fried, slow-cooked or barbecued, all had our testers
raving for days over their "must-try" juicy, fork-tender taste.

From hundreds of prime possibilities, our judges narrowed the field to a few
choice dishes. Finally, they concurred on a cut-above entree—Tangy Beef Brisket
was chosen as the Grand Prize Winner.

"The secret's in the sauce," says Jacque Watkins from Green River, Wyoming.
"The sweetness of brown sugar and bite of horseradish don't disguise the flavor of the
meat—in fact, they enhance it. The meat is so juicy and tender, everyone requests seconds."

"The meat is so juicy and tender, everyone requests seconds."

1 large onion, diced
1/2 cup butter
1 bottle (28 ounces) ketchup
1-1/2 cups packed brown sugar
1/2 cup Worcestershire sauce
1/3 cup lemon juice
2 tablespoons chili powder
1-1/2 teaspoons hot pepper sauce
1 teaspoon prepared horseradish
1 teaspoon salt
1/2 teaspoon garlic powder
1 boneless beef brisket (6 pounds)

In a saucepan, saute onion in butter until tender. Add the next nine ingredients; bring to a boil. Reduce heat; simmer, uncovered, for 30-40 minutes.

Place brisket in a roasting pan. Add 3 cups of sauce. Cover and bake at 350° for 4 hours, basting occasionally. Skim fat. Remove brisket; thinly slice the beef and return to pan. Add remaining sauce if desired. **Yield:** 12-14 servings (6 cups sauce).

Editor's Note: This is a fresh beef brisket, not corned beef.

BEEFING IT UP

#1

BEEF AND
ASPARAGUS
STIR-FRY

beef and asparagus stir-fry
GRAND PRIZE WINNER

If you're at home by the range, you'll have no problem rustlin' up a delicious dinner for your crew when you rely on the roundup of award-winning recipes from *Taste of Home's* beef contest.

This collection was selected from more than 3,600 recipes for roasts, steaks, ribs and more shared by great cooks from coast to coast.

"...this mouth-watering stir-fry was designated 'a keeper' by my husband the first time I made it."

Our judges had the tricky but tasty job of choosing the winners. Now, when you cook any of these satisfying beef recipes, your hungry herd will stampede to the table!

Beef and Asparagus Stir-Fry was selected as the Grand Prize Winner. "With tender slices of beef and fresh, colorful vegetables, this mouth-watering stir-fry was designated 'a keeper' by my husband the first time I made it," says JoLynn Hill of Roosevelt, Utah. "He loves beef and asparagus, and I appreciate how simple this dish is to make."

 2 tablespoons cornstarch
 2 tablespoons plus 1/2 cup water, *divided*
 1/2 teaspoon salt
 1/4 teaspoon pepper
 1/8 teaspoon hot pepper sauce
 1 pound boneless round steak (3/4 inch thick)
 3 tablespoons vegetable oil, *divided*
 2 cups fresh asparagus pieces *or* broccoli florets
 1 cup sliced cauliflower
 1 small sweet red *or* green pepper, julienned
 1 small onion, cut into 1/4-inch wedges
 2 teaspoons beef bouillon granules
 1 tablespoon soy sauce
 1 tablespoon ketchup
 1 teaspoon red wine vinegar
Hot cooked rice

Combine cornstarch, 2 tablespoons water, salt, pepper and hot pepper sauce. Slice beef into thin 3-in. strips; toss with the cornstarch mixture.

In a large skillet or wok over medium-high heat, stir-fry half of the beef in 1 tablespoon oil until cooked as desired; remove from the skillet. Repeat with the remaining beef and 1 tablespoon oil.

Stir-fry the asparagus and cauliflower in remaining oil for 4 minutes. Add red pepper and onion; stir-fry for 2 minutes. Return beef to skillet.

Combine the bouillon, soy sauce, ketchup, vinegar and remaining water; add to the skillet. Cook and stir for 2 minutes or until heated through. Serve over rice. **Yield:** 6 servings.

party beef casserole

Kelly Hardgrave, Hartman, Arkansas
Round steak is economical and delicious. That's why I was thrilled to find the recipe for this comforting, meal-in-one casserole. With a salad and rolls, it's an inexpensive, hearty dinner.

- 3 tablespoons all-purpose flour
- 1 teaspoon salt
- 1/2 teaspoon pepper
- 2 pounds boneless round steak, cut into 1/2-inch cubes
- 2 tablespoons vegetable oil
- 1 cup water
- 1/2 cup beef broth
- 1 garlic clove, minced
- 1 tablespoon dried minced onion
- 1/2 teaspoon dried thyme
- 1/4 teaspoon dried rosemary, crushed
- 2 cups sliced fresh mushrooms
- 2 cups frozen peas, thawed
- 3 cups mashed potatoes (mashed with milk and butter)
- 1 tablespoon butter, melted

Paprika

In a large resealable plastic bag, combine flour, salt and pepper; add beef cubes and shake to coat. In a skillet, brown beef in oil over medium heat. Place beef and drippings in a greased shallow 2-1/2-qt. baking dish.

To skillet, add water, broth, garlic, onion, thyme and rosemary; bring to a boil. Simmer, uncovered, for 5 minutes; stir in mushrooms. Pour over meat; mix well.

Cover and bake at 350° for 1-1/2 to 1-3/4 hours or until the beef is tender. Sprinkle peas over the meat. Spread potatoes evenly over the top. Brush with butter; sprinkle with paprika. Bake 15-20 minutes longer. **Yield:** 6-8 servings.

scott's beef brisket

Scott Post, Clayton, North Carolina
My brother and I made special grills to cook 20 briskets at a time for parties. I created this recipe to achieve a similar fork-tender brisket using the oven.

- 1/2 teaspoon *each* sugar, onion powder, seasoned salt, garlic powder, paprika, chili powder and ground allspice
- 1/4 teaspoon pepper
- 1 fresh beef brisket (3 to 4 pounds)
- 1/2 cup cola
- 1/3 cup Worcestershire sauce
- 1/2 cup cider vinegar
- 1/2 cup butter, melted
- 1/3 cup soy sauce
- 3/4 cup barbecue sauce

Additional barbecue sauce, optional

Combine the dry seasonings; cover and set aside. Place brisket in a large resealable plastic bag. Combine cola and Worcestershire sauce; pour over meat. Seal bag and turn to coat; refrigerate overnight.

Drain meat; discard marinade. Rub seasoning mix over brisket; place in a large shallow roasting pan. Combine vinegar, butter and soy sauce; pour over meat. Cover and bake at 325° for 2 hours, basting occasionally. Drain drippings. Pour barbecue sauce over meat.

Cover and bake for 1 hour or until the meat is tender. Remove meat from pan; let stand for 15 minutes before slicing. Serve with additional barbecue sauce if desired. **Yield:** 6-8 servings.

Editor's Note: This is a fresh brisket, not corned beef.

peppered beef tenderloin

Margaret Ninneman, La Crosse, Wisconsin
When you're cooking for a crowd that really savors the flavor of beef, this peppery, tempting tenderloin is perfect! It's no fuss since it comes together quickly. It's important to let it rest for a few minutes before carving to allow the juices to work through the meat.

  1 teaspoon salt, optional
  1 teaspoon dried oregano
  1 teaspoon dried thyme
  1 teaspoon paprika
1/2 teaspoon garlic powder
1/2 teaspoon onion powder
1/2 teaspoon white pepper
1/2 teaspoon pepper
1/8 to 1/4 teaspoon cayenne pepper
  1 beef tenderloin (3 pounds)

Combine seasonings and rub over entire tenderloin. Place on a rack in a roasting pan.

Bake, uncovered, at 425° until meat is cooked as desired. Allow approximately 45-50 minutes for medium-rare or until a meat thermometer reads 145°, 62-65 minutes for medium (160°) and 67-70 minutes for well-done (170°). Let stand for 10 minutes before carving. **Yield:** 8-10 servings.

fabulous fajitas

Janie Reitz, Rochester, Minnesota
I've enjoyed cooking since I was a girl growing up in the Southwest. When friends call to ask me for new recipes to try, I suggest these flavorful fajitas. It's wonderful to put the beef in the slow cooker before church and come home to a hot, delicious main dish.

1-1/2 pounds boneless beef sirloin steak, cut into
      thin strips
    2 tablespoons vegetable oil
    2 tablespoons lemon juice
    1 garlic clove, minced
1-1/2 teaspoons ground cumin
    1 teaspoon seasoned salt
  1/2 teaspoon chili powder
  1/4 to 1/2 teaspoon crushed red pepper flakes
    1 large green pepper, julienned
    1 large onion, julienned
    6 to 8 flour tortillas (8 inches)
Shredded cheddar cheese, salsa, sour cream,
      lettuce and tomatoes, optional

In a skillet, brown the steak in oil over medium heat. Place steak and drippings in a 3-qt. slow cooker. Add lemon juice, garlic, cumin, salt, chili powder and red pepper flakes; mix well.

Cover and cook on high for 2-1/2 to 3 hours or until meat is almost tender. Add green pepper and onion; cover and cook for 1 hour or until meat and vegetables are tender.

Warm tortillas according to package directions; spoon beef and vegetables down the center of tortillas. Top each with cheese, salsa, sour cream, lettuce and tomatoes if desired. **Yield:** 6-8 servings.

stew with confetti dumplings

Lucile Cline, Wichita, Kansas

If you want a stew that will warm you to the bone, try this. My family particularly likes the dumplings.

- 2 pounds boneless chuck roast, cut into cubes
- 2 tablespoons vegetable oil
- 1/2 pound fresh mushrooms, halved
- 1 large onion, thinly sliced
- 1 garlic clove, minced
- 2 cans (14-1/2 ounces *each*) beef broth
- 1 teaspoon *each* Italian seasoning and salt
- 1/4 teaspoon pepper
- 1 bay leaf
- 1/3 cup all-purpose flour
- 1/2 cup water
- 1 package (10 ounces) frozen peas

DUMPLINGS:
- 1-1/2 cups biscuit/baking mix
- 2 tablespoons diced pimientos, drained
- 1 tablespoon minced chives
- 1/2 cup milk

In a Dutch oven, brown meat in oil. Add mushrooms, onion and garlic; cook until onion is tender, stirring occasionally. Stir in broth, Italian seasoning, salt, pepper and bay leaf; bring to a boil. Cover and simmer for 1-1/2 hours. Discard bay leaf. Combine the flour and water until smooth; stir into stew. Bring to a boil; cook and stir for 1 minute. Reduce heat. Stir in peas.

For dumplings, combine biscuit mix, pimientos and chives in a bowl. Stir in enough milk to form a soft dough. Drop by tablespoonfuls onto the simmering stew. Cover and simmer for 10-12 minutes or until dumplings test done (do not lift lid while simmering). Serve immediately. **Yield:** 10-12 servings (about 3 quarts).

old-fashioned pot roast

Georgia Edgington, Crystal, Minnesota

Every time I fix this recipe for friends, it's asked for—and usually by the husbands! As a mom who works full time, I also like how easy it is to prepare. It's one of our favorites. Some people I've shared the recipe with have used a beef brisket in place of the regular roast. For a bit different taste, I at times add red wine vinegar. My mom started me cooking young. I made my first from-scratch Thanksgiving dinner at age 13. After that, I figured I could tackle just about any cooking!

- 1 eye of round roast (3 to 4 pounds)
- 1 bottle (12 ounces) chili sauce
- 1 cup water
- 1 envelope onion soup mix
- 4 medium potatoes, cut into 1-inch pieces
- 5 medium carrots, cut into 1-inch pieces
- 2 celery ribs, cut into 1-inch pieces

Place roast in an ungreased roasting pan. Combine the chili sauce, water and onion soup mix; pour over roast. Cover and bake at 350° for 2 hours.

Cut roast into 1/2-in. slices; return to pan. Top with potatoes, carrots and celery. Cover and bake 1 hour longer or until vegetables are tender, stirring the vegetables once. **Yield:** 8 servings.

pasta salad with steak

Julie DeRuwe, Oakville, Washington

While there are quite a few ingredients in this recipe, it doesn't take too long to make—and cleanup afterward is a snap.

    3/4 cup olive oil
      2 tablespoons lemon juice
      2 teaspoons dried oregano
      1 tablespoon Dijon mustard
      2 teaspoons red wine vinegar
      1 teaspoon sugar
    1/2 teaspoon salt
    1/2 teaspoon pepper
      3 cups cooked small shell pasta
      1 boneless beef sirloin steak (1 pound)
RUB:
      1 tablespoon olive oil
      3 garlic cloves, minced
      2 teaspoons dried oregano
      2 teaspoons pepper
      1 teaspoon sugar
SALAD:
    2/3 cup diced cucumber
    1/2 cup crumbled blue *or* feta cheese
    1/4 cup sliced ripe olives
    1/4 cup chopped red onion
    1/4 cup minced fresh parsley
      1 jar (2 ounces) diced pimientos, drained
Iceberg *or* romaine lettuce

Combine the first eight ingredients; set half of the dressing aside. Place pasta in a bowl; add remaining dressing. Toss to coat; cover and refrigerate.

Pierce steak with a fork. Combine rub ingredients; rub over steak. Cover and refrigerate for at least 15 minutes. Grill steak, uncovered, over medium heat for 9-10 minutes on each side or until meat reaches desired doneness (for medium-rare, a meat thermometer should read 145°; medium, 160°; well-done, 170°). Let stand 10 minutes.

Meanwhile, add cucumber, cheese, olives, onion, parsley and pimientos to pasta; mix well. Spoon onto a lettuce-lined platter. Slice steak and arrange over salad. Serve with reserved dressing. **Yield:** 4 servings.

---

prize winning tips

✱ One way to tenderize flank steak is to score it. Make shallow crisscrossed diamond-shaped cuts on both sides of the meat before cooking it.

Margaret Herz, Hastings, Nebraska

✱ I often use a steak pinwheel recipe when I'm unsure about the number of dinner guests to expect. You can feed as few or as many as you like simply by adjusting the number you prepare.

Ellen Baird, Kennewick, Washington

✱ A can of carbonated cola will tenderize and add flavor to pot roast.

Pam Rush, Salina, Kansas

herbed pot roast

Christel McKinley, East Liverpool, Ohio
I prepare this delicious main dish several times a month. The herbs give the beef an excellent taste. Adding the onion, carrots and potatoes makes this a meal-in-one dish. My husband, Jack, a real meat-and-potatoes man, even enjoys the leftovers, which isn't always the case with other recipes.

  1 boneless beef rump *or* chuck roast
      (3 to 3-1/2 pounds)
  1 tablespoon vegetable oil
  1 teaspoon salt
  1 teaspoon dried marjoram
  1 teaspoon dried thyme
1/2 teaspoon garlic powder
1/2 teaspoon dried oregano
1/2 teaspoon pepper
  1 can (10-1/2 ounces) condensed beef broth
  8 carrots, cut into thirds
  8 medium potatoes, peeled and quartered
  1 large onion, quartered
  1 cup water

In a Dutch oven, brown roast in oil over medium heat. Combine the seasonings; sprinkle over meat. Add broth and bring to a boil.

Cover and bake at 325° for 2 hours, basting occasionally. Add carrots, potatoes, onion and water.

Cover and bake for 1 hour or until the vegetables are tender. Thicken the pan juices for gravy if desired. **Yield:** 8 servings.

southwestern stew

Linda Russell, Forest Lakes, Arizona
Romping in the national forest amid tall ponderosa pines around our home gives my husband and our two little boys big appetites. They really like this savory stew. Because I'm a busy firefighter, I often make it ahead and serve it when I need a meal in a hurry.

    2 pounds beef stew meat, cut into 1-inch cubes
    2 tablespoons vegetable oil
    2 cups water
1-1/4 cups chopped onion
    1 cup salsa
    2 garlic cloves, minced
    1 tablespoon dried parsley flakes
    2 teaspoons beef bouillon granules
    1 teaspoon ground cumin
  1/2 teaspoon salt
    3 medium carrots, cut into 1-inch pieces
    1 can (14-1/2 ounces) diced tomatoes,
        undrained
1-1/2 cups frozen cut green beans
1-1/2 cups frozen corn
    1 can (4 ounces) chopped green chilies
Hot pepper sauce, optional
Hot cooked rice, optional

In a 4-qt. Dutch oven, brown meat in oil over medium heat; drain. Add the next eight ingredients; bring to a boil. Reduce heat; cover and simmer for 1 hour. Add carrots; return to a boil.

Reduce heat and simmer for 20 minutes. Add tomatoes, beans, corn and chilies; return to a boil. Reduce heat; cover and simmer for 15-20 minutes or until beef and vegetables are tender. Season with hot pepper sauce if desired. Serve over rice if desired. **Yield:** 8 servings.

oven swiss steak

Lorna Dickau, Vanderhoof, British Columbia
I was really glad to find this recipe since it's a great way to use economical round steak and it picks up fabulous flavor from one of my favorite herbs—tarragon.

    8 bacon strips
    2 pounds round steak (3/4 inch thick)
    2 cups sliced fresh mushrooms
    1 can (14-1/2 ounces) diced tomatoes,
      undrained
  1/2 cup chopped onion
    1 to 2 teaspoons dried tarragon
    2 tablespoons cornstarch
    2 tablespoons water
    1 cup heavy whipping cream

In a large ovenproof skillet, cook bacon over medium heat until crisp. Remove to paper towels to drain, reserving 1/4 cup drippings. Crumble bacon and set aside. Trim beef; cut into serving-size pieces. Brown on both sides in drippings. Top meat with mushrooms, tomatoes and onion. Sprinkle with tarragon and bacon. Cover and bake at 325° for 1-1/4 to 1-3/4 hours or until meat is tender, basting twice.

Remove meat to a serving platter; keep warm. Combine cornstarch and water until smooth; add to skillet. Bring to a boil; cook and stir for 2 minutes or until thickened. Reduce heat; stir in cream. Simmer, uncovered, for 3-4 minutes or until heated through. Serve over meat. **Yield: 6-8 servings.**

marinated sirloin steak

Karren Mattern, Spokane, Washington
I once knew a nun who cooked the very best marinated steaks. I found this wonderful, easy recipe in my quest to fix steaks as good as hers. This delicious, versatile meat makes a special holiday main dish or a super camping supper. It always gets compliments.

    2 to 2-1/2 pounds boneless beef sirloin steak
      (about 1 inch thick)
1-1/2 cups water
  3/4 cup soy sauce
  1/4 cup Worcestershire sauce
    1 medium onion, chopped
    2 tablespoons white wine vinegar
    2 tablespoons lemon juice
    2 tablespoons Dijon mustard
    2 garlic cloves, minced
    2 teaspoons dried parsley flakes
    1 teaspoon dried thyme
    1 teaspoon Italian seasoning
    1 teaspoon pepper

Place steak in a large resealable plastic bag. Combine remaining ingredients; pour over the meat. Seal bag and turn to coat; refrigerate overnight.

Remove meat; discard marinade. Grill, uncovered, over medium heat for 6-7 minutes on each side or until meat reaches desired doneness (for medium-rare, a meat thermometer should read 145°; medium, 160°; well-done, 170°). **Yield:** 6 servings.

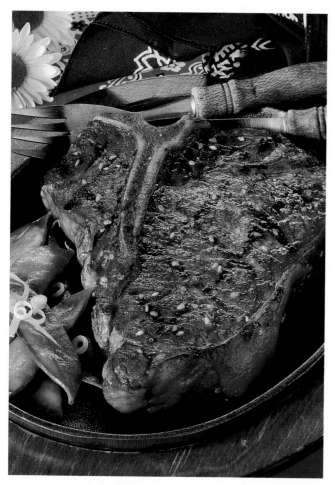

sesame steaks

Elaine Anderson, Aliquippa, Pennsylvania
There's enough flavor in these steaks to allow the side dish to be simple. So consider serving them with baked potatoes, rice pilaf or another plain vegetable and salad. The meal has always gone over big when I've fixed it for my husband and friends helping out with his latest home construction project.

> 1/2 cup soy sauce
> 2 tablespoons brown sugar
> 2 tablespoons vegetable oil
> 2 tablespoons sesame seeds
> 2 teaspoons onion powder
> 2 teaspoons lemon juice
> 1/4 teaspoon ground ginger
> 4 T-bone steaks (about 1 inch thick)

In a large resealable plastic bag or shallow glass container, combine the first seven ingredients; mix well. Add steaks and turn to coat. Cover and refrigerate for at least 4 hours.

Drain and discard marinade. Grill steaks, uncovered, over medium heat for 5-7 minutes on each side or until meat reaches desired doneness (for medium-rare, a meat thermometer should read 145°; medium, 160°; well-done, 170°). **Yield:** 4 servings.

sour cream swiss steak

Barb Benting, Grand Rapids, Michigan
One year, after we'd purchased half a beef from a local cattle raiser, I went on a full-scale search for new and different recipes. This is one I found—my family loved it from the very first bite. I've shared it with friends at work, too (I'm a waitress). They agree it's a nice change from regular Swiss steak.

> 1/3 cup all-purpose flour
> 1-1/2 teaspoons *each* salt, pepper, paprika and ground mustard
> 3 pounds boneless round steak, cut into serving-size pieces
> 3 tablespoons vegetable oil
> 3 tablespoons butter
> 1-1/2 cups water
> 1-1/2 cups (12 ounces) sour cream
> 1 cup finely chopped onion
> 2 garlic cloves, minced
> 1/3 cup soy sauce
> 1/4 to 1/3 cup packed brown sugar
> 3 tablespoons all-purpose flour
> **Additional paprika, optional**

In a shallow bowl, combine flour, salt, pepper, paprika and mustard; dredge the steak. In a large skillet, heat oil and butter. Cook steak on both sides until browned. Carefully add water; cover and simmer for 30 minutes.

In a bowl, combine the sour cream, onion, garlic, soy sauce, brown sugar and flour; stir until smooth. Transfer steak to a greased 2-1/2-qt. baking dish; add sour cream mixture. Cover and bake at 325° for 1-1/2 hours or until tender. Sprinkle with paprika if desired. **Yield:** 6-8 servings.

chicken-fried cube steaks

Toni Holcomb, Rogersville, Missouri
Here in the Ozarks, country-fried steak is a staple. These are wonderful served with mashed potatoes and some freshly baked rolls. I developed the recipe to meet the spicy tastes of my family.

2-1/2 cups all-purpose flour, *divided*
   2 tablespoons black pepper
   1 to 2 tablespoons white pepper
   2 tablespoons garlic powder
   1 tablespoon paprika
1-1/2 teaspoons salt
   1 teaspoon ground cumin
 1/4 to 1/2 teaspoon cayenne pepper
   2 cups buttermilk
   2 cans (12 ounces *each*) evaporated milk
   8 cube steaks (4 ounces *each*)
Oil for frying
   1 teaspoon Worcestershire sauce
Dash hot pepper sauce

In a shallow bowl, combine 2 cups flour and seasonings; set aside. In another bowl, combine buttermilk and evaporated milk. Remove 3-1/2 cups for gravy and set aside. Dip cube steaks into buttermilk mixture, then into flour mixture, coating well. Repeat.

In a skillet, heat 1/2 in. of oil on high. Fry steaks, a few at a time, for 5-7 minutes. Turn carefully and cook 5 minutes longer or until coating is crisp and meat is no longer pink. Remove steaks and keep warm.

Drain, reserving 1/3 cup drippings in the skillet; stir remaining flour into drippings until smooth. Cook and stir over medium heat for 5 minutes or until golden brown. Whisk in reserved buttermilk mixture; bring to a boil. Cook and stir for 2 minutes. Add Worcestershire sauce and hot pepper sauce. Serve with steaks. **Yield:** 8 servings (4 cups gravy).

herb-crusted roast beef

Teri Lindquist, Gurnee, Illinois
It's more than 20 years now I've been married to a man who loves beef. For a long time, though, I was reluctant to cook a roast for fear of ruining it. Finally, I started buying roasts on sale and experimenting. This recipe was the fabulous result.

   1 boneless rump roast (4-1/2 to 5 pounds)
   2 garlic cloves, minced
   2 tablespoons Dijon mustard
   2 tablespoons lemon juice
   2 tablespoons olive oil
   2 tablespoons Worcestershire sauce
   1 tablespoon dried parsley flakes
   1 teaspoon dried basil
   1 teaspoon salt
   1 teaspoon coarsely ground pepper
 1/2 teaspoon dried tarragon
 1/2 teaspoon dried thyme
2-1/3 cups water, *divided*
   2 teaspoons beef bouillon granules
 1/4 to 1/3 cup all-purpose flour

Place roast with fat side up in an ungreased roasting pan. Combine the next five ingredients; pour over roast. Combine parsley, basil, salt, pepper, tarragon and thyme; rub over roast. Bake, uncovered, at 325° for 1-3/4 to 2-1/4 hours or until meat reaches desired doneness (for medium-rare, a meat thermometer should read 145°; medium, 160°; well-done, 170°). Remove to a warm serving platter. Let stand for 10-15 minutes.

Meanwhile, add 2 cups water and bouillon to pan drippings; bring to a boil. Combine flour and remaining water until smooth; gradually add to pan. Cook and stir until bubbly and thickened. Slice roast; serve with gravy. **Yield:** 10-12 servings.

savory beef sandwiches

Lynn Williamson, Hayward, Wisconsin
Before heading to work in the morning, I'll get this going in the slow cooker. Then it's all ready to serve, usually with hard rolls and potato salad or another salad, as soon as my husband and I walk in. When my son—one of three children—moved to another state recently, I cut up beef roast in smaller portions, repackaged it and sent seasonings for a two-person slow cooker as his housewarming present.

> 1 tablespoon dried minced onion
> 2 teaspoons salt
> 2 teaspoons garlic powder
> 2 teaspoons dried oregano
> 1 teaspoon dried rosemary, crushed
> 1 teaspoon caraway seeds
> 1 teaspoon dried marjoram
> 1 teaspoon celery seed
> 1/4 teaspoon cayenne pepper
> 1 boneless chuck roast (3 to 4 pounds), halved
> 8 to 10 sandwich rolls, split

Combine seasonings; rub over roast. Place in a slow cooker. Cover and cook on low for 6-8 hours or until meat is tender. Shred with a fork. Serve on rolls. **Yield:** 8-10 servings.

Editor's Note: No liquid is added to the slow cooker. The moisture comes from the roast.

tenderloin with creamy garlic sauce

Beth Taylor, Chapin, South Carolina
Served with green beans, garlic mashed potatoes and seven-layer salad, this is the main course at my family's annual Christmas gathering. Even those who aren't fond of meat comment on its tenderness and flavor. Likely, since garlic goes well with everything, the sauce would also be good with pork or poultry.

> 1 jar (8 ounces) Dijon mustard, *divided*
> 10 garlic cloves, *divided*
> 2 tablespoons whole black peppercorns, coarsely crushed, *divided*
> 3 tablespoons vegetable oil, *divided*
> 1 beef tenderloin (4 to 5 pounds), halved
> 2 cups heavy whipping cream
> 1 cup (8 ounces) sour cream

In a blender, combine half of the mustard, eight garlic cloves and 1 tablespoon peppercorns. Cover; process 1 minute, scraping sides occasionally. Add 1 tablespoon oil; process until a paste forms. Spread over beef.

In a large skillet, heat the remaining oil over medium-high heat. Brown beef on all sides. Transfer to an ungreased 13-in. x 9-in. x 2-in. baking dish. Cover and bake at 375° for 40-50 minutes or until meat reaches desired doneness (for medium-rare, a meat thermometer should read 145°; medium, 160°; well-done, 170°). Remove to a warm serving platter. Let stand for 10-15 minutes.

Meanwhile, mince remaining garlic. In a saucepan, combine garlic, whipping cream, sour cream and remaining mustard and peppercorns. Cook and stir over low heat until heated through. Slice beef; serve with the sauce. **Yield:** 12-15 servings.

barbecued short ribs

Cheryl Niemela, Cokato, Minnesota
People like the blending of many different flavors in this recipe. I consider it a very special one and generally fix it for company. It receives rave reviews. I'm sure the sauce would also taste good with other meats.

 5 pounds bone-in short ribs, trimmed
 2 medium onions, finely chopped
 2 garlic cloves, minced
 2 tablespoons olive oil
 1 can (14-1/2 ounces) diced tomatoes, undrained
 1 cup chili sauce
1/3 cup soy sauce
1/3 cup honey
1/4 cup packed brown sugar
1/4 cup ketchup
 2 teaspoons chili powder
1/2 teaspoon ground ginger
1/8 teaspoon cayenne pepper
1/8 teaspoon dried oregano
1/8 teaspoon Liquid Smoke, optional

Place ribs in a Dutch oven; add water to cover by 2 in. Bring to a boil. Reduce heat; simmer, uncovered, for 1-1/2 to 2 hours or until tender.

Meanwhile, in a saucepan, saute onions and garlic in oil until tender. Add remaining ingredients; bring to a boil. Reduce heat; simmer, uncovered, for 30 minutes, stirring occasionally.

Drain ribs. Arrange on a broiler pan and baste with barbecue sauce. Broil 4 to 5 in. from the heat for 5-10 minutes on each side or until sauce is bubbly. **Yield:** 6-8 servings.

tender beef and noodles

Nancy Peterson, Farmington, British Columbia
Because I often work outside with my husband on our cattle ranch, I appreciate convenient recipes like this. The main dish cooks by itself and is ready for us when we come in the house. If you like, substitute stew meat for the roast. Either way, it's a hearty, everyday meal with a special tasty twist.

 1 boneless chuck roast (2 to 2-1/2 pounds), cut into 1-inch cubes
 2 large onions, chopped
 3 tablespoons butter
 1 can (8 ounces) tomato sauce
 2 teaspoons sugar
 2 teaspoons paprika
 2 teaspoons Worcestershire sauce
 1 to 2 teaspoons salt
1-1/2 teaspoons caraway seeds
 1 teaspoon dill weed
1/4 teaspoon pepper
1/8 teaspoon garlic powder
 1 cup (8 ounces) sour cream
Hot cooked noodles

In a large saucepan or Dutch oven, cook beef and onions in butter until the meat is browned. Add the next nine ingredients; bring to a boil. Reduce heat; cover and simmer for 1-3/4 to 2 hours or until meat is tender. Remove from the heat; stir in sour cream. Serve over noodles. **Yield:** 4-6 servings.

GROUND BEEF ROUNDUP

#1

MEATBALL PIE

meatball pie
GRAND PRIZE WINNER

Mention meatballs, and most folks think of spaghetti. Sure enough, there were some super sauces entered in our Ground Beef Roundup contest. There were other delicious meatball dishes as well. It was a meatball pie, however, that caught our judges' eyes and tantalized their taste buds the most.

> "The combination of tomatoes, carrots and peas is colorful and appetizing."

After sampling dozens of different ground beef dishes, they awarded the Grand Prize to Susan Keith of Fort Plain, New York for her hearty and satisfying Meatball Pie.

"Meatball Pie looks as good as it tastes," says Susan. "The combination of tomatoes, carrots and peas is colorful and appetizing—so pretty on the table as a meal with a salad or coleslaw as a side dish.

"My roots in New England are likely what sparked my fondness for meat pies," she concludes. "I make pies with everything from chicken and pork to tuna."

3/4 cup soft bread crumbs
1/4 cup chopped onion
2 tablespoons minced fresh parsley
1 teaspoon salt
1/2 teaspoon dried marjoram
1/8 teaspoon pepper
1/4 cup milk
1 egg, lightly beaten
1 pound ground beef
1 can (14-1/2 ounces) stewed tomatoes
1 tablespoon cornstarch
2 teaspoons beef bouillon granules
1 cup frozen peas
1 cup sliced carrots, cooked
CRUST:
2-2/3 cups all-purpose flour
1/2 teaspoon salt
1 cup shortening
7 to 8 tablespoons ice water
Half-and-half cream

In a bowl, combine the first eight ingredients; crumble beef over mixture and mix well (mixture will be soft). Divide into fourths; shape each portion into 12 small meatballs. Brown meatballs, a few at a time, in a large skillet; drain and set aside.

Drain tomatoes, reserving liquid. Combine the liquid with cornstarch; pour into the skillet. Add tomatoes and bouillon; bring to a boil over medium heat, stirring constantly. Stir in peas and carrots. Remove from the heat and set aside.

For crust, combine flour and salt in a bowl. Cut in shortening until the mixture resembles coarse crumbs. Add water, 1 tablespoon at a time, tossing lightly with a fork until dough forms a ball.

On a lightly floured surface, roll half of dough to fit a 10-in. pie plate. Place in ungreased plate; add meatballs. Spoon tomato mixture over top. Roll remaining pastry to fit top of pie. Place over filling; seal and flute edges. Cut vents in top crust. Brush with cream.

Bake at 400° for 45-50 minutes or until golden brown. If needed, cover edges with foil for the last 10 minutes to prevent overbrowning. Let stand for 10 minutes before cutting. **Yield:** 6 servings.

chili with potato dumplings

Shirley Marshall, Michigantown, Indiana
Now that my husband has retired, we eat out a lot. If we stay home, though, he asks if we can have this chili!

- 1 pound ground beef
- 1 pound ground turkey
- 1/2 cup chopped onion
- 1 can (15-1/2 ounces) kidney beans, rinsed and drained
- 1 can (15-1/2 ounces) mild chili beans, undrained
- 1/2 cup chopped green pepper
- 4 teaspoons chili powder
- 1 teaspoon salt
- 1 teaspoon paprika
- 1 teaspoon cumin seed
- 1/2 teaspoon garlic salt
- 1/2 teaspoon dried oregano
- 1/4 teaspoon crushed red pepper flakes
- 3 cups V8 juice

DUMPLINGS:
- 1 cup mashed potato flakes
- 1 cup all-purpose flour
- 1 tablespoon minced fresh parsley
- 2 teaspoons baking powder
- 1/2 teaspoon salt
- 1 cup milk
- 1 egg, beaten

In a 5-qt. Dutch oven, cook beef, turkey and onion over medium heat until meat is no longer pink; drain. Add the next 11 ingredients; bring to a boil. Reduce heat; cover and simmer for 30 minutes, stirring occasionally.

In a medium bowl, combine the first five dumpling ingredients. Add milk and egg; stir just until moistened. Let rest for 3 minutes. Drop by tablespoonfuls into simmering chili. Cover and cook for 15 minutes. **Yield: 8 servings (2 quarts).**

inside-out brussels sprouts

Shirley Max, Cape Girardeau, Missouri
There were seven of us children when I was a girl, and I was the second oldest. I began cooking as soon as I could reach the stove and stir a pot. I'm a widow, so I usually make this for large gatherings. It's so quick and easy. The recipe was given to me when my husband and I were caring for foster children who enjoyed beef dishes.

- 1-1/2 cups uncooked instant rice
- 1 medium onion, chopped
- 2 eggs, lightly beaten
- 1-1/2 teaspoons garlic salt
- 1/2 teaspoon pepper
- 2 pounds ground beef
- 1 package (10 ounces) frozen brussels sprouts
- 2 cans (15 ounces *each*) tomato sauce
- 1 cup water
- 1 teaspoon dried thyme

In a large bowl, combine the first five ingredients; crumble beef over mixture and mix well. Cut an X in the core of each brussels sprout. Shape a scant 1/4 cupful around each frozen brussels sprout to form a meatball. Place in an ungreased 15-in. x 10-in. x 1-in. baking dish.

Combine tomato sauce, water and thyme; pour over meatballs. Cover and bake at 350° for 1 hour and 15 minutes or until meatballs are no longer pink. **Yield: 8-10 servings.**

beefy taco dip

Faye Parker, Bedford, Nova Scotia
This taco dip is actually a combination of several different recipes I received from friends. I just experimented until I came up with my favorite! It's always a hit when I carry it to family gatherings, church potlucks, etc.

  1 package (8 ounces) cream cheese, softened
  1 cup (8 ounces) sour cream
3/4 cup mayonnaise
  1 pound ground beef
  1 envelope taco seasoning mix
  1 can (8 ounces) tomato sauce
  2 cups (8 ounces) shredded cheddar *or* taco
    cheese
  4 cups shredded lettuce
  2 medium tomatoes, diced
  1 small onion, diced
  1 medium green pepper, diced
Tortilla chips

In a small mixing bowl, beat the cream cheese, sour cream and mayonnaise until smooth. Spread on a 12- to 14-in. pizza pan or serving dish. Refrigerate for 1 hour.

In a saucepan over medium heat, cook beef until no longer pink; drain. Add taco seasoning and tomato sauce; cook and stir for 5 minutes. Cool completely. Spread over cream cheese layer. Refrigerate. Just before serving, sprinkle with cheese, lettuce, tomatoes, onion and green pepper. Serve with chips. **Yield:** 16-20 servings.

beef and sauerkraut dinner

Marilyn Dietz, White, South Dakota
I've been making this one-dish meal for more than 30 years. The original recipe called for a single can of sauerkraut—but that wasn't enough for us! My husband is the pastor to two small-town congregations. Among other occasions, I enjoy preparing this for church potlucks.

    1 egg, lightly beaten
1-1/2 cups soft rye bread crumbs
  1/3 cup milk
  1/4 cup chopped onion
    1 tablespoon cider vinegar
1-1/2 teaspoons caraway seed
    1 teaspoon salt
1-1/2 pounds ground beef
    1 tablespoon vegetable oil
    2 cans (15 ounces *each*) sliced potatoes, drained
    2 cans (14 ounces *each*) sauerkraut, undrained
    2 tablespoons minced fresh parsley
  1/4 cup *each* mayonnaise and horseradish,
      optional

In a bowl, combine the first seven ingredients; crumble beef over mixture and mix well. Shape into 1-1/2-in. balls. In a Dutch oven over medium heat, brown meatballs in oil; drain.

Add potatoes and sauerkraut; mix well. Bring to a boil. Reduce heat; cover and simmer for 15-20 minutes or until meatballs are no longer pink. Sprinkle with parsley. If sauce is desired, combine mayonnaise and horseradish; serve on the side. **Yield:** 6-8 servings.

spaghetti 'n' meatballs

Mary Lou Koskella, Prescott, Arizona
One evening, we had unexpected company. Since I had some of these meatballs left over in the freezer, I warmed them up as appetizers. Everyone raved!

1-1/2 cups chopped onion
   3 garlic cloves, minced
   2 tablespoons vegetable oil
   3 cups water
   1 can (29 ounces) tomato sauce
   2 cans (12 ounces *each)* tomato paste
1/3 cup minced fresh parsley
   1 tablespoon dried basil
   1 tablespoon salt
1/2 teaspoon pepper
MEATBALLS:
   4 eggs, lightly beaten
   2 cups soft bread cubes (1/4-inch pieces)
1-1/2 cups milk
   1 cup grated Parmesan cheese
   3 garlic cloves, minced
   1 tablespoon salt
1/2 teaspoon pepper
   3 pounds ground beef
   2 tablespoons vegetable oil
Hot cooked spaghetti

In a Dutch oven over medium heat, saute onion and garlic in oil. Add water, tomato sauce and paste, parsley, basil, salt and pepper; bring to a boil. Reduce heat; cover and simmer for 50 minutes.

Combine the first seven meatball ingredients; crumble beef over mixture and mix well. Shape into 1-1/2-in. balls. In a skillet over medium heat, brown meatballs in oil; drain. Add to sauce; bring to a boil. Reduce heat; cover and simmer for 1 hour, stirring occasionally. Serve over spaghetti. **Yield:** 12-16 servings.

crispy beef tostadas

Joy Rackham, Chimacum, Washington
This one-dish ground beef meal that I created myself is a family favorite.

   3 cups all-purpose flour
   5 teaspoons baking powder
1-1/4 cups milk
   1 pound ground beef
   2 garlic cloves, minced
   1 can (4 ounces) chopped green chilies
   1 envelope taco seasoning mix
3/4 cup water
   1 can (16 ounces) refried beans
Oil for deep-fat frying
Picante sauce *or* salsa, shredded lettuce, finely chopped green onions, diced tomatoes and shredded cheddar cheese

In a large bowl, combine flour and baking powder; add the milk to form a soft dough. Cover and let rest for 1 hour. About 30 minutes before serving, cook beef and garlic in a skillet until meat is no longer pink; drain. Stir in chilies, taco seasoning and water; simmer for 10 minutes. Stir in beans; heat through and keep warm.

Divide dough into sixths. On a lightly floured surface, roll each portion into a 7-in. circle. In a deep-fat fryer, preheat oil to 375°. Fry tostadas in hot oil until golden, turning once; drain on paper towels.

Top each with meat mixture, picante sauce or salsa, lettuce, onions, tomatoes and cheese; serve immediately. **Yield:** 6 servings.

pasta meatball stew

Pat Jelinek, Kitchener, Ontario

Growing up on the farm, I participated in 4-H cooking club activities. Nowadays, I like to visit Mom, Dad and all of their varied animals.

   1 egg, lightly beaten
1/4 cup dry bread crumbs
1/4 cup milk
1/2 teaspoon ground mustard
1/2 teaspoon salt
1/2 teaspoon pepper
   1 pound ground beef
   1 tablespoon vegetable oil

SAUCE:
   1 cup chopped onion
   2 garlic cloves, minced
   1 tablespoon vegetable oil
   2 tablespoons all-purpose flour
1-1/2 cups beef broth
   1 can (14-1/2 ounces) diced tomatoes, undrained
   2 tablespoons tomato paste
   1 bay leaf
3/4 teaspoon dried thyme
1/2 teaspoon salt
1-1/2 cups sliced carrots
1-1/2 cups chopped zucchini
   1 cup chopped green pepper
   1 cup chopped sweet red pepper
   1 tablespoon minced fresh parsley
   2 cups cooked pasta

Combine first six ingredients; crumble beef over mixture and mix well. Shape into 1-in. balls. In a Dutch oven over medium heat, brown meatballs in oil; drain and set aside.

In same pan, saute onion and garlic in oil until onion is tender. Blend in flour. Gradually add broth, stirring constantly; bring to a boil. Cook and stir 1-2 minutes or until thickened. Add tomatoes, paste, bay leaf, thyme and salt; mix well. Add meatballs and carrots; bring to a boil. Reduce heat; cover and simmer 30 minutes. Add zucchini and peppers; bring to a boil. Reduce heat; cover and simmer 10-15 minutes or until vegetables are tender and meatballs are no longer pink. Add parsley and pasta; heat through. Remove bay leaf. **Yield:** 6-8 servings.

---

prize winning tips

* Save both time and money by buying ground beef in a large quantity and cooking it. Freeze serving-size portions in airtight containers for use in a variety of recipes during the months ahead.

Kathy Beliveau, Middletown, Connecticut

---

* When preparing meatballs, be careful not to overmix the meat with the other ingredients or the meatballs will become very firm and tough.

Joy Rackham, Chimacum, Washington

ground beef turnovers

Wendy Tomlinson, Echo Bay, Ontario
My husband likes these turnovers so much that he even eats them cold!

    4 cups all-purpose flour
    1 tablespoon sugar
    2 teaspoons salt
1-3/4 cups shortening
    1/2 cup ice water
    1 egg, lightly beaten
    1 tablespoon vinegar
FILLING:
    2 pounds uncooked ground beef
    1 cup diced carrots
    2 medium potatoes, peeled and cut
      into 1/4-inch cubes
    1 medium onion, chopped
    1 to 2 teaspoons salt
    1/4 teaspoon pepper
Half-and-half cream

In a bowl, combine flour, sugar and salt; cut in shortening until mixture resembles coarse crumbs. Combine the water, egg and vinegar; mix well. Add to shortening mixture, 1 tablespoon at a time, tossing lightly with a fork until mixture forms a ball. Cover and chill for 30 minutes. Meanwhile, combine the first six filling ingredients.

Divide pastry into 15 equal portions. On a lightly floured surface, roll out one portion into a 6-1/2-in. circle. Mound a heaping 1/3 cup filling on half of circle. Moisten edges with water; fold dough over filling and press edges with a fork to seal. Transfer to a greased baking sheet. Repeat with remaining pastry and filling.

Cut three slits in top of each turnover; brush with cream. Bake at 375° for 35-40 minutes or until vegetables are tender and crust is golden. **Yield:** 15 turnovers.

sloppy joe pie

Kathy McCreary, Goddard, Kansas
To be honest, I don't hear many compliments on this dish…folks are always too busy eating! I developed the recipe by grabbing ingredients from my refrigerator and cupboards one "crunch time" when I needed an easy dish.

    1 pound ground beef
    1/2 cup chopped onion
    1 can (8 ounces) tomato sauce
    1 can (8-3/4 ounces) whole kernel corn, drained
    1/4 cup water
    1 envelope sloppy joe seasoning mix
    1 can (10 ounces) refrigerated biscuits
    2 tablespoons milk
    1/3 cup cornmeal
    1 cup (8 ounces) shredded cheddar cheese,
      divided

In a skillet, cook beef with onion until meat is no longer pink; drain. Stir in the tomato sauce, corn, water and sloppy joe seasoning; cook over medium heat until bubbly. Reduce heat and simmer for 5 minutes; remove from the heat and set aside.

Separate biscuits and roll or flatten each to a 3-1/2-in. circle; dip both sides into milk and then into the cornmeal. Place seven biscuits around the sides and three on the bottom of an ungreased 9-in. pie plate. Press biscuits together to form a crust, leaving a scalloped edge around rim. Sprinkle with 1/2 cup cheese. Spoon meat mixture over cheese.

Bake at 375° for 20-25 minutes or until crust is deep golden brown. Sprinkle with remaining cheese. Let stand for 5 minutes before serving. **Yield:** 7 servings.

cajun burgers

Julie Culbertson, Bensalem, Pennsylvania
*I found the original recipe for these burgers in a cookbook,
then added and subtracted ingredients until they suited
my family's taste.*

CAJUN SEASONING BLEND:
 3 tablespoons ground cumin
 3 tablespoons dried oregano
 1 tablespoon garlic powder
 1 tablespoon paprika
 2 teaspoons salt
 1 teaspoon cayenne pepper
BURGERS:
 1/4 cup finely chopped onion
 1 teaspoon salt
 1 teaspoon Cajun Seasoning Blend (recipe
   above)
 1/2 to 1 teaspoon hot pepper sauce
 1/2 teaspoon dried thyme
 1/4 teaspoon dried basil
 1 garlic clove, minced
 1 pound ground beef
 4 hamburger buns
Sauteed onions, optional

Combine all seasoning blend ingredients in a small
bowl or resealable plastic bag; mix well. In a bowl, combine the first seven burger ingredients; crumble beef over
mixture and mix well. Shape into four patties.

 Cook in a skillet or grill over medium-hot heat for
4-5 minutes per side or until burgers reach desired doneness. Serve on buns; top burgers with sauteed onions if
desired. Store remaining seasoning blend in an airtight
container. **Yield:** 4 servings.

all-purpose meat sauce

Sonja Fontaine, Winnipeg, Manitoba
*Experimenting with different herbs and spices led to this
sauce…my husband does not like bland food! I now make
it for him and our three children at least once a week.*

 1 pound ground beef
 1 to 2 garlic cloves, minced
 1 can (15 ounces) tomato sauce
 1 can (10-3/4 ounces) tomato soup, undiluted
 1/4 cup grated Parmesan cheese
 1 tablespoon Worcestershire sauce
1-1/2 teaspoons dried oregano
 1 teaspoon dried basil
 1/2 teaspoon sugar
 1/2 teaspoon salt
 1/2 teaspoon dried parsley flakes
 1/4 teaspoon crushed red pepper flakes
**Pinch *each* dried thyme, tarragon and ground
  cinnamon**
Hot pepper sauce and cayenne pepper to taste

In a large skillet or Dutch oven, cook the beef and garlic
until meat is no longer pink; drain. Stir in remaining
ingredients. Simmer, uncovered, for 30 minutes or until
sauce is as thick as desired, stirring occasionally.

 Serve over pasta or rice, or use for making lasagna,
pizza, chili dogs, tacos or sloppy joes. **Yield:** 4 cups.

CHOICE CHICKEN RECIPES

#1

NUTTY OVEN-FRIED
CHICKEN

nutty oven-fried chicken

Choosing a winner in *Taste of Home's* first-ever national recipe contest—Choice Chicken Recipes held in 1993—was quite a challenge. Nearly 1,000 home-style recipes were entered by great family cooks from coast to coast.

"*...the chicken comes out so moist, tasty and crispy.*"

Our panel of judges spent weeks narrowing the pleasing poultry selection to a few dozen of the most promising entries, which were then carefully prepared and enthusiastically taste-tested.

When the votes were finally tallied, the Grand Prize was awarded to Diane Hixon of Niceville, Florida. Flavored with a hint of sage and sporting a delightful pecan coating, Nutty Oven-Fried Chicken was picked the fairest of the fowl.

"The pecans that give this dish its unique, nutty flavor are plentiful in the South, and so is chicken," says Diane. "I love to make and serve this easy dish because the chicken comes out so moist, tasty and crispy."

  1 **cup biscuit/baking mix**
1/3 **cup finely chopped pecans**
  2 **teaspoons paprika**
1/2 **teaspoon salt**
1/2 **teaspoon poultry seasoning**
1/2 **teaspoon rubbed sage**
  1 **broiler-fryer chicken (2 to 3 pounds), cut up**
1/2 **cup evaporated milk**
1/3 **cup butter, melted**

In a shallow dish, combine biscuit mix, pecans and seasonings; mix well. Dip chicken pieces in milk; coat generously with pecan mixture.

Place in a lightly greased 13-in. x 9-in. x 2-in. baking dish. Drizzle butter over chicken. Bake, uncovered, at 350° for 1 hour or until juices run clear. **Yield:** 6-8 servings.

chicken fajitas

Lindsay St. John, Plainfield, Indiana
Fresh flavor with a flair describes this quick and easy recipe. Fajitas are great for hot summer evenings when you want to serve something fun and tasty, yet keep cooking to a minimum. Try topping them with sour cream, guacamole or both. My family loves them!

1/4	cup lime juice
1	garlic clove, minced
1	teaspoon chili powder
1/2	teaspoon ground cumin
2	whole boneless skinless chicken breasts, cut into strips
1	medium onion, cut into thin wedges
1/2	medium sweet red pepper, cut into strips
1/2	medium yellow pepper, cut into strips
1/2	medium green pepper, cut into strips
1/2	cup salsa
12	flour tortillas (8 inches)
1-1/2	cups (6 ounces) shredded cheddar *or* Monterey Jack cheese

In a small bowl, combine lime juice, garlic, chili powder and cumin. Add chicken; stir. Marinate for 15 minutes.

In a nonstick skillet, cook onion, chicken and marinade for 3 minutes or until chicken is no longer pink. Add peppers; saute for 3-5 minutes or until crisp-tender. Stir in salsa. Divide mixture among tortillas; top with cheese. Roll up and serve. **Yield:** 6 servings.

chicken chili with black beans

Jeanette Urbom, Overland Park, Kansas
Because this dish looks different from traditional chili, my family was a little hesitant to try it at first. But thanks to full, hearty flavor, it's become a real favorite around our house. I like to serve it with warm corn bread.

3	whole boneless skinless chicken breasts (about 1-3/4 pounds), cubed
2	medium sweet red peppers, chopped
1	large onion, chopped
4	garlic cloves, minced
3	tablespoons olive oil
1	can (4 ounces) chopped green chilies
2	tablespoons chili powder
2	teaspoons ground cumin
1	teaspoon ground coriander
2	cans (15 ounces *each*) black beans, rinsed and drained
1	can (28 ounces) Italian plum tomatoes, chopped, undrained
1	cup chicken broth *or* beer

In a Dutch oven, saute chicken, red peppers, onion and garlic in oil for 5 minutes or until chicken is no longer pink. Add green chilies, chili powder, cumin and coriander; cook for 3 minutes.

Stir in beans, tomatoes and broth or beer; bring to a boil. Reduce heat and simmer, uncovered, for 15 minutes, stirring often. **Yield:** 10 servings (3 quarts).

barbecued chicken

Linda Scott, Hahira, Georgia

I adapted my mother's recipe for barbecue sauce to suit our tastes. Every summer, we have a neighborhood cookout. I take this chicken and watch it disappear!

 2 broiler-fryer chickens (2 to 3 pounds *each*), cut up

SEASONING MIX:
 3 tablespoons salt
 2 tablespoons onion powder
 1 tablespoon paprika
 2 teaspoons garlic powder
 1-1/2 teaspoons chili powder
 1-1/2 teaspoons pepper
 1/4 teaspoon ground turmeric
Pinch ground red pepper

SAUCE:
 2 cups ketchup
 3 tablespoons brown sugar
 2 tablespoons dried minced onion
 2 tablespoons frozen orange juice concentrate, thawed
 1 tablespoon Seasoning Mix (recipe above)
 1/2 teaspoon Liquid Smoke, optional

Pat chicken pieces dry so seasoning coats well; set aside. Combine seasoning mix ingredients; sprinkle over both sides of the chicken. Reserve 1 tablespoon mix for sauce. Store leftovers in a covered container.

Grill chicken, skin side down, uncovered, over medium heat for 20 minutes. Turn; grill 20-30 minutes more or until chicken is no longer pink and juices run clear. Meanwhile, combine sauce ingredients in a small bowl. During the last 10 minutes of grilling, brush chicken often with sauce. **Yield:** 12 servings.

chinese chicken salad

Shirley Smith, Yorba Linda, California

Here's a cool, easy entree perfect for steamy summer days! You can do most of the preparation for this dish ahead of time and just mix it together before serving. The crispy lettuce and wonton strips keep this dish light, while the chicken and dressing give it wonderful flavor.

 1/2 package wonton wrappers, cut into 1/4-inch strips
Oil for deep-fat frying
 3 cups cubed cooked chicken
 1 head lettuce, shredded
 4 green onions with tops, sliced
 4 tablespoons sesame seeds, toasted

DRESSING:
 1/3 cup white wine vinegar
 1/4 cup sugar
 3 tablespoons vegetable oil
 2 tablespoons sesame oil
 1 teaspoon salt
 1/2 teaspoon pepper

Deep-fry wonton strips in oil until brown and crisp. Drain on paper towels; set aside. In a large salad bowl, combine chicken, lettuce, green onions and sesame seeds.

In a small bowl, whisk together all of the dressing ingredients. Just before serving, add fried wonton strips to salad; pour dressing over and toss to coat. **Yield:** 6-8 servings.

Editor's Note: For faster preparation, a can of chow mein noodles can be substituted for the wonton strips.

artichoke chicken

Ruth Stenson, Santa Ana, California
Rosemary, mushrooms and artichokes combine to give chicken a wonderful, savory flavor. It's always a big hit with everyone—especially my family!

    8 boneless skinless chicken breast halves
    2 tablespoons butter
    2 jars (6 ounces *each*) marinated artichoke
       hearts, drained
    1 jar (4-1/2 ounces) whole mushrooms, drained
  1/2 cup chopped onion
  1/3 cup all-purpose flour
1-1/2 teaspoons dried rosemary
    1 teaspoon salt
  1/4 teaspoon pepper
    2 cups chicken broth *or* 1 cup broth and 1 cup
       dry white wine
Hot cooked noodles
Chopped fresh parsley

In a skillet, brown chicken in butter. Remove chicken to an ungreased 13-in. x 9-in. x 2-in. baking dish; do not drain pan juices. Cut the artichokes into quarters. Arrange artichokes and mushrooms on top of chicken; set aside.

Saute onion in pan juices; blend in flour, rosemary, salt and pepper. Add chicken broth; cook until thickened and bubbly. Remove from heat; spoon over chicken.

Cover and bake at 350° for 50-60 minutes or until chicken is tender. Place noodles on serving platter; top with chicken and sauce. Sprinkle with parsley. **Yield:** 8 servings.

chicken tetrazzini

Kelly Heusmann, Cincinnati, Ohio
My husband is not a casserole lover, but this creamy, cheesy dish is one of his favorites! Nutmeg gives it a wonderful, different taste.

    2 cups sliced mushrooms
  1/4 cup butter
  1/4 cup all-purpose flour
    2 cups chicken broth
  1/4 cup half-and-half cream
    1 tablespoon chopped fresh parsley
    1 teaspoon salt
  1/8 to 1/4 teaspoon ground nutmeg
  1/4 teaspoon pepper
    3 tablespoons dry white wine *or* additional
       chicken broth
    3 cups cubed cooked chicken
    8 ounces spaghetti, cooked and drained
  3/4 cup shredded Parmesan cheese
Additional parsley

In a skillet, cook mushrooms in butter until tender. Stir in flour; gradually add the chicken broth. Cook, stirring constantly, until sauce comes to a boil. Remove from the heat; stir in cream, parsley, salt, nutmeg, pepper and wine or additional broth. Fold in the chicken and spaghetti.

Turn into a greased 12-in. x 8-in. x 2-in. baking dish; sprinkle with Parmesan cheese. Bake, uncovered, at 350° for 30 minutes or until heated through. Garnish with parsley. **Yield:** 8 servings.

chicken cheese lasagna

Mary Ann Kosmas, Minneapolis, Minnesota

This creamy pasta dish gives an old favorite a new twist! Three cheeses and chicken blended with the fresh taste of spinach make it a real crowd-pleaser. Try it served with a green salad and a light dessert.

- 1 medium onion, chopped
- 1 garlic clove, minced
- 1/2 cup butter
- 1/2 cup all-purpose flour
- 1 teaspoon salt
- 2 cups chicken broth
- 1-1/2 cups milk
- 4 cups (16 ounces) shredded part-skim mozzarella cheese, *divided*
- 1 cup grated Parmesan cheese, *divided*
- 1 teaspoon dried basil
- 1 teaspoon dried oregano
- 1/2 teaspoon white pepper
- 2 cups ricotta cheese
- 1 tablespoon minced fresh parsley
- 9 lasagna noodles (8 ounces), cooked and drained
- 2 packages (10 ounces *each*) frozen spinach, thawed and well drained
- 2 cups cubed cooked chicken

In a saucepan, saute the onion and garlic in butter until tender. Stir in the flour and salt; cook until bubbly. Gradually stir in the broth and milk. Bring to a boil, stirring constantly. Boil 1 minute. Stir in 2 cups mozzarella cheese, 1/2 cup Parmesan cheese, basil, oregano and pepper; set aside.

In a bowl, combine the ricotta cheese, parsley and remaining mozzarella; set aside.

Spread one-quarter of the cheese sauce into a greased 13-in. x 9-in. x 2-in. baking dish; cover with one-third of the noodles. Top with half of ricotta mixture, half of spinach and half of chicken. Cover with one-quarter of cheese sauce and one-third of noodles. Repeat layers of ricotta mixture, spinach, chicken and one-quarter cheese sauce. Cover with remaining noodles and cheese sauce. Sprinkle remaining Parmesan cheese over all. Bake at 350°, uncovered, for 35-40 minutes. Let stand 15 minutes. **Yield:** 12 servings.

★★★★★ prize winning tips

★ Chicken is easier to cut into strips if it's semi-frozen.

Amy Wolfe, Kittanning, Pennsylvania

★ A fresh lemon makes a nice rub for a whole chicken. Then simply add a dusting of sage.

Anna Moore, Howell, New Jersey

★ When making your favorite coating mix for chicken, double or triple the amount and store the extra in resealable plastic bags.

Opal Bobo, Cincinnati, Ohio

runners-up

cashew chicken

Ena Quiggle, Goodhue, Minnesota
We love eating ethnic foods, especially Oriental dishes. This chicken stir-fry is my family's favorite! The cashews add crunch and a sweet, nutty flavor, and the tasty sauce adds richness to garden-fresh carrots and broccoli.

- 1 tablespoon sesame oil
- 1/4 cup rice wine vinegar
- 1/4 cup sherry *or* 3 tablespoons chicken broth plus 1 tablespoon apple juice
- 1 teaspoon garlic powder
- 1-1/2 pounds boneless skinless chicken, cubed
- 3 tablespoons vegetable oil
- 3 cups broccoli florets
- 1 cup thinly sliced carrots
- 2 teaspoons cornstarch
- 1/3 cup soy sauce
- 1/3 cup hoisin sauce
- 1 tablespoon ground ginger
- 1 cup roasted salted cashews
Hot cooked rice

In a large bowl, combine first four ingredients; add chicken and toss to coat. Cover and refrigerate for 2 hours.

Remove chicken from marinade and reserve marinade. Heat oil in a wok or large skillet. Stir-fry chicken for 2-3 minutes or until it is no longer pink. With a slotted spoon, remove chicken and set aside.

In the same skillet, stir-fry broccoli and carrots for 3 minutes or just until crisp-tender. Combine cornstarch, soy sauce, hoisin sauce, ginger and reserved marinade; stir into vegetables. Cook and stir until slightly thickened and bubbly. Stir in cashews and chicken; heat through. Serve over rice. **Yield:** 6 servings.

sweet gingered chicken wings

Debbie Dougal, Roseville, California
I first tasted this delicious chicken dish years ago when I attended a class on using honey in cooking. When I prepare this recipe for a party, it's one of the very first dishes to disappear.

- 1 cup all-purpose flour
- 2 teaspoons salt
- 2 teaspoons paprika
- 1/4 teaspoon pepper
- 24 chicken wings
SAUCE:
- 1/4 cup honey
- 1/4 cup frozen orange juice concentrate, thawed
- 1/2 teaspoon ground ginger
Snipped fresh parsley, optional

In a bowl, combine flour, salt, paprika and pepper. Coat chicken wings in flour mixture; shake off excess. Place wings on a large greased baking sheet. Bake at 350° for 30 minutes. Remove from the oven and drain.

Combine honey, orange juice concentrate and ginger; brush generously over chicken wings. Reduce heat to 325°.

Bake for 30-40 minutes or until chicken tests done, basting occasionally with more sauce. Sprinkle with parsley before serving if desired. **Yield:** 2 dozen.

phyllo chicken

Joyce Mummau, Mt. Airy, Maryland
Some years ago I found this recipe and streamlined it to fit our busy family. The broccoli adds a lot to the great flavor. Phyllo is fun to work with, and its flakiness turns standard ingredients into a special entree.

- 1/2 cup butter, melted, *divided*
- 12 sheets phyllo pastry dough
- 3 cups diced cooked chicken
- 1/2 pound bacon, cooked and crumbled
- 1 package (10 ounces) frozen chopped broccoli, thawed and drained
- 2 cups (8 ounces) shredded cheddar *or* Swiss cheese
- 6 eggs
- 1 cup half-and-half cream *or* evaporated milk
- 1/2 cup milk
- 1 teaspoon salt
- 1/2 teaspoon pepper

Brush sides and bottom of a 13-in. x 9-in. x 2-in. baking dish with some of the melted butter. Place one sheet of phyllo in bottom of dish; brush with butter. Repeat with five more sheets of phyllo. (Keep remaining phyllo dough covered with a damp cloth to avoid drying out.)

In a bowl, combine chicken, bacon, broccoli and cheese; spread evenly over phyllo in baking dish. In another bowl, whisk together eggs, cream, milk, salt and pepper; pour over chicken mixture.

Cover filling with one sheet of phyllo; brush with butter. Repeat with remaining phyllo dough. Brush top with remaining butter. Bake, uncovered, at 375° for 35-40 minutes or until a knife inserted near the center comes out clean. **Yield:** 10-12 servings.

cheesy chicken chowder

Hazel Fritchie, Palestine, Illinois
I like to serve this hearty chowder with garlic bread and a salad. It's a wonderful dish to prepare when company drops in. The rich flavor and tender chicken and vegetables appeal even to children and picky eaters.

- 3 cups chicken broth
- 2 cups diced peeled potatoes
- 1 cup diced carrots
- 1 cup diced celery
- 1/2 cup diced onion
- 1-1/2 teaspoons salt
- 1/4 teaspoon pepper
- 1/4 cup butter
- 1/3 cup all-purpose flour
- 2 cups milk
- 2 cups (8 ounces) shredded cheddar cheese
- 2 cups diced cooked chicken

In a 4-qt. saucepan, bring chicken broth to a boil. Reduce heat; add potatoes, carrots, celery, onion, salt and pepper. Cover and simmer for 15 minutes or until vegetables are tender.

Meanwhile, melt butter in a medium saucepan; add flour and mix well. Gradually stir in milk; cook over low heat until slightly thickened. Stir in cheese and cook until melted; add to broth along with chicken. Cook and stir over low heat until heated through. **Yield:** 6-8 servings.

TALKING TURKEY

#1

HERBED TURKEY
AND DRESSING

herbed turkey and dressing
GRAND PRIZE WINNER

Tempting turkey is the choice of many cooks for an impressive holiday entree or a delicious dish to pass. It's a marvelous meat since it goes so well with a variety of flavors and cooks up tender and tasty. With many versatile serving options, turkey is always pleasing to the palate.

"**...guests fill their plates and I'm buried in compliments.**"

Our Talking Turkey contest certainly proved that point. Super cooks entered over 2,100 recipes featuring drumsticks, ground turkey and more.

The judges' satisfying choices, like Grand Prize Winner Herbed Turkey and Dressing, will make it easy for you to proudly prepare this popular poultry for meals your family will "gobble up."

"Whenever I serve this succulent, golden turkey and delectable dressing, guests fill their plates and I'm buried in compliments," says Marilyn Clay of Palatine, Illinois, who shares the recipe. "This special entree makes any dinner one to remember."

BASTING SAUCE:
2-1/4 cups chicken broth
1/2 cup butter
1/2 teaspoon salt
1 teaspoon dried thyme
1/4 teaspoon *each* dried marjoram, rosemary and rubbed sage
1/4 cup chopped fresh parsley
2 tablespoons dried chives

DRESSING:
1 loaf (1 pound) sliced bread
1 pound bulk pork sausage
1/2 cup butter
4 cups thinly sliced celery
3 cups thinly sliced carrots
1/2 pound fresh mushrooms, chopped
1/2 pound cubed fully cooked ham
2 cups sliced green onions
2 cups chopped pecans
1 large tart apple, chopped
1 cup chopped dried apricots
1 tablespoon rubbed sage
2 teaspoons dried marjoram
1 teaspoon dried rosemary
1 teaspoon salt
1/8 teaspoon ground nutmeg
1 cup egg substitute
1 turkey (16 to 18 pounds)

In a pan, bring broth, butter and salt to a boil. Add herbs; set aside.

Toast bread; cut into 1/2-in. cubes. Place in a bowl. In a skillet, cook sausage over medium heat until no longer pink; remove with slotted spoon and add to bread. Add butter to drippings; saute celery, carrots, mushrooms, ham and onions for 15 minutes.

Add to bread mixture; stir in the nuts, fruit and seasonings. Add egg substitute and 3/4 cup basting sauce; mix lightly.

Stuff turkey with about 8 cups dressing. Skewer openings; tie drumsticks together. Place on rack in roasting pan. Baste with some of remaining basting sauce.

Bake, uncovered, at 325° for 5 to 5-1/2 hours or until thermometer reads 180° for the turkey and 165° for the stuffing, basting every 30 minutes. When turkey begins to brown, cover lightly with foil.

Add broth to remaining dressing; mix lightly. Place in a greased 2-1/2-qt. baking dish; refrigerate. Remove from the refrigerator 30 minutes before baking. Cover and bake at 325° for 1 hour; uncover and bake 10 minutes. **Yield:** 14-16 servings (18 cups dressing).

creamy turkey soup

Kathleen Harris, Galesburg, Illinois

My mother always prepared a holiday turkey much larger than our family could ever eat in one meal so there'd be plenty of leftovers. That's one tradition I've kept up. This hearty soup uses a lot of turkey and is great after watching football games and raking leaves.

- 1 large onion, chopped
- 3 celery ribs with leaves, cut into 1/4-inch pieces
- 6 tablespoons butter
- 6 tablespoons all-purpose flour
- 1 teaspoon salt
- 1/4 teaspoon pepper
- 1/4 teaspoon garlic powder
- 1/2 teaspoon *each* dried thyme, savory and parsley flakes
- 1-1/2 cups milk
- 4 cups cubed cooked turkey
- 5 medium carrots, cut into 1/4-inch pieces
- 1 to 2 cups turkey *or* chicken broth
- 1 package (10 ounces) frozen peas

In a large kettle, saute onion and celery in butter until tender, about 10 minutes. Stir in the flour and seasonings; gradually add milk. Bring to a boil; cook and stir for 2 minutes or until thickened. Add turkey and carrots. Add enough broth until soup is desired consistency. Cover and simmer for 15 minutes.

Add peas; cover and simmer for 15 minutes or until vegetables are tender. **Yield:** 6-8 servings (2 quarts).

turkey primavera

Zita Wilensky, North Miami Beach, Florida

We grow herbs and vegetables in our garden, so I incorporate them into recipes whenever possible. This creation has tender turkey and mushrooms, onions and green pepper covered in a zippy tomato sauce. It's become a real favorite for us.

- 1/4 cup all-purpose flour
- 2 teaspoons minced fresh parsley
- 1-1/2 pounds turkey tenderloins, cubed
- 2 tablespoons olive oil
- 1/2 cup chicken broth
- 1 cup sliced fresh mushrooms
- 1 medium onion, chopped
- 4 garlic cloves, minced
- 1/2 medium green pepper, chopped
- 1 can (14-1/2 ounces) beef broth
- 3/4 cup tomato puree
- 1/2 teaspoon dried thyme
- 1/2 teaspoon dried rosemary, crushed
- 1/2 teaspoon dried basil
- 1 bay leaf
- 1/4 teaspoon salt
- 1/8 teaspoon pepper

Hot cooked fettuccine *or* spaghetti
Parmesan cheese, optional

Combine flour and parsley; add turkey and toss to coat. In a skillet, brown turkey in oil; remove with a slotted spoon and set aside.

In the same skillet, combine chicken broth, mushrooms, onion, garlic and green pepper. Cook and stir for 3-4 minutes. Add beef broth, tomato puree and seasonings. Cook and stir for 20-25 minutes or until sauce is desired consistency.

Add turkey; heat through. Discard the bay leaf. Serve over pasta; sprinkle with Parmesan if desired. **Yield:** 4-6 servings.

honey-mustard turkey meatballs

Bonnie Durkin, Nescopeck, Pennsylvania
I serve this appetizer often during the holidays. It's nice to have a turkey meatball that doesn't taste like you should have used beef. These tangy meatballs can be prepared ahead and frozen, so even drop-in guests can be treated to a hot snack.

    1 pound ground turkey
    1 egg, lightly beaten
  3/4 cup crushed butter-flavored crackers
  1/2 cup shredded part-skim mozzarella cheese
  1/4 cup chopped onion
  1/2 teaspoon ground ginger
    6 tablespoons Dijon mustard, *divided*
    1 tablespoon cornstarch
  1/4 teaspoon onion powder
1-1/4 cups unsweetened pineapple juice
  1/4 cup chopped green pepper
    2 tablespoons honey

In a bowl, combine turkey, egg, cracker crumbs, cheese, onion, ginger and 3 tablespoons mustard. Shape into 30 (1-in.) balls. Place in a greased 13-in. x 9-in. x 2-in. baking dish. Bake, uncovered, at 350° for 20-25 minutes or until juices run clear.

In a saucepan, combine the cornstarch and onion powder. Stir in the pineapple juice until smooth. Add the pepper and honey. Bring to a boil; cook and stir for 2 minutes or until thickened. Reduce heat; stir in remaining mustard until smooth.

Brush meatballs with about 1/4 cup sauce and bake 10 minutes longer. Serve remaining sauce as a dip for meatballs. **Yield:** 2-1/2 dozen.

turkey drumstick dinner

Alice Balliet, Kane, Pennsylvania
I discovered this recipe a long time ago and love it since it uses tasty, economical turkey drumsticks. Our family and friends enjoy this savory meat and potatoes meal. The flavorful sauce turns plain drumsticks into a feast.

  4 uncooked turkey drumsticks
    (about 3 pounds)
  2 tablespoons vegetable oil
  1 tablespoon butter
  1 medium onion, sliced
  1 can (14-1/2 ounces) stewed tomatoes
  3 chicken bouillon cubes
  1 teaspoon garlic salt
1/2 teaspoon dried oregano
1/2 teaspoon dried basil
  4 large potatoes, peeled, cooked and quartered
  2 medium zucchini, cut into 3/4-inch slices
  2 tablespoons cornstarch
  2 tablespoons water
Chopped fresh parsley

In a large skillet, brown drumsticks in oil and butter. Place in a 3-qt. Dutch oven. Top with onion slices. In the same skillet, heat tomatoes, bouillon and seasonings until bouillon is dissolved. Pour over the drumsticks. Cover and bake at 325° for 2 hours, basting once or twice.

Add potatoes and zucchini. Cover and bake for 20 minutes. Remove drumsticks and vegetables to a serving dish and keep warm.

Combine cornstarch and water until smooth; stir into tomato mixture. Return to oven, uncovered, for 10-15 minutes or until slightly thickened. Pour over drumsticks and vegetables. Sprinkle with parsley. **Yield:** 4 servings.

runners-up

turkey potpie

Cheryl Arnold, Lake Zurich, Illinois
Family and guests rave about this hearty, comforting potpie and its light, flaky crust. The "secret" crust ingredients are Parmesan cheese and instant mashed potato flakes. On busy days, I prepare this entree in the morning and just bake it in the evening.

- 1 can (10-3/4 ounces) condensed cream of mushroom soup, undiluted
- 1 can (5 ounces) evaporated milk
- 1/4 cup minced fresh parsley *or* 1 tablespoon dried parsley flakes
- 1/2 teaspoon dried thyme
- 3 cups cubed cooked turkey
- 1 package (10 ounces) frozen mixed vegetables, thawed
- 1/4 teaspoon salt
- 1/4 teaspoon pepper

CRUST:
- 3/4 cup instant mashed potato flakes
- 3/4 cup all-purpose flour
- 1/4 cup grated Parmesan cheese
- 1/3 cup butter
- 1/4 cup ice water

Half-and-half cream

In a bowl, combine the first four ingredients. Stir in turkey, vegetables, salt and pepper. Spoon into a greased 11-in. x 7-in. x 2-in. baking dish.

For crust, combine potato flakes, flour and Parmesan in a bowl; cut in butter until crumbly. Add water, 1 tablespoon at a time, tossing lightly with a fork until the dough forms a ball.

On a lightly floured surface, roll the dough to fit baking dish. Cut vents in crust, using a small tree or star cut-

ter if desired. Place over filling; flute edges. Brush pastry with cream.

Bake at 400° for 25-30 minutes or until golden brown. If necessary, cover edges of crust with foil to prevent over-browning. **Yield:** 6 servings.

turkey pasta supreme

Cassie Dion, South Burlington, Vermont
Since this dish combines turkey and pasta, even our children love it. It's fun to make turkey a different way, and you can't beat the creamy, cheesy sauce. This recipe also helps stretch my meal budget.

- 3/4 pound uncooked turkey breast
- 2 garlic cloves, minced
- 2 tablespoons butter
- 1-1/4 cups heavy whipping cream
- 2 tablespoons minced fresh basil *or* 2 teaspoons dried basil
- 1/4 cup grated Parmesan cheese

Dash pepper
- 3 to 4 cups hot cooked pasta

Cut turkey into 2-in. x 1/4-in. pieces. In a skillet, saute turkey and garlic in butter until turkey is browned and no longer pink, about 6 minutes.

Add the cream, basil, Parmesan and pepper; bring to a boil. Reduce heat; simmer for 3 minutes, stirring frequently. Stir in the pasta and toss to coat. Serve immediately. **Yield:** 4 servings.

turkey potato pancakes

Kathi Duerr, Fulda, Minnesota

My husband and our four children like pancakes, and I appreciate quick suppers…so I gave this recipe a try when I saw it. The addition of turkey turns golden side-dish potato pancakes into a simple main dish we all savor.

3 eggs
3 cups shredded peeled potatoes
1-1/2 cups finely chopped cooked turkey
1/4 cup sliced green onions with tops
2 tablespoons all-purpose flour
1-1/2 teaspoons salt
Vegetable oil
Cranberry sauce, optional

In a bowl, beat the eggs. Add potatoes, turkey, onions, flour and salt; mix well.

Heat about 1/4 in. of oil in a large skillet. Pour batter by 1/3 cupfuls into hot oil. Fry 5-6 minutes on each side or until the potatoes are tender and the pancakes are golden brown. Serve with cranberry sauce if desired.
Yield: 12 pancakes.

✳ ✳ ✳ ✳ ✳ prize winning tips

✳ "Turkey splits" are a hit at my house. Line a microwave-safe banana split dish with cooked turkey. Top with a scoop of mashed potatoes, a scoop of stuffing and a scoop of sweet potatoes. Drizzle with gravy. Cover and microwave until hot. Garnish with cranberry sauce and enjoy.

Diane Bullis, Grant, Michigan

✳ I purchase fresh turkey when it's on sale, then bone it and freeze the meat in small packages for future use. I make turkey broth from the bones and freeze that, too.

Sharon Brown, Gillett, Pennsylvania

✳ You can perk up canned baked beans by adding cooked ground turkey.

Joan Jackson, Fixfire Village, North Carolina

✳ For Reuben sandwiches with a down-home change of pace, I use sliced cooked turkey instead of corned beef. My family loves it.

Lucie Buse, Snohomish, Washington

✳ Make an extra flavorful and nutritious turkey soup by adding lots of vegetables.

Phyllis Stewart, Good Wood, Ontario

PICK OF THE PORK

\#1

FARMHOUSE PORK
AND APPLE PIE

farmhouse pork and apple pie

GRAND PRIZE WINNER

Practical, patate-pleasing pork is the choice of many cooks for a hearty main dish. It's such a popular meat because it goes well with a wide variety of flavors and cooks up tender and juicy. And pork is so versatile it can be served often without boring the taste buds.

> " I've always loved pork and apples together, and this recipe combines them nicely... "

Nothing proves that point better than our Pick of the Pork contest. Great cooks from across the country entered over 2,500 recipes in all, featuring ribs, chops, roasts, tenderloins and more. Our judges had the difficult but delicious job of selecting the winners. Farmhouse Pork and Apple Pie won the Grand Prize.

"I've always loved pork and apples together, and this recipe combines them nicely to create a comforting main dish," says Suzanne Strocsher of Bothell, Washington. "It calls for a bit of preparation, but my family and I agree that its wonderful flavor makes it well worth the extra effort."

1 pound sliced bacon, cut into 2-inch pieces
3 medium onions, chopped
3 pounds boneless pork, cubed
3/4 cup all-purpose flour
Vegetable oil, optional
3 tart cooking apples, peeled and chopped
1 teaspoon rubbed sage
1/2 teaspoon ground nutmeg
1 teaspoon salt
1/4 teaspoon pepper
1 cup apple cider
1/2 cup water
4 medium potatoes, peeled and cubed
1/2 cup milk
5 tablespoons butter, *divided*
Additional salt and pepper
Snipped fresh parsley, optional

Cook bacon in an ovenproof 12-in. skillet until crisp. Remove with a slotted spoon to paper towels to drain. In drippings, saute onions until tender; remove with a slotted spoon and set aside.

Dust pork lightly with flour. Brown a third at a time in drippings, adding oil if needed. Remove from the heat and drain. To pork, add bacon, onions, apples, sage, nutmeg, salt and pepper. Stir in apple cider and water. Cover and bake at 325° for 2 hours or until the pork is tender.

In a saucepan, cook potatoes in boiling water until tender. Drain and mash with milk and 3 tablespoons butter. Add salt and pepper to taste. Remove skillet from the oven and spread potatoes over pork mixture. Melt remaining butter; brush over potatoes.

Broil 6 in. from the heat for 5 minutes or until topping is browned. Sprinkle with parsley if desired. **Yield:** 10 servings.

sweet-and-sour pork

Cherry Williams, St. Albert, Alberta
After my sister moved away to the university, I used to visit her on weekends. She often made this wonderful and tangy pork dish. Now, every time I make it for my family, it reminds me of those special visits.

      1 **pound pork tenderloin**
      2 **cans (8 ounces *each*) pineapple tidbits**
    1/3 **cup ketchup**
    1/3 **cup water**
      2 **tablespoons *each* soy sauce, vinegar, brown sugar and cornstarch**
    3/4 **teaspoon salt**
    1/4 **teaspoon pepper**
    1/4 **teaspoon ground ginger**
      2 **tablespoons vegetable oil**
      1 **medium onion, chopped**
      1 **green pepper, cut into thin strips**
Hot cooked rice

Cut the tenderloin into 1-1/2-in. x 1/4-in. strips; set aside. Drain pineapple, reserving juice in a small bowl. Set pineapple aside. To juice, add ketchup, water, soy sauce, vinegar, brown sugar, cornstarch, salt, pepper and ginger; stir until smooth.

Heat oil in a large skillet or wok on high; stir-fry pork and onion for 5-7 minutes or until pork is no longer pink. Stir pineapple juice mixture; add to skillet. Cook and stir until thickened and bubbly. Add pineapple and green pepper. Reduce heat; cover and cook for 5 minutes. Serve immediately over rice. **Yield:** 4 servings.

spicy pork chili

Christine Hartry, Emo, Ontario
This zippy chili is a pleasant change from the traditional beef chili recipes I've tried. It tastes so good served with garden-fresh steamed green beans, sliced cucumbers and hot crusty bread. It's satisfying on a cold day.

      1 **pound ground pork**
      2 **large onions, chopped**
      4 **garlic cloves, minced**
      1 **medium sweet red pepper, chopped**
      1 **medium green pepper, chopped**
      1 **cup chopped celery**
      2 **cans (14-1/2 ounces *each*) diced tomatoes, undrained**
      1 **can (16 ounces) kidney beans, rinsed and drained**
      1 **can (6 ounces) tomato paste**
    3/4 **cup water**
      2 **teaspoons brown sugar**
      1 **teaspoon dried oregano**
      1 **teaspoon chili powder**
    1/4 **teaspoon dried red pepper flakes**
    1/4 **teaspoon cayenne pepper**
Dash hot pepper sauce

In a Dutch oven, cook pork and onions until pork is no longer pink; drain. Stir in the garlic, peppers and celery; cook for 5 minutes. Add remaining ingredients; bring to a boil. Reduce heat; cover and simmer for 45 minutes. **Yield:** 6-8 servings (2-1/2 quarts).

pork with mustard sauce

Irma Pomeroy, Enfield, Connecticut

Back when I was a young girl, I couldn't wait until I was grown up and could start cooking for my own family! Now that I am, I really enjoy using pork in a variety of dishes. I think that the tender meat and the rich mustard sauce in this recipe are simply delectable together.

- 1 pound pork tenderloin
- 2 tablespoons butter
- 1/2 cup beef broth
- 3/4 teaspoon dried tarragon
- 1/2 cup heavy whipping cream
- 1 tablespoon Dijon mustard

Salt and pepper to taste
Hot cooked noodles, optional

Cut the pork tenderloin into eight pieces. Slice each piece of pork again, but do not cut all of the way through; open and flatten each piece, pounding slightly with meat mallet.

In a large skillet over medium-high heat, cook the pork in butter until no longer pink, about 5-6 minutes per side. Remove to a serving dish and keep warm; discard the drippings.

In the same skillet, cook broth and tarragon over high heat until reduced by half. Reduce heat; stir in whipping cream and mustard. Season with salt and pepper. Spoon over the pork. Serve with noodles if desired. **Yield:** 4 servings.

---

prize winning tips

✳ Leftover pork chops make wonderful sandwiches. Just remove meat from the bones and chop in a food processor. Reheat the meat and serve on buns.

Deborah Imioli-Schriver, Amherst, New York

✳ If you're preparing a pork dish in a slow cooker, add fresh herbs at the end of the cooking time for pleasing taste and pretty color.

Elizabeth Mullett, Haverhill, Massachusetts

✳ Here's an easy marinade for grilled pork chops: for 4 chops, combine 1/2 cup each soy sauce, water and honey. Pour over chops and marinate, covered, in the refrigerator overnight. Drain and discard marinade and grill the pork chops.

Rhea Lease, Colman, South Dakota

✳ If you want succulent chops, choose those that are about 1 inch thick. Thin pork chops have a tendency to dry out no matter how careful you are.

Elaine Williams, Sebastopol, California

pork chow mein

Helen Carpenter, Marble Falls, Texas

I give all the credit for my love of cooking and baking to my mother, grandmother and mother-in-law. That trio inspired delicious dishes like this hearty skillet dinner. When we get a taste for stir-fry, this dish hits the spot.

- 1 pound boneless pork loin
- 2 garlic cloves, minced
- 4 tablespoons soy sauce, *divided*
- 1 cup chicken broth
- 2 tablespoons cornstarch
- 1/2 to 1 teaspoon ground ginger
- 1 tablespoon vegetable oil
- 1 cup thinly sliced carrots
- 1 cup thinly sliced celery
- 1 cup chopped onion
- 1 cup coarsely chopped cabbage
- 1 cup coarsely chopped fresh spinach

Hot cooked rice, optional

Cut pork into 4-in. x 1/2-in. x 1/4-in. strips; place in a bowl. Add garlic and 2 tablespoons soy sauce. Cover and refrigerate 2-4 hours. Meanwhile, combine broth, cornstarch, ginger and remaining soy sauce; mix well and set aside.

Heat oil in a large skillet or wok on high; stir-fry pork until no longer pink. Remove and keep warm. Add carrots and celery; stir-fry 3-4 minutes. Add onion, cabbage and spinach; stir-fry 2-3 minutes. Stir broth mixture and add to skillet along with pork. Cook and stir until the broth thickens, about 3-4 minutes. Serve immediately over rice if desired. **Yield:** 6 servings.

pork tenderloin diane

Janie Thorpe, Tullahoma, Tennessee

We have pork at least once a week, and this is one dish we especially enjoy. Moist tender pork "medallions" are served up in a savory sauce for a combination that's irresistible. I'm not sure where the recipe came from, but I'm glad I have it.

- 1 pork tenderloin (about 1 pound)
- 1 tablespoon lemon-pepper seasoning
- 2 tablespoons butter
- 2 tablespoons lemon juice
- 1 tablespoon Worcestershire sauce
- 1 teaspoon Dijon mustard
- 1 tablespoon minced fresh parsley

Cut tenderloin into eight pieces; place each piece between two pieces of plastic wrap or waxed paper and flatten to 1/2-in. thickness. Sprinkle with lemon-pepper seasoning.

Melt butter in a large skillet over medium heat; cook pork for 3-4 minutes on each side or until no longer pink and juices run clear. Remove to a serving platter and keep warm.

To the pan juices, add lemon juice, Worcestershire sauce and mustard; heat through, stirring occasionally. Pour over the pork and sprinkle with parsley. Serve immediately. **Yield:** 4 servings.

tuscan pork roast

Elinor Stabile, Canmore, Alberta

Everyone's eager to eat after the wonderful aroma of this well-seasoned pork roast baking in the oven tempts us all afternoon. This is a great Sunday dinner with little fuss to prepare. Since I found this recipe a few years ago, it's become a favorite with our seven grown children and their families.

> 5 to 8 garlic cloves, peeled
> 1 tablespoon dried rosemary
> 1 tablespoon olive oil
> 1/2 teaspoon salt
> 1 boneless whole pork loin roast (3 to 4 pounds)

In a food processor, combine the garlic, rosemary, olive oil and salt; cover and process until the mixture becomes a paste. Rub over the roast; cover and let stand for 30 minutes.

Place roast fat side up on a greased baking rack in a shallow roasting pan. Bake, uncovered, at 350° for 1 to 1-1/4 hours or until a meat thermometer reads 160°. Let stand for 10 minutes before slicing. **Yield:** 10-12 servings.

old-world stuffed pork chops

Jeanne Schuyler, Wauwatosa, Wisconsin

Years ago, a relative ran a restaurant, and this is one of the recipes she developed. The savory stuffing and juicy pork chops are always a hit.

> 4 pork chops (1/2 inch thick)
> 1 to 2 tablespoons vegetable oil
> Salt and pepper to taste
> 3 cups dry unseasoned bread cubes
> 1 can (16 ounces) cream-style corn
> 1 egg, lightly beaten
> 1 teaspoon grated onion
> 1/2 teaspoon rubbed sage
> 1/2 teaspoon dried basil
> 1/2 teaspoon salt
> 1/4 teaspoon pepper

In a skillet, brown pork chops in oil on both sides; sprinkle with salt and pepper. Meanwhile, in a bowl, combine remaining ingredients and mix well. Alternate the pork chops and stuffing lengthwise in a greased 3-qt. or 11-in. x 7-in. x 2-in. baking dish. Bake, uncovered, at 350° for 1 hour. **Yield:** 4 servings.

> ✳ To make pork roast even tastier, top it with a jar of all-fruit apricot preserves. Pour 1/2 cup apple juice over all and sprinkle with lemon-pepper seasoning.
> Bettyrae Easley, Anchorage, Alaska

HEARTY HAM

#1

DILLY HAM BALLS

dilly ham balls
GRAND PRIZE WINNER

When word of mouth focuses on kitchen classics, ham's full-flavored taste is always included. But even a succulent standby can stand freshening-up occasionally.

So, starting here with the winners of our Hearty Ham contest, you'll find good, practical ideas for making an old favorite a new favorite.

> " I have handed out this recipe many, many times. "

From breakfast to dinner and from appetizers to filling main dishes, great cooks have shared their most-requested ham recipes (many of them can help you use up leftover ham). Let ham create a stir at your house, too.

The recipe for Dilly Ham Balls was chosen the Grand Prize Winner. "To come up with a meal my grandchildren would enjoy, I shaped a ham loaf into balls and added a sauce," says Dixie Terry of Marion, Illinois. "The kids raved—and so did the adults. I have handed out this recipe many, many times."

    1 pound ground fully cooked ham
1/2 cup dry bread crumbs
1/4 cup finely chopped green onions
    3 tablespoons finely chopped fresh dill *or* 3
      teaspoons dried dill, *divided*
1/4 cup milk
    1 egg, lightly beaten
    1 teaspoon Dijon mustard
1/2 teaspoon pepper, *divided*
    1 to 2 tablespoons butter
    1 to 2 tablespoons vegetable oil
    2 tablespoons all-purpose flour
    1 cup water
    1 cup (8 ounces) sour cream
Hot cooked noodles

In a bowl, combine ham, bread crumbs, onions, 1 tablespoon fresh dill (or 1 teaspoon dried), milk, egg, mustard and 1/4 teaspoon pepper. Shape into 1-in. balls.

In a large skillet, heat 1 tablespoon butter and 1 tablespoon oil. Brown ham balls, adding remaining butter and oil as needed. Remove ham balls to a serving dish; cover and keep warm.

Pour ham drippings into a saucepan; blend in flour. Gradually add water and stir until smooth. Bring to a boil; cook and stir for 2 minutes or until thickened. Reduce heat to low. Add sour cream and remaining dill and pepper; heat through, but do not boil. Pour over the ham balls. Serve over noodles. **Yield:** 6 servings.

festive ham glaze

Becky Magee, Chandler, Arizona

As long as I can remember, my favorite room's been the kitchen. My glaze dates back to shortly after my husband and I were married. My parents were visiting; I cooked a Sunday ham with this glaze—and I've done it that same way from then on. Since my husband made his career in the Air Force, we spent years in the city or living in close quarters. When he retired, we decided to plant roots here where we could experience the daily rise and set of the sun, silhouetting the mountains in the distance.

　1　bone-in fully cooked ham (5 to 8 pounds)
1-1/2　cups orange juice
1-1/4　cups packed brown sugar
　1　tablespoon grated orange peel
　1　teaspoon ground mustard
1/4　teaspoon ground cloves

Score surface of ham, making diamond shapes 1/2 in. deep. Place in a large baking dish.

In a bowl, mix remaining ingredients; pour over ham. Cover and refrigerate overnight, turning the ham occasionally.

Reserving glaze, remove ham to a rack in a shallow roasting pan. Insert meat thermometer. Bake, uncovered, at 325° until thermometer registers 140°, about 2-4 hours, brushing occasionally with glaze. **Yield:** 10-16 servings.

ham pasta salad

Deanna Mitchell, Independence, Kansas

I invented this salad as I went along. It's a combination of various pasta salad recipes I've seen. It can be served as a side dish, of course. In summer, however, my husband doesn't care for hot meals, so I make it as a main dish.

　1　package (7 ounces) shell macaroni, cooked and drained
　2　cups cubed fully cooked ham
　1　cup chopped green pepper
　1　cup chopped tomato
1/4　cup chopped onion
DRESSING:
1/2　cup mayonnaise
1/4　cup grated Parmesan cheese
　2　tablespoons milk
1/4　teaspoon salt
Additional Parmesan cheese

In a large bowl, toss macaroni with ham, green pepper, tomato and onion. In a small bowl, combine mayonnaise, Parmesan cheese, milk and salt. Pour over pasta mixture and stir to coat. Cover and refrigerate. Sprinkle with additional Parmesan before serving. **Yield:** 4-6 servings.

ham and potato frittata

Katie Dreibelbis, State College, Pennsylvania
Easy and delicious, this hearty dish's been appreciated whenever I've served it…breakfast, lunch or dinner. Reheated or cold, the leftovers are also great! We live in a suburb, but our back windows look out at mountains, farms, horses and cows.

        3 tablespoons butter, *divided*
        1 pound red potatoes, cooked and sliced
    1-1/2 cups thinly sliced fresh mushrooms
        1 cup thinly sliced onion
        1 sweet red pepper, cut into thin strips
        2 cups diced fully cooked ham
        2 teaspoons minced fresh garlic
        1 tablespoon olive oil
      1/2 cup minced fresh parsley *or* basil
        8 eggs
Salt and pepper to taste
    1-1/2 cups (6 ounces) shredded cheddar *or* Swiss cheese

In a 10-in. castiron or other ovenproof skillet, melt 2 tablespoons butter. Brown potatoes over medium-high heat. Remove and set aside.

In the same skillet, melt the remaining butter; saute mushrooms, onion, red pepper, ham and garlic over medium-high heat until vegetables are tender. Remove and set aside. Wipe skillet clean.

Heat oil over medium-low. Add potatoes, ham/vegetable mixture and parsley or basil. In a bowl, beat eggs, salt and pepper. Pour into skillet; cover and cook for 10-15 minutes or until eggs are nearly set.

Preheat broiler; place uncovered skillet 6 in. from the heat for 2 minutes or until eggs are set. Sprinkle with cheese and broil until cheese is melted. Cut into wedges to serve. **Yield:** 6 servings.

ham and lentil soup

Andi Haug, Hendrum, Minnesota
This is a combination of two soup recipes I came across and adapted. I often serve it for Sunday dinner, making enough so there are leftovers for my husband's lunch thermos. He's a bricklayer and regularly works outside during winter.

        1 meaty ham bone
        6 cups water
    1-1/4 cups dried lentils, rinsed
        1 can (28 ounces) diced tomatoes, undrained
        2 to 3 carrots, sliced
        2 celery ribs, sliced
      1/4 cup chopped green onions
      1/2 teaspoon salt
      1/2 teaspoon garlic powder
      1/2 teaspoon dried oregano
      1/8 teaspoon pepper
       12 ounces bulk pork sausage, cooked and drained
        2 tablespoons chopped fresh parsley

In a Dutch oven, bring ham bone and water to a boil. Reduce heat; cover and simmer for 1-1/2 hours.

Remove ham bone. To broth, add lentils, tomatoes, carrots, celery, onions and seasonings; bring to a boil. Reduce heat; cover and simmer for 30-40 minutes or until lentils and vegetables are tender.

Meanwhile, remove ham from bone; coarsely chop. Add ham, sausage and parsley to soup; heat through. **Yield:** 10-12 servings (3 quarts).

creamed ham and asparagus

Linda Hartline, Marietta, Ohio

To be truthful, asparagus is my least favorite vegetable. But I make an exception with this recipe my mom and I came up with together because it's so delicious. The ham and cheese really lend a tasty difference. Now that our parents are retired, my brothers and I have taken over the family farm. We milk 200 Holsteins.

> 1 pound fresh *or* frozen asparagus, cut into 1-inch pieces
> 2 tablespoons butter
> 1 tablespoon cornstarch
> 1 teaspoon salt
> 1/2 teaspoon pepper
> 1-1/2 cups milk
> 1/2 teaspoon dried parsley flakes
> 1-1/2 pounds fully cooked ham, cubed
> 3 hard-cooked eggs, chopped
> 2 cups (8 ounces) shredded cheddar cheese
> Toast points *or* biscuits

In a saucepan, cook asparagus in a small amount of water until tender; drain and set aside.

In a large saucepan, melt butter. Stir in cornstarch, salt and pepper until smooth. Gradually add milk. Bring to a boil over medium heat; cook and stir for 2 minutes or until thickened.

Add parsley, ham, eggs, cheese and asparagus; cook and stir over low heat until ham is warmed and cheese is melted. Serve over toast points or biscuits. **Yield:** 4-6 servings.

cheddar ham chowder

Ann Heine, Mission Hill, South Dakota

Life on a farm can get hectic—along with my husband's four brothers, we custom-feed 5,000 head of cattle and grow 5,000 acres of crops. So I often freeze this soup and thaw it for a fast, easy meal. Since it's hearty, all I need to add are rolls or bread and a salad.

> 2 cups water
> 2 cups cubed peeled potatoes
> 1/2 cup sliced carrots
> 1/2 cup sliced celery
> 1/4 cup chopped onion
> 1 teaspoon salt
> 1/4 teaspoon pepper
> 1/4 cup butter
> 1/4 cup all-purpose flour
> 2 cups milk
> 2 cups (8 ounces) shredded sharp cheddar cheese
> 1 can (15-3/4 ounces) whole kernel corn, drained
> 1-1/2 cups cubed fully cooked ham

In a large saucepan, bring the water, potatoes, carrots, celery, onion, salt and pepper to a boil. Reduce heat; cover and simmer for 8-10 minutes or until vegetables are just tender. Remove from the heat; do not drain.

Meanwhile, in a large saucepan, melt the butter. Stir in flour until smooth; gradually add milk. Bring to a boil; cook and stir for 2 minutes or until thickened.

Add cheese and stir until melted. Stir into the undrained vegetables; return large saucepan to the heat. Add corn and ham; heat through, stirring occasionally. **Yield:** 6-8 servings (2 quarts).

ham and cheese calzones

Shelby Marino, Neptune Beach, Florida

I keep the convenient ingredients on hand whenever family requests this dish, which they do quite often! This sort of inside-out pizza is something I concocted one evening when I had leftover baked ham and needed to fix something quick and simple. My husband loved it—so did all his friends when he took some to work for lunch.

- 2 tubes (10 ounces *each*) refrigerated pizza crust
- 1 cup ricotta cheese
- 4 to 6 ounces sliced pepperoni
- 2 cups diced fully cooked ham
- 2 cups (8 ounces) shredded part-skim mozzarella cheese

Shredded Parmesan cheese, optional
Dried basil, optional
Meatless spaghetti sauce, warmed

Unroll one pizza crust, stretching gently to make a 14-in. x 11-in. rectangle. Spread half of the ricotta on half of the dough lengthwise, to within 1 in. of the edges.

Sprinkle with half of the pepperoni, ham and mozzarella. Fold the unfilled side of the dough over the filled half and press edges together firmly to seal. Transfer to a greased baking sheet. Repeat with the remaining crust and filling ingredients.

Bake at 400° for 20-25 minutes or until golden brown. Sprinkle with Parmesan and basil if desired. Slice into serving-size pieces. Serve with spaghetti sauce. **Yield:** 8 servings.

★ ★ ★ ★ ★ prize winning tips

★ To dress up a ham dinner, make dressing as you would for chicken or turkey—but without seasoning. Bake it with your ham, letting the juices flavor the dressing. Green beans also make a nice complement to baked ham. Add them to the roaster with the ham about an hour before you eat and bake.

Laura Ann Nelson, Kenyon, Minnesota

★ Here's a way to make thick ham slices special. Dust them with flour, dip in beaten egg and coat both sides with bread crumbs. Brown them in butter over medium heat until both sides are golden. I like to serve them with cranberry sauce on the side.

Tina Principato, Hampton, New Hampshire

★ For a little variety, try replacing ground beef with ham in your stuffed green peppers.

Cindy Hartley, Norfolk, Virginia

★ For a hearty change of pace for your next party, add a bit of ground ham to your favorite cheese dip, ball or spread.

Kathy Weisbrod, Regina, Saskatchewan

runners-up

MEAT-AND-POTATO COMBOS

#1

BEEF STEW WITH
POTATO DUMPLINGS

beef stew with potato dumplings
GRAND PRIZE WINNER

The dictionary may define meat and potatoes as "basic," but there's nothing ordinary about the winners of our Meat-and-Potato Combos contest! Plain and simple, they're all hearty good eating with a deliciously unexpected dash of pizzazz added.

"**Everyone who tries it loves this flavorful stew...**"

Pleasing pairings of beef, pork or poultry with potatoes had our panel of tasters smiling, nodding and asking for second helpings. Comparing notes on their favorites later, the judges easily agreed on a Grand Prize Winner—Beef Stew with Potato Dumplings from Shawn Asiala of Boca Raton, Florida.

Shawn's rich, meaty stew, topped with fluffy herb-flavored potato dumplings, is a stick-to-the-ribs feast impossible to resist. "Everyone who tries it loves this flavorful stew and asks me to share the recipe," says Shawn. "Sometimes, all I have to do is describe the stew and people ask for the recipe even before tasting it!"

1/4 **cup all-purpose flour**
3/4 **teaspoon salt**
1/2 **teaspoon pepper**
2 **pounds beef stew meat, cubed**
2 **medium onions, chopped**
2 **tablespoons vegetable oil**
2 **cans (10-1/2 ounces *each*) condensed beef broth, undiluted**
3/4 **cup water**
1 **tablespoon red wine vinegar**
6 **medium carrots, cut into 2-inch chunks**
2 **bay leaves**
1 **teaspoon dried thyme**
1/4 **teaspoon garlic powder**
DUMPLINGS:
1 **egg**
3/4 **cup seasoned dry bread crumbs**
1 **tablespoon all-purpose flour**
1 **tablespoon minced fresh parsley**
1 **tablespoon minced onion**
1/2 **teaspoon dried thyme**
1/2 **teaspoon salt**
1/2 **teaspoon pepper**
2-1/2 **cups finely shredded raw potatoes**
Additional all-purpose flour

In a plastic bag, combine flour, salt and pepper. Add meat; toss to coat. In a 4-qt. Dutch oven, cook meat and onions in oil until the meat is browned and onions are tender. Stir in broth, water, vinegar, carrots and seasonings; bring to a boil. Reduce heat; cover and simmer for 1-1/2 hours or until meat is almost tender. Remove bay leaves.

In a bowl, beat egg; add the bread crumbs, flour, parsley, onion and seasonings. Stir in potatoes; mix well. With floured hands, shape into 1-1/2-in. balls. Dust with flour.

Bring stew to a boil; drop dumplings onto stew. Cover and simmer for 30 minutes (do not lift cover) or until dumplings are done. Serve immediately. **Yield:** 6 servings.

hot german potato salad

Inez Senner, Glendive, Montana
I enjoy sharing favorite dishes at church and family potlucks. This one has won raves whenever I've served it. I've also found it makes a good lunch that's better the second time around!

     9 medium potatoes
 1-1/2 pounds fully cooked smoked sausage *or* precooked bratwurst
     6 bacon strips
   3/4 cup chopped onion
     2 tablespoons all-purpose flour
     1 teaspoon salt
   1/2 teaspoon celery seed
   1/8 teaspoon pepper
   1/4 cup sugar
 1-1/3 cups water
   2/3 cup cider vinegar

In a saucepan, cook potatoes in boiling salted water until tender. Meanwhile, cut sausage into 1/2-in. slices; saute in a skillet until browned. Drain and place in a large bowl. Drain potatoes; peel and cut into 3/4-in. cubes. Add to sausage; keep warm.

Cook bacon until crisp; crumble and set aside. Drain all but 3 tablespoons of drippings; saute onion in drippings until tender. Stir in the flour, salt, celery seed and pepper; blend well. Add sugar, water and vinegar; bring to a boil. Boil for 2 minutes. Pour over potato mixture and stir gently to coat. Sprinkle with bacon. Serve warm. **Yield:** 12-14 servings.

meat loaf potato surprise

Lois Edwards, Citrus Heights, California
Although I'm retired after years of teaching school, my days continue to be full. So easy dishes like this still are a blessing to me.

     1 cup soft bread crumbs
   1/2 cup beef broth
     1 egg, beaten
     4 teaspoons dried minced onion
     1 teaspoon salt
   1/4 teaspoon Italian seasoning
   1/4 teaspoon pepper
 1-1/2 pounds ground beef
     4 cups frozen shredded hash browns, thawed
   1/3 cup grated Parmesan cheese
   1/4 cup minced fresh parsley
     1 teaspoon onion salt
SAUCE:
     1 can (8 ounces) tomato sauce
   1/4 cup beef broth
     2 teaspoons prepared mustard
Additional Parmesan cheese, optional

In a bowl, combine bread crumbs, broth, egg and seasonings; let stand for 2 minutes. Add the beef and mix well. On a piece of waxed paper, pat meat mixture into a 10-in. square.

Combine hash browns, cheese, parsley and onion salt; spoon over meat. Roll up jelly-roll style, removing waxed paper as you roll. Pinch edges and ends to seal; place with seam side down in an ungreased shallow baking pan.

Bake at 375° for 40 minutes. Combine the first three sauce ingredients; spoon over meat loaf. Return to the oven for 10 minutes. Sprinkle with Parmesan cheese if desired. **Yield:** 8 servings.

roast pork and potatoes

Denise Collins, Chillicothe, Ohio
We used to raise our own hogs. This recipe was given to me by a fellow farmer who also had pork on the dinner table a couple of times a week. I'm a dietitian at the local VA hospital. Cooking, of course, is one of my top pastimes!

 1 envelope onion soup mix
 2 garlic cloves, minced
 1 tablespoon dried rosemary, crushed
 1/2 teaspoon salt
 1/2 teaspoon pepper
 1/4 teaspoon ground cloves
 3 cups water, *divided*
 1 pork loin roast with bone (4 to 5 pounds)
 24 small red potatoes, halved (2 to 3 pounds)
 1-1/2 cups sliced onions

In a bowl, combine the first six ingredients. Stir in 1/2 cup water; let stand for 3 minutes. Place roast fat side up on a greased rack in a roasting pan. Pour remaining water into the pan. Combine potatoes and onions; spoon around the roast. Brush vegetables and roast with seasoning mixture.

Bake, uncovered, at 325° for 2-1/2 to 3 hours or until a meat thermometer reads 160°-170° and the potatoes are tender. Baste and stir the potatoes occasionally. Tent with foil if browning too fast. Thicken juices for gravy if desired. Let stand for 10 minutes before slicing. **Yield:** 8-10 servings.

beef and potato boats

Linda Wheeler, Harrisburg, Pennsylvania
Back when I was teaching elementary school (I'm now a busy stay-at-home mom), my class would put together a Mother's Day cookbook. Many of the dishes are still my favorites—this one included.

 4 large baking potatoes (8 to 10 ounces *each*)
 2 tablespoons butter
1-1/4 teaspoons salt, *divided*
Dash pepper
 1/4 to 1/3 cup milk
 1 pound ground beef
 1 small onion, chopped
 6 bacon strips, cooked and crumbled
 1/2 cup sour cream
 1/4 cup shredded cheddar cheese

Wash potato skins and prick with a fork. Bake at 400° for 60-70 minutes or until tender. Allow potatoes to cool to the touch. Slice a small portion off the top of each potato. Carefully scoop out the pulp, leaving a 1/4-in. shell. In a bowl, mash the pulp with butter, 1/2 teaspoon salt, pepper and milk; set aside.

In a saucepan over medium heat, cook the beef and onion until meat is no longer pink; drain. Cool 10 minutes. Add bacon, sour cream and remaining salt. Spoon into potato shells. Top each with a fourth of the mashed potato mixture; sprinkle with cheese.

Place potatoes on an ungreased baking sheet. Bake at 400° for 20-25 minutes or until heated through. **Yield:** 4 servings.

chicken potato bake

Myrtle Nelson, Wetaskiwin, Alberta
When I came up with this recipe, I was looking for something that didn't require last-minute fuss. It's great getting compliments on something so simple!

    1 cup dry bread crumbs
  1/2 cup all-purpose flour
    2 teaspoons salt
    2 teaspoons paprika
    1 teaspoon seasoned salt
    1 teaspoon sugar
    1 teaspoon onion powder
    1 teaspoon rubbed sage
    1 teaspoon dried oregano
  1/2 teaspoon pepper
  1/2 teaspoon celery seed
  1/2 teaspoon dried parsley flakes
  1/4 teaspoon garlic powder
3-1/2 to 4 pounds chicken pieces, skin removed
    3 tablespoons vegetable oil
POTATOES:
    1 teaspoon vegetable oil
    1 teaspoon seasoned salt
    1 teaspoon dried parsley flakes
  1/2 teaspoon paprika
  1/8 teaspoon garlic powder
  1/8 teaspoon pepper
    4 medium red potatoes, cut into 1-inch cubes

In a shallow bowl, combine the first 13 ingredients. Dip chicken in oil; coat with crumb mixture. Place on a greased 15-in. x 10-in. x 1-in. baking pan.

For potatoes, combine oil, salt, parsley, paprika, garlic powder and pepper in a bowl. Add potatoes; stir until coated. Place around chicken. Bake, uncovered, at 350° for 1 hour or until potatoes are tender and chicken juices run clear. **Yield:** 4 servings.

potato lasagna

Mara Beaumont, South Milwaukee, Wisconsin
At our house, this is a regular—it's as much fun to fix as it is to eat! It's perfect for potlucks as well.

    2 tablespoons olive oil
    2 garlic cloves, minced
  1/2 teaspoon *each* salt and pepper
    7 medium potatoes, sliced 1/4 inch thick
    1 pound bulk Italian sausage
    1 large onion, chopped
    2 packages (10 ounces *each*) frozen chopped spinach, thawed and drained
    1 cup ricotta cheese
  1/4 cup Italian-seasoned dry bread crumbs
Dash cayenne pepper
Additional salt and pepper to taste
    2 cups (8 ounces) shredded part-skim mozzarella cheese
  1/2 cup chicken broth
    2 tablespoons grated Parmesan cheese

In a large bowl, combine oil, garlic, salt and pepper. Add the potatoes and toss to coat; spread evenly in an ungreased 15-in. x 10-in. x 1-in. baking pan. Cover tightly with foil. Bake at 425° for 35-40 minutes or until tender. Cool at least 15 minutes.

Meanwhile, in a large skillet, cook sausage and onion over medium heat until no longer pink; drain. Combine spinach, ricotta, crumbs, cayenne, salt and pepper.

Arrange a third of the potatoes evenly in a greased 13-in. x 9-in. x 2-in. baking dish. Layer with half of the spinach mixture, half of the sausage and half of the mozzarella. Repeat with a third of the potatoes and the remaining spinach mixture, sausage and mozzarella. Pour broth over all. Top with remaining potatoes; sprinkle with Parmesan. Bake, uncovered, at 350° for 30-35 minutes. Let stand 5 minutes before serving. **Yield:** 8-10 servings.

herbed cornish pasties

Maribeth Edwards, Follansbee, West Virginia

These hand-held golden pockets are packed with the irresistible combination of beef and potatoes.

- 2 cups all-purpose flour
- 1 teaspoon salt
- 1/2 teaspoon *each* dried basil and thyme
- 1/2 cup shortening
- 1/4 cup butter
- 5 to 6 tablespoons ice water

FILLING:
- 1 pound boneless beef chuck, cut into 1/2-inch cubes
- 2 tablespoons vegetable oil, *divided*
- 1 teaspoon salt
- 1/8 teaspoon pepper
- 2 tablespoons all-purpose flour
- 1 cup water
- 2 medium potatoes, peeled and diced
- 1/2 cup *each* diced carrot and onion
- 1 egg, lightly beaten

In a bowl, combine flour, salt, basil and thyme; cut in shortening and butter until crumbly. Add water, 1 tablespoon at a time, tossing lightly with a fork until mixture forms a ball. Cover and chill for at least 30 minutes.

Meanwhile, brown beef in a skillet in 1 tablespoon oil; sprinkle with salt and pepper. Remove with a slotted spoon; set aside. Add remaining oil to skillet; gradually stir in flour until smooth. Cook and stir over medium heat for about 2-3 minutes or until lightly browned. Gradually add water; whisk until smooth.

Return beef to skillet. Reduce heat; cover and simmer for 20 minutes. Add potatoes, carrot and onion. Cover and simmer for 25 minutes or until tender. Remove from the heat; cool.

Divide pastry into four equal portions. On a lightly floured surface, roll out one portion into a 9-in. circle. Mound 3/4 cup filling on half of circle. Moisten edges with water; fold dough over filling and press edges with a fork to seal. Place on an ungreased baking sheet. Repeat with remaining pastry and filling. Cut three slits in top of each; brush with egg. Bake at 400° for 25-30 minutes or until golden brown. **Yield:** 4 servings.

✳✳✳✳✳ prize. winning tips

✳ For a hearty but quick one-pot dinner, spread four or five medium sliced potatoes over the bottom of a large saucepan. Lightly salt and top with a pound of hamburger made into a large patty the size of the pan lid. Add a sliced onion and two or three sliced carrots. Cover and cook on low for 1 hour.

Marj Ridgeway, Brashear, Texas

✳ When I'm in a hurry, I make hash by browning a package of smoked sausage, a small onion and six sliced potatoes in a little oil.

Donna Brandt, Churubusco, Indiana

---

runners-up

shepherd's pie

Diane Gillingham, Carman, Manitoba
As the second oldest of eight children in a farm family, I had plenty of opportunity to cook while I was growing up. For "country eaters," this hearty pie is perfect!

    1 pound ground beef
  3/4 cup chopped onion
    2 garlic cloves, minced
    3 tablespoons vegetable oil, *divided*
    1 cup chopped fresh mushrooms
    1 tablespoon tomato paste
  1/2 cup beef broth
    2 teaspoons prepared horseradish
    1 teaspoon ground mustard
1-1/2 teaspoons salt, *divided*
  1/4 teaspoon pepper
  1/2 cup diced green pepper
  1/2 cup diced sweet red pepper
    8 medium potatoes, peeled and cubed
  1/3 cup hot milk
    1 cup (4 ounces) shredded cheddar cheese
    2 egg whites

In a skillet, cook beef, onion and garlic in 2 tablespoons of oil. Add mushrooms. Cook and stir for 3 minutes; drain. Place tomato paste in a bowl. Gradually whisk in broth until smooth. Stir in horseradish, mustard, 1 teaspoon salt and pepper. Add to meat mixture. Pour into a greased 11-in. x 7-in. x 2-in. baking pan; set aside.

In same skillet, saute peppers in remaining oil until tender, about 3 minutes. Drain and spoon over meat mixture.

Cook potatoes in boiling salted water until tender; drain. Mash with milk, cheese and remaining salt. Beat egg whites until stiff peaks form; gently fold into potatoes. Spoon over pepper layer. Bake, uncovered, at 425° for 15 minutes. Reduce heat to 350°; bake 20 minutes longer or until meat layer is bubbly. **Yield:** 4-6 servings.

steak potpie

Pattie Bonner, Cocoa, Florida
When I hear "meat and potatoes," this is the recipe that immediately comes to mind. I've made it for years.

  3/4 cup sliced onions
    4 tablespoons vegetable oil, *divided*
  1/4 cup all-purpose flour
    1 teaspoon salt
  1/2 teaspoon pepper
  1/2 teaspoon paprika
Pinch *each* ground allspice and ginger
    1 pound boneless round steak, cut into 1/2-inch pieces
2-1/2 cups boiling water
    3 medium potatoes, peeled and diced
Pastry for single-crust pie

In a large skillet, saute the onions in 2 tablespoons oil until golden. Drain and set aside. In a plastic bag, combine dry ingredients; add meat and shake to coat. Brown meat in remaining oil in the same skillet. Add water; cover and simmer until meat is tender, about 1 hour. Add potatoes; simmer, uncovered, for 15-20 minutes or until the potatoes are tender. Pour into a greased 1-1/2-qt. baking dish. Top with onion slices.

Roll pastry to fit baking dish. Place over hot filling; seal to edges of dish. Make slits in the crust. Bake at 450° for 25-30 minutes or until golden brown. If necessary, cover edges of crust with foil to prevent overbrowning. **Yield:** 4-6 servings.

chicken with potato stuffing

Carla Kreider, Quarryville, Pennsylvania
This is a great Sunday meal or company dish—as long as you're prepared with second helpings!

- 6 medium red potatoes, cut into 1-inch cubes
- 1 pound Italian sausage
- 1 cup finely chopped onion
- 1 tablespoon butter
- 4 teaspoons dried parsley flakes, *divided*
- 1 teaspoon salt
- 3/4 teaspoon dried rosemary, crushed
- 2-3/4 teaspoons dried thyme, *divided*
- 1/2 teaspoon pepper
- 1 roasting chicken (7 to 7-1/2 pounds)
- 1 tablespoon vegetable oil
- 1 cup water

Cook potatoes in boiling salted water until almost tender; drain and set aside. Cook sausage in boiling water for 10 minutes; drain. Halve each sausage lengthwise, then cut into 1/2-in. pieces.

In a large skillet over medium heat, cook potatoes, sausage and onion in butter until sausage is browned and the onion is tender. Add 2 teaspoons parsley, salt, rosemary, 3/4 teaspoon thyme and pepper.

Stuff chicken. Place remaining stuffing in a greased 1-1/2-qt. baking dish; cover and refrigerate. Place chicken in a roasting pan; brush with oil and sprinkle with remaining parsley and thyme. Add water to pan. Bake, uncovered, at 350° for 1-1/2 hours.

Place baking dish of stuffing in oven. Bake chicken and stuffing for 45 minutes or until a meat thermometer reads 180°. Thicken drippings if desired. **Yield:** 8 servings.

ham 'n' spuds salad

Jo Baker, Litchfield, Illinois
Not only does this make a hearty salad that's a favorite of men and good for carrying to picnics and church suppers...it's also a tasty way to use up ham!

- 2 cups cubed cooked potatoes
- 2 cups cubed fully cooked ham
- 4 hard-cooked eggs, chopped
- 1/2 cup pitted ripe olives
- 1/2 cup sliced celery
- 1/4 cup finely chopped green pepper
- 1/4 cup finely chopped onion
- 1/2 cup mayonnaise
- 1/4 cup sweet pickle relish
- 2 tablespoons minced pimientos
- 1 tablespoon prepared spicy brown *or* yellow mustard
- 2 teaspoons cider vinegar

Lettuce leaves, optional

In a bowl, combine potatoes, ham, eggs, olives, celery, green pepper and onion. In a small bowl, combine mayonnaise, relish, pimientos, mustard and vinegar; pour over potato mixture. Toss lightly to coat. Chill for several hours. Serve in a lettuce-lined bowl if desired. **Yield:** 6-8 servings.

COMFORTING CASSEROLES

#1

CHICKEN AND
DUMPLING
CASSEROLE

chicken and dumpling casserole

GRAND PRIZE WINNER

A hearty casserole can take the chill out of a cold evening, lift spirits and warm hearts. The versatility and convenience of casseroles, along with their stick-to-your-ribs goodness, have made them a mainstay in family meals.

> "This savory meal-in-one is one of my husband's favorites."

Our Comforting Casseroles contest stirred the interest of readers from coast to coast, resulting in a kitchen full of recipes—over 6,000 in all!

The casseroles our judges selected as the winners will surely make regular appearances on your table whenever a warm, filling meal is in order...especially Grand Prize Winner Chicken and Dumpling Casserole shared by Sue Mackey of Galesburg, Illinois.

"This savory meal-in-one is one of my husband's favorites," says Sue. "He loves the fluffy dumplings with plenty of gravy poured over them. The basil adds just the right touch of flavor and makes the whole house smell so good while this dish cooks."

1/2 cup chopped onion
1/2 cup chopped celery
  2 garlic cloves, minced
1/4 cup butter
1/2 cup all-purpose flour
  2 teaspoons sugar
  1 teaspoon salt
  1 teaspoon dried basil
1/2 teaspoon pepper
  4 cups chicken broth
  1 package (10 ounces) frozen green peas
  4 cups cubed cooked chicken
DUMPLINGS:
  2 cups biscuit/baking mix
  2 teaspoons dried basil
2/3 cup milk

In a large saucepan, saute onion, celery and garlic in butter until tender. Add flour, sugar, salt, basil, pepper and broth; bring to a boil. Cook and stir for 1 minute; reduce heat. Add peas and cook for 5 minutes, stirring constantly. Stir in chicken. Pour into a greased 13-in. x 9-in. x 2-in. baking dish.

For dumplings, combine biscuit mix and basil in a bowl. Stir in milk with a fork until moistened. Drop by tablespoonfuls onto casserole (12 dumplings).

Bake, uncovered, at 350° for 30 minutes. Cover and bake 10 minutes more or until dumplings are done.
Yield: 6-8 servings.

cheese potato puff

Beverly Templeton, Garner, Iowa
I enjoy entertaining and always look for recipes that can be made ahead of time. I got this comforting potato recipe from my mother-in-law. It's wonderful because I can prepare it the night before. It contains basic ingredients that everyone loves like potatoes, milk and cheddar cheese.

12 medium potatoes, peeled (about 5 pounds)
 1 teaspoon salt, *divided*
3/4 cup butter
 2 cups (8 ounces) shredded cheddar cheese
 1 cup milk
 2 eggs, beaten
Fresh *or* dried chives, optional

Place potatoes in a large kettle; cover with water. Add 1/2 teaspoon salt; cook until tender. Drain; mash potatoes until smooth.

In a saucepan, cook and stir the butter, cheese, milk and remaining salt until smooth. Stir into the potatoes; fold in eggs.

Pour mixture into a greased 3-qt. baking dish. Bake, uncovered, at 350° for 40 minutes or until puffy and golden brown. Sprinkle with chives if desired. **Yield:** 8-10 servings.

Editor's Note: Casserole may be covered and refrigerated overnight. Allow to stand at room temperature for 30 minutes before baking.

tuna mushroom casserole

Jone Furlong, Santa Rosa, California
I love to serve this dressed-up version of a tuna casserole. The green beans add nice texture, color and flavor.

1/2 cup water
 1 teaspoon chicken bouillon granules
 1 package (10 ounces) frozen green beans
 1 cup chopped onion
 1 cup sliced fresh mushrooms
1/4 cup chopped celery
 1 garlic clove, minced
1/2 teaspoon dill weed
1/2 teaspoon salt
1/8 teaspoon pepper
 4 teaspoons cornstarch
1-1/2 cups milk
1/2 cup shredded Swiss cheese
1/4 cup mayonnaise
2-1/2 cups medium egg noodles, cooked and drained
 1 can (12-1/4 ounces) tuna, drained and flaked
1/3 cup dry bread crumbs
 1 tablespoon butter

In a large saucepan, bring water and bouillon to a boil, stirring to dissolve. Add the next eight ingredients; bring to a boil. Reduce heat; cover and simmer 5 minutes or until vegetables are tender. Dissolve cornstarch in milk; add to vegetable mixture, stirring constantly. Bring to a boil; boil 2 minutes or until thickened.

Remove from the heat; stir in cheese and mayonnaise until the cheese is melted. Fold in noodles and tuna. Pour into a greased 2-1/2-qt. baking dish. Brown bread crumbs in butter; sprinkle on top of casserole. Bake, uncovered, at 350° for 25-30 minutes or until heated through. **Yield:** 4-6 servings.

cordon bleu casserole

Joyce Paul, Moose Jaw, Saskatchewan
Whenever I'm invited to attend a potluck, people usually ask me to bring this tempting casserole. The turkey, ham and cheese are delectable combined with the crunchy topping.

> 4 cups cubed cooked turkey
> 3 cups cubed fully cooked ham
> 1 cup (4 ounces) shredded cheddar cheese
> 1 cup chopped onion
> 1/4 cup butter
> 1/3 cup all-purpose flour
> 2 cups half-and-half cream
> 1 teaspoon dill weed
> 1/8 teaspoon ground mustard
> 1/8 teaspoon ground nutmeg

TOPPING:
> 1 cup dry bread crumbs
> 2 tablespoons butter, melted
> 1/4 teaspoon dill weed
> 1/4 cup shredded cheddar cheese
> 1/4 cup chopped walnuts

In a large bowl, combine turkey, ham and cheese; set aside. In a saucepan, saute onion in butter until tender. Add flour; stir to form a paste. Gradually add cream, stirring constantly. Bring to a boil; boil 1 minute or until thick. Add dill, mustard and nutmeg; mix well. Remove from the heat and pour over meat mixture.

Spoon into a greased 13-in. x 9-in. x 2-in. baking dish. Toss bread crumbs, butter and dill; stir in cheese and walnuts. Sprinkle over the casserole. Bake, uncovered, at 350° for 30 minutes or until heated through. **Yield:** 8-10 servings.

spaghetti squash casserole

Myna Dyck, Boissevain, Manitoba
Spaghetti squash, like zucchini, can take over a backyard garden. This casserole is an excellent way to put that abundance to good use.

> 1 small spaghetti squash (1-1/2 to 2 pounds)
> 1/2 cup water
> 1 pound ground beef
> 1/2 cup chopped onion
> 1/2 cup chopped sweet red pepper
> 1 garlic clove, minced
> 1 can (8 ounces) diced tomatoes, undrained
> 1/2 teaspoon dried oregano
> 1/4 teaspoon salt
> 1/8 teaspoon pepper
> 1 cup (4 ounces) shredded part-skim mozzarella *or* cheddar cheese
> 1 tablespoon chopped fresh parsley

Cut squash in half lengthwise; scoop out seeds. Place with cut side down in a baking dish; add water. Cover and bake at 375° for 20-30 minutes or until it is easily pierced with a fork. When cool enough to handle, scoop out squash, separating the strands with a fork.

In a skillet, cook beef, onion, red pepper and garlic until meat is no longer pink and the vegetables are tender. Drain; add tomatoes, oregano, salt, pepper and squash. Cook and stir for 1-2 minutes or until liquid is absorbed. Transfer to an ungreased 1-1/2-qt. baking dish.

Bake, uncovered, at 350° for 25 minutes. Sprinkle with the cheese and parsley; let stand a few minutes. **Yield:** 6-8 servings.

pork and green chili casserole

Dianne Esposite, New Middletown, Ohio
I work at a local hospital and also part time for some area doctors, so I'm always on the lookout for good, quick recipes to fix for my family. Some of my co-workers and I exchange recipes. This zippy casserole is one that was brought to a picnic at my house. People raved over it.

1-1/2   **pounds boneless pork, cut into 1/2-inch cubes**
  1   **tablespoon vegetable oil**
  1   **can (15 ounces) black beans, rinsed and drained**
  1   **can (10-3/4 ounces) condensed cream of chicken soup, undiluted**
  1   **can (14-1/2 ounces) diced tomatoes, undrained**
  2   **cans (4 ounces *each*) chopped green chilies**
  1   **cup quick-cooking brown rice**
1/4   **cup water**
  2   **to 3 tablespoons salsa**
  1   **teaspoon ground cumin**
1/2   **cup shredded cheddar cheese**

In a large skillet, saute pork in oil until no pink remains; drain. Add the beans, soup, tomatoes, chilies, rice, water, salsa and cumin; cook and stir until bubbly. Pour into an ungreased 2-qt. baking dish.

Bake, uncovered, at 350° for 30 minutes or until bubbly. Sprinkle with cheese; let stand a few minutes before serving. **Yield:** 6 servings.

butternut squash bake

Julie Jahn, Decatur, Indiana
If I ask our two girls what to fix for a special meal, this dish is always requested. I discovered this slightly sweet and crunchy-topped casserole at a church dinner about 20 years ago, and now I take it to potluck dinners and come home with an empty dish! Crisp rice cereal and pecans are unusual but tasty toppings.

1/3   **cup butter, softened**
3/4   **cup sugar**
  2   **eggs**
  1   **can (5 ounces) evaporated milk**
  1   **teaspoon vanilla extract**
  2   **cups mashed cooked butternut squash**
TOPPING:
1/2   **cup crisp rice cereal**
1/4   **cup packed brown sugar**
1/4   **cup chopped pecans**
  2   **tablespoons butter, melted**

In a mixing bowl, cream the butter and sugar. Beat in the eggs, milk and vanilla. Stir in the squash (mixture will be thin). Pour into a greased 11-in. x 7-in. x 2-in. baking pan.

Bake, uncovered, at 350° for 45 minutes or until almost set. Combine topping ingredients; sprinkle over casserole. Return to the oven for 5-10 minutes or until bubbly. **Yield:** 6-8 servings.

lasagna with white sauce

Angie Price, Bradford, Tennessee

I'm an old-fashioned country cook and love preparing recipes like this one that use staples I normally keep on hand. Unlike most lasagnas, this one doesn't call for precooking the noodles. It's so simple my children sometimes make it after school and have it ready when I get home from work.

- 1 pound ground beef
- 1 large onion, chopped
- 1 can (14-1/2 ounces) diced tomatoes, undrained
- 2 tablespoons tomato paste
- 1 beef bouillon cube
- 1-1/2 teaspoons Italian seasoning
- 1 teaspoon salt
- 1/2 teaspoon pepper
- 1/4 teaspoon ground red *or* cayenne pepper

WHITE SAUCE:

- 2 tablespoons butter
- 3 tablespoons all-purpose flour
- 1 teaspoon salt
- 1/4 teaspoon pepper
- 2 cups milk
- 1-1/4 cups shredded part-skim mozzarella cheese, *divided*
- 10 to 12 uncooked lasagna noodles

In a Dutch oven, cook beef and onion until meat is no longer pink and onion is tender; drain. Add tomatoes, tomato paste, bouillon and seasonings. Cover; cook over medium-low heat 20 minutes, stirring occasionally.

Meanwhile, melt butter in a medium saucepan; stir in flour, salt and pepper. Gradually add milk; bring to a boil, stirring constantly. Reduce heat and cook for 1 minute. Remove from the heat and stir in half of the cheese; set aside.

Pour half of the meat sauce into an ungreased 13-in. x 9-in. x 2-in. baking dish. Cover with half of the lasagna noodles. Cover with remaining meat sauce. Top with remaining noodles. Pour white sauce over noodles. Sprinkle with remaining cheese. Cover and bake at 400° for 40 minutes or until noodles are done. **Yield:** 10-12 servings.

prize winning tips

✳ Lasagna takes on a whole different twist if you spread frozen chopped spinach that has been thawed, well drained and squeezed dry on the middle layer. It adds great flavor and color.

Kris Martinell, Dell, Montana

✳ Like a flavorful change of pace? Top your favorite ground beef casserole with butter-flavored cracker crumbs instead of potato chips.

Michelle Gazaw, Wynantskill, New York

✳ Add some dried marjoram the next time you make a creamy ham casserole. It's just the right complement.

Caryn Hasbrouck, Wheaton, Illinois

monterey spaghetti

Janet Hibler, Cameron, Missouri

I'm a working mother with two young boys. Our family leads a very active life, so I make a lot of casseroles. It's so nice to have a hearty, nutritious side dish the kids will eat. Topped with cheese and french-fried onions, this tasty casserole is a hit at our house.

- 4 ounces spaghetti, broken into 2-inch pieces
- 1 egg
- 1 cup (8 ounces) sour cream
- 1/4 cup grated Parmesan cheese
- 1/4 teaspoon garlic powder
- 2 cups (8 ounces) shredded Monterey Jack cheese
- 1 package (10 ounces) frozen chopped spinach, thawed and drained
- 1 can (2.8 ounces) french-fried onions, *divided*

Cook the spaghetti according to package directions. Meanwhile, in a medium bowl, beat the egg. Add the sour cream, Parmesan cheese and garlic powder. Drain spaghetti; add to egg mixture with Monterey Jack cheese, spinach and half of the onions. Pour into a greased 2-qt. baking dish.

Cover and bake at 350° for 30 minutes or until heated through. Top with remaining onions; return to the oven for 5 minutes or until onions are golden brown. **Yield:** 6-8 servings.

pan burritos

Joyce Kent, Grand Rapids, Michigan

Our family loves Mexican food, so this flavorful, satisfying casserole is a favorite.

- 2 packages (1-1/2 ounces *each*) enchilada sauce mix
- 3 cups water
- 1 can (12 ounces) tomato paste
- 1 garlic clove, minced
- 1/4 teaspoon pepper
- Salt to taste
- 2 pounds ground beef
- 9 large flour tortillas (9 inches)
- 4 cups (16 ounces) shredded cheddar cheese *or* taco cheese
- 1 can (16 ounces) refried beans, warmed
- Taco sauce, sour cream, chili peppers, chopped onion *and/or* guacamole, optional

In a saucepan, combine the first six ingredients; simmer for 15-20 minutes. In a skillet, cook the beef over medium heat until no longer pink. Drain; stir in one-third of the sauce. Spread another third on the bottom of a greased 13-in. x 9-in. x 2-in. baking pan.

Place three tortillas over sauce, tearing to fit bottom of pan. Spoon half of meat mixture over tortillas; sprinkle with 1-1/2 cups cheese. Add three more tortillas. Spread refried beans over tortillas; top with remaining meat. Sprinkle with 1-1/2 cups of cheese. Layer remaining tortillas; top with the remaining sauce. Sprinkle with remaining cheese.

Bake, uncovered, at 350° for 35-40 minutes. Let stand 10 minutes before cutting. Serve with taco sauce, sour cream, chili peppers, chopped onion and/or guacamole if desired. **Yield:** 8-10 servings.

*runners-up

hungarian noodle side dish

Betty Sugg, Akron, New York

I first served this creamy, rich casserole at our ladies meeting at church. Everyone liked it and many of the ladies wanted the recipe. The original recipe was from a friend, but I changed it a bit to suit our tastes.

    3 chicken bouillon cubes
  1/4 cup boiling water
    1 can (10-3/4 ounces) condensed cream of
      mushroom soup, undiluted
  1/2 cup chopped onion
    2 tablespoons Worcestershire sauce
    2 tablespoons poppy seeds
  1/8 to 1/4 teaspoon garlic powder
  1/8 to 1/4 teaspoon hot pepper sauce
    2 cups (16 ounces) cottage cheese
    2 cups (16 ounces) sour cream
    1 package (16 ounces) medium egg noodles,
      cooked and drained
  1/4 cup shredded Parmesan cheese
Paprika

In a large bowl, dissolve bouillon in water. Add the next six ingredients; mix well. Stir in cottage cheese, sour cream and noodles and mix well. Pour into a greased 2-1/2-qt. baking dish. Sprinkle with the Parmesan cheese and paprika. Cover and bake at 350° for 45 minutes or until heated through. **Yield:** 8-10 servings.

Editor's Note: Casserole may be covered and refrigerated overnight. Allow to stand at room temperature for 30 minutes before baking.

spanish rice and chicken

Cindy Clark, Mechanicsburg, Pennsylvania

My mother has always been an avid cook, and my sister, two brothers and I were raised on this casserole. When I polled our family to see which recipe I should share, this fresh-tasting, well-seasoned chicken casserole came out on the top of the list. I know you'll enjoy it as much as we do.

    1 broiler/fryer chicken (2-1/2 to 3 pounds),
      cut up
    1 teaspoon garlic salt
    1 teaspoon celery salt
    1 teaspoon paprika
    1 cup uncooked rice
  3/4 cup chopped onion
  3/4 cup chopped green pepper
  1/4 cup minced fresh parsley
1-1/2 cups chicken broth
    1 cup chopped tomatoes
1-1/2 teaspoons salt
1-1/2 teaspoons chili powder

Place chicken in a greased 13-in. x 9-in. x 2-in. baking pan. Combine garlic salt, celery salt and paprika; sprinkle over chicken. Bake, uncovered, at 425° for 20 minutes. Remove chicken from pan. Combine rice, onion, green pepper and parsley; spoon into the pan.

In a saucepan, bring broth, tomatoes, salt and chili powder to a boil. Pour over rice mixture; mix well. Place chicken pieces on top. Cover and bake for 45 minutes or until chicken and rice are tender. **Yield:** 4-6 servings.

SLOW-COOKED SPECIALTIES

#1

TANGY PORK CHOPS

tangy pork chops

Clever cooks who take advantage of a slow cooker know the joy of coming into the kitchen after a busy day away to find a hot, delicious meal waiting.

In addition to handy main-dish preparation, slow cookers can also serve up a no-fuss soup, side dish or dessert. In our Slow-Cooked Specialties contest, home cooks entered 3,500 of their favorites. Your slow cooker may take its time with any of the 12 winners featured here, but your family will be sure to gobble them up fast!

Tangy Pork Chops from Karol Hines of Kitty Hawk, North Carolina took the Grand Prize. "Fancy enough for company, these mouth-watering pork chops also make a great family meal," say Karol. "I usually have all the ingredients on hand. When my husband and I had our first child, this recipe was so convenient—I started it during naptime for a no-fuss supper later."

> "Fancy enough for company, these mouth-watering pork chops also make a great family meal."

4 pork chops (1/2 inch thick)
1/2 teaspoon salt
1/8 teaspoon pepper
2 medium onions, chopped
2 celery ribs, chopped
1 large green pepper, sliced
1 can (14-1/2 ounces) stewed tomatoes
1/2 cup ketchup
2 tablespoons cider vinegar
2 tablespoons brown sugar
2 tablespoons Worcestershire sauce
1 tablespoon lemon juice
1 beef bouillon cube
2 tablespoons cornstarch
2 tablespoons water
Hot cooked rice, optional

Place chops in a slow cooker; sprinkle with salt and pepper. Add the onions, celery, green pepper and tomatoes. Combine ketchup, vinegar, sugar, Worcestershire sauce, lemon juice and bouillon; pour over vegetables. Cover and cook on low for 5-6 hours.

Mix cornstarch and water until smooth; stir into liquid in slow cooker. Cover and cook on high for 30 minutes or until thickened. Serve over rice if desired. **Yield:** 4 servings.

stuffed chicken rolls

Jean Sherwood, Kenneth City, Florida
The wonderful aroma of this moist, delicious chicken cooking sparks our appetites. The ham and cheese rolled inside is a tasty surprise. When I prepared this impressive main dish for a church luncheon, I received lots of compliments. The rolls are especially nice served over rice or pasta.

      6 large boneless skinless chicken breast halves
      6 slices fully cooked ham
      6 slices Swiss cheese
    1/4 cup all-purpose flour
    1/4 cup grated Parmesan cheese
    1/2 teaspoon rubbed sage
    1/4 teaspoon paprika
    1/4 teaspoon pepper
    1/4 cup vegetable oil
      1 can (10-3/4 ounces) condensed cream of
         chicken soup, undiluted
    1/2 cup chicken broth
Chopped fresh parsley, optional

Flatten chicken to 1/8-in. thickness. Place ham and cheese on each breast. Roll up and tuck in ends; secure with a toothpick. Combine the flour, Parmesan cheese, sage, paprika and pepper; coat chicken on all sides. Cover and refrigerate for 1 hour.

In a large skillet, brown chicken in oil over medium-high heat. Transfer to a 5-qt. slow cooker. Combine soup and broth; pour over chicken. Cover and cook on low for 4-5 hours. Remove toothpicks. Garnish with parsley if desired. **Yield:** 6 servings.

teriyaki sandwiches

Bernice Muilenburg, Molalla, Oregon
The meat for these sandwiches comes out of the slow cooker tender and flavorful. Living as we do in the foothills of the Cascades, we frequently have deer and elk in the freezer. I sometimes substitute that in this recipe, and it never tastes like game.

      2 pounds boneless chuck steak
    1/4 cup soy sauce
      1 tablespoon brown sugar
      1 teaspoon ground ginger
      1 garlic clove, minced
      4 teaspoons cornstarch
      2 tablespoons water
      8 French rolls, split
    1/4 cup butter, melted
Pineapple rings
Chopped green onions

Cut steak into thin bite-size slices. In a slow cooker, combine soy sauce, sugar, ginger and garlic. Add steak. Cover and cook on low for 7-9 hours or until meat is tender.

Remove meat with a slotted spoon; set aside. Carefully pour liquid into a 2-cup measuring cup; skim fat. Add water to liquid to measure 1-1/2 cups. Pour into a large saucepan. Combine cornstarch and water until smooth; add to pan. Cook and stir until thick and bubbly, about 2 minutes. Add meat and heat through.

Brush rolls with butter; broil 4-5 in. from the heat for 2-3 minutes or until lightly toasted. Fill with meat, pineapple and green onions. **Yield:** 8 servings.

★runners-up

nutty apple streusel dessert

Jacki Every, Rotterdam, New York
Many people don't think of using a slow cooker to make dessert, but I like finishing up our dinner and having this hot, scrumptious apple treat waiting to be served up. I can start it in the morning and not think about it all day.

      6 cups sliced peeled tart apples
1-1/4 teaspoons ground cinnamon
   1/4 teaspoon ground allspice
   1/4 teaspoon ground nutmeg
   3/4 cup milk
      2 tablespoons butter, softened
   3/4 cup sugar
      2 eggs
      1 teaspoon vanilla extract
   1/2 cup biscuit/baking mix
TOPPING:
      1 cup biscuit/baking mix
   1/3 cup packed brown sugar
      3 tablespoons cold butter
   1/2 cup sliced almonds
Ice cream *or* whipped cream, optional

In a large bowl, toss apples with cinnamon, allspice and nutmeg. Place in a greased slow cooker. In a mixing bowl, combine milk, butter, sugar, eggs, vanilla and baking mix; mix well. Spoon over apples.

For topping, combine biscuit mix and brown sugar in a bowl; cut in butter until crumbly. Add almonds; sprinkle over apples. Cover and cook on low for 6-7 hours or until the apples are tender. Serve with ice cream or whipped cream if desired. **Yield:** 6-8 servings.

hearty new england dinner

Claire McCombs, San Diego, California
This favorite slow cooker recipe came from a friend. The horseradish in the gravy adds zip.

      2 medium carrots, sliced
      1 medium onion, sliced
      1 celery rib, sliced
      1 boneless chuck roast (about 3 pounds)
      1 teaspoon salt, *divided*
   1/4 teaspoon pepper
      1 envelope onion soup mix
      2 cups water
      1 tablespoon vinegar
      1 bay leaf
   1/2 small head cabbage, cut into wedges
      3 tablespoons butter
      2 tablespoons all-purpose flour
      1 tablespoon dried minced onion
      2 tablespoons prepared horseradish

Place carrots, onion and celery in a 5-qt. slow cooker. Place the roast on top; sprinkle with 1/2 teaspoon salt and pepper. Add soup mix, water, vinegar and bay leaf. Cover and cook on low for 7-9 hours or until beef is tender.

Remove beef and keep warm; discard bay leaf. Add cabbage. Cover and cook on high for 30-40 minutes or until cabbage is tender.

Meanwhile, melt butter in a small saucepan; stir in flour and onion. Add 1-1/2 cups cooking liquid from the slow cooker. Stir in horseradish and remaining salt; bring to a boil. Cook and stir over low heat until thick and smooth, about 2 minutes. Serve with roast and vegetables. **Yield:** 6-8 servings.

egg and broccoli casserole

Janet Sliter, Kennewick, Washington
For years, I've prepared this filling egg casserole —which is delicious for brunch—in my slow cooker. It's an unusual recipe for this appliance but is welcomed wherever I serve it. Folks always go back for second and third helpings.

- 1 carton (24 ounces) small-curd cottage cheese
- 1 package (10 ounces) frozen chopped broccoli, thawed and drained
- 2 cups (8 ounces) shredded cheddar cheese
- 6 eggs, beaten
- 1/3 cup all-purpose flour
- 1/4 cup butter, melted
- 3 tablespoons finely chopped onion
- 1/2 teaspoon salt

Additional shredded cheddar cheese, optional

In a large bowl, combine the first eight ingredients. Pour into a greased slow cooker. Cover and cook on high for 1 hour.

Stir. Reduce heat to low; cover and cook 2-1/2 to 3 hours longer or until a thermometer placed in the center reads 160° and the eggs are set. Sprinkle with additional cheese if desired. **Yield:** 6 servings.

partytime beans

Jean Cantner, Boston, Virginia
A friend brought this colorful bean dish to my house for a church circle potluck dinner a number of years ago. As soon as I tasted these slightly sweet baked beans, I had to have the recipe. I've served this and shared the recipe many times since.

- 1-1/2 cups ketchup
- 1 medium onion, chopped
- 1 medium green pepper, chopped
- 1 medium sweet red pepper, chopped
- 1/2 cup water
- 1/2 cup packed brown sugar
- 2 bay leaves
- 2 to 3 teaspoons cider vinegar
- 1 teaspoon ground mustard
- 1/8 teaspoon pepper
- 1 can (16 ounces) kidney beans, rinsed and drained
- 1 can (15-1/2 ounces) great northern beans, rinsed and drained
- 1 can (15 ounces) lima beans, rinsed and drained
- 1 can (15 ounces) black beans, rinsed and drained
- 1 can (15-1/2 ounces) black-eyed peas, rinsed and drained

In a slow cooker, combine the first 10 ingredients; mix well. Add the beans and peas; mix well. Cover and cook on low for 5-7 hours or until onion and peppers are tender. Remove bay leaves. **Yield:** 14-16 servings.

black and blue cobbler

Martha Creveling, Orlando, Florida

It never occurred to me that I could bake a cobbler in my slow cooker until I saw some recipes and decided to try my favorite fruity dessert recipe. It took a bit of experimenting, but the results are "berry" well worth it.

      1 cup all-purpose flour
1-1/2 cups sugar, *divided*
      1 teaspoon baking powder
  1/4 teaspoon salt
  1/4 teaspoon ground cinnamon
  1/4 teaspoon ground nutmeg
      2 eggs, beaten
      2 tablespoons milk
      2 tablespoons vegetable oil
      2 cups fresh *or* frozen blackberries
      2 cups fresh *or* frozen blueberries
  3/4 cup water
      1 teaspoon grated orange peel
Whipped cream *or* ice cream, optional

In a bowl, combine flour, 3/4 cup sugar, baking powder, salt, cinnamon and nutmeg. Combine eggs, milk and oil; stir into dry ingredients just until moistened. Spread the batter evenly onto the bottom of a greased 5-qt. slow cooker.

In a saucepan, combine berries, water, orange peel and remaining sugar; bring to a boil. Remove from the heat; immediately pour over batter. Cover and cook on high for 2 to 2-1/2 hours or until a toothpick inserted into the batter comes out clean.

Turn cooker off. Uncover and let stand for 30 minutes before serving. Serve with whipped cream or ice cream if desired. **Yield:** 6 servings.

---

prize winning tips

* * * * *

* To avoid heating up your kitchen during the hot summer months, try cooking pot roast in a slow cooker. All you lose is extra heat!

  Caroline Christensen, Richfield, Utah

* Economical, less-tender cuts of beef like round steak, stew meat and cube steak are perfect for the slow cooker. The long, slow cooking process ensures fork-tender, moist and flavorful meat even on cuts that would be tough and chewy prepared using other cooking methods. For meats to cook evenly in the slow cooker, allow some space between the pieces so the heat can circulate.

  Teona Miller, Phoenix, Arizona

* For a super-easy slow cooker recipe, try adding a couple envelopes of Italian salad dressing mix to a roast, and nothing else.

  Sharon Wilging, Mountain, Wisconsin

---

runners-up

championship bean dip

Wendi Wavrin Law, Omaha, Nebraska
My friends and neighbors always expect me to bring this irresistible dip to every gathering. When I arrive, they ask, "You brought your bean dip along, didn't you?" If there are any leftovers, we use them to make bean and cheese burritos the next day. I've given out this recipe a hundred times.

- 1 can (16 ounces) refried beans
- 1 cup picante sauce
- 1 cup (4 ounces) shredded Monterey Jack cheese
- 1 cup (4 ounces) shredded cheddar cheese
- 3/4 cup sour cream
- 1 package (3 ounces) cream cheese, softened
- 1 tablespoon chili powder
- 1/4 teaspoon ground cumin

Tortilla chips
Salsa

In a large bowl, combine the first eight ingredients, then transfer to a slow cooker. Cover and cook on high for 2 hours or until the dip is heated through, stirring once or twice. Serve with tortilla chips and salsa. **Yield:** 4-1/2 cups.

slow-cooker enchiladas

Mary Luebbert, Benton, Kansas
As a busy wife and mother of two young sons, I rely on this handy recipe. I layer enchilada ingredients in the slow cooker, turn it on and forget about it. With a bit of spice, these hearty enchiladas are especially nice during the colder months.

- 1 pound ground beef
- 1 cup chopped onion
- 1/2 cup chopped green pepper
- 1 can (16 ounces) pinto *or* kidney beans, rinsed and drained
- 1 can (15 ounces) black beans, rinsed and drained
- 1 can (10 ounces) diced tomatoes and green chilies, undrained
- 1/3 cup water
- 1 teaspoon chili powder
- 1/2 teaspoon ground cumin
- 1/2 teaspoon salt
- 1/4 teaspoon pepper
- 1 cup (4 ounces) shredded sharp cheddar cheese
- 1 cup (4 ounces) shredded Monterey Jack cheese
- 6 flour tortillas (6 *or* 7 inches)

In a skillet, cook beef, onion and green pepper until beef is no longer pink and vegetables are tender; drain. Add next eight ingredients; bring to a boil. Reduce heat; cover and simmer for 10 minutes. Combine cheeses.

In a 5-qt. slow cooker, layer about 3/4 cup beef mixture, one tortilla and about 1/3 cup cheese. Repeat layers. Cover and cook on low for 5-7 hours or until heated through. **Yield:** 4 servings.

sesame pork ribs

Sandy Alexander, Fayetteville, North Carolina

No one ever believes how little effort it takes to make these tender, juicy country-style ribs. The flavor of the lightly sweet and tangy sauce penetrates through the meat as the ribs simmer in the slow cooker all day.

- 3/4 cup packed brown sugar
- 1/2 cup soy sauce
- 1/2 cup ketchup
- 1/4 cup honey
- 2 tablespoons white wine vinegar
- 3 garlic cloves, minced
- 1 teaspoon ground ginger
- 1 teaspoon salt
- 1/4 to 1/2 teaspoon crushed red pepper flakes
- 5 pounds country-style pork ribs
- 1 medium onion, sliced
- 2 tablespoons sesame seeds, toasted
- 2 tablespoons chopped green onions

In a large bowl, combine the first nine ingredients. Add ribs and turn to coat. Place the onion in a 5-qt. slow cooker; arrange ribs on top and pour sauce over.

Cover and cook on low for 5-6 hours or until a meat thermometer reads 160°-170°. Place ribs on a serving platter; sprinkle with sesame seeds and green onions. **Yield:** 6 servings.

texican chili

Stacy Law, Cornish, Utah

This flavorful, meaty chili is my favorite...and it's so easy to prepare in the slow cooker. It's a great way to serve a crowd without last-minute preparation. I got the idea from my mother, who used her slow cooker often for soups and stews.

- 8 bacon strips, diced
- 2-1/2 pounds beef stew meat, cut into 1/2-inch cubes
- 2 cans (one 28 ounces, one 14-1/2 ounces) stewed tomatoes
- 2 cans (8 ounces *each*) tomato sauce
- 1 can (16 ounces) kidney beans, rinsed and drained
- 2 cups sliced carrots
- 1 medium onion, chopped
- 1 cup chopped celery
- 1/2 cup chopped green pepper
- 1/4 cup minced fresh parsley
- 1 tablespoon chili powder
- 1 teaspoon salt
- 1/2 teaspoon ground cumin
- 1/4 teaspoon pepper

In a skillet, cook bacon until crisp. Remove to paper towel to drain. Brown beef in the drippings over medium heat; drain. Transfer to a 5-qt. slow cooker; add bacon and remaining ingredients. Cover and cook on low for 9-10 hours or until the meat is tender, stirring occasionally. **Yield:** 16-18 servings.

GREAT GRILLING
#1

TERIYAKI SHISH KABOBS

teriyaki shish kabobs

Summer wouldn't be the same without the delicious taste of foods cooked to perfection on the outdoor grill. The appetizing aroma and satisfying sizzle of a cookout bring family and friends together for warm-weather food and fun.

For *Taste of Home's* Great Grilling recipe contest, cooks shared hot-off-the-grill recipes for burgers, chops, ribs, roasts, fish, vegetables and more. The tempting recipes here and on the following pages are sure to become summertime favorites at your house.

> "The tender beef, tangy sauce, sweet pineapple and flavorful vegetables make this main dish a memorable one."

The Grand Prize Winner is Teriyaki Shish Kabobs shared by Suzanne Pelegrin of Ocala, Florida. "The tender beef, tangy sauce, sweet pineapple and flavorful vegetables make this main dish a memorable one," Suzanne says.

"In the 1960s, when I was a teenager, my father worked for an airline, and my family lived on the island of Guam in the South Pacific. That's when a friend of my mother gave her this wonderful recipe. We ate this delicious warm-weather dish often, and now I prepare it for my family."

1/2 cup ketchup
1/2 cup sugar
1/2 cup soy sauce
1 teaspoon garlic powder
1 teaspoon ground ginger
2 pounds boneless beef sirloin steak (1-1/2 inches thick), cut into 1-1/2-inch cubes
1/2 fresh pineapple, trimmed and cut into 1-inch chunks
2 to 3 small zucchini, cut into 1-inch chunks
1/2 pound whole fresh mushrooms (medium size work best)
1/2 pound boiling onions, peeled
1 large green or sweet red pepper, cut into 1-inch pieces

Combine first five ingredients in a large resealable plastic bag; add beef. Seal bag and turn to coat; refrigerate overnight.

Drain beef, reserving marinade. Thread meat, pineapple and vegetables alternately on long skewers. Grill over hot coals for 15-20 minutes, turning often, or until meat reaches desired doneness and vegetables are tender.

In a saucepan, bring reserved marinade to a full rolling boil; boil for 1 minute. Remove meat and vegetables from skewers; serve with marinade. **Yield:** 6-8 servings.

GREAT GRILLING

#1

TANGY
GRILLED PORK

tangy grilled pork

I f you can't stand the heat, get out of the kitchen. When the weather is too warm, many cooks heed that safe advice by heading outdoors to the frill. Our Test Kitchen staff got fired up to do the same.

Their goal was to grill up dozens of family favorite dishes from among the thousands entered in *Country Woman's* own grilling contest—and the competition was hot!

"As it's cooking, the aroma of the pork is mouth-watering..."

When the smoke cleared, the panel of judges had sampled savory grilled ribs, roasts, kabobs, burgers, chicken, fish and more. After comparing notes, they agreed the Grand Prize should go to Ginger Johnson of Farmington, Illinois for her flavorful Tangy Grilled Pork that's served with a mustard sauce.

"Everyone who's tried it loves the bite of the mustard horseradish sauce mixed with the sweet-sour taste of the fruit preserves," says Ginger. "As it's cooking, the aroma of the pork is mouth-watering, and the sauce forms a glaze that is so appetizing."

1 boneless pork loin roast (2-1/2 to 3 pounds)
2 teaspoons olive oil
1-1/4 teaspoons ground mustard
3/4 teaspoon garlic powder
1/4 teaspoon ground ginger
1/2 cup horseradish mustard
1/2 cup apricot *or* pineapple preserves

Rub roast with oil, combine mustard, garlic powder and ginger; rub over the roast. Place the in a large resealable plastic bag or shallow glass container; seal bag or cover container. Refrigerate overnight.

Grill roast, covered, over indirect heat for 60 minutes. Combine the horseradish mustard and preserves. Continue grilling for 15-30 minutes basting twice with sauce, or until a meat thermometer reads 160°-170°. Let stand for 10 minutes before slicing. Heat remaining sauce to serve with roast. **Yield:** 10-12 servings.

Editor's Note: As a substitute for the horseradish mustard, combine 1/4 cup spicy brown mustard and 1/4 cup prepared horseradish.

dilly barbecued turkey

Sue Walker, Greentown, Indiana
This is one of my brother-in-law's special cookout recipes. The onions, garlic and herbs in the marinade make a tasty, tender turkey, and the tempting aroma always prompts the family to gather around the grill.

- 1 turkey breast half with bone (2-1/2 to 3 pounds)
- 2 cups plain yogurt
- 1/2 cup lemon juice
- 1/3 cup vegetable oil
- 1/2 cup minced fresh parsley
- 1/2 cup chopped green onions
- 4 garlic cloves, minced
- 4 tablespoons fresh minced dill *or* 4 teaspoons dill weed
- 1 teaspoon crushed dried rosemary
- 1 teaspoon salt
- 1/2 teaspoon pepper

Place the turkey in a glass baking dish. In a small bowl, combine all of the remaining ingredients; spread half over the turkey. Cover and refrigerate the remaining yogurt mixture. Cover and refrigerate the turkey for 6-8 hours or overnight.

Remove turkey, discarding marinade. Grill turkey, covered, over medium-hot heat, basting often with reserved marinade, for 1 to 1-1/4 hours or until juices run clear or internal temperature reaches 170°. **Yield:** 6 servings.

scrum-delicious burgers

Wendy Sommers, West Chicago, Illinois
I'm not sure where this recipe originated, but it's one of my family's summertime favorites. I usually serve these juicy burgers when we have company. The guests rave about the cheesy topping. It's fun to serve a burger like this one that's a little more special.

- 1-1/2 pounds ground beef
- 3 tablespoons finely chopped onion
- 1/2 teaspoon garlic salt
- 1/2 teaspoon pepper
- 1 cup (4 ounces) shredded cheddar cheese
- 1/3 cup canned sliced mushrooms
- 6 bacon strips, cooked and crumbled
- 1/4 cup mayonnaise
- 6 hamburger buns, split

Lettuce leaves and tomato slices, optional

In a medium bowl, combine beef, onion, garlic salt and pepper; mix well. Shape into six patties, 3/4 in. thick.

In a small bowl, combine the cheese, mushrooms, bacon and mayonnaise; refrigerate.

Grill burgers, covered, over medium heat for 5-7 minutes on each side.

During the last 3 minutes, spoon 1/4 cup of the cheese mixture onto each burger. Serve on buns with lettuce and tomato if desired. **Yield:** 6 servings.

kathy's herbed corn

Kathy Von Korff, North College Hill, Ohio
My husband and I agreed that the original recipe for this corn needed a little jazzing up, so I added the thyme and cayenne pepper to suit our tastes. Now fresh summer corn makes a regular appearance on our grill. And because the corn is covered with herbed butter before cooking, there is no need to add it afterwards.

        1/2 cup butter, softened
          2 tablespoons minced fresh parsley
          2 tablespoons minced fresh chives
          1 teaspoon dried thyme
        1/2 teaspoon salt
        1/4 teaspoon cayenne pepper
          8 ears sweet corn, husked

In a small bowl, combine first six ingredients. Spread 1 tablespoon over each ear of corn. Wrap corn individually in heavy-duty foil.

Grill, covered, over medium heat for 10-15 minutes, turning frequently, or until tender. **Yield:** 8 servings.

> *I could never get my ribs tender enough on the grill, until I tried precooking them in a slow cooker on high heat for 2 to 3 hours. Since racks of ribs don't fit in a slow cooker very well, I roll them up and place them in the pot standing up.
> Loyda Coulombe, Federal Way, Washington

marinated flank steak

Debbie Bonczek, Tariffville, Connecticut
I copied this recipe from a friend's collection 15 years ago. Since then I've gotten married and had two children. Now when we make steak on the grill, this is the recipe we usually use. It's also a tempting dish to serve when entertaining. It's earned me many compliments.

          3 tablespoons ketchup
          1 tablespoon vegetable oil
          1 tablespoon chopped onion
          1 teaspoon brown sugar
          1 teaspoon Worcestershire sauce
          1 garlic clove, minced
        1/8 teaspoon pepper
          1 beef flank steak (about 2 pounds)

In a large resealable plastic bag, combine the first seven ingredients; add beef. Seal bag and turn to coat; refrigerate for at least 4 hours.

Drain meat and discard marinade. Grill, covered, over medium heat until meat reaches desired doneness, about 6 minutes per side for medium, 8 minutes per side for medium-well. Slice into thin strips across the grain to serve. **Yield:** 8 servings.

tangy barbecue sauce

Mary Kaye Rackowitz, Marysville, Washington
My mother-in-law created this recipe, and we just can't get enough of the delectable sauce! I always take some out of the basting dish prior to using it on the grill so we have some to serve at the table. It tastes terrific on any grilled meat.

- 1 cup ketchup
- 2 tablespoons lemon juice
- 2 tablespoons cider vinegar
- 1/4 cup packed brown sugar
- 2 teaspoons prepared mustard
- 1 teaspoon salt
- 1/2 to 1 teaspoon hot pepper sauce
- 1 bay leaf
- 1 garlic clove, minced
- 1/2 cup water
- 2 teaspoons Worcestershire sauce

Combine all of the ingredients in a small saucepan; bring to a boil, stirring occasionally. Reduce heat; cover and simmer for 30 minutes.

Discard bay leaf. Use as a basting sauce when grilling chicken, pork or beef. **Yield:** 1-1/2 cups.

> *Presoak bamboo skewers in water for at least 20 minutes before threading with meat, vegetables or fruit to prevent them from scorching or burning. Or better yet, use metal skewers.
>
> Sally Hook, Houston, Texas

barbecued trout

Vivian Wolfram, Mountain Home, Arkansas
This delicious recipe came from a friend. The tangy sauce really gives the fish a wonderful flavor. Even those who aren't that fond of fish will like it prepared this way. My husband and I have been married for over 45 years and still look forward to dinner together.

- 2/3 cup soy sauce
- 1/2 cup ketchup
- 2 tablespoons lemon juice
- 2 tablespoons vegetable oil
- 1 teaspoon crushed dried rosemary
- 6 pan-dressed trout
Lemon wedges, optional

Combine the soy sauce, ketchup, lemon juice, oil and rosemary; pour two-thirds of marinade into a large resealable plastic bag; add fish. Seal bag and turn to coat; refrigerate bag for 1 hour, turning once. Cover and refrigerate remaining marinade for basting. Drain fish and discard marinade.

Place fish in a single layer in a well-greased hinged wire grill basket. Grill, covered, over medium heat for 8-10 minutes or until fish is browned on the bottom. Turn and baste with reserved marinade; grill 5-7 minutes longer or until fish flakes easily with a fork. Serve with lemon if desired. **Yield:** 6 servings.

*runners-up

grilled chicken salad

Juli Stewart, Coppell, Texas

A few years back, I found this easy, light salad recipe and made it for a picnic for my boyfriend and myself. Now that guy is my husband, and we still enjoy going on picnics and having this satisfying salad.

    6 boneless skinless chicken breast halves
    2 tablespoons fresh lemon juice
    1 pound penne pasta, cooked and drained
    1 medium sweet red pepper, chopped
2-1/2 cups sliced celery
    1 medium red onion, chopped
  1/4 cup minced fresh dill *or* 5 teaspoons dill weed
    3 tablespoons white wine vinegar
    2 tablespoons mayonnaise
    2 tablespoons Dijon mustard
  1/2 teaspoon salt
  1/4 teaspoon pepper
  2/3 cup olive oil
Leaf lettuce, optional

Grill chicken breasts, uncovered, over medium heat for 5-8 minutes on each side or until juices run clear. Remove from the grill and place in a single layer on a platter; sprinkle with lemon juice and set aside.

In a large bowl, toss pasta, red pepper, celery, onion and dill. Remove chicken from platter; pour juices into a bowl. Slice chicken crosswise into thin strips; add to pasta mixture.

To the juices, add vinegar, mayonnaise, mustard, salt and pepper; whisk well. Whisk in oil very slowly in a stream until dressing is thickened.

Pour over salad and toss. Serve in a lettuce-lined bowl or on individual lettuce-lined plates. **Yield:** 6 servings.

My family enjoys eating veggies grilled in foil packets. After placing vegetables in the center of a piece of aluminum foil, I seal the foil by folding along the sides to create a seam in the middle, then fold over the sides. These packets can also be baked in the oven on a baking sheet. After cooling, cautiously open the packets to let the steam escape and prevent burns.

Lynna Snider, Nipawin, Saskatchewan

grilled mushrooms

Melanie Knoll, Marshalltown, Iowa

Mushrooms cooked over hot coals always taste good, but this easy recipe makes the mushrooms taste fantastic. As the mother of two children, I love to cook entire meals on the grill. It's fun spending time outdoors with the kids.

  1/2 pound whole fresh mushrooms
        (medium size work best)
  1/4 cup butter, melted
  1/2 teaspoon dill weed
  1/2 teaspoon garlic salt

Thread mushrooms on skewers. Combine butter, dill and garlic salt; brush over mushrooms.

Grill over hot heat for 10-15 minutes, basting and turning every 5 minutes. **Yield:** 4 servings.

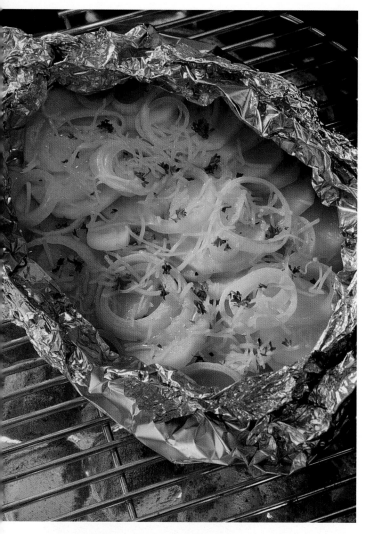

spicy pork tenderloin

Diana Steger, Prospect, Kentucky
A friend shared this recipe for marvelously flavorful pork years ago. It really sparks up a barbecue and has been popular whenever I've served it. I guarantee you'll get many requests for the recipe.

    1 to 3 tablespoons chili powder
    1 teaspoon salt
  1/4 teaspoon ground ginger
  1/4 teaspoon ground thyme
  1/4 teaspoon pepper
    2 pork tenderloins (about 1 pound *each*)

Combine the first five ingredients; rub over tenderloins. Cover and refrigerate for 2-4 hours.

Grill, covered over medium-hot indirect heat for 25-40 minutes or until meat thermometer reads 160°. **Yield:** 8 servings.

campfire potatoes

Joann Dettbarn, Brainerd, Minnesota
We like grilling because it's a no-fuss way to make a meal. This pleasing potato recipe is one we use often! The onion, cheddar cheese and Worcestershire sauce combine to make a super side dish for any grilled meat. Plus, cooking in the foil makes cleanup a breeze.

    5 medium potatoes, peeled and thinly sliced
    1 medium onion, sliced
    6 tablespoons butter
  1/3 cup shredded cheddar cheese
    2 tablespoons minced fresh parsley
    1 tablespoon Worcestershire sauce
Salt and pepper to taste
  1/3 cup chicken broth

Place the potatoes and onion on a large piece of heavy-duty foil (about 20 in. x 20 in.); dot with butter.

Combine the cheese, parsley, Worcestershire sauce, salt and pepper; sprinkle over potatoes. Fold foil up around the potatoes and add broth. Seal the edges of foil well.

Grill, covered, over medium heat for 35-40 minutes or until potatoes are tender. **Yield:** 4-6 servings.

*runners-up

zesty grilled ham

Mary Ann Lien, Tyler, Texas
This is my children's first choice of ham dishes. The mixture of sweet and tangy flavors is mouth-watering on a grilled piece of ham. Even the small ones eat adult-sized portions, so be sure to make plenty!

- 1 cup packed brown sugar
- 1/3 cup prepared horseradish
- 1/4 cup lemon juice
- 1 fully cooked ham steak (1 to 1-1/2 pounds and 1 inch thick)

In a small saucepan, bring the brown sugar, horseradish and lemon juice to a boil. Brush over both sides of ham.

Grill over medium-hot heat for 10-12 minutes on each side or until heated through and well glazed. **Yield:** 4 servings.

✳When making hamburger patties, place them on waxed paper on a tray. Once you start grilling, you can just lift the corner of the waxed paper to easily remove them.
Ruth Ann Miller, Sugarcreek, Ohio

✳It's simple to grill acorn squash for an inviting side dish. Pierce the skin with a fork a few times, then wrap the whole squash in aluminum foil. Grill over direct heat for 1 hour, turning once. Remove from the grill. Cut in half. Remove seeds. Season with butter, salt and pepper.
Bonnie Isaacs, Kalkaska, Michigan

---

pizza on the grill

Lisa Boettcher, Columbus, Wisconsin
Pizza is such a favorite at our house I make it at least once a week. When the heat and humidity are up there, though, the last thing that I want to do is turn on the oven. So I just move my recipe to the grill—the barbecue flavor mingling with the cheese tastes delicious.

CRUST:
- 1 package (1/4 ounce) active dry yeast
- 1 cup warm water (110° to 115°)
- 2 tablespoons vegetable oil
- 2 teaspoons sugar
- 1 teaspoon baking soda
- 1 teaspoon salt
- 2-3/4 to 3 cups all-purpose flour

TOPPINGS:
- 2 cups cubed cooked chicken
- 1/2 to 3/4 cup barbecue sauce
- 1/2 cup julienned green pepper
- 2 cups (8 ounces) shredded Monterey Jack cheese

In a mixing bowl, dissolve yeast in water. Add the oil, sugar, baking soda, salt and 2 cups flour. Stir in enough remaining flour to form a soft dough. Turn onto a floured surface; knead until smooth and elastic, about 6-8 minutes. Cover and let rest for 10 minutes.

On a floured surface, roll dough into a 13-in. circle. Transfer to a greased 12-in. pizza pan. Build up edges slightly. Grill, covered, over medium heat for 5 minutes. Remove from the grill.

Combine chicken and barbecue sauce; spread over the crust. Sprinkle with green pepper and cheese. Grill, covered, 5-10 minutes longer or until crust is golden and cheese is melted. **Yield:** 4 servings.

grilled cheese loaf

Debbi Baker, Green Springs, Ohio
Generally, I serve this with steaks and salads. The loaf's so quick to make, in fact, I often grill two of them.

- 1 package (3 ounces) cream cheese, softened
- 2 tablespoons butter, softened
- 1 cup (4 ounces) shredded part-skim mozzarella cheese
- 1/4 cup chopped green onions with tops
- 1/2 teaspoon garlic salt
- 1 loaf (1 pound) French bread, sliced

In a mixing bowl, beat cream cheese and butter. Add cheese, onions and garlic salt; mix well. Spread on both sides of each slice of bread. Wrap loaf in a large piece of heavy-duty foil (about 28 in. x 18 in.); seal tightly.

Grill, covered, over medium heat for 8-10 minutes, turning once. Unwrap foil; grill 5 minutes longer. **Yield:** 10-12 servings.

> *My husband makes grilled burgers guests rave about. He adds about 1/4 cup brown sugar and 1 tablespoon of ketchup to a pound of ground beef. These patties smell great while sizzling on the grill. The brown sugar seems to enhance the flavors of the condiments and toppings as well.
>
> Maria Abrams, Amherst, New Hampshire

barbecued spareribs

Jane Uphoff, Idalia, Colorado
All of us—my husband, our two sons and I—love to eat barbecued ribs. But the closest rib restaurant to us is in Denver, 150 miles away. So I came up with this recipe. It's now our traditional meal on the Fourth of July.

- 1 tablespoon ground mustard
- 1 tablespoon chili powder
- 1/2 teaspoon cayenne pepper
- 1/4 teaspoon garlic powder
- 3 pounds pork spareribs
- 2/3 cup ketchup
- 1/2 cup water
- 1/2 cup chopped onion
- 1/4 cup lemon juice
- 2 tablespoons vegetable oil
- 1 teaspoon dried oregano
- 1 teaspoon Liquid Smoke, optional
- 1/2 teaspoon salt
- 1/4 teaspoon pepper

Combine the first four ingredients; rub over ribs. For sauce, combine the remaining ingredients; mix well and set aside.

Grill ribs, covered, over indirect heat and medium-low heat for 1 hour, turning occasionally. Add 10 briquettes to coals. Grill 30 minutes longer, basting both sides several times with sauce, or until meat is tender. **Yield:** 4 servings.

*runners-up

marinated catfish fillets

Pauletta Boese, Macon, Mississippi
A number of years ago, we hosted a group of young people from Canada. Since we wanted to give them a taste of the South, this was served. They raved about it.

- 6 catfish fillets (about 8 ounces *each*)
- 1 bottle (16 ounces) Italian salad dressing
- 1 can (10-3/4 ounces) condensed tomato soup, undiluted
- 3/4 cup vegetable oil
- 3/4 cup sugar
- 1/3 cup vinegar
- 3/4 teaspoon celery seed
- 3/4 teaspoon salt
- 3/4 teaspoon pepper
- 3/4 teaspoon ground mustard
- 1/2 teaspoon garlic powder

Place fillets in a large resealable plastic bag or shallow glass container; cover with salad dressing. Seal bag or cover container; refrigerate for 1 hour, turning occasionally. Drain and discard marinade.

Combine remaining ingredients; mix well. Remove 1 cup for basting. (Refrigerate remaining sauce for another use.) Grill fillets, covered, over medium-hot heat for 3 minutes on each side. Brush with the basting sauce. Continue grilling for 6-8 minutes or until fish flakes easily with a fork, turning once and basting several times. **Yield:** 6 servings.

Editor's Note: Reserved sauce may be used to brush on grilled or broiled fish, chicken, turkey or pork.

teriyaki beef kabobs

Lisa Hector, Estevan, Saskatchewan
My sister-in-law once brought this recipe on a family camping trip and we fixed it for an outdoor potluck. It was so delicious that I asked if I could have a copy. It's become a summer standard for us. Making this dish is a team effort…I put the ingredients together, and my husband handles the grilling.

- 1/4 cup vegetable oil
- 1/4 cup orange juice
- 1/4 cup soy sauce
- 1 teaspoon garlic powder
- 1 teaspoon ground ginger
- 1-3/4 pounds beef tenderloin, cut into 1-inch cubes
- 3/4 pound cherry tomatoes
- 1/2 pound fresh whole mushrooms
- 2 large green peppers, cubed
- 1 large red onion, cut into wedges

Hot cooked rice, optional

In a resealable plastic bag or shallow glass container, combine the first five ingredients and mix well. Reserve 1/2 cup for basting and refrigerate. Add beef to remaining marinade; turn to coat. Seal bag or cover container; refrigerate for 1 hour, turning occasionally. Drain and discard the marinade.

On metal or soaked bamboo skewers, alternate beef, tomatoes, mushrooms, green peppers and onions. Grill, uncovered, over medium heat for 3 minutes on each side. Baste with reserved marinade. Continue turning and basting for 8-10 minutes or until meat reaches desired doneness (for medium-rare, a meat thermometer should read 145°; medium, 160°; well-done, 170°). Serve the meat and vegetables over rice if desired. **Yield:** 6-8 servings.

barbecued chuck roast

Ardis Gautier, Lamont, Oklahoma
Whether I serve this roast for church dinners, company or just family, it is always a hit. To go along with it, my family likes scalloped potatoes, tossed salad and pie. If there's ever any left over, it makes good sandwiches, too.

    1/3 cup cider vinegar
    1/4 cup ketchup
      2 tablespoons vegetable oil
      2 tablespoons soy sauce
      1 tablespoon Worcestershire sauce
      1 teaspoon garlic powder
      1 teaspoon prepared mustard
      1 teaspoon salt
    1/4 teaspoon pepper
      1 boneless chuck roast (2-1/2 to 3 pounds)
    1/2 cup applesauce

In a large resealable plastic bag or shallow glass container, combine the first nine ingredients; mix well. Add roast and turn to coat. Seal bag or cover container; refrigerate for at least 3 hours, turning occasionally.

Remove roast. Pour marinade into a small saucepan; bring to a boil. Reduce heat; simmer for 15 minutes.

Meanwhile, grill roast, covered, over indirect heat for 20 minutes, turning occasionally. Add applesauce to marinade; brush over roast. Continue basting and turning the roast several times for 1 to 1-1/2 hours or until meat reaches desired doneness (for medium-rare, a meat thermometer should read 145°; medium, 160°; well-done, 170°). **Yield:** 6-8 servings.

spicy grilled chicken

Edith Maki, Hancock, Michigan
Very near the top of the list of foods I prepare for company is this chicken. It's easy to fix and has never flopped. It is a family favorite, too—any leftovers are great in a salad or sandwich.

    3/4 cup finely chopped onion
    1/2 cup grapefruit juice
      2 tablespoons olive oil
      2 tablespoons soy sauce
      1 tablespoon honey
      1 garlic clove, minced
  1-1/2 teaspoons salt
  1-1/2 teaspoons rubbed sage
  1-1/2 teaspoons dried thyme
      1 teaspoon ground allspice
      1 teaspoon garlic powder
    1/2 teaspoon ground cinnamon
    1/2 teaspoon ground nutmeg
    1/4 teaspoon cayenne pepper
    1/4 teaspoon pepper
      6 boneless skinless chicken breast halves

In a large resealable plastic bag or shallow glass container, combine the first 15 ingredients; mix well. Reserve 1/3 cup for basting and refrigerate. Add chicken to remaining marinade and turn to coat. Seal bag or cover container; refrigerate overnight.

Drain and discard marinade. Grill chicken, uncovered, over medium heat for 3 minutes on each side. Baste with reserved marinade. Continue grilling for 6-8 minutes or until juices run clear, basting and turning several times. **Yield:** 6 servings.

hawaiian honey burgers

Sheryl Creech, Lancaster, California
These burgers were a favorite when I was growing up. I now use them as a way to "fancy up" a barbecue without a lot of extra preparation. They keep me out of a hot kitchen yet let me serve a nice meal. Fresh fruit and corn on the cob are wonderful accompaniments. As the oldest of six children, I began cooking when I was very young. But I really started enjoying cooking when I married a very appreciative husband. He inspires me!

- 1/2 cup honey
- 1/4 teaspoon ground cinnamon
- 1/4 teaspoon paprika
- 1/4 teaspoon curry powder
- 1/8 teaspoon ground ginger
- 1/8 teaspoon ground nutmeg
- 2 pounds ground beef
- 1/4 cup soy sauce
- 1 can (23 ounces) sliced pineapple, drained
- 8 hamburger buns, split and toasted

Lettuce leaves, optional

In a bowl, combine the first six ingredients; crumble beef over mixture and mix well. Shape into eight 3/4-in.-thick patties. Grill the burgers, uncovered, over medium-hot heat for 3 minutes on each side. Brush with soy sauce. Continue grilling for 4-6 minutes or until juices run clear, basting and turning several times.

During the last 4 minutes, grill the pineapple slices until browned, turning once. Serve burgers and pine-apple on buns with lettuce if desired. **Yield:** 8 servings.

campfire bundles

Lauri Krause, Jackson, Nebraska
A family camping trip's where I "invented" this recipe. I'd brought along a hodgepodge of ingredients, so I just threw them all together. Everyone said that the bundles were delicious. Ever since, I've also grilled them at home. I also prepare them often for our Ladies' Home Extension meetings.

- 1 large sweet onion, sliced
- 1 large green pepper, sliced
- 1 large sweet red pepper, sliced
- 1 large sweet yellow pepper, sliced
- 4 medium potatoes, sliced 1/2 inch thick
- 6 medium carrots, sliced 1/4 inch thick
- 1 small cabbage, sliced
- 2 medium tomatoes, chopped
- 1 to 1-1/2 pounds fully cooked kielbasa *or* Polish sausage, cut into 1/2-inch pieces
- 1/2 cup butter
- 1 teaspoon salt
- 1/2 teaspoon pepper

Place the vegetables in the order listed on three pieces of double-layered heavy-duty foil (about 18 in. x 18 in.). Add the sausage; dot with butter. Sprinkle with salt and pepper. Fold foil around the mixture and seal tightly.

Grill, covered, over medium heat for 30 minutes. Turn and grill 30 minutes longer or until vegetables are tender. **Yield:** 6 servings.

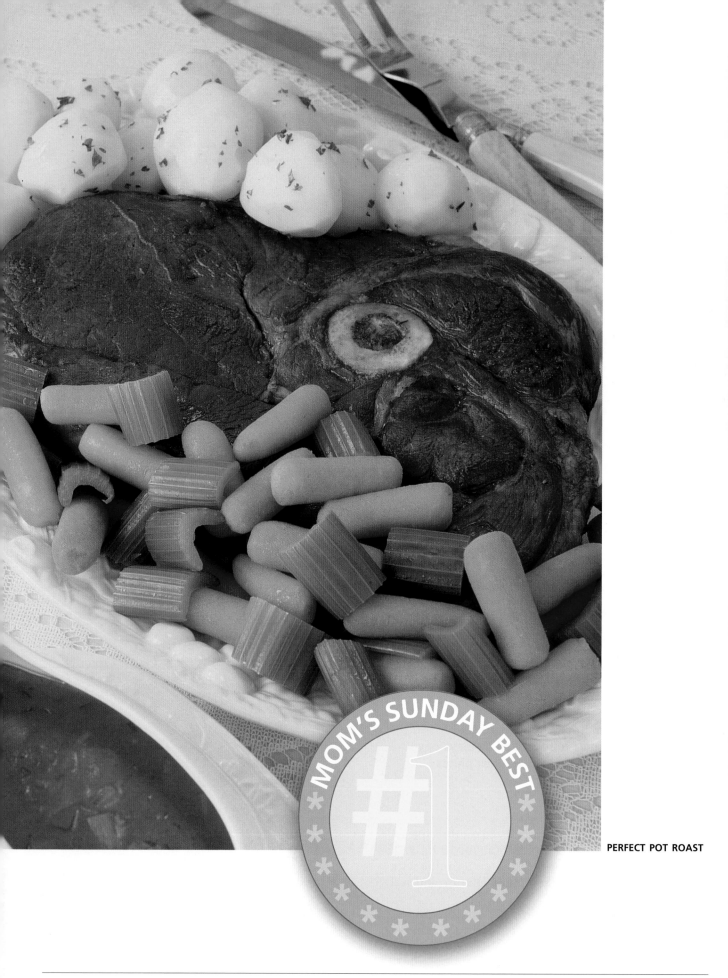

PERFECT POT ROAST

perfect pot roast
GRAND PRIZE WINNER

Home cooking is delicious anytime, but Sunday often means dinner is extra special. We asked readers to share the dishes they considered "Mom's Sunday Best" with their families each week. Here you'll find make-ahead food and dishes that easily cook while you visit. Whatever you choose, your family's sure to agree there's none better!

> "...everyone who tries this pot roast asks for seconds."

Try Perfect Pot Roast, the Grand Prize Winner. "I serve this flavorful, fork-tender beef with its rich gravy at least once a month," says Melody Sroufe of Wichita, Kansas. "Although I wouldn't say meaty main dishes are my specialty, everyone who tries this pot roast asks for seconds."

1 teaspoon seasoned salt
1/2 teaspoon onion powder
1/4 teaspoon pepper
1/8 teaspoon garlic powder
1 beef chuck pot roast (3 to 4 pounds)
1 tablespoon olive oil
3/4 cup water
1 large onion, chopped
1/4 cup chopped green pepper
2 garlic cloves, minced
2 bay leaves
2 teaspoons dried parsley flakes
1/4 teaspoon dried thyme
All-purpose flour

Combine first four ingredients; rub onto roast. In skillet, brown roast in oil. Place in a roasting pan. Add water, onion, green pepper and seasonings. Cover and bake at 325° for 2-1/2 to 3 hours or until roast is tender.

Remove and keep warm. Discard bay leaf. Skim fat from pan juices. Measure juices and transfer to a saucepan.

For each cup of juices, combine 1 tablespoon flour with 2 tablespoons water; mix well. Stir flour mixture into pan. Bring to a boil; cook and stir for 2 minutes or until thickened. Serve gravy with roast. **Yield:** 8-10 servings.

broccoli bacon salad

Joyce Blakley, Windsor Locks, Connecticut
Try this salad with baked ham or pork roast. I like serving it at Sunday dinners. My family just loves it, and our friends rave about its taste, too. I learned to cook from my grandmother (she was an expert!). I still love trying new recipes.

    1 large bunch broccoli, separated into florets
    1 small red onion, coarsely chopped
    1 cup raisins
   10 to 12 bacon strips, cooked and crumbled
DRESSING:
    3 tablespoons white vinegar
  1/3 cup mayonnaise
  1/3 cup sugar

In a large serving bowl, combine the broccoli, onion, raisins and bacon; set aside.

In a mixing bowl, combine dressing ingredients. Just before serving, pour dressing over broccoli mixture; toss to coat. **Yield:** 6-8 servings.

apple roly-poly

Megan Newbombe, Cookstown, Ontario
Apple Roly-Poly isn't very fancy, but it's genuine "Down East" fare. It came from my grandmother. With 13 children plus the men at Grampa's sawmill, she had to do lots of cooking each day!

1-3/4 cups all-purpose flour
  1/4 cup sugar
    4 teaspoons baking powder
  1/2 teaspoon salt
  1/4 cup shortening
  1/4 cup cold butter
  2/3 cup sour cream
FILLING:
  1/4 cup butter, softened
    1 cup packed brown sugar
    2 teaspoons ground cinnamon
    6 medium Granny Smith apples, peeled, cored and coarsely shredded (about 5 cups)
TOPPING:
2-1/2 cups water
    2 tablespoons brown sugar
    1 teaspoon ground cinnamon
  1/2 cup half-and-half cream

In a mixing bowl, combine flour, sugar, baking powder and salt. Cut in shortening and butter until crumbly. Add sour cream and blend until a ball forms.

Roll out on a floured surface into a 15-in. x 10-in. rectangle. Spread with softened butter; sprinkle with remaining filling ingredients.

Roll up jelly-roll style, starting with a long side. Cut into 12 slices. Place slices cut side down in a 13-in. x 9-in. x 2-in. baking pan.

For topping, combine water, brown sugar and cinnamon in a saucepan. Bring to a boil; remove from the heat. Stir in the cream.

Carefully pour hot topping over dumplings. Bake, uncovered, at 350° for 35 minutes or until bubbly. (Center will jiggle when dumplings are hot out of the oven but will set as dumplings stand for a few minutes.) Serve warm. **Yield:** 12 servings.

one-dish pork chop dinner

Pat Waymire, Yellow Springs, Ohio
The apple juice in this gives the pork a wonderful flavor, and the cabbage taste isn't too strong.

> 8 pork chops (1/2 inch thick)
> 1/3 cup all-purpose flour, *divided*
> 1/4 cup butter
> Salt and pepper to taste
> 2 cups apple juice, *divided*
> 2 pounds small red potatoes
> 1 pound *or* 1 jar (16 ounces) small whole onions, drained
> 1 pound carrots, peeled and cut into 3-inch pieces
> 6 to 8 cups shredded cabbage

Coat pork chops with 1/4 cup flour. In a large Dutch oven, melt butter over medium-high heat. Brown chops on both sides. Season with salt and pepper. Remove and set aside. Stir remaining flour into pan; cook and stir until a paste forms. Gradually whisk in 1-1/2 cups apple juice; blend until smooth.

Return chops to Dutch oven; cover and bake at 350° for 30 minutes. Add potatoes, onions, carrots and remaining apple juice. Cover and bake 30 minutes longer.

Top with cabbage; cover and bake for 1 to 1-1/2 hours or until the pork chops are tender, basting occasionally with juices. **Yield:** 8 servings.

---

prize winning tips

* * * * *

*When guests are coming for Sunday dinner, I'll set the table as soon as the breakfast dishes are cleared...prepare and chill relish trays...chill a large pitcher of water to cut down on ice use...and get out serving bowls and utensils.

Lila Schmidt, Mobridge, South Dakota

*If you're planning on serving fresh-from-the-oven dinner rolls on Sunday, try setting them to rise before leaving for church. When you come home, they'll be ready to bake.

Betty Cannell, Reading, Pennsylvania

*For a tender, juicy meat loaf, first mix all the ingredients except for the beef. Then add the meat and mix lightly. When shaping the loaf, handle only as much as necessary.

Ethel Bregant, La Salle, Illinois

*When I make a batch of mashed potatoes, I heat up the milk and butter before adding them. The potatoes stay nice and hot this way.

Kimberly Dean, San Diego, California

pecan-chocolate chip pound cake

Ruth Ann Vernon, Hobe Sound, Florida
This cake is one I prepare frequently for Sunday dinner. I also make it for church meetings and to take to friends who are sick. It goes a long way—unless you have some real "chocoholics!"

1-1/4 cups butter, softened
2-3/4 cups sugar
   5 eggs
   1 teaspoon almond extract
   3 cups all-purpose flour
   1 teaspoon baking powder
1/4 teaspoon salt
   1 cup milk
   1 cup mini semisweet chocolate chips
   1 cup chopped pecans

In a large mixing bowl, cream butter and sugar; add eggs and almond extract on low just until mixed. Beat on high for 5 minutes, scraping bowl occasionally.

In a separate bowl, combine flour, baking powder and salt. On low speed, add flour mixture alternately with milk, mixing just until blended. Fold in chocolate chips.

Sprinkle pecans in the bottom of a greased and floured 10-in. tube pan. Carefully pour batter over pecans. Bake at 325° for 1 hour and 40 minutes or until a toothpick inserted into the center comes out clean. Cool 20 minutes in pan before removing to a wire rack to cool completely. **Yield:** 16-20 servings.

autumn apple salad

Melissa Bowers, Sidney, Ohio
Whether I make it for a Sunday dinner, a company dinner or a covered-dish dinner, people like the blend of flavor in this salad. The ladies ask for the recipe...the men ask me to make sure their wives get a copy of it!

   1 can (20 ounces) crushed pineapple, undrained
2/3 cup sugar
   1 package (3 ounces) lemon gelatin
   1 package (8 ounces) cream cheese, softened
   1 cup diced unpeeled apples
1/2 to 1 cup chopped nuts
   1 cup chopped celery
   1 cup whipped topping
Lettuce leaves

In a saucepan, combine pineapple and sugar; bring to a boil and boil for 3 minutes. Add gelatin; stir until dissolved. Add cream cheese; stir until mixture is thoroughly combined. Cool.

Fold in apples, nuts, celery and whipped topping. Pour into a 9-in. square pan. Refrigerate until firm. Cut into squares and serve on lettuce leaves. **Yield:** 9-12 servings.

sour cream 'n' dill chicken

Rebekah Brown, Three Hills, Alberta

With six children and two boarders, it seems I'm always cooking for a crowd. (My husband says that we must have a revolving door!) So almost every recipe I use is doubled or tripled. This one is an updated version of the Sunday dinner my mother would have prepared—and the latest favorite with my family. You can easily get it ready Sunday morning, slip it in the oven, set the timer and let it cook while you're away at church.

  8 to 10 chicken pieces, skinned
Pepper to taste
  **1 can (10-3/4 ounces) condensed cream of
     mushroom soup, undiluted**
  1 envelope dry onion soup mix
  1 cup (8 ounces) sour cream
  1 tablespoon lemon juice
  **1 tablespoon fresh dill, chopped *or* 1 teaspoon
     dill weed**
  1 can (4 ounces) sliced mushrooms, drained
Paprika
Cooked wide egg noodles, optional

Place chicken in a single layer in a 13-in. x 9-in. x 2-in. baking pan. Sprinkle with pepper. Combine soup, soup mix, sour cream, lemon juice, dill and mushrooms; pour over chicken. Sprinkle with paprika.

Bake, uncovered, at 350° for 1 hour or until chicken is tender. Serve over egg noodles if desired. **Yield:** 4-6 servings.

cheddar parmesan potatoes

Nellie Web, Athens, Tennessee

People in my part of Tennessee love potato dishes! This one tickles my fancy so much I couldn't help sharing it. I'm a widow with five grown children and grandchildren. I make these potatoes when they come to visit for family suppers and holidays. Most often, I serve them alongside meat and vegetables—but, with the cheese, they could even be a main dish all by themselves.

  1/4 cup butter
  1/4 cup all-purpose flour
    2 cups milk
  1/2 teaspoon salt
    1 cup (4 ounces) shredded cheddar cheese
  1/2 cup grated Parmesan cheese
    **5 cups sliced cooked peeled potatoes
      (about 5 medium)**
  1/4 cup buttered bread crumbs

In a saucepan, melt the butter over low heat. Stir in the flour until smooth. Gradually add milk. Bring to a boil; cook and stir for 2 minutes or until thickened. Remove from the heat.

Add the salt, cheddar cheese and Parmesan cheese; stir until the cheese is melted. Add the potatoes; stir gently to mix.

Place in a greased 2-qt. baking dish. Sprinkle bread crumbs on top. Bake, uncovered, at 350° for 30-35 minutes. **Yield:** 6-8 servings.

ALMOND CHICKEN
SALAD

almond chicken salad

Picnics and potlucks are perfect for sampling a variety of delicious foods while enjoying the company of friends and family.

For this recipe contest, plenty of "take-along" family favorites came rolling in, from super salads and sandwiches of all kinds to casseroles,

> "You can't beat the tasty combination of chicken, grapes and almonds."

desserts, flavorful finger foods and thirst-quenching beverages. Readers shared over 6,500 of their favorite recipes. The judges top picks, like Grand Prize Winner Almond Chicken Salad, will surely be welcome additions to the buffet at your next gathering.

"My mother used to prepare this salad for an evening meal during the warm summer months," says Kathy Kittell of Lenexa, Kansas. "It's also wonderful to serve as a delicious but quick luncheon or potluck dish. You can't beat the tasty combination of chicken, grapes and almonds."

4 cups cubed cooked chicken
1-1/2 cups seedless green grapes, halved
1 cup chopped celery
3/4 cup sliced green onions
3 hard-cooked eggs, chopped
1/2 cup mayonnaise
1/4 cup sour cream
1 tablespoon prepared mustard
1 teaspoon salt
1/2 teaspoon pepper
1/4 teaspoon onion powder
1/4 teaspoon celery salt
1/8 teaspoon ground mustard
1/8 teaspoon paprika
1/2 cup slivered almonds, toasted
1 kiwifruit, peeled and sliced, optional

In a large bowl, combine chicken, grapes, celery, onions and eggs. In another bowl, combine the next nine ingredients; stir until smooth.

Pour over the chicken mixture and toss gently. Stir in almonds and serve immediately, or refrigerate and add the almonds just before serving. Garnish with kiwi if desired. **Yield:** 6-8 servings.

aunt frances' lemonade

Debbie Blackburn, Camp Hill, Pennsylvania

My sister and I spent a week each summer with Aunt Frances, who always had this thirst-quenching lemonade in the refrigerator.

- 5 **lemons**
- 5 **limes**
- 5 **oranges**
- 3 **quarts water**
- 1-1/2 **to 2 cups sugar**

Squeeze the juice from four of the lemons, limes and oranges; pour into a gallon container. Thinly slice remaining fruit; set aside for garnish. Add water and sugar; mix well. Store in the refrigerator. Serve on ice with fruit slices. **Yield:** 12-16 servings (about 1 gallon).

maple-glazed ribs

Linda Kobeluck, Ardrossan, Alberta

I love maple syrup and so does my family, so I gave this recipe a try. It's well worth the effort! I make these ribs often, and I never have leftovers. With two boys who like to eat, this main dish is a real winner.

- 3 **pounds pork spareribs, cut into serving-size pieces**
- 1 **cup maple syrup**
- 3 **tablespoons orange juice concentrate**
- 3 **tablespoons ketchup**
- 2 **tablespoons soy sauce**
- 1 **tablespoon Dijon mustard**
- 1 **tablespoon Worcestershire sauce**
- 1 **teaspoon curry powder**
- 1 **garlic clove, minced**
- 2 **green onions, minced**
- 1 **tablespoon sesame seeds, toasted**

Place ribs meaty side up on a rack in a greased 13-in. x 9-in. x 2-in. baking pan. Cover pan tightly with foil. Bake at 350° for 1-1/4 hours.

Meanwhile, combine the next nine ingredients in a saucepan. Bring to a boil over medium heat. Reduce heat; simmer for 15 minutes, stirring occasionally.

Drain ribs; remove rack and return ribs to pan. Cover with sauce. Bake, uncovered, for 35 minutes, basting occasionally. Sprinkle with sesame seeds just before serving. **Yield:** 6 servings.

golden chocolate cake

Kay Hansen, Escondido, California
At our Wisconsin farm, dessert was just as important as the main course. This idea has followed us to California, where I'm still on the lookout for good dessert recipes. This moist cake is a favorite since it's chock-full of fun ingredients like chocolate candy bars, pecans and coconut.

    1   package (18-1/4 ounces) yellow cake mix
        without pudding
    1   package (3.4 ounces) instant vanilla
        pudding mix
  1/2   cup vegetable oil
  1/2   cup water
    4   eggs
    1   cup (8 ounces) sour cream
    3   milk chocolate candy bars (1.55 ounces *each*),
        chopped
    1   cup (6 ounces) semisweet chocolate chips
    1   cup chopped pecans
    1   cup flaked coconut
Confectioners' sugar, optional

In a large mixing bowl, combine cake and pudding mixes, oil, water and eggs; beat on low speed for about 30 seconds or until moistened. Beat 2 minutes on high.

Blend in the sour cream. Stir in the candy bars, chocolate chips, nuts and coconut. Pour into a greased and floured 10-in. fluted tube pan. Bake at 350° for 60-65 minutes or until a toothpick inserted near the center comes out clean.

Cool for 15 minutes before removing from pan to a wire rack. Cool completely. Chill before slicing. Dust with confectioners' sugar if desired. **Yield:** 12-16 servings.

zesty sloppy joes

Sandy Abrams, Greenville, New York
For a big family gathering, these sandwiches are a hit. I have never served them without getting recipe requests. A fantastic blend of seasonings in a hearty sandwich means no one can eat just one.

    4   pounds ground beef
    1   cup chopped onion
    1   cup finely chopped green pepper
    2   cans (10-3/4 ounces *each*) condensed
        tomato soup, undiluted
    1   can (15 ounces) thick and zesty tomato sauce
    1   can (8 ounces) tomato sauce
  3/4   cup packed brown sugar
  1/4   cup ketchup
    3   tablespoons Worcestershire sauce
    1   tablespoon prepared mustard
    1   tablespoon ground mustard
    1   teaspoon chili powder
    1   teaspoon garlic salt
   20   to 25 hamburger buns

In a large saucepan or Dutch oven, cook beef and onion over medium heat until meat is no longer pink. Add green pepper. Cook and stir for 5 minutes; drain.

Add the next 10 ingredients; bring to a boil. Reduce heat; cover and simmer for 1 hour, stirring occasionally. Serve on buns. **Yield:** 20-25 servings.

chocolate chip brownies

Brenda Kelly, Ashburn, Virginia
People love these very rich brownies so much that I never take them anywhere without bringing along several copies of the recipe to hand out. These treats are wonderful to take on picnics because you don't have to worry about any frosting melting.

    1 cup butter, softened
    3 cups sugar
    6 eggs
    1 tablespoon vanilla extract
 2-1/4 cups all-purpose flour
  1/2 cup baking cocoa
    1 teaspoon baking powder
  1/2 teaspoon salt
    1 cup (6 ounces) semisweet chocolate chips
    1 cup (about 6 ounces) vanilla *or* white chips
    1 cup chopped walnuts

In a mixing bowl, cream butter and sugar. Add eggs and vanilla; mix well. Combine the flour, cocoa, baking powder and salt; stir into creamed mixture just until blended (do not overmix).

Pour into two greased 9-in. square baking pans. Sprinkle with chips and nuts. Bake at 350° for 30-35 minutes or until a toothpick inserted near the center comes out clean. Cool. **Yield:** 36-38 brownies.

baked potato salad

Barbara O'Kane, Greenwood Lake, New York
I was tired of the ordinary potato salads served so often in summer, so I came up with this hearty, flavorful variation. My family has enjoyed it for several years.

 4-1/2 pounds potatoes, peeled and cut into
        3/4-inch chunks
   1/4 cup olive oil
     2 envelopes Italian salad dressing mix
     1 medium green pepper, chopped
     1 medium sweet red pepper, chopped
     1 bunch green onions, chopped
     2 large tomatoes, chopped
     4 hard-cooked eggs, chopped
     5 bacon strips, cooked and crumbled
 1-1/2 cups mayonnaise
     1 tablespoon white vinegar
     1 tablespoon lemon juice
     2 teaspoons dried basil
     1 teaspoon salt
   1/2 teaspoon pepper
   1/4 teaspoon garlic powder

In a large bowl, toss the potatoes with oil and dressing mixes. Place in two greased 13-in. x 9-in. x 2-in. baking pans. Bake, uncovered, at 400° for 45 minutes or until tender. Cool. Transfer to a large bowl; add peppers, onions, tomatoes, eggs and bacon. Toss gently.

Combine remaining ingredients in a small bowl. Pour over salad and stir gently. Cover and refrigerate for at least 1 hour. **Yield:** 16-20 servings.

*runners-up

calico corn salad

Henry Tindal, Red Bank, New Jersey
With a full-time job and my own catering business, I appreciate delicious food that can be made ahead, like this zippy salad.

- 2 packages (16 ounces *each*) frozen corn, thawed
- 4 small zucchini, diced
- 1 large sweet red pepper, diced
- 2 cans (4 ounces *each*) chopped green chilies, drained
- 1 medium onion, chopped
- 2/3 cup olive oil
- 1/4 cup fresh lime juice
- 2 tablespoons cider vinegar
- 2 to 2-1/2 teaspoons ground cumin
- 1-1/2 teaspoons salt
- 1 teaspoon pepper
- 1/2 teaspoon garlic salt

In a bowl, toss the corn, zucchini, red pepper, chilies and onion. In a jar with a tight fitting lid, combine remaining ingredients; shake well. Pour over the salad and stir gently. Chill for several hours or overnight. **Yield:** 8-10 servings.

---

prize winning tips

✳ ✳ ✳ ✳

✳ When covering a casserole or meat dish for traveling to a potluck, coat the lid (or sheet of aluminum foil) with nonstick cooking spray. This keeps food, especially cheese, from sticking to the covering.

Marlis Tribby, Estherville, Iowa

✳ For a picnic or potluck tossed salad, mix all the salad fixings and the dressing in a clean plastic bag (as large as you need). It's easy to pack in a cooler since it's not in a big bowl. To serve, set the bagful of salad inside an empty box and pull the edges of the bag over the box. No dishes to wash!

Marge Oliverius, Roy, Utah

✳ Preparing a decorated sheet cake to serve a large group? Before frosting and decorating, cut the cooled cake into serving-size pieces in the pan. Then frost and decorate as usual. To serve, remove one piece at a time. The rest of the cake stays pretty without cuts going through the frosting.

Mary Skaggs, Milton, Wisconsin

---

runners-up

10 MINUTES TO THE TABLE

#1

SWEET 'N' SPICY
CHICKEN

sweet 'n' spicy chicken
GRAND PRIZE WINNER

Some days when you're running late, 10 minutes is all the time you have to get a homemade tasting meal on the table. So we invited subscribers to enter their rapid recipes in our 10 Minutes to the Table contest. Eligible were dishes that can be made from start to finish in 10 minutes or less.

"...I'm always looking for easy-to-prepare dishes that everyone likes."

Sheri White of Higley, Arizona won the Grand Prize for her Sweet 'n' Spicy Chicken. Fast-to-fix dishes, especially those that take just minutes to make, are a must for this working mother.

"No matter what day of the week, mealtime is hectic at our house," says Sheri. "So I'm always looking for easy-to-prepare dishes that everyone likes."

Her chicken fits the bill on both counts. With its quick cooking time and zesty flavor, this marvelous main dish dazzled our judges. Peach preserves add just a touch of sweetness, while taco seasoning and salsa give the dish some kick.

1 **pound boneless skinless chicken breasts, cut into 1/2-inch cubes**
3 **tablespoons taco seasoning**
1 **to 2 tablespoons vegetable oil**
1 **jar (11 ounces) chunky salsa**
1/2 **cup peach preserves**
Hot cooked rice

Place the chicken in a large resealable plastic bag; add taco seasoning and toss to coat. In a skillet, brown chicken in oil. Combine salsa and preserves; stir into skillet. Bring to a boil. Reduce heat; cover and simmer for 2-3 minutes or until meat juices run clear. Serve over rice. **Yield:** 4 servings.

chocolate berry parfaits

Lynn McAllister, Mount Ulla, North Carolina

This creamy dessert is easy to make for weekday dinners, yet pretty enough for company. Instant chocolate pudding is layered with a mixture of pureed strawberries and whipped cream to create yummy parfaits. For quicker results, use whipped topping rather than whipping cream…or serve in a single bowl.

- 2 cups cold milk
- 1 package (3.9 ounces) instant chocolate pudding mix
- 1 package (10 ounces) frozen sweetened strawberries, thawed
- 1 cup heavy whipping cream
- 1/4 cup confectioners' sugar

Sliced fresh strawberries, optional

In a mixing bowl, beat milk and pudding mix until thick and smooth, about 2 minutes; set aside. Drain strawberries (discard the juice or save for another use); place berries in a blender. Cover and process until smooth; set aside.

In a mixing bowl, beat cream and sugar until stiff peaks form. Gently fold in strawberry puree. Divide half of the chocolate pudding among four or six parfait glasses or bowls. Top with half of the strawberry mixture. Repeat layers. Garnish with a strawberry slice if desired. **Yield:** 4-6 servings.

Editor's Note: 2 cups of whipped topping may be substituted for the whipping cream and sugar.

honey-mustard pork scallopini

Stephanie Moon, Green Bay, Wisconsin

This is one of the quickest entrees I have…and one of the most delicious, too. My family loves honey and mustard. Paired with crispy pork, it's even more mouth-watering. Pounding the boneless chops tenderizes them and makes them cook quickly. It's wonderful to have something as tasty as this to serve my family whenever time is short.

- 4 boneless pork chops (about 4 ounces *each*), trimmed
- 2 tablespoons honey
- 2 tablespoons spicy brown mustard
- 1/3 cup crushed butter-flavored crackers (about 8 crackers)
- 1/3 cup dry bread crumbs
- 1 tablespoon vegetable oil
- 1 tablespoon butter

Flatten pork to 1/8-in. thickness. Combine honey and mustard; brush over both sides of pork. In a shallow bowl, combine cracker and bread crumbs; add pork and turn to coat.

In a skillet, heat oil and butter. Fry pork for 2-3 minutes on each side or until crisp and juices run clear. **Yield:** 4 servings.

chicken mushroom fettuccine

Susanne Stevens, Cedar City, Utah
I depend on this recipe when I get home late from work and my hungry family wants something rich and delicious to eat for dinner. It's quick to make, too, because it uses canned chicken and fresh mushrooms that I buy presliced. It's easy but looks like I fussed.

- 1 package (16 ounces) fettuccine
- 1 pound fresh mushrooms, sliced
- 4 garlic cloves, minced
- 1/4 cup butter
- 2 cans (5 ounces *each*) chunk white chicken, drained
- 1/2 cup milk
- 1-1/3 cups grated Parmesan cheese

Cook fettuccine according to package directions. Meanwhile, in a skillet, saute mushrooms and garlic in butter for 2-3 minutes. Add chicken and milk; cook for 5-7 minutes or until heated through. Drain fettuccine; add to skillet. Sprinkle with cheese and toss to coat. **Yield:** 6 servings.

cheesy squash

Randy Lawrence, Clinton, Mississippi
I'm a retired police officer and now a deputy sheriff who loves to cook. But with my busy schedule, I must rely on speedy side dishes like this one. The squash retains its fresh taste and cooks to a perfect tender-crispness. You can give this cheesy treatment to other fresh veggies, as well.

- 1 small zucchini
- 1 small yellow summer squash
- Salt and pepper to taste
- 1 cup (4 ounces) shredded part-skim mozzarella cheese
- 1/4 cup grated Parmesan cheese

Cut zucchini and yellow squash into 1/4-in. slices. Place in a greased shallow 1-qt. baking dish. Sprinkle with salt and pepper. Top with cheeses.

Broil 4 in. from the heat for 7-10 minutes or until squash is crisp-tender and cheese is bubbly. Serve immediately. **Yield:** 2 servings.

> *I keep ingredients for a few favorite fast-to-make main dishes on hand. That way I can fall back on one of these recipes if time keeps me from making what I originally planned for that night's meal.
> Karin Bailey, Golden, Colorado

ranch chicken salad

Valerie Leist, Bulverde, Texas

I'm a wife and mother of two girls, and my weeknights are busy. So I rely on quick meals like this flavorful main-dish salad. It's a snap to saute the seasoned chicken strips and toss them with salad greens and shredded cheese. Topped with corn chips and an easy dressing, this is one hurry-up meal that the whole family enjoys.

> 1 pound boneless skinless chicken breasts, cut into 1/4-inch strips
> 2 teaspoons chili powder
> 1 tablespoon vegetable oil
> 1 package (16 ounces) ready-to-serve salad
> 1 cup (4 ounces) shredded cheddar cheese
> 3/4 cup ranch salad dressing
> 3/4 cup salsa
> 1/2 cup corn chips *or* crushed tortilla chips

Sprinkle the chicken with chili powder. In a skillet, cook the chicken in oil for 6 minutes or until the juices run clear.

Meanwhile, place salad greens in a large bowl or on individual plates. Top with cheese and chicken. Combine salad dressing and salsa; drizzle over chicken. Top with chips. **Yield:** 8 servings.

curried tuna sandwiches

Lorene Corbett, Tryon, Nebraska

If you're looking for a change from more traditional tuna sandwiches, try this recipe I developed. It includes my favorite ingredients from a few different tuna salad recipes, including apples, raisins and curry. The first time I combined them, I loved the results, and now I won't make tuna salad any other way.

> 1 can (6 ounces) tuna, drained and flaked
> 1/4 cup chopped apple
> 2 tablespoons raisins
> 2 tablespoons mayonnaise
> 1/4 teaspoon onion salt
> 1/8 teaspoon curry powder
> 2 sandwich rolls, split
> **Additional mayonnaise, optional**
> **Lettuce leaves**

In a bowl, combine the first six ingredients; mix well. Spread rolls with additional mayonnaise if desired; top each with 1/2 cup tuna mixture and lettuce. **Yield:** 2 servings.

★runners-up

quick elephant ears

Terry Lynn Ayers, Anderson, Indiana

Our eight children love helping me make these sweet and crunchy treats. First we fry flour tortillas for a few seconds in oil, then sprinkle them with cinnamon and sugar. They're fun to make for a large group. I usually do the frying, then have one of the older kids add the sweet coating.

1-1/2 cups sugar
   2 teaspoons ground cinnamon
Oil for deep-fat frying
  10 flour tortillas (7 inches)

Combine sugar and cinnamon in a shallow bowl or large plate; set aside. In a skillet, heat 1/2 in. of oil. Place one tortilla at a time in skillet. Cook for 5 seconds; turn and cook 10 seconds longer or until browned. Place in sugar mixture and turn to coat. Serve immediately. **Yield:** 10 servings.

---

prize winning tips

* I always have pasta in the pantry and ground beef in the freezer for fixing fast meals. I also keep a convenient brownie or cake mix on hand for times I need a speedy dessert or the kids need to take treats to school or other activities.

Beth Stephas, Eagle Grove, Iowa

* Before starting a recipe, I put all the ingredients and supplies on the counter. As I use each item, I put the ingredient away and any dirty bowls or utensils in the dishwasher. When I'm ready to cook the dish, my counter is clear so I know there's nothing left to add to the recipe. It's a great way to avoid losing your place if you get interrupted while cooking…and it gives you a head start on cleanup, too.

Diana Richards, Buffalo, Wyoming

* A visit to the supermarket salad bar saves me a great deal of time after a busy day. For a tossed salad, I buy a head of lettuce and pick up the rest of the vegetable fixings already chopped and ready to serve. It's also a great place to get a small amount of an item when a recipe doesn't call for the entire vegetable.

TerryAnn Moore, Oaklyn, New Jersey

* As a working mom, I'm always on the lookout for speedy meals. I like to mix leftover meat loaf with prepared macaroni and cheese. I stir in a small can of tomato sauce and heat through. The yummy dinner is ready in minutes, and my kids love its cheeseburger taste!

Joanie O'Neill, Eureka, California

5-INGREDIENT RECIPES

#1

TACO PUFFS

taco puffs

Fewer ingredients mean faster meals for busy cooks. So we invited readers to send in favorite family-pleasing recipes that are short on ingredients but long on flavor.

Home cooks by the hundreds took time from their schedules to enter our 5-Ingredient Recipes contest. Our kitchen staff selected the most promising entries that call for five ingredients or fewer and prepared them for the judges. It was a challenge, but those taste-testers narrowed the list to the top 12 dishes.

"Preparing Taco Puffs for dinner is a snap because they rely on refrigerated biscuits."

The Grand Prize went to Jan Schmid of Hibbing, Minnesota for her easy-to-eat Taco Puffs. "This recipe is a real time-saver in two ways," says Jan. "Preparing Taco Puffs for dinner is a snap because they rely on refrigerated biscuits…and the leftovers save minutes the next day packed in our lunches. I got the recipe from a friend years ago and still make these cheesy sandwiches regularly."

1 pound ground beef
1/2 cup chopped onion
1 envelope taco seasoning
2 tubes (16.3 ounces *each*) large refrigerated flaky biscuits
8 ounces cheddar cheese, cut into 16 slices *or* 2 cups (8 ounces) shredded cheddar cheese

In a skillet, cook beef and onion over medium heat until meat is no longer pink; drain. Add the taco seasoning and prepare according to package directions. Cool slightly.

Flatten half of the biscuits into 4-in. circles; place in greased 15-in. x 10-in. x 1-in. baking pans. Spoon 1/4 cup meat mixture onto each; top with two cheese slices or 1/4 cup shredded cheese. Flatten the remaining biscuits; place on top and pinch edges to seal tightly. Bake at 400° for 15 minutes or until golden brown. **Yield:** 8 servings.

spinach cheese swirls

Mary Nichols, Dover, New Hampshire

My family loves dividing up this super-easy sandwich, which is brimming with great spinach and onion flavor. Refrigerated pizza dough shaves minutes off prep time and creates a golden brown crust. The cheesy slices taste terrific warm or cold, so they're great for lunches, picnics or trips.

    1 package (10 ounces) frozen chopped
      spinach, thawed and drained
    2 cups (8 ounces) shredded part-skim
      mozzarella cheese
    1 cup finely chopped onion
    1 garlic clove, minced
    1 tube (10 ounces) refrigerated pizza
      crust

In a bowl, combine the first four ingredients and mix well. On a greased baking sheet, roll the pizza dough into a 14-in. x 10-in. rectangle and seal any holes.

Spoon filling over crust to within 1 in. of edge. Roll up jelly-roll style, starting with a long side; seal the ends and place the seam side down. Bake at 400° for 25-27 minutes or until golden brown. Cut into slices. **Yield:** 4 servings.

tropical bananas

Kathleen Jones, Chicago, Illinois

Lime provides the refreshing twist to this exotic-tasting dessert that's quick, healthy and delicious. I sometimes like to serve it as a midday snack.

    1 medium lime
    2 medium firm bananas, sliced
    2 tablespoons salted peanuts
    1 tablespoon honey
    1 tablespoon flaked coconut

Grate lime peel; set aside. Squeeze lime; measure 1 tablespoon of juice (save remaining juice for another use).

In a bowl, toss bananas with lime juice. Add peanuts and honey; mix well. Spoon into individual dishes. Sprinkle with coconut and lime peel. Serve immediately. **Yield:** 2 servings.

> *When making instant vanilla pudding, simply add a cup of cooked rice and a dash or two of cinnamon as you mix in the milk. It's a fast and delicious dessert.
> Melanie Hartpence, Nampa, Idaho

runners-up

chicken chili

Yvonne Morgan, Grand Rapids, Michigan
My aunt gave me the recipe for this thick "instant" chili a number of years ago. To save time, I usually cook and cube the chicken the night before or use leftovers. The next day, it's simple to simmer the ingredients on the stovetop. I serve the hearty results with crunchy corn or tortilla chips or provide warm bread on the side.

> 2 cans (15 ounces *each*) great northern beans, rinsed and drained
> 2 jars (16 ounces *each*) picante sauce
> 4 cups cubed cooked chicken
> 1 to 2 teaspoons ground cumin

Shredded Monterey Jack cheese

In a saucepan, combine beans, picante sauce, chicken and cumin. Bring to a boil. Reduce heat; cover and simmer for 20 minutes. Sprinkle individual servings with cheese. **Yield:** 6 servings.

cran-apple salad

Lucille Foster, Grant, Nebraska
This tart and tasty salad goes so wonderfully with lots of different meals. Folks will think you spent hours on it, but with fewer than five ingredients, preparation takes only minutes! Crunchy walnuts, celery and apples are a special way to dress up canned cranberry sauce. I especially like to serve it for the holidays.

> 1 can (16 ounces) whole-berry cranberry sauce
> 1 medium unpeeled tart apple, diced
> 1 celery rib, thinly sliced
> 1/2 cup chopped walnuts

In a bowl, combine the cranberry sauce, apple and celery. Cover and refrigerate. Stir in walnuts just before serving. **Yield:** 4-6 servings.

> ∗The next time you have extra carrots and onions after serving a roast, use them the following day to make mashed potatoes. Just mash the carrots and onions right with the potatoes, then add milk and butter if desired. It's a nice change from regular mashed potatoes.
>
> Violet Thompson, Scio, Oregon

double chocolate torte

Naomi Treadwell, Swans Island, Maine
If you love chocolate, you won't be able to resist this rich and fudgy torte. I often make it for company because it's easy to prepare yet looks so impressive when served. For special occasions, I place it on a fancy cake plate and use a can of whipped topping to decorate it right before I serve it. It looks and tastes awesome!

- 1 package fudge brownie mix (13-inch x 9-inch pan size)
- 1 cup (6 ounces) semisweet chocolate chips, melted
- 1/2 cup butter, softened
- 2 cups whipped topping
- 1 teaspoon chocolate sprinkles

Prepare brownie mix according to package directions for fudge-like brownies. Spread batter in a greased and floured 9-in. round baking pan. Bake at 350° for 38-42 minutes or until center springs back when lightly touched. Cool for 10 minutes. Invert onto a serving plate; cool completely.

In a bowl, stir the chocolate and butter until smooth. Spread over brownie layer; refrigerate for 30 minutes. Just before serving, top with whipped topping. Decorate with sprinkles. **Yield:** 9-12 servings.

seafood stuffing

Marcy Thrall, Haddam Neck, Connecticut
For an easy and elegant side dish, I add canned crab and shrimp to a boxed stuffing mix. When I served this to my mom as part of her birthday dinner a number of years ago, she said it was the best stuffing she had ever tasted…and next time she wanted just the stuffing for her meal!

- 1 package (6 ounces) instant chicken-flavored stuffing mix
- 1 can (6 ounces) crabmeat, drained and cartilage removed *or* 1 cup imitation crabmeat
- 1 can (6 ounces) small shrimp, rinsed and drained *or* 1 cup frozen small cooked shrimp
- 1 teaspoon lemon juice

Prepare stuffing according to package directions. Gently stir in crab, shrimp and lemon juice. Serve immediately. **Yield:** 4-6 servings.

nutty peach crisp

Nancy Carpenter, Sidney, Montana

A co-worker brought this easy, delicious dessert to work, and I couldn't resist asking for the recipe. A moist bottom layer made with canned peaches and boxed cake mix is covered with a lovely golden topping of coconut and pecans. It tastes just wonderful served warm with ice cream on top.

  1 can (29 ounces) sliced peaches,
     undrained
  1 package (18-1/4 ounces) yellow *or*
     butter pecan cake mix
1/2 cup butter, melted
  1 cup flaked coconut
  1 cup chopped pecans

Arrange peaches in an ungreased 13-in. x 9-in. x 2-in. baking dish. Sprinkle dry cake mix over top. Drizzle with butter; sprinkle with coconut and pecans.

Bake at 325° for 55-60 minutes or until golden brown. Let stand for 15 minutes. Serve warm or cold. **Yield:** 12-15 servings.

prize winning tips

✶ ✶ ✶ ✶ ✶

✶Dab a few teaspoons of maple syrup onto ham slices when they're almost done frying. Turn the slices several times so the syrup glazes the meat. It gives it a candied flavor.

Alfred Seltz Jr., Fergus Falls, Minnesota

✶For a deliciously different side dish, I stir a can of peach pie filling into 2 pounds of cooked sliced carrots.

Gladys Gierl, Pittsburgh, Pennsylvania

✶When preparing hamburgers for the grill, I add a package of dry onion soup mix to about 2 pounds of ground beef. It really brings out the flavor in these tasty burgers.

Marilyn Lee, Richmond, Missouri

✶I cube cooked chicken and put a layer in a baking dish. I cover it with a box of prepared stuffing mix, then pour undiluted cream of chicken or cream of mushroom soup over it. I bake it until the casserole is warmed through.

Minnie Riley, Portsmouth, Virginia

✶To give some zip to plain cooked noodles, add enough butter and French onion dip until coated.

Joanie Wiesbrock, Leonore, Illinois

easy baked chicken

Susan Adair, Muncie, Indiana

I was surprised when my sister-in-law told me she used just three simple ingredients to make this tender, flavorful chicken. The pretty, crispy coating seals in the juices to keep the chicken moist and delicious while it bakes in the oven. Open a can or two of veggies, and you have an easy but delicious dinner.

    1 broiler/fryer chicken (3-1/2 to 4 pounds),
      cut up
    1 cup Italian salad dressing
1-1/4 cups crushed cornflakes

Place chicken in a large resealable plastic bag or shallow glass container; add salad dressing. Seal or cover and turn to coat. Refrigerate for at least 1 hour. Drain and discard marinade.

Coat the chicken with cornflakes; place in a greased 13-in. x 9-in. x 2-in. baking dish. Bake, uncovered, at 350° for 1 hour or until the chicken juices run clear. **Yield:** 4 servings.

ravioli casserole

Mary Ann Rothert, Austin, Texas

The whole family will love the fun, cheesy flavor of this main dish which tastes just like lasagna but without all the fuss to make it. Time-saving ingredients, including prepared spaghetti sauce and frozen ravioli, hurry the preparation along.

    1 jar (28 ounces) spaghetti sauce
    1 package (25 ounces) frozen cheese ravioli,
      cooked and drained
    2 cups (16 ounces) small-curd cottage cheese
    4 cups (16 ounces) shredded part-skim
      mozzarella cheese
  1/4 cup grated Parmesan cheese

Spread 1/2 cup of spaghetti sauce in an ungreased 13-in. x 9-in. x 2-in. baking dish. Layer with half of the ravioli, 1-1/4 cups of sauce, 1 cup of cottage cheese and 2 cups of mozzarella cheese. Repeat layers. Sprinkle with the Parmesan cheese.

Bake, uncovered, at 350° for 30-40 minutes or until bubbly. Let stand 5-10 minutes before serving. **Yield:** 6-8 servings.

Editor's Note: 4-5 cups of any style cooked ravioli may be substituted for the frozen cheese ravioli.

quick caramel rolls

Jeannette Westphal, Gettysburg, South Dakota
Refrigerated crescent rolls and caramel ice cream topping make these yummy, gooey treats a snap to assemble. I used to whip up a huge panful for our kids when they were growing up...now our grandchildren love them, too. They are easy to reheat in the microwave for a speedy snack.

- 1/4 cup butter
- 1/2 cup chopped pecans
- 1 cup caramel ice cream topping
- 2 tubes (8 ounces *each*) refrigerated crescent rolls

Place butter in a 13-in. x 9-in. x 2-in. baking pan; heat in a 375° oven until melted. Sprinkle with pecans. Add ice cream topping and mix well.

Remove dough from tubes (do not unroll); cut each section of dough into six rolls. Arrange rolls in prepared pan with cut side down. Bake at 375° for 20-25 minutes or until golden. Immediately invert onto a serving plate. Serve warm. **Yield:** 2 dozen.

scandinavian pecan cookies

Laurie Knoke, DeKalb, Illinois
We enjoyed these rich, buttery cookies at a bed-and-breakfast, and the hostess was kind enough to share her simple recipe. The pretty nut-topped treats are so special you could give a batch as a gift.

- 1 cup butter, softened
- 3/4 cup packed brown sugar
- 1 egg, *separated*
- 2 cups all-purpose flour
- 1/2 cup finely chopped pecans

In a mixing bowl, cream butter, brown sugar and egg yolk. Gradually add flour. Shape into 1-in. balls. In a small bowl, beat egg white. Dip balls in egg white, then roll in pecans.

Place 2 in. apart on ungreased baking sheets; flatten slightly. Bake at 375° for 8-12 minutes or until edges are lightly browned. Cool on wire racks. **Yield:** 4-5 dozen.

---

*I have two small kids who enjoy their hot dogs sliced, which means we often have extra hot dog buns.

To use them up, I open the buns flat and butter them. Next I sprinkle the buns with garlic salt and parsley flakes before setting them a few inches beneath the broiler.
Kathy Marples, Chandler, Arizona

EXCEPTIONAL EGGS #1

CREAMY
CARAMEL FLAN

creamy caramel flan
GRAND PRIZE WINNER

Some dishes—especially those touted as "trendy"—can be a disappointment when they get to the table. Not these, though. The best-of-the-best in our Exceptional Eggs recipe contest, they're all they're cracked up to be!

Plus, you can choose from such a wide variety. There are plenty of rise-and-shine breakfast specialties.

"Flan can be served year-round with most any meal."

But in addition, here and on the following pages, you'll find new ideas for lunch and brunch...dinner...even dessert! For every occasion, one of these dishes will surely be "eggsactly" right.

The Grand Prize Winner is Creamy Caramel Flan, an elegant and delicious dessert that is a local favorite shared by Pat Forte of Miami, Florida.

"We enjoy many foods of Spanish and Cuban origin here, so flan is served often," Pat says. "I recently made this oh-so-creamy treat for my family back in Massachusetts and they loved it as much as our Florida friends.

"Flan can be served year-round with most any meal. It looks so pretty when you prepare it in a mold, then invert it and let the caramelized sugar glaze the top."

3/4 cup sugar
1 package (8 ounces) cream cheese, softened
5 eggs
1 can (14 ounces) sweetened condensed milk
1 can (12 ounces) evaporated milk
1 teaspoon vanilla extract

In a heavy saucepan, cook and stir sugar over medium-low heat until melted and golden, about 15 minutes. Quickly pour into an ungreased 2-qt. round baking or souffle dish, tilting to coat the bottom; let stand for 10 minutes.

In a mixing bowl, beat the cream cheese until smooth. Beat in eggs, one at a time, until thoroughly combined. Add remaining ingredients; mix well. Pour over caramelized sugar.

Place dish in a larger baking pan. Pour boiling water into larger pan to a depth of 1 in. Bake at 350° for 50-60 minutes or until center is just set (mixture will jiggle).

Remove dish from larger pan to a wire rack; cool for 1 hour. Refrigerate overnight.

To unmold, run a knife around edges and invert onto a large rimmed serving platter. Cut into wedges or spoon onto dessert plates; spoon the sauce over each serving. **Yield:** 8-10 servings.

bacon and eggs casserole

Deanna Durward-Orr, Windsor, Ontario
Because it requires so little time to prepare and is such a great hit with adults and children alike, this is ideal to make for brunches. Served with a green or fruit salad, hot muffins and croissants, the hot dish is excellent for an after-church Easter brunch. At Christmas, I sprinkle on red and green peppers!

     4 bacon strips
    18 eggs
     1 cup milk
     1 cup (4 ounces) shredded cheddar cheese
     1 cup (8 ounces) sour cream
    1/4 cup sliced green onions
     1 to 1-1/2 teaspoons salt
    1/2 teaspoon pepper

In a skillet, cook bacon over medium heat until crisp. Remove to paper towel to drain. In a large bowl, beat eggs. Add milk, cheese, sour cream, onions, salt and pepper.

Pour into a greased 13-in. x 9-in. x 2-in. baking dish. Crumble bacon and sprinkle on top.

Bake, uncovered, at 325° for 40-45 minutes or until a knife inserted near the center comes out clean. Let stand for 5 minutes. **Yield:** 8-10 servings.

puffy apple omelet

Melissa Davennport, Campbell, Minnesota
With all the eggs our chickens produce, I could make this omelet every day! I guess I consider it a festive dish, but you could fix it anytime…including for a light supper. Growing up in a big family—seven children—of hearty eaters, I started cooking early. Now, I have a husband who likes to eat satisfying dishes like this!

     3 tablespoons all-purpose flour
    1/4 teaspoon baking powder
    1/8 teaspoon salt
     2 eggs, *separated*
     3 tablespoons milk
     1 tablespoon lemon juice
     3 tablespoons sugar
TOPPING:
     1 large tart apple, thinly sliced
     1 teaspoon sugar
    1/4 teaspoon ground cinnamon

In a small bowl, combine flour, baking powder and salt. Add egg yolks, milk and lemon juice; mix well and set aside.

In a small mixing bowl, beat egg whites on medium speed until soft peaks form. Gradually add sugar, beating on high until stiff peaks form. Fold into yolk mixture.

Pour into a greased 1-1/2-qt. shallow baking dish. Arrange apple slices on top. Combine sugar and cinnamon; sprinkle over all.

Bake, uncovered, at 375° for 18-20 minutes or until a knife inserted near the center comes out clean. Serve immediately. **Yield:** 2 servings.

easter bread

Rose Kostynuik, Calgary, Alberta

While I most often make this traditional Ukrainian bread for breakfast, I've also served it for an afternoon tea.

    2 packages (1/4 ounce *each*) active dry yeast
  1/2 cup warm water (110° to 115°)
    4 eggs
    6 egg yolks
    1 cup sugar
  3/4 cup butter, melted
    2 teaspoons salt
    1 teaspoon vanilla extract
    1 teaspoon lemon juice
    2 tablespoons grated lemon peel
    2 cups warm milk (110° to 115°)
9-3/4 to 10-1/4 cups all-purpose flour
    1 cup golden raisins

In a small bowl, dissolve yeast in water; set aside. In a large mixing bowl, beat the eggs and yolks until lemon-colored; gradually add sugar. Add butter, salt, vanilla, lemon juice and peel; beat well. Blend in milk and yeast mixture. Add 6 cups flour; beat until smooth. By hand, stir in enough remaining flour to form a soft dough.

Turn onto a lightly floured surface; knead until smooth and elastic, about 10 minutes. Sprinkle with raisins; knead for 5 minutes longer. Place in a greased bowl, turning once to grease top. Cover and let rise in a warm place until doubled, about 1 hour.

Punch dough down. Turn onto a lightly floured surface; divide into thirds. Cover and let rest for 10 minutes. Shape each portion into a loaf and place in greased 8-in. x 4-in. x 2-in. loaf pans. Cover and let rise in a warm place until almost doubled, about 30 minutes.

Bake at 325° for 45 minutes or until golden brown. Remove from pans to cool on wire racks. **Yield:** 3 loaves.

almond deviled eggs

Martha Baechle, Nipomo, California

This recipe's one I've used many times for potlucks, during the holidays and several times a month when entertaining. The reactions have ranged from "These eggs slide down gently" from one young man to just "Scrumptious!" Though this dish is good on its own, you might also want to consider adding it to a salad plate or serving it with soup and sandwich for lunch.

    6 hard-cooked eggs
  1/4 cup mayonnaise
    1 teaspoon Dijon mustard
  1/4 teaspoon garlic salt
    3 tablespoons finely chopped roasted almonds
   12 whole roasted almonds
Fresh parsley

Slice eggs in half lengthwise; remove yolks and set whites aside. In a small bowl, mash yolks, mayonnaise, mustard, garlic salt and chopped almonds.

Stuff or pipe into egg whites. Garnish with whole almonds and parsley. Chill until serving. **Yield:** 12 servings.

egg-filled buns

Kathy Wells, Brodhead, Wisconsin

As the cook for our local volunteer fire department, I'm a nonstop recipe clipper. This one's been a constant in my file for years. It's great for grabbing and going, and a good lunch dish, too. Here on our farm, my husband—who's also a teacher—and I have cattle and hogs plus one chicken who furnishes many of our eggs.

    2 tablespoons butter
    4 eggs, beaten
    2 packages (2-1/2 ounces *each*) sliced smoked
      beef, chopped
  1/3 cup mayonnaise
  1/4 teaspoon salt
  1/4 teaspoon pepper
    1 package (16 ounces) hot roll mix
    1 tablespoon milk

Melt butter in a medium skillet. Add the eggs; cook and stir gently until set. Remove from the heat. Add beef, mayonnaise, salt and pepper; mix well. Chill.

Prepare roll mix according to package directions. Divide dough into six portions; roll each portion into an 8-in. x 3-in. rectangle. Spoon 1/3 cup of egg mixture on half of each rectangle. Fold over and seal edges. Place on a greased baking sheet. Cover and let rise in a warm place until doubled, about 30 minutes.

Brush tops with milk. Bake at 350° for 20-25 minutes or until golden brown. Serve warm. **Yield:** 6 servings.

overnight french toast

Catherine Buehre, Weeping Water, Nebraska

Youngsters who won't eat eggs cooked the traditional ways go crazy for this breakfast dish. I should know—I have four children.

    1 loaf (1 pound) unsliced cinnamon-raisin bread
    5 eggs
    2 egg yolks
    1 cup half-and-half cream
  3/4 cup packed brown sugar
    2 teaspoons pumpkin pie spice
    1 teaspoon maple flavoring
    1 teaspoon vanilla extract
    3 cups milk
  1/4 cup butter, melted
Fresh strawberries *or* maple syrup, optional

Slice ends from bread and discard or save for another use. Slice remaining loaf into eight 1-in. slices and arrange in the bottom of two greased 8-in. square baking pans.

In a large bowl, beat eggs, yolks, cream, brown sugar, pie spice and flavorings. Gradually add milk, beating until well blended; pour over bread. Cover and chill overnight.

Remove from the refrigerator 30 minutes before baking. Drizzle with butter. Bake, uncovered, at 350° for 45-60 minutes or until a knife inserted near the center comes out clean. Serve warm; top with strawberries or syrup if desired. **Yield:** 6-8 servings.

Editor's Note: If cinnamon-raisin bread is unavailable, substitute raisin bread and add 1/4 teaspoon ground cinnamon to the egg mixture.

salmon quiche

Deanna Baldwin, Bermuda Dunes, California
This recipe came to me from my mother—it's the kind you request after just one bite! Unlike some quiches, it's also hearty enough that it appeals equally to both women and men. Cooking is something that I've always liked. I pore over cookbooks the way other people read novels! In addition, I collect antique kitchen utensils.

1 unbaked pastry shell (10 inches)
1 medium onion, chopped
1 tablespoon butter
2 cups (8 ounces) shredded Swiss cheese
1 can (14-3/4 ounces) salmon, drained, flaked and cartilage removed
5 eggs
2 cups half-and-half cream
1/4 teaspoon salt
Minced fresh parsley, optional

Line unpricked pastry shell with a double thickness of heavy-duty foil. Bake at 450° for 8 minutes. Remove foil; bake 5 minutes longer. Cool on a wire rack.

In a small skillet, saute onion in butter until tender. Sprinkle Swiss cheese in the crust; top with the salmon and onion.

In a bowl, beat eggs, cream and salt; pour over salmon mixture. Bake at 350° for 45-50 minutes or until a knife inserted near the center comes out clean. Sprinkle with parsley if desired. Let stand for 5 minutes before cutting. **Yield:** 6-8 servings.

---

prize winning tips

★ ★ ★ ★

★ To make sure your scrambled eggs come out tender and light, use an electric fry pan. Its controlled heat keeps eggs from becoming tough. It's also good for keeping eggs warm while serving—use the "warm" setting.

Gerry Ebert, Milwaukee, Wisconsin

★ For best volume, egg whites should be separated when the eggs are cold and allowed to come to room temperature before beating. Leftover separated egg whites and yolks can be frozen for future use.

Joyce Ruce, Mena, Arkansas

★ Never wash eggs before storing; it removes their natural protective coating.

Clara Pelletier, Victoria Harbour, Ontario

★ Refrigerate eggs with the large end up. When I do this, the yolk centers when hard-cooked and makes a better presentation when sliced for deviled eggs.

Jo Ann Jones, Statesville, North Carolina

MARVELOUS MUFFINS

#1

PUMPKIN
CHIP MUFFINS

pumpkin chip muffins

They can be sweet or savory...cheesy, chunky or chewy. They're perfect for breakfast...with a meal...as a snack or even for dessert. We mean muffins, of course.

And our Marvelous Muffins contest included each of those types along with many others.

Our judges had their hands full—literally—sampling the abundance of hand-sized treats subscribers entered.

"**Most people tell me these are the best muffins they've ever eaten.**"

Between bites, they agreed there's much more to muffins than meets the eye. Later, after eyeing their notes, they awarded the Grand Prize to Cindy Middleton of Champion, Alberta for her Pumpkin Chip Muffins.

"Most people tell me these are the best muffins they've ever eaten," says Cindy. "Needless to say, I've shared the recipe often. They're also a hit at church bake sales and potlucks."

Now it's your turn...almost anytime. Breakfast, brunch, snacks, potlucks or packed for lunch—you can "make the day" with muffins!

---

4 **eggs**
2 **cups sugar**
1 **can (15 ounces) solid-pack pumpkin**
1-1/2 **cups vegetable oil**
3 **cups all-purpose flour**
2 **teaspoons baking soda**
2 **teaspoons baking powder**
1 **teaspoon ground cinnamon**
1 **teaspoon salt**
2 **cups (12 ounces) semisweet chocolate chips**

In a large mixing bowl, beat eggs, sugar, pumpkin and oil until smooth. Combine flour, baking soda, baking powder, cinnamon and salt; add to pumpkin mixture and mix well. Fold in chocolate chips.

Fill greased or paper-lined muffin cups three-fourths full. Bake at 400° for 16-20 minutes or until a toothpick comes out clean. Cool in pan 10 minutes before removing to a wire rack. **Yield:** about 24 muffins.

Prize Winning Recipes 123

poppy seed muffins

Kathy Smith, Granger, Indiana
Because these muffins are a bit heavier than many of the snack type, they are perfect for when you wake up hungry. They're quick and easy, too. I adapted them from a poppy seed quick bread I was served once at a neighbor's house.

- 3 cups all-purpose flour
- 2-1/2 cups sugar
- 2 tablespoons poppy seeds
- 1-1/2 teaspoons baking powder
- 1-1/2 teaspoons salt
- 3 eggs
- 1-1/2 cups milk
- 1 cup vegetable oil
- 1-1/2 teaspoons vanilla extract
- 1-1/2 teaspoons almond extract

In a large bowl, combine flour, sugar, poppy seeds, baking powder and salt. In another bowl, beat eggs, milk, oil and extracts; stir into dry ingredients just until moistened.

Fill greased or paper-lined muffin cups two-thirds full. Bake at 350° for 20-25 minutes or until a toothpick comes out clean. Cool in pan for 10 minutes before removing to a wire rack. **Yield:** about 8 dozen mini-muffins or 24 standard-size muffins.

snappy ginger muffins

Marlene Falsetti, Lowbanks, Ontario
To tell the truth, I cook out of necessity but enjoy myself when I bake! I make these for school lunches and my husband to take with him to work. They are nice to serve for breakfast besides.

- 1/2 cup vegetable oil
- 1/4 cup sugar
- 1/4 cup packed brown sugar
- 1 cup molasses
- 1 egg
- 3 cups all-purpose flour
- 1-1/2 teaspoons baking soda
- 1 teaspoon ground cinnamon
- 1 teaspoon ground ginger
- 1/2 teaspoon salt
- 1 cup water

In a mixing bowl, beat the oil and sugars. Beat in molasses and egg. Combine the flour, baking soda, cinnamon, ginger and salt; stir into molasses mixture alternately with water.

Fill greased or paper-lined muffin cups two-thirds full. Bake at 350° for 20-25 minutes or until a toothpick comes out clean. Cool in pan for 10 minutes before removing to a wire rack. **Yield:** about 20 muffins.

*runners-up

apple butter muffins

Anita Bell, Gallatin, Tennessee

As an ex-farm girl, I have fond memories of making apple butter with my grandmother. I often bake muffins for my husband and me to eat during job breaks.

1-3/4 cups all-purpose flour
1/3 cup sugar
2 teaspoons baking powder
1/2 teaspoon ground cinnamon
1/4 teaspoon salt
1/4 teaspoon ground nutmeg
1/8 teaspoon ground allspice
1/8 teaspoon ground ginger
1 egg, lightly beaten
3/4 cup milk
1/4 cup vegetable oil
1/2 cup thick apple butter
TOPPING:
1/2 cup chopped pecans
3 tablespoons sugar

In a medium bowl, combine the first eight ingredients. Combine egg, milk and oil; stir into dry ingredients just until moistened.

Fill greased or paper-lined muffin cups with a rounded tablespoon of batter. Top each with a rounded teaspoon of apple butter and the remaining batter. Combine topping ingredients; sprinkle over muffins. Bake at 400° for 15-18 minutes. Cool in pan 10 minutes before removing to a wire rack. **Yield:** about 12 muffins.

Editor's Note: This recipe was tested with commercially prepared apple butter.

cheddar dill muffins

Bernadaette Colvin, Houston, Texas

Unlike many other baked goods, these muffins aren't sweet…that's one of the reasons I like this recipe. I serve them with soups and stews, just like bread. Cooking for family and friends is something I truly enjoy doing.

3-1/2 cups all-purpose flour
3 tablespoons sugar
2 tablespoons baking powder
2 teaspoons dill weed
1 teaspoon salt
1 cup (4 ounces) shredded cheddar cheese
1-3/4 cups milk
2 eggs, lightly beaten
1/4 cup butter, melted

In a bowl, combine the first six ingredients. Combine milk, eggs and butter; stir into dry ingredients just until moistened.

Fill greased or paper-lined muffin cups almost full. Bake at 400° for 25-30 minutes or until a toothpick comes out clean. Cool in pan for 10 minutes before removing to a wire rack. **Yield:** about 9 jumbo muffins or 12 standard-size muffins.

runners-up

berry cream muffins

Linda Gilmore, Hampstead, Maryland

The sour cream makes these muffins so nice and light that you can serve them as a bread with a meal. But, here at our house, I've fixed them for everything from breakfast up to midnight snacks.

> 2 cups all-purpose flour
> 1 cup sugar
> 1/2 teaspoon baking powder
> 1/2 teaspoon baking soda
> 1/2 teaspoon salt
> 1-1/2 cups fresh *or* frozen raspberries *or* blueberries
> 2 eggs, lightly beaten
> 1 cup (8 ounces) sour cream
> 1/2 cup vegetable oil
> 1/2 teaspoon vanilla extract

In a large bowl, combine flour, sugar, baking powder, baking soda and salt; add berries and toss gently. Combine eggs, sour cream, oil and vanilla; mix well. Stir into dry ingredients just until moistened.

Fill greased muffin cups two-thirds full. Bake at 400° for 18-22 minutes or until a toothpick comes out clean. Cool for 5 minutes before removing from pan to a wire rack. **Yield:** about 14 muffins.

honey bran muffins

Pauline Rohloff, Endeavor, Wisconsin

There's a deliciously different taste to these muffins, thanks to the pineapple juice and raisins they contain. We have them for breakfast, lunch and snacks.

> 2 cups lukewarm pineapple juice
> 2 cups golden raisins
> 1 cup packed brown sugar
> 1/2 cup vegetable oil
> 1/2 cup honey
> 5 eggs, beaten
> 2 cups all-purpose flour
> 2 teaspoons baking soda
> 1 teaspoon salt
> 4 cups All-Bran cereal

In a small bowl, combine pineapple juice and raisins; set aside. In a large mixing bowl, combine the brown sugar, oil, honey and eggs; mix well. Combine the flour, baking soda and salt; stir in the cereal. Add to sugar mixture and mix well. Fold in the raisin mixture (batter will be thin).

Cover and refrigerate at least 3 hours or overnight. Stir (batter will thicken).

Fill greased or paper-lined muffin cups three-fourths full. Bake at 400° for 20-25 minutes or until a toothpick comes out clean. Cool in pan for 10 minutes before removing to a wire rack. **Yield:** about 12 jumbo muffins or 20 standard-size muffins.

cinnamon doughnut muffins

Sharon Pullen, Alvinston, Ontario

All five of our children are grown…in fact, we now have five grandchildren. But, back when they were youngsters, they loved these muffins as after-school treats and as part of Sunday brunch.

1-3/4 cups all-purpose flour
1-1/2 teaspoons baking powder
   1/2 teaspoon salt
   1/2 teaspoon ground nutmeg
   1/4 teaspoon ground cinnamon
   3/4 cup sugar
   1/3 cup vegetable oil
     1 egg, lightly beaten
   3/4 cup milk
Jam
TOPPING:
   1/4 cup butter, melted
   1/3 cup sugar
     1 teaspoon ground cinnamon

In a large bowl, combine flour, baking powder, salt, nutmeg and cinnamon. Combine sugar, oil, egg and milk; stir into dry ingredients just until moistened.

Fill greased or paper-lined muffin cups half full; place 1 teaspoon jam on top. Cover jam with enough batter to fill muffin cups three-fourths full. Bake at 350° for 20-25 minutes or until a toothpick comes out clean.

Place melted butter in a small bowl; combine sugar and cinnamon in another bowl. Immediately after removing muffins from the oven, dip tops in butter, then in cinnamon-sugar. Serve warm. **Yield:** 10 muffins.

---

prize winning tips

✳ To keep paper baking cups from clinging to muffins, coat the inside of the cups with nonstick cooking spray before filling.

                                     Helen Wolt, Black Forest, Colorado

✳ To add a little extra sweetness and flavor to plain muffins, dip them while warm in melted butter and roll in cinnamon-sugar. Cool on a wire rack.

                                   Laura Reigel, Sheboygan, Wisconsin

✳ To keep muffins moist, store them in an airtight plastic ice cream pail with a seal-tight lid.

                                Hayley Whelpton, Moosomin, Saskatchewan

✳ Instead of pumpkin muffins, try substituting pureed sweet potatoes or winter squash.
                                   Judy Langdon, Sheridan, Indiana

SWEET BREAD TREATS #1

ALMOND STREUSEL
ROLLS

almond streusel rolls
GRAND PRIZE WINNER

How sweet they are! Our sweet bread contest brought in a bounty of baked goods to please any palate. Whether yeast breads, quick breads or fried creations, many of the recipes that follow will provide extra enjoyment at an Easter breakfast, Mother's Day brunch, Christmas Day gathering or any special occasion morning meal.

> "Often, the rolls don't even get to cool before the pan is empty."

Of course, they'd also be scrumptiously popular as snacks for family, friends or co-workers.

A perfect example is the recipe for Almond Streusel Rolls, the Grand Prize Winner shared by Perlene Hoekema of Lynden, Washington. Says Perlene of these old-fashioned, comforting rolls, "They're just wonderful sweet rolls."

Perlene makes the rolls, originally created by herself and her grown daughter Janis, for Sunday family breakfasts and to give as gifts as well. "I've used them as a deliciously different dessert also," she says. "Often, the rolls don't even get to cool before the pan is empty!"

---

  2 packages (1/4 ounce *each*) active dry yeast
3/4 cup warm water (110° to 115°)
3/4 cup warm milk (110° to 115°)
1/4 cup butter, softened
1/2 cup sugar
  2 eggs
  1 teaspoon salt
5-1/4 to 5-1/2 cups all-purpose flour
FILLING:
1/2 cup almond paste
1/4 cup butter, softened
1/2 cup packed brown sugar
1/4 teaspoon almond extract
TOPPING:
  3 tablespoons sugar
  1 tablespoon all-purpose flour
  1 tablespoon butter
ICING:
1-1/2 cups confectioners' sugar
1/4 teaspoon almond extract
  1 to 2 tablespoons milk

In a mixing bowl, dissolve yeast in water; let stand for 5 minutes. Add milk, butter, sugar, eggs and salt; mix well. Add 2 cups of flour; beat until smooth. Stir in enough of the remaining flour to form a soft dough.

Turn onto a floured surface; knead until smooth and elastic, about 6-8 minutes. Place in a greased bowl, turning once to grease top. Cover and let rise in a warm place until doubled, about 1 hour.

Punch dough down; roll out to a 15-in. x 10-in. rectangle. In a mixing bowl, beat the filling ingredients until smooth. Spread over the dough. Roll up jelly-roll style, starting with a short side; seal seams. Cut into 12 slices. Place in a greased 13-in. x 9-in. x 2-in. baking pan. Cover and let rise in a warm place until doubled, about 30 minutes.

Combine topping ingredients; sprinkle over rolls. Bake at 350° for 35-40 minutes or until golden brown. Cool on a wire rack. Combine confectioners' sugar, extract and enough milk to achieve drizzling consistency; drizzle over rolls. **Yield:** 1 dozen.

swedish doughnuts

Lisa Bates, Dunham, Quebec

One day, my father got a hankering for doughnuts and asked me to make him some. I ended up trying these. Dad—and everyone else—loved the results. They come out so golden and plump.

2 eggs
1 cup sugar
2 cups cold mashed potatoes (mashed with milk and butter)
3/4 cup buttermilk
2 tablespoons butter, melted
1 teaspoon vanilla *or* almond extract
4-1/2 cups all-purpose flour
4 teaspoons baking powder
1 teaspoon baking soda
1 teaspoon salt
2 teaspoons ground nutmeg
1/8 teaspoon ground ginger
Oil for deep-fat frying
Additional sugar, optional

In a mixing bowl, beat eggs and sugar. Add the potatoes, buttermilk, butter and vanilla; mix well. Combine the flour, baking powder, baking soda, salt, nutmeg and ginger; add to egg mixture and mix well. Cover and refrigerate for 1-2 hours.

On a floured surface, roll dough to 1/2-in. thickness. Cut with a 2-1/2-in. doughnut cutter. In an electric skillet or deep-fat fryer, heat oil to 375°.

Fry doughnuts, a few at a time, for 2 minutes on each side or until browned. Drain on paper towels. Roll in sugar if desired. **Yield:** about 2-1/2 dozen.

banana yeast bread

Maralee Meyer, Milford, Nebraska

Though our two children dislike bananas, they've always enjoyed these loaves. The recipe has been a standby since my grandmother shared it before I was married. Cooking is fun for me but I have to admit I would rather bake than make a meal. Yeast breads are my favorites!

3/4 cup milk
1/2 cup butter
1/2 cup sugar
5-1/4 to 6 cups all-purpose flour
2 packages (1/4 ounce *each*) active dry yeast
1 teaspoon salt
3 eggs
3 medium ripe bananas, mashed
1 teaspoon water

In a saucepan, cook and stir milk, butter and sugar over medium heat until butter is melted; cool to 120°-130°. In a mixing bowl, combine 2 cups of flour, yeast, salt, 2 eggs, bananas and milk mixture; beat on low speed until combined. Beat on medium for 3 minutes. Stir in enough of the remaining flour to form a firm dough.

Turn onto a floured surface; knead until smooth and elastic, about 4-6 minutes. Place in a greased bowl, turning once to grease top. Cover and let rise in a warm place until doubled, about 45 minutes.

Divide dough in half; shape each into a round loaf. Place on a greased baking sheet; cut slits in tops. Cover and let rise until doubled, about 45 minutes.

Beat remaining egg with water; brush over the loaves. Bake at 375° for 30-35 minutes or until golden brown. **Yield:** 2 loaves.

martha washington's fan

Susan Peck, Springfield, Missouri
These exceptional pastries, with pecans and coconut in the filling, taste as wonderful as they look.

    6 to 7 cups all-purpose flour, *divided*
    1/2 cup sugar
    2 tablespoons instant nonfat dry milk powder
    2 packages (1/4 ounce *each*) active dry yeast
1-1/4 teaspoons salt
    2/3 cup butter, softened
1-1/4 cups warm water (120° to 130°)
    3 eggs

FILLING:

1-1/2 cups flaked coconut
    1 cup chopped pecans
    1/2 cup packed brown sugar
    6 tablespoons butter, melted, *divided*

ICING:

    1 cup confectioners' sugar
    2 to 3 tablespoons milk

In a mixing bowl, combine 2 cups flour, sugar, dry milk, yeast and salt. Add butter and water; beat on low for 2 minutes. Add eggs; beat on high for 2 minutes. Stir in enough remaining flour to form a soft dough.

Turn onto a floured surface; knead until smooth and elastic, 6-8 minutes. Place in a greased bowl; turn once to grease top. Cover and let rise in a warm place until doubled, about 1 hour.

Combine coconut, pecans and brown sugar in a bowl. Blend in 3 tablespoons butter; set aside. Punch dough down; divide into thirds. Roll one portion into a 20-in. x 6-in. rectangle, with a short side facing you. Brush top two-thirds of dough with 1 tablespoon of remaining butter; sprinkle buttered portion with one-third of filling. Starting at plain short side, fold dough over half of filling; fold over again. Seal edges and end.

Place on a greased baking sheet with folded edge facing away from you. With scissors, cut into eight strips to within 1 in. from folded edge. Separate strips slightly; twist to allow filling to show. Pinch ends into points. Repeat with remaining dough and filling. Cover and let rise until doubled, about 45 minutes.

Bake at 350° for 20-25 minutes. Remove to wire racks to cool. Combine confectioners' sugar with enough milk to achieve drizzling consistency; drizzle over fans. **Yield:** 3 loaves.

***** prize.winning**tips**

＊Quick breads will slice better if you prepare them a day ahead of serving, wrap them tightly and refrigerate. You'll love the rich flavor, moist texture and perfect slices!

Cathy Burgdoerfer, Connersville, Indiana

＊For an easy spread for quick breads or muffins, combine softened cream cheese, a small can of drained crushed pineapple, some chopped walnuts and a little milk or pineapple juice.

Dorothy Jasper, Washington, Missouri

＊If you need chopped nuts for a recipe, don't fuss with the nut chopper. Just put the nuts in a plastic bag and roll them with a rolling pin. Then just pour them from the bag into your measuring cup.

Dorothy Baxter, Brush Prairie, Washington

runners-up

cherry danish

Christie Cochran, Canyon, Texas

These extra special pastries make any breakfast or brunch a memorable one. They're also perfect for a ladies' luncheon or shower.

- 1 package (1/4 ounce) active dry yeast
- 1/4 cup warm water (110° to 115°)
- 1 cup warm milk (110° to 115°)
- 3/4 cup shortening, *divided*
- 1/3 cup sugar
- 3 eggs
- 1 teaspoon salt
- 1/4 teaspoon *each* ground mace, lemon extract and vanilla extract
- 4 to 4-1/2 cups all-purpose flour
- 1 can (21 ounces) cherry pie filling

GLAZE:
- 1-1/2 cups confectioners' sugar
- 2 to 3 tablespoons milk
- 1/2 teaspoon vanilla extract
- 1/3 cup chopped almonds

In a mixing bowl, dissolve yeast in water. Add milk, 1/4 cup shortening, sugar, 2 eggs, salt, mace, extracts and 2 cups of flour; beat until smooth. Add enough remaining flour to form a soft dough.

Turn onto a floured surface and knead until smooth and elastic, about 6-8 minutes. Place in a greased bowl, turning once to grease top. Cover and let rise in a warm place until doubled, about 1 hour.

Punch dough down. On a large floured surface, roll dough out to a 24-in. x 16-in. rectangle. Dot half of the dough with 1/4 cup of shortening; fold dough lengthwise.

Fold the dough three times lengthwise, then two times widthwise, each time dotting with some of the remaining shortening. Place dough in a greased bowl; cover and let rise 20 minutes.

On a floured surface, roll dough into a 16-in. x 15-in.

rectangle. Cut into 8-in. x 3/4-in. strips; coil into a spiral shape, tucking end underneath the coil. Place in two greased 15-in. x 10-in. x 1-in. baking pans. Cover and let rise in a warm place until doubled, about 1 hour.

Beat remaining egg. Make a depression in the center of each roll; brush with egg. Fill with 1 tablespoon of pie filling. Bake at 375° for 15-18 minutes or until golden brown. Cool on a wire rack. Combine the first three glaze ingredients; drizzle over rolls. Sprinkle with almonds. **Yield:** 40 rolls.

citrus streusel quick bread

Debra White, Williamson, West Virginia

I do a lot of baking and cooking and often make copies of recipes to share. This one's generally in demand.

- 1 (18-1/4 ounces) lemon *or* orange cake mix, *divided*
- 2 tablespoons brown sugar
- 1 teaspoon ground cinnamon
- 1 tablespoon cold butter
- 1/2 cup chopped pecans
- 1 package (3.4 ounces) instant vanilla pudding mix
- 4 eggs
- 1 cup (8 ounces) sour cream
- 1/3 cup vegetable oil

GLAZE:
- 1 cup confectioners' sugar
- 2 to 3 tablespoons milk

In a small bowl, combine 2 tablespoons cake mix, brown sugar and cinnamon; cut in butter until crumbly. Stir in pecans; set aside. In a mixing bowl, combine pudding mix, eggs, sour cream, oil and remaining cake mix; beat on medium speed 2 minutes.

Pour into two greased 8-in. x 4-in. x 2-in. loaf pans. Sprinkle with pecan mixture. Bake at 350° for 45-50 minutes or until a toothpick inserted near the center comes out clean. Cool in pans for 10 minutes before removing to wire racks. Combine glaze ingredients; drizzle over warm bread. **Yield:** 2 loaves.

runners-up

pineapple cheese braid

Shirley Kensinger, Roaring Spring, Pennsylvania
Not only cheese but sweet pineapple is tucked into these tender, golden loaves. They're always a hit.

   2 packages (1/4 ounce *each*) active dry yeast
   1 cup warm water (110° to 115°)
   1/2 cup butter, softened
   5 tablespoons sugar
   2 eggs
   1/4 teaspoon salt
4-1/4 to 4-1/2 cups all-purpose flour
PINEAPPLE FILLING:
   1 can (8 ounces) crushed pineapple, undrained
   1/2 cup sugar
   3 tablespoons cornstarch
CREAM CHEESE FILLING:
   2 packages (8 ounces *each*) cream cheese, softened
   1/3 cup sugar
   1 tablespoon lemon juice
   1/2 teaspoon vanilla extract
ICING (optional):
   1 cup confectioners' sugar
   2 to 3 tablespoons milk

In a mixing bowl, dissolve yeast in water; let stand for 5 minutes. Add butter, sugar, eggs, salt and 2 cups flour; beat on low speed for 3 minutes. Stir in enough remaining flour to form a soft dough.

Turn onto a floured surface; knead until smooth and elastic, about 6-8 minutes. Place in a greased bowl, turning once to grease top. Cover and let rise in a warm place until doubled, about 45 minutes.

Meanwhile, combine pineapple filling ingredients in a saucepan. Bring to a boil; reduce heat. Cook and stir until thickened. Cool.

Combine cream cheese filling ingredients. Punch dough down. Divide dough in half. On a floured surface, roll each portion into a 15-in. x 9-in. rectangle. Place on greased baking sheets. Spread the cream cheese filling lengthwise down center third of each rectangle. Spread the pineapple filling on top.

On each long side, cut 1-in.-wide strips 3 in. into center. Starting at one end, fold alternating strips at an angle across filling. Seal ends. Cover and let rise for 20 minutes.

Bake at 350° for 25-30 minutes or until golden brown. Cool. If desired, combine icing ingredients and drizzle over braids. **Yield:** 2 loaves.

cocoa ripple squares

Phyllid Rank, Wapato, Washington
When my four children were growing up, this was a frequent birthday treat. Now, my grandchildren request it. It also could be served at a tea or at a card party.

   1/2 cup shortening
   1 cup sugar, *divided*
   2 eggs
1-1/2 cups all-purpose flour
   2 teaspoons baking powder
   3/4 teaspoon salt
   2/3 cup milk
   2 tablespoons baking cocoa
   2/3 cup chopped walnuts, *divided*
   3 tablespoons butter

In a mixing bowl, cream shortening and 3/4 cup sugar. Add eggs; beat until light and fluffy. Combine the flour, baking powder and salt; add to creamed mixture alternately with milk, beating well after each addition. Set aside.

Combine cocoa, 1/3 cup walnuts and remaining sugar. Spoon a third of the batter into a greased 9-in. square baking pan. Sprinkle with half of the cocoa mixture. Dot with half of the butter. Repeat layers; top with remaining batter.

Sprinkle with remaining walnuts. Bake at 350° for 35-40 minutes or until a toothpick inserted near the center comes out clean. Serve warm. **Yield:** 9 servings.

ABSOLUTELY ASPARAGUS #1

ASPARAGUS
PUFF RING

asparagus puff ring

When tender asparagus is bountiful in your garden or at the store, marvelous meals will soon be cropping up! This versatile vegetable adds fresh, distinctive flavor and lovely green color to many dishes. Several thousand recipes spotlighting these spears came in for our Absolutely Asparagus recipe contest.

> "It's delectable yet deceivingly simple to prepare."

After selecting the most promising recipes, our kitchen staff began slicing, sauteing, mixing and marinating tempting appetizers, side dishes and main dishes studded with asparagus. Then our judges had the demanding job of selecting the winners.

They selected Asparagus Puff Ring, shared by Shirley De Lange of Byron Center, Michigan, as the Grand Prize Winner. This tempting dish and all of the other delicious asparagus recipes on the following pages are sure to put a "spring" in your step.

"Every time I make this family-favorite entree, I'm struck by how impressive it looks," says Shirley. "Ham and asparagus in a creamy sauce are piled high in a cheesy cream puff shell. It's delectable yet deceivingly simple to prepare."

3/4 **cup water**
6 **tablespoons butter**
3/4 **cup all-purpose flour**
1/2 **teaspoon salt**
3 **eggs**
1/4 **cup grated Parmesan cheese,** *divided*
FILLING:
1 **pound fresh asparagus, cut into 1-inch pieces**
1/4 **cup diced onion**
2 **tablespoons butter**
2 **tablespoons all-purpose flour**
1/2 **teaspoon salt**
1/4 **teaspoon pepper**
1-1/2 **cups milk**
1/2 **cup shredded Swiss cheese**
2 **tablespoons grated Parmesan cheese**
2 **cups diced fully cooked ham**

In a saucepan over medium heat, bring water and butter to a boil. Add flour and salt all at once; stir until a smooth ball forms. Remove from the heat; let stand for 5 minutes. Add eggs, one at a time, beating well after each; beat until smooth. Stir in 3 tablespoons Parmesan cheese.

Using 1/4 cupfuls of dough, form a ring around the sides of a greased 10-in. quiche pan or pie plate (mounds should touch). Top with the remaining cheese. Bake at 400° for 35 minutes.

Meanwhile, cook asparagus in a small amount of water until crisp-tender, 3-4 minutes; drain. In a saucepan, saute onion in butter until tender. Stir in flour, salt and pepper. Gradually add milk; bring to a boil over medium heat, stirring constantly. Reduce heat; add cheeses and stir until melted.

Stir in ham and asparagus; spoon into ring. Serve immediately. **Yield:** 6 servings.

Prize Winning Recipes 135

asparagus mornay

Linda McKee, Big Prairie, Ohio

When I was growing up on my parents' dairy farm, we always had a large asparagus patch. I still love asparagus, but my husband and children weren't that eager to eat it until I found this recipe. Now we enjoy these savory spears.

- 1-1/2 pounds fresh asparagus, trimmed
- 1 tablespoon butter
- 1 tablespoon all-purpose flour
- 1 cup half-and-half cream
- 1/2 teaspoon chicken bouillon granules
- 1/8 teaspoon ground nutmeg
- 1/8 teaspoon salt
- 1/2 cup shredded Swiss cheese
- 2 tablespoons crushed butter-flavored crackers

In a skillet, cook asparagus in a small amount of water until crisp-tender, about 6-8 minutes; drain. Arrange spears in the bottom of a greased 1-1/2-qt. baking dish; set aside and keep warm.

In a small saucepan, melt butter. Stir in flour until smooth. Gradually whisk in the cream, bouillon, nutmeg and salt. Bring to a boil over medium heat; cook and stir for 2 minutes or until thickened.

Remove from the heat; add cheese and stir until melted. Pour over asparagus. Sprinkle with cracker crumbs. Broil 6 in. from the heat for 3-5 minutes or until lightly browned. **Yield:** 4-6 servings.

gingered pork and asparagus

Kathleen Purvis, Franklin, Tennessee

My husband and I really enjoy fresh asparagus. So we were thrilled when I found this recipe for asparagus and juicy pork slices smothered in a snappy ginger sauce.

- 6 tablespoons apple juice
- 6 tablespoons soy sauce
- 4 garlic cloves, minced
- 1 tablespoon ground ginger
- 1 pound pork tenderloin, thinly sliced
- 2 tablespoons vegetable oil, *divided*
- 1 pound fresh asparagus, cut into 1-inch pieces
- 1-1/2 teaspoons cornstarch
- Hot cooked rice, optional

Combine the first four ingredients. Reserve 1/3 cup. Pour remaining marinade into large resealable plastic bag; add pork. Seal bag and turn to coat; refrigerate for 1 hour. Cover and refrigerate reserved marinade.

Drain and discard marinade from pork. In a large skillet or wok, stir-fry half of the pork in 1 tablespoon oil for 2-3 minutes or until no longer pink. Remove pork with a slotted spoon; set aside. Repeat with remaining pork and oil.

In the same skillet, stir-fry the asparagus for 2-3 minutes or until crisp-tender. Combine cornstarch and reserved marinade until smooth; stir into the skillet. Bring to a boil; cook and stir for 2 minutes or until thickened. Return pork to skillet and heat through. Serve over rice if desired. **Yield:** 4 servings.

asparagus ham swirls

Nancy Ingersol, Midlothian, Illinois
I came across the recipe for this hot appetizer years ago and have made it many times to share with friends and co-workers. Asparagus, ham and cheese combine to create a fun finger food.

- 16 fresh asparagus spears, trimmed
- 3 tablespoons Dijon mustard
- 16 thin slices fully cooked ham
- 16 slices process Swiss cheese
- 2 eggs, beaten
- 1 cup dry bread crumbs

Vegetable oil

In a skillet, cook asparagus in a small amount of water until crisp-tender, about 6-8 minutes; drain well.

Spread about 1 teaspoon of mustard on each ham slice. Top with one slice of cheese. Place an asparagus spear at one end (trim to fit if needed). Roll up each ham slice tightly; secure with three toothpicks.

Dip ham rolls in egg, then roll in bread crumbs. In an electric skillet, heat 1 in. of oil to 350°. Fry rolls, a few at a time, until golden brown, about 3-4 minutes. Drain on paper towels; keep warm. Cut each roll between the toothpicks into three pieces. **Yield:** 4 dozen.

lemon asparagus soup

Darlene Swille, Green Bay, Wisconsin
We have a small asparagus patch and my husband and I wait eagerly for this tasty vegetable to appear every spring. We're pleased to use our precious harvest in this soup.

- 1 medium onion, chopped
- 1/2 cup chopped celery
- 1/4 cup butter
- 2 tablespoons cornstarch
- 1 cup water
- 2 chicken bouillon cubes
- 3/4 pound fresh asparagus, trimmed and cut into 1-inch pieces
- 2 cups milk
- 1/4 to 1/2 teaspoon grated lemon peel
- 1/8 teaspoon ground nutmeg

Dash seasoned salt

In a 2-qt. saucepan, saute the onion and celery in butter until tender. Combine cornstarch and water; stir into the saucepan with bouillon. Bring to a boil over medium heat; cook and stir for 2 minutes or until thickened.

Add asparagus. Reduce heat; cover and simmer until asparagus is crisp-tender, about 3-4 minutes. Stir in the milk, lemon peel, nutmeg and seasoned salt.

Cover and simmer for 25 minutes, stirring occasionally. **Yield:** 4 servings.

asparagus bacon quiche

Suzanne McKinley, Lyons, Georgia
Lovely asparagus peeks out of every slice of this hearty quiche, which is delicious and a little different. I like to make it for special occasions—it's a welcome addition to any brunch buffet.

- 1 unbaked pastry shell (9 inches)
- 1 pound fresh asparagus, trimmed and cut into 1-inch pieces
- 6 bacon strips, cooked and crumbled
- 3 eggs
- 1-1/2 cups half-and-half cream
- 1 cup grated Parmesan cheese, *divided*
- 1 tablespoon sliced green onions
- 1 teaspoon sugar
- 1/2 teaspoon salt
- 1/4 teaspoon pepper

Pinch ground nutmeg

Line the unpricked pastry shell with a double thickness of heavy-duty foil. Bake at 450° for 5 minutes; remove foil. Bake 5 minutes longer; remove from the oven and set aside.

Cook asparagus in a small amount of water until crisp-tender, about 3-4 minutes; drain well. Arrange the bacon and asparagus in the crust.

In a bowl, beat eggs; add cream, 1/2 cup cheese, onions, sugar, salt, pepper and nutmeg. Pour over asparagus. Sprinkle with remaining cheese.

Bake at 400° for 10 minutes. Reduce heat to 350°; bake 23-25 minutes longer or until a knife inserted near the center comes out clean. **Yield:** 6-8 servings.

asparagus, apple and chicken salad

Nancy Horsburgh, Everett, Ontario
This cool, refreshing salad is a palate-pleaser. Apples and asparagus seem an unlikely match, but they form a terrific trio with chicken. I make this salad often while asparagus is in sesaon.

- 1 cup cut fresh asparagus (1-inch pieces)
- 2 tablespoons cider vinegar
- 2 tablespoons vegetable oil
- 2 teaspoons honey
- 2 teaspoons minced fresh parsley
- 1/2 teaspoon salt
- 1/4 teaspoon pepper
- 1 cup cubed cooked chicken
- 1/2 cup diced red apple
- 2 cups torn mixed greens

Cook asparagus in a small amount of water until crisp-tender, about 3-4 minutes; drain and cool. In a bowl, combine the next six ingredients. Stir in chicken, apple and asparagus; toss. Serve over greens. **Yield:** 3 servings.

cream of asparagus soup

Veva Hepler, Walla Walla, Washington

It's not difficult to fix a batch of this smooth, comforting soup. It has wonderful homemade goodness. A single steaming bowl really warms me up…but I usually can't resist going back for seconds.

- 1/2 cup chopped onion
- 1 tablespoon vegetable oil
- 2 cans (14-1/2 ounces *each*) chicken broth
- 2-1/2 pounds fresh asparagus, trimmed and cut into 1-inch pieces
- 1/4 teaspoon dried tarragon
- 1/4 cup butter
- 1/4 cup all-purpose flour
- 1/2 teaspoon salt
- 1/4 teaspoon white pepper
- 3 cups half-and-half cream
- 1-1/2 teaspoons lemon juice
- Shredded Swiss cheese

In a large saucepan, saute onion in oil until tender. Add broth, asparagus and tarragon. Bring to a boil. Reduce heat; simmer, uncovered, until asparagus is tender, about 8-10 minutes. Cool for 10 minutes.

In a blender or food processor, puree the asparagus, a third at a time; set aside.

In a Dutch oven or soup kettle, melt butter; stir in flour, salt and pepper until smooth. Cook and stir for 2 min-utes or until golden. Gradually add cream. Bring to a boil; cook and stir for 2 minutes or until thickened. Reduce heat.

Stir in the pureed asparagus and lemon juice; heat through. Garnish with cheese if desired. **Yield:** 8 servings (about 2 quarts).

---

* * * * * prize winning tips

★ Fresh asparagus stores longer if kept standing, cut side down, in an inch of water in the refrigerator. Use a tall pitcher or large beverage container and replace the water as needed.

Sheryl Sue Keefer, Papillion, Nebraska

★ To make quick soup that tastes homemade, chop, then cook asparagus spears until tender. Drain the liquid and add the asparagus to a prepared can of cream of mushroom, cream of chicken or cream of asparagus soup. Garnish with cooked and crumbled bacon.

Lucy Euvrard, Okeana, Ohio

★ To remove the woody asparagus ends, gently bend each stalk near the stem until it snaps—the stalk will break where the tender section starts. A pound of fresh asparagus yields 1/2 to 3/4 pound trimmed.

Edna Hoffman, Hebron, Indiana

runners-up

FRESH CORN SALAD

fresh corn salad

GRAND PRIZE WINNER

When the garden corn's as high as an elephant's eye (or cheap and plentiful at the grocery or farm stand), you might wonder what in the world you're going to do with all those ears. Wonder no more! Our Country Corn contest brought in bushels of bright ideas for corn that will have your family clamoring for seconds through all four seasons.

> "It tastes best when you make it ahead..."

From robust soups to hearty and meaty main courses, sunny side dishes and salads, moist muffins and more, you truly have struck "gold" by turning to this section of recipes.

Fresh Corn Salad, with tangy flavor and appealing color, was selected the Grand Prize Winner. The recipe was shared by Carol Shaffer of Cape Girardeau, Missouri, who enjoys gardening as much as she does cooking. "I love recipes that call for homegrown ingredients," she says. "I make this corn salad often for family get-togethers. It's always a hit at barbecues, too. It tastes best when you make it ahead and let it sit in the refrigerator overnight. Then just put it in your picnic cooler and go."

8 ears fresh corn, husked and cleaned
1/2 cup vegetable oil
1/4 cup cider vinegar
1-1/2 teaspoons lemon juice
1/4 cup minced fresh parsley
2 teaspoons sugar
1 teaspoon salt
1/2 teaspoon dried basil
1/8 to 1/4 teaspoon cayenne pepper
2 large tomatoes, seeded and coarsely chopped
1/2 cup chopped onion
1/3 cup chopped green pepper
1/3 cup chopped sweet red pepper

In a large saucepan, cook corn in enough boiling water to cover for 5-7 minutes or until tender. Drain, cool and set aside.

In a large bowl, mix the oil, vinegar, lemon juice, parsley, sugar, salt, basil and cayenne pepper. Cut cooled corn off the cob (should measure 4 cups).

Add corn, tomatoes, onion and peppers to the oil mixture. Mix well. Cover and chill for several hours or overnight. **Yield:** 10 servings.

pork chops with corn dressing

June Hassler, Sultan, Washington

As a new bride, I came across the original version of this recipe in a newspaper. I changed it around and tried it out on my groom. It became a family staple—not to mention a great, easy main course for unexpected company. With our children both grown, my husband's still my "guinea pig." I love to experiment with new dishes.

- 1 egg, beaten
- 2 cups soft bread crumbs
- 1 can (15-1/4 ounces) whole kernel corn, drained *or* 1-1/2 cups cooked whole kernel corn
- 1/4 cup water
- 1/2 cup chopped green pepper
- 1 small onion, chopped
- 1 teaspoon Worcestershire sauce
- 2 tablespoons vegetable oil
- 6 butterfly pork chops (about 1 inch thick)
- Salt and pepper to taste
- 1 can (10-3/4 ounces) condensed cream of mushroom soup, undiluted
- 2/3 cup milk

In a bowl, combine egg, bread crumbs, corn, water, green pepper, onion and Worcestershire sauce; set aside.

In a large ovenproof skillet or a Dutch oven, heat oil over medium heat. Lightly brown pork chops on both sides. Season with salt and pepper. Top with corn dressing mixture. Add enough water to cover bottom of pan.

Bake, uncovered, at 350° for about 1 hour or until pork is tender. Add additional water to pan if necessary. Remove pork chops and dressing to a serving platter; keep warm. Skim fat from drippings. Add soup and milk to pan drippings. Cook and stir over medium heat until hot and bubbly. Serve with pork chops. **Yield:** 6 servings.

> *To freeze fresh corn: blanch ears, then cool them. Place an ear of corn on the cone of an angel food cake pan and cut off the kernels with an electric knife. The cake pan will catch the kernels without making a mess of your kitchen counter.
> Marilyn McDonnell, San Andreas, California

corn balls

Sharon Knicely, Harrisonburg, Virginia

Whenever I serve my Corn Balls, it's just about certain someone will ask for the recipe—I've gotten more requests for it than any other I've ever tried. I usually make them when we have company as a nice change-of-pace side dish. They're great with ham, steak or roast beef.

- 1/2 cup chopped onion
- 1 cup chopped celery
- 1/2 cup butter
- 3-1/2 cups herb-seasoned stuffing croutons
- 3 cups cooked whole kernel corn
- 3 eggs, beaten
- 1/2 cup water
- 1/2 teaspoon salt
- 1/4 teaspoon pepper

In a saucepan, cook onion and celery in butter until tender; set aside to cool.

In a bowl, combine croutons, corn, eggs, water, salt, pepper and onion mixture; mix well. Shape into eight to 10 balls.

Place in an ungreased shallow baking dish. Bake, uncovered, at 375° for 25-30 minutes. **Yield:** 8-10 servings.

halibut chowder

Mary Davis, Palmer, Alaska

This rich, creamy chowder is so good you won't believe it starts with canned soup and frozen vegetables. It showcases tender chunks of halibut, but salmon or most any type of whitefish will do. I double the recipe for large gatherings, and guests almost lick the pot clean!

- 8 to 10 green onions, thinly sliced
- 2 garlic cloves, minced
- 2 tablespoons butter
- 4 cans (10-3/4 ounces *each*) condensed cream of potato soup, undiluted
- 2 cans (10-3/4 ounces *each*) condensed cream of mushroom soup, undiluted
- 4 cups milk
- 2 packages (8 ounces *each*) cream cheese, cubed
- 1-1/2 pounds halibut *or* salmon fillets, cubed
- 1-1/2 cups frozen sliced carrots
- 1-1/2 cups frozen corn
- 1/8 to 1/4 teaspoon cayenne pepper, optional

In a Dutch oven or soup kettle, saute onions and garlic in butter until tender. Add soups, milk and cream cheese; cook and stir until cheese is melted. Bring to a boil.

Stir in fish, carrots and corn. Reduce heat; simmer, uncovered, for 5-10 minutes or until fish flakes easily and the vegetables are tender. Add cayenne pepper if desired. **Yield:** 16 servings (about 4 quarts).

hush puppies

Karyl Goodhart, Geraldine, Montana

Some years ago, I was a cook on a large cattle ranch. One day, I thought back to the hush puppies I'd had as a child on a Southern trip...and ended up creating my own version of them. They go well as part of an old-fashioned ham, sausage or fried chicken dinner. They're great when mashed potatoes and gravy, biscuits and corn on the cob are on the menu.

- 2 cups yellow cornmeal
- 1/2 cup all-purpose flour
- 2 tablespoons sugar
- 2 teaspoons baking powder
- 1 teaspoon salt
- 1/2 teaspoon baking soda
- 1 egg, beaten
- 3/4 cup milk
- 3/4 cup cream-style corn

Vegetable oil for frying
Confectioners' sugar, optional

In a bowl, combine cornmeal, flour, sugar, baking powder, salt and baking soda. Add egg, milk and corn; stir just until mixed.

In a deep-fat fryer, heat oil to 375°. Drop batter by teaspoonfuls into oil. Fry until golden brown.

Allow to cool slightly and roll in confectioners' sugar if desired. Serve immediately. **Yield:** 12-15 servings.

colossal cornburger

Lesley Colgan, London, Ontario
I don't even remember where this recipe came from! Cooking's something I thoroughly enjoy. When I'm finished, my husband always wonders whether or not a truck ran through our kitchen. Somehow, I manage to cover every bit of counter space.

- 1 egg, beaten
- 1 cup cooked whole kernel corn
- 1/2 cup coarsely crushed cheese crackers
- 1/4 cup sliced green onions
- 1/4 cup chopped fresh parsley
- 1 teaspoon Worcestershire sauce
- 2 pounds ground beef
- 1 teaspoon salt
- 1/2 teaspoon pepper
- 1/2 teaspoon ground sage

In a medium bowl, combine egg, corn, crackers, green onions, parsley and Worcestershire sauce; set aside. In a large bowl, combine ground beef and seasonings. On sheets of waxed paper, pat half of the beef mixture at a time into an 8-1/2-in. circle. Spoon corn mixture onto one circle of meat to within 1 in. of the edge. Top with second circle of meat; remove top sheet of waxed paper and seal edges. Invert onto a well-greased wire grill basket; peel off waxed paper.

Grill, covered, over medium heat, for 12-15 minutes on each side or until thermometer reads 160°. For oven method, place burger on a baking pan. Bake at 350° for 40-45 minutes or until thermometer reads 160°. Cut into wedges to serve. **Yield:** 6 servings.

company vegetable casserole

Leora Clark, Lincoln, Nebraska
A neighbor passed this on to me. I make my casserole for family dinners, reunions and potlucks, and the response is almost always the same when people taste it—"Can I have the recipe?"

- 1 can (14-1/2 ounces) cut green beans, drained *or* 2 cups frozen cut green beans, thawed
- 1 can (15-1/4 ounces) whole kernel corn, drained *or* 2 cups cooked fresh *or* frozen whole kernel corn
- 1 can (10-3/4 ounces) condensed cream of celery soup, undiluted
- 1/2 cup sour cream
- 1/2 cup shredded cheddar cheese
- 1/2 cup chopped onion
- 1/4 cup butter, melted
- 3/4 cup saltine crumbs
- 1/4 cup sliced almonds, toasted

In a bowl, combine beans, corn, soup, sour cream, cheese and onion. Pour into an ungreased 2-qt. baking dish.

Combine butter, crumbs and almonds; sprinkle over vegetables. Bake, uncovered, at 350° for 35-40 minutes or until bubbly. **Yield:** 6-8 servings.

corn and sausage chowder

Joanne Watts, Kitchener, Ontario

I've had several cooking teachers over the years—my Irish grandmother, my mother, and the restaurant my husband and I once operated in Manitoba.

- 3 ears fresh corn, husked and cleaned
- 4 cups heavy whipping cream
- 2 cups chicken broth
- 4 garlic cloves, minced
- 10 fresh thyme sprigs
- 1 bay leaf
- 1-1/2 medium onions, finely chopped, *divided*
- 1/2 pound hot Italian sausage links
- 2 teaspoons minced jalapeno peppers with seeds
- 1/2 teaspoon ground cumin
- 2 tablespoons butter
- 2 medium potatoes, peeled and cut into 1/2-inch cubes
- 2 tablespoons all-purpose flour

Salt and pepper to taste
- 1-1/2 teaspoons snipped fresh chives

Using a small sharp knife, cut corn from cobs; set corn aside. Place the corncobs, cream, broth, garlic, thyme, bay leaf and 1/2 cup onions in a large saucepan. Heat almost to boiling. Reduce heat; cover and simmer for 1 hour, stirring occasionally.

Remove and discard corncobs. Strain cream mixture through a sieve set over a large bowl, pressing solids with back of spoon. Discard solids and reserve corn broth.

Meanwhile, cook sausage over medium heat until browned. Cool and cut into 1/2-in. slices. In a large saucepan, cook jalapenos, cumin and remaining onions in butter for 5 minutes. Set aside 1/4 cup corn stock. Add remaining corn stock along with potatoes and sausage to saucepan. Bring to a boil. Reduce heat; cover and cook for 25 minutes or until potatoes are tender. Combine flour with reserved corn stock until smooth. Stir into chowder. Bring to a boil; cook and stir for 2 minutes or until thickened.

Add corn and cook just until tender, about 5 minutes. Discard bay leaf. Season with salt and pepper. For a thinner chowder, add additional chicken broth. Sprinkle with chives before serving. **Yield:** 8 servings (2 quarts).

Editor's Note: When cutting or seeding hot peppers, use rubber or plastic gloves to protect your hands. Avoid touching your face.

---

prize winningtips

★ Make herb butter to spread on corn on the cob. Combine 2 sticks of butter softened to room temperature with 1 teaspoon chopped fresh basil or 1/2 teaspoon dried basil. This makes enough for 12 ears and is especially tasty with corn cooked on the grill.

Ellen Bower, Taneytown, Maryland

★ For an oven method of preparing corn for the freezer, consider this: combine 9 cups corn, 2 cups water, 2 teaspoons salt and 1/4 cup sugar in a roasting pan. Bake at 350° for 30-45 minutes, stirring every 15 minutes or so. Cool, then package it in serving-size portions and freeze.

Sue Beiswanger, Wolcottville, Indiana

corn muffins with honey butter

Marilyn Platner, Marion, Iowa

There's an interesting country story behind this recipe. I've worked at our local Farm Bureau office for over 15 years. A friend on our women's committee developed it to give people new ideas for using farm commodities. I especially like preparing these muffins for my family on a winter night—along with a big pot of chili, they make for a very hearty meal!

- 2 cups all-purpose flour
- 2 cups yellow cornmeal
- 1 cup nonfat dry milk powder
- 1/4 cup sugar
- 2 tablespoons baking powder
- 1 teaspoon salt
- 1/2 teaspoon baking soda
- 2-2/3 cups water
- 1/2 cup butter, melted
- 2 eggs, beaten
- 1 tablespoon lemon juice

HONEY BUTTER:
- 2 tablespoons honey
- 1/2 cup butter, softened

In a bowl, combine flour, cornmeal, milk powder, sugar, baking powder, salt and baking soda. Add water, butter, eggs and lemon juice; stir until dry ingredients are moistened.

Spoon into 24 greased muffin cups. Bake at 425° for 13-15 minutes. Cool for 5 minutes before removing from pans to wire racks.

In a small mixing bowl, beat together honey and softened butter. Serve with the muffins. **Yield:** 2 dozen.

fresh corn cakes

Gaynelle Fritsch, Welches, Oregon

Corn's always been the basis of my favorite recipes— in fact, these corn cakes were one of the first things I prepared for my husband. For dinner, they're nice with fresh fruit salad and ham. They're also great with breakfast sausage and orange juice.

- 1 cup all-purpose flour
- 1/2 cup yellow *or* blue cornmeal
- 1 tablespoon sugar
- 1 tablespoon baking powder
- 1/2 teaspoon salt
- 2 eggs, *separated*
- 1 cup milk
- 1/4 cup butter, melted
- 1 cup cooked whole kernel corn
- 4 green onions, thinly sliced
- 1/2 medium sweet red pepper, finely chopped
- 1 can (4 ounces) chopped green chilies

Vegetable oil for frying
Maple syrup, optional

In a medium bowl, combine flour, cornmeal, sugar, baking powder and salt. In a small bowl, beat egg yolks; blend in milk and butter. Add to dry ingredients; stir until just mixed. (Batter may be slightly lumpy.)

Stir in the corn, green onions, red pepper and green chilies; set aside.

In a small mixing bowl, beat egg whites until stiff peaks form. Gently fold into batter.

For each pancake, pour about 1/4 cup batter onto a lightly greased hot griddle; turn when bubbles form on tops of cakes. Cook second side until golden brown. Serve immediately with syrup if desired. **Yield:** 20 pancakes.

calico potato salad

Christine Hartry, Emo, Ontario
One of the nice things about this colorful, tangy salad is how versatile it is. I've taken it to a potluck...to a square dance gathering...and to the field for my husband and the men during haying season! As part of a lunch, it is a refreshing side dish with roast beef, chicken or ham sandwiches.

DRESSING:
- 1/2 cup olive oil
- 1/4 cup vinegar
- 1 tablespoon sugar
- 1-1/2 teaspoons chili powder
- 1 teaspoon salt, optional

Dash hot pepper sauce

SALAD:
- 4 large red potatoes (about 2 pounds), peeled and cooked
- 1-1/2 cups cooked whole kernel corn
- 1 cup shredded carrot
- 1/2 cup chopped red onion
- 1/2 cup diced green pepper
- 1/2 cup diced sweet red pepper
- 1/2 cup sliced pitted ripe olives

In a jar with a lid, combine all dressing ingredients. Shake well. Chill.

Cube potatoes; combine with corn, carrot, onion, peppers and olives in a salad bowl.

Pour dressing over; toss lightly. Cover and chill. **Yield:** 14 servings.

corn and chicken dinner

Doralee Pinkerton, Milford, Indiana
My interests are reading, gardening and growing most of the ingredients I use in this dinner! There's something for every taste in this recipe. It would be great as a meal-in-one dish for a picnic or a reunion.

- 3 garlic cloves, minced, *divided*
- 1/2 cup butter, *divided*
- 3 pounds chicken legs and thighs (about 8 pieces)
- 3 ears fresh corn, husked, cleaned and cut into thirds
- 1/4 cup water
- 2 teaspoons dried tarragon, *divided*
- 1/2 teaspoon salt
- 1/4 teaspoon pepper
- 2 medium zucchini, sliced into 1/2-inch pieces
- 2 tomatoes, seeded and cut into chunks

In a Dutch oven or large skillet, saute 2 of the garlic cloves in 2 tablespoons butter. Add the chicken and brown on both sides. Reduce heat. Add corn and water. Sprinkle with 1 teaspoon tarragon, salt and pepper. Cover and simmer for 20-25 minutes or until chicken is tender and the juices run clear.

Meanwhile, in a small saucepan, melt remaining butter. Add remaining garlic and tarragon; simmer for 3 minutes. Layer zucchini and tomatoes over the chicken mixture.

Drizzle seasoned butter over all; cover and cook for 3-5 minutes. **Yield:** 6-8 servings.

RED PEPPER SOUP

red pepper soup

I f variety is the spice of life, this section with winners from the Peck of Peppers contest might be the zestiest one. It stars one of the most full-flavored pleasures—peppers—in all sorts of forms and force, from sweet to sizzling.

"Smooth and savory, this packed-with-peppers soup is a versatile favorite at my house."

Here and on the following pages, you'll find the top finishers in our coast-to-coast quest for the best of the best, family-favorite pepper recipes. Any of these dishes would be perfect for when the heat's on to prepare a great meal.

The Grand Prize Winner is Red Pepper Soup, shared by Barb Nelson of Victoria, British Columbia. "Smooth and savory, this packed-with-peppers soup is a versatile favorite at my house," says Barb. It's easy to make ahead and freezes well so you can make big batches when summer's garden peppers are abundant.

"When we have company, I often make this soup as a first course," says Barb. "For a casual, family supper, it's the main dish. I'll usually serve it along with a salad and focaccia bread."

6 medium sweet red peppers, chopped
2 medium carrots, chopped
2 medium onions, chopped
1 celery rib, chopped
4 garlic cloves, minced
1 tablespoon olive oil
2 cans (one 49-1/2 ounces, one 14-1/2 ounces) chicken broth
1/2 cup uncooked long grain rice
2 tablespoons minced fresh thyme *or* 2 teaspoons dried thyme
1-1/2 teaspoons salt
1/4 teaspoon pepper
1/8 to 1/4 teaspoon cayenne pepper
1/8 to 1/4 teaspoon crushed red pepper flakes

In a large Dutch oven or soup kettle, saute the red peppers, carrots, onions, celery and garlic in oil until tender.

Stir in the broth, rice, thyme, salt, pepper and cayenne; bring to a boil. Reduce heat; cover and simmer for 20-25 minutes or until the vegetables and rice are tender.

Cool for 30 minutes. Puree in small batches in a blender; return to pan. Add red pepper flakes; heat through. **Yield:** 10-12 servings (about 3 quarts).

grilled three-pepper salad

Ruth Wickard, York, Pennsylvania
I have been cooking since my mother taught me how at an early age. I enjoy it, and I'm always trying new recipes. This one's both flavorful and pretty.

    2 *each* large green, sweet red and yellow
      peppers, cut into 1-inch pieces
    1 large red onion, halved and thinly sliced
    1 pound bulk mozzarella cheese, cut into
      bite-size cubes
    1 can (6 ounces) pitted ripe olives, drained and
      halved
VINAIGRETTE:
  2/3 cup olive oil
  1/3 cup red wine vinegar
    2 tablespoons lemon juice
    2 tablespoons Dijon mustard
    1 tablespoon minced fresh basil *or* 1 teaspoon
      dried basil
  1/2 teaspoon cayenne pepper
  1/2 teaspoon garlic powder

Thread peppers onto metal or soaked wooden skewers; grill or broil for 10-12 minutes or until edges are browned. Remove from skewers and place in a large bowl.

Add onion, mozzarella and olives; toss gently. Cover and refrigerate.

In a jar with tight-fitting lid, combine vinaigrette ingredients, shake well. Pour over the pepper mixture just before serving; toss to coat. **Yield:** 10-12 servings.

pickled peppers

Heather Prendergast, Sundre, Alberta
Well received at potlucks, this colorful, tasty dish adds zest to the menu. I also make it as a salad or accompaniment for a luncheon or dinner at home. My husband and I manage a campground and these peppers are popular at barbecues.

    2 *each* medium green, sweet red and yellow
      peppers, cut into 1-inch pieces
    1 large red onion, halved and thinly sliced
    1 cup cider vinegar
    1 cup sugar
  1/3 cup water
    2 teaspoons mixed pickling spices
  1/2 teaspoon celery seed

In a large glass bowl, combine peppers and onion; set aside.

In a saucepan, combine the vinegar, sugar and water. Place the pickling spices and celery seed in a double thickness of cheesecloth; bring up the corners of cloth and tie with string to form a bag. Add to saucepan. Bring to a boil; boil for 1 minute.

Transfer spice bag to pepper mixture. Pour the vinegar mixture over all. Cover and refrigerate for 24 hours, stirring occasionally.

Discard spice bag. Peppers may be stored in the refrigerator for up to 1 month. **Yield:** 4 cups.

bell pepper enchiladas

Melissa Cowser, Greenville, Texas
Peppers are probably the vegetable that gets used most frequently in my kitchen. My freezer's constantly stocked in case I discover a new recipe to try or want to whip up an old favorite. In a way, my parents helped create this recipe. They always taught never to waste. So one day when my husband and I had prepared a Mexican meal and had peppers, cheese, salsa and tortillas left over, these were the result!

> 2 medium green peppers, chopped
> 1/2 cup shredded cheddar cheese
> 1/2 cup shredded Monterey Jack cheese
> 1/2 cup diced process cheese (Velveeta)
> 4 flour tortillas (8 inches)
> 1 small jalapeno pepper, minced, optional
> 1 cup salsa, *divided*

Additional shredded cheese, optional

Sprinkle the green peppers and cheeses down the center of tortillas; add jalapeno if desired. Roll up.

Spread 1/2 cup salsa in a shallow baking dish. Place tortillas seam side down over salsa. Top with remaining salsa.

Bake, uncovered, at 350° for 20 minutes or until heated through. Sprinkle with additional cheese if desired. **Yield:** 4 enchiladas.

Editor's Note: When cutting or seeding hot peppers, use rubber or plastic gloves to protect your hands. Avoid touching your face.

pepper avocado salsa

Theresa Mullens, Gill, Massachusetts
Much of our summer menu is done on the grill, and peppers and avocados are favorites in my family. That led me to create this recipe to help spice up our barbecued entrees. I have also served the salsa as an appetizer on thin wedges of bread and as a topping for easy country-style dishes like chicken and rice pilaf.

> 2 medium tomatoes, diced
> 1/4 cup *each* diced green, sweet red and yellow pepper
> 1/4 cup diced red onion
> 2 tablespoons olive oil
> 2 tablespoons lime juice
> 1 tablespoon white wine vinegar
> 1 garlic clove, minced
> 1 tablespoon minced fresh basil *or* 1 teaspoon dried basil
> 1 tablespoon minced fresh dill *or* 1 teaspoon dill weed
> 1 teaspoon sugar
> 3/4 teaspoon minced fresh thyme *or* 1/4 teaspoon dried thyme
> Dash hot pepper sauce
> 1 large ripe avocado

In a bowl, combine the first 12 ingredients. Cover and refrigerate. Just before serving, peel and chop the avocado; stir into the salsa.

Serve with chips or as an accompaniment to meat, poultry or fish. **Yield:** 3-1/2 cups.

hearty tortilla casserole

Terri Nelsom, Warren, Minnesota

Being single, I often halve this recipe to yield a meal for one plus a lunch I can take to work. When co-workers remark on how good it looks, I ask them over to try it, then pass along the recipe. It's hot but not overpowering.

- 1/2 pound ground beef
- 2 tablespoons taco seasoning
- 1/3 cup water
- 1 small onion, finely chopped
- 1 to 2 Anaheim *or* Poblano chilies, roasted, peeled and finely chopped *or* 1 can (4 ounces) chopped green chilies
- 1 jalapeno pepper, seeded and finely chopped
- 1 garlic clove, minced
- 1 tablespoon vegetable oil
- 1/4 cup heavy whipping cream
- 1/8 teaspoon salt
- 4 flour tortillas (8 inches)
- 1 can (16 ounces) refried beans
- 1 cup (4 ounces) shredded Monterey Jack cheese, *divided*
- 1 cup (4 ounces) shredded cheddar cheese, *divided*

Sour cream and salsa, optional

In a skillet over medium heat, cook beef until no longer pink; drain. Add taco seasoning and water. Simmer, uncovered, for 5 minutes; remove from the heat and set aside.

In a saucepan, saute onion, chilies, jalapeno and garlic in oil until tender, about 8 minutes. Stir in cream and salt. Cover and simmer for 5 minutes.

Spread 3 tablespoons sauce in an ungreased 8-in. round or square baking dish. Spread about 2 teaspoons sauce on each tortilla; layer with beans, beef mixture and 2 table-spoons of each kind of cheese. Roll up and place seam side down in baking dish. Top with the remaining sauce.

Bake, uncovered, at 350° for 25 minutes. Sprinkle with remaining cheeses; bake 5 minutes longer. Serve with sour cream and salsa if desired. **Yield:** 2-4 servings.

Editor's Note: When cutting or seeding hot peppers, use rubber or plastic gloves to protect your hands. Avoid touching your face.

peppery philly steaks

Edie Fitch, Clifton, Arizona

Since we love to cook and eat, my husband and I are always developing new recipes. This is one we especially enjoy when we have fresh peppers. Our home is a small mountain cabin that's 3 hours from town. We have no electricity or phone and we cook about half the time on a wood stove.

- 1-1/2 pounds boneless sirloin steak, cut into 1/4-inch strips
- 1 *each* medium green and sweet red peppers, julienned
- 1 large onion, thinly sliced
- 3 tablespoons vegetable oil
- 2 tablespoons butter
- 5 to 6 French *or* Italian sandwich rolls, split
- 2 cans (4 ounces *each*) whole green chilies, drained and halved
- 5 to 6 slices Swiss cheese

In a large skillet, cook steak, peppers and onion in oil until meat reaches desired doneness and vegetables are soft.

Spread butter on rolls; top with meat mixture, chilies and cheese. Wrap in heavy-duty foil.

Bake at 350° for 10-12 minutes or until heated through and cheese is melted. **Yield:** 5-6 servings.

chicken-stuffed green peppers

Shelley Armstrong, Buffalo Center, Iowa

Both for a family meal and for entertaining, this is a dish I serve frequently. It's very appealing to the eye, and people like the wild rice and the peppers. What I learned about cooking came from an expert—my husband! He's the real chef in the family.

- 4 large green peppers
- 1/3 cup chopped onion
- 1 garlic clove, minced
- 2 tablespoons butter
- 3 cups diced cooked chicken
- 2 cups chicken broth
- 1 package (6 ounces) long grain brown and wild rice blend
- 1/3 cup sliced celery
- 1/4 cup finely chopped carrot
- 1/4 teaspoon dried basil
- 1/4 teaspoon dried thyme
- 1 can (14-1/2 ounces) diced tomatoes, undrained
- 1 cup chopped fresh mushrooms
- 1/2 cup chopped zucchini
- 1/4 cup grated Parmesan cheese

Cut tops off peppers; remove seeds. In a large kettle, cook peppers in boiling water for 3 minutes. Drain and rinse in cold water. Place upside down on paper towels; set aside.

In a large saucepan, saute onion and garlic in butter until tender. Add chicken, broth, rice with contents of seasoning packet, celery, carrot, basil and thyme; bring to a boil. Reduce heat; cover and simmer for 25 minutes or until the rice is almost tender.

Remove from the heat; stir in tomatoes, mushrooms and zucchini. Spoon rice mixture into the peppers; place in a greased 2-qt. baking dish. Spoon the remaining rice mixture around peppers.

Cover and bake at 350° for 25-30 minutes or until the peppers are tender and filling is heated through. Uncover and sprinkle with Parmesan cheese; bake 5 minutes longer. **Yield:** 4 servings.

---

prize winning tips

* To easily roast 10-12 peppers at a time, rub them with vegetable oil and place them over the highest heat on an outdoor grill until the skins blacken completely. Remove from the grill and place in a bowl, then cover with plastic wrap. Let stand for 15-20 minutes. Peel and seed cooled peppers.

Bronwyn Morgan, Blytheville, Arkansas

* Since many recipes call for chopped peppers, I freeze them that way. After chopping peppers, I place them in a metal mesh strainer, blanch for 1 minute in a pot of boiling water, drain, then put them in ice cube trays (each cube contains about 2 tablespoons). Once they're frozen, I put the cubes in freezer bags. Then I can easily pick the color and amount I need for my recipes.

Ann McKellips, Lynchburg, Virginia

pork 'n' pepper tacos

Jacquie Baldwin, Raleigh, North Carolina
As a Texas native, I prefer spicy food. But since my husband and I both work nights (I'm a nurse), I also need quick dishes like this. I've taken it to parties at work, too, and most tasters enjoy it—with an icy cold soda in most cases!

- 1 medium onion, chopped
- 2 medium jalapeno peppers, diced
- 3 tablespoons vegetable oil
- 2 pounds boneless pork, cut into bite-size pieces
- 1 tablespoon chili powder
- 1/2 teaspoon salt
- 1/4 teaspoon pepper
- 8 taco shells, warmed

Shredded lettuce and cheddar cheese, chopped tomato and salsa

In a large skillet, saute the onion and jalapenos in oil for 3-4 minutes or until tender. Add the pork; cook and stir over medium heat until meat is no longer pink, about 8 minutes.

Stir in chili powder, salt and pepper. Reduce heat; cover and simmer for 25-30 minutes or until the meat is tender, stirring occasionally.

Serve in taco shells with lettuce, cheese, tomato and salsa. **Yield:** 8 tacos.

Editor's Note: When cutting or seeding hot peppers, use rubber or plastic gloves to protect your hands. Avoid touching your face.

spicy sausage spaghetti

Nancy Rollag, Kewaskum, Wisconsin
Served with crusty bread and a green salad, this is a good summer supper. It has lots of heat (my husband likes that) and it's colorful on the plate besides.

- 1 pound bulk Italian sausage
- 3 tablespoons olive oil, *divided*
- 3 dried whole red chilies
- 1 can (28 ounces) plum tomatoes, drained and chopped
- 3 garlic cloves, minced
- 2 tablespoons minced fresh oregano *or* 2 teaspoons dried oregano
- 1/2 teaspoon salt
- 1/4 teaspoon pepper
- 3 large sweet red peppers, thinly sliced
- 4 cups hot cooked spaghetti
- 1/2 cup minced fresh parsley
- 1/2 cup shredded Parmesan cheese

In a skillet, cook sausage over medium heat, until no longer pink; drain. Set the sausage aside and keep warm.

In a skillet, heat 2 tablespoons of oil; saute red chilies for 5-8 minutes or until they turn black. Discard chilies; cool oil slightly. Add the tomatoes, garlic, oregano, salt and pepper; simmer for 15 minutes. Stir in red peppers and sausage; heat through.

Toss spaghetti with remaining oil. Add tomato sauce; toss to coat. Sprinkle with parsley and Parmesan cheese. **Yield:** 4 servings.

colorful apricot chutney

Lucile Cline, Wichita, Kansas

You can use this chutney as an appetizer on cracker bread or mix it with cream cheese into a spread. When the local Extension office held a "Pepper Day," I entered it in the recipe contest. It won first prize.

     3 large sweet red peppers, diced
    12 ounces dried apricots, diced
     1 cup raisins
     1 cup sugar
     1 large onion, finely chopped
   3/4 cup red wine vinegar
     5 garlic cloves, minced
 1-1/2 teaspoons salt
 1-1/2 teaspoons crushed red pepper flakes
   1/4 teaspoon ground ginger
   1/4 teaspoon ground cumin
   1/4 teaspoon ground mustard

In a large heavy saucepan, combine all ingredients; bring to a boil. Reduce heat; simmer, uncovered, for 25-30 minutes or until thickened, stirring occasionally. Cover and refrigerate.

Serve as an accompaniment to pork or chicken. Chutney may be stored in the refrigerator for up to 1 month. **Yield:** 4 cups.

jalapeno cranberry jelly

Karen Bunzow, Saginaw, Michigan

The thing that inspires most of my recipes is getting an item that I don't know what to do with and trying to cobble together something to use it up. With this one, my brother giving me several jalapeno peppers was the beginning. Fortunately for me, my husband is a willing guinea pig for my experiments!

     3 cups cranberry juice
     1 cup chopped seeded jalapeno peppers
     1 cup white vinegar
     7 cups sugar
     2 pouches (3 ounces *each*) liquid fruit pectin
    10 drops red food coloring, optional

Place cranberry juice and peppers in a blender; cover and process until peppers are fully chopped. Strain through a double thickness of cheesecloth. Pour the strained juice into a large kettle; add vinegar. Stir in sugar. Bring to a full rolling boil, stirring constantly.

Stir in pectin; return to a full rolling boil. Boil for 1 minute, stirring constantly. Remove from the heat; skim foam.

Add food coloring if desired. Pour into hot sterilized jars, leaving 1/4-in. headspace. Adjust caps.

Process for 5 minutes in a boiling-water bath. Serve the jelly with cream cheese on crackers or use as a condiment with meat or poultry. **Yield:** 8 half-pints.

Editor's Note: When cutting or seeding hot peppers, use rubber or plastic gloves to protect your hands. Avoid touching your face.

ROOTING FOR ROOT VEGETABLES

#1

HUNGARIAN
GOULASH SOUP

hungarian goulash soup
GRAND PRIZE WINNER

Eat your vegetables! is an enjoyable order—for the cook as well—with the mouth-watering root vegetable dishes featured in our Rooting for Root Vegetables recipe contest. With an appetizing array of soups, salads, side dishes and hearty main dishes, you now have new recipes for all occasions throughout the year. But, in late summer and fall, these delicious dishes are especially welcome. They make great use of the bounty from your garden (and delicious vegetables available at their freshest at farm stands and the grocery store). Any of the recipes here and on the following pages will help you get to the root of good eating!

"...it's a rich, flavorful meal in a bowl!"

Enjoy Hungarian Goulash Soup, the Grand Prize Winner, shared by Julie Polakowski of West Allis, Wisconsin. She went to her roots for this best-of-the-best recipe. "Brimming with beef, potatoes, rutabagas, carrots and onions, it's a rich, flavorful meal in a bowl!" says Julie.

"It may not be glamorous, but it's certainly hearty. This soup is similar to one my mother made years ago. We loved the flavor, and Dad appreciated that it used an inexpensive cut of meat and homegrown vegetables.

"For convenience, make it up a day ahead and let the flavors mingle. Even if you're only cooking for one, make a big batch since this soup freezes so well."

1-1/4 **pounds beef stew meat, cut into 1-inch cubes**
   2 **tablespoons olive oil,** *divided*
   4 **medium onions, chopped**
   6 **garlic cloves, minced**
   2 **teaspoons paprika**
1/2 **teaspoon caraway seed, crushed**
1/2 **teaspoon pepper**
1/4 **teaspoon cayenne pepper**
   1 **teaspoon salt, optional**
   2 **cans (14-1/2 ounces** *each***) beef broth**
   2 **cups cubed peeled potatoes**
   2 **cups sliced carrots**
   2 **cups cubed peeled rutabagas**
   2 **cans (28 ounces** *each***) diced tomatoes, undrained**
   1 **large sweet red pepper, chopped**
Sour cream, optional

In a Dutch oven over medium heat, brown beef in 1 tablespoon oil. Remove beef; drain drippings. Heat remaining oil in the same pan; saute onions and garlic for 8-10 minutes over medium heat or until lightly browned.

Add paprika, caraway, pepper, cayenne and salt if desired; cook and stir 1 minute. Return beef to pan. Add broth, potatoes, carrots and rutabagas; bring to a boil. Reduce heat; cover and simmer for 1-1/2 hours or until vegetables are tender and meat is almost tender.

Add tomatoes and red pepper; return to a boil. Reduce heat; cover and simmer 30-40 minutes or until meat and vegetables are tender. Serve with sour cream if desired. **Yield:** 15 servings.

upper peninsula pasties

Carole Lynn Derifield, Valdez, Alaska
I grew up in Michigan's Upper Peninsula, where many people are of English ancestry. Pasties—traditional meat pies often eaten by hand—are popular.

- 2 cups shortening
- 2 cups boiling water
- 5-1/2 to 6 cups all-purpose flour
- 2 teaspoons salt

FILLING:
- 12 large red potatoes (about 6 pounds), peeled
- 4 medium rutabagas (about 3 pounds), peeled
- 2 medium onions, chopped
- 2 pounds ground beef
- 1 pound ground pork
- 1 tablespoon salt
- 2 teaspoons pepper
- 2 teaspoons garlic powder
- 1/4 cup butter

Half-and-half cream, optional

In a large bowl, stir shortening and water until shortening is melted. Gradually stir in flour and salt until a very soft dough is formed; cover and refrigerate for 1-1/2 hours.

Quarter and thinly slice potatoes and rutabagas; place in a large bowl with onions, beef, pork and seasonings. Divide dough into 12 equal portions. On a floured surface, roll out one portion at a time into a 10-in. circle. Mound about 2 cups filling on half of each circle; dot with 1 teaspoon butter. Moisten edges with water; fold dough over filling and press edges with a fork to seal.

Place on ungreased baking sheets. Cut several slits in top of pasties. Brush with cream if desired. Bake at 350° for 1 hour or until golden brown. Cool on wire racks. Serve hot or cold. Store in the refrigerator. **Yield:** 12 servings.

italian potato salad

Ardis Kohnen, Rudolph, Wisconsin
With six grown daughters who visit us frequently, I have plenty of chances to serve this family favorite—whether we are making steaks, pork chops, burgers or bratwurst. I've even served it with more formal ham dinners. The recipe comes from my mom, who was a cook at local restaurants and resorts. Here on the tree farm my husband and I run, we also grow potatoes. They are a staple that are always as close as my root cellar when I prepare this dish.

- 3 pounds potatoes
- 1/3 cup Italian salad dressing
- 4 hard-cooked eggs, chopped
- 3/4 cup chopped celery
- 1/3 cup chopped onion
- 1/4 cup chopped cucumber
- 1/4 cup chopped green pepper
- 1/2 cup mayonnaise
- 1/4 cup sour cream
- 1 teaspoon prepared horseradish

Chopped fresh tomatoes

Place potatoes in a saucepan; cover with water. Bring to a boil. Reduce heat; cover and cook for 15-20 minutes or until tender. Drain and cool.

Peel and cube potatoes; place in a large bowl. Add dressing and toss to coat. Cover and chill for 2 hours. Add eggs, celery, onion, cucumber and green pepper; mix well.

In a small bowl, combine mayonnaise, sour cream and horseradish; mix well. Pour over potato mixture and toss to coat. Chill for at least 1 hour. Top with tomatoes. **Yield:** 8-10 servings.

root vegetable medley

Marilyn Smudzinski, Peru, Illinois

Equally good with pork or beef roast—or with a Thanksgiving turkey—this dish is one my husband requests at least once a month. It's a tasty alternative to plain potatoes.

- 6 small red potatoes, quartered
- 1 medium rutabaga, peeled and cut into 1-inch cubes
- 1/2 teaspoon salt
- 3 medium carrots, cut into 1/2-inch slices
- 1 medium turnip, peeled and cut into 1-inch cubes
- 1 to 2 medium parsnips, peeled and cut into 1/2-inch slices
- 1 medium onion, cut into eighths

GLAZE:
- 1 tablespoon butter
- 3 tablespoons brown sugar
- 1 teaspoon cornstarch
- 1/4 cup water
- 3 tablespoons lemon juice
- 1/2 teaspoon dill weed
- 1/8 teaspoon pepper
- 1/2 teaspoon salt

Place potatoes and rutabaga in a large saucepan; cover with water. Add salt. Bring to a boil. Reduce heat; cover and cook for 8 minutes.

Add remaining vegetables; return to a boil. Reduce heat; cover and simmer for 10 minutes or until vegetables are tender; drain.

For glaze, melt butter in a saucepan; stir in brown sugar and cornstarch until smooth. Stir in water, lemon juice, dill, pepper and salt. Bring to a boil; cook and stir for 2 minutes or until thickened.

Pour over vegetables and toss to coat. **Yield:** 8 servings.

zippy radish salad

Carol Stevens, Basye, Virginia

I admit to it—the first time I prepared this salad for my husband, he was skeptical! He loved it, though. Served with a rich entree or hot barbecue, it makes a light and refreshing side dish. Growing up during World War II when food and money were scarce, I learned from my mother how to make a little go a long way. Now that we've retired and moved from the city, we're living in a mountain home we built on the side of the Shenandoah Valley.

- 2 cups thinly sliced radishes
- 1/2 cup cubed Swiss cheese
- 2 green onions, thinly sliced
- 1 garlic clove, minced
- 1 tablespoon tarragon vinegar
- 1/2 teaspoon Dijon mustard
- 1/4 teaspoon salt
- 1/8 teaspoon pepper
- 3 tablespoons olive oil

Leaf lettuce

In a bowl, combine radishes, cheese and onions. In a small bowl, combine garlic, vinegar, mustard, salt and pepper; whisk in oil until smooth.

Pour over radish mixture; toss to coat. Chill for 2 hours. Serve on a bed of lettuce. **Yield:** 4 servings.

fried onion rings

Marsha Moore, Poplar Bluff, Missouri

Try these as an accompaniment to hamburgers, fried fish or steaks on the grill. The recipe is from my mom, and it's one of her most popular. This side dish has wonderful homemade flavor.

  2 large sweet onions
  1 egg, lightly beaten
2/3 cup water
  1 tablespoon vegetable oil
  1 teaspoon lemon juice
  1 cup all-purpose flour
1-1/2 teaspoons baking powder
  1 to 1-1/4 teaspoons salt
1/8 to 1/4 teaspoon cayenne pepper
Vegetable oil for deep-fat frying

Cut onions into 1/2-in. slices; separate into rings. Place in a bowl; cover with ice water and soak for 30 minutes.

Meanwhile, combine egg, water, oil and lemon juice in a bowl. Combine flour, baking powder, salt and cayenne; stir into egg mixture until smooth.

Drain onion rings; dip into batter. In an electric skillet or deep-fat fryer, heat 1 in. of oil to 375°. Fry onion rings, a few at a time, for 1 to 1-1/2 minutes per side or until golden brown. Drain on paper towels. **Yield:** 4-6 servings.

Editor's Note: Onion rings may be kept warm in a 300° oven while frying remainder of batch.

✳Here's a simple but tasty way to make mashed potatoes. Cook equal amounts of peeled and diced potatoes and parsnips in boiling salted water until tender. Mash as usual with milk and butter. Delicious!

Harriet Bennett, Hodgkins, Illinois

---

creamy mushroom-potato bake

Kathy Smith, Granger, Indiana

The day I first made this, we'd invited a neighbor—a bachelor farmer—over, and I wanted to fix something hearty. It was a hit instantly. These days, our three sons enjoy it as a change from regular mashed potatoes. We've found that it's best served with beef…either with or without gravy.

2-1/2 to 3 pounds white potatoes, peeled and cubed
  1 teaspoon salt, *divided*
  1 medium onion, finely chopped
1/2 pound fresh mushrooms, chopped
  3 tablespoons butter, *divided*
1/2 cup sour cream
1/4 teaspoon pepper
1/4 cup grated Parmesan cheese

Place potatoes in a large saucepan; cover with water. Add 1/2 teaspoon salt. Bring to a boil. Reduce heat; cover and cook for 15-20 minutes or until tender. Drain and mash (do not add butter or milk).

In a skillet, saute onion and mushrooms in 2 tablespoons butter for 3-4 minutes or until just tender. Stir into potatoes along with sour cream, pepper and remaining salt.

Spoon into a greased 2-qt. baking dish. Sprinkle with cheese; dot with remaining butter.

Bake, uncovered, at 400° for 20-25 minutes or until heated through and golden brown. **Yield:** 10 servings.

Editor's Note: Potatoes can be prepared the day before and refrigerated overnight. Remove from refrigerator 30 minutes before baking.

vegetable meatball stew

Elaine Grose, Elmira, New York

People who try this comment on how much they love the sweet potatoes. But they can never quite seem to pinpoint my secret ingredient—the parsnips!

- 4 cups water
- 2 medium potatoes, cut into 1-inch cubes
- 2 medium carrots, cut into 3/4-inch slices
- 1 large onion, cut into eighths
- 2 tablespoons beef bouillon granules
- 1 bay leaf
- 1 teaspoon dried thyme
- 1 teaspoon dried basil
- 1/2 teaspoon salt
- 1/2 teaspoon pepper
- 1/2 cup seasoned dry bread crumbs
- 1 egg, beaten
- 1 teaspoon Worcestershire sauce
- 1 pound ground beef
- 2 medium sweet potatoes, peeled and cut into 1-inch cubes
- 2 medium parsnips, peeled and cut into 3/4-inch slices
- 1 cup frozen peas
- 1/3 cup all-purpose flour
- 1/2 cup cold water
- 1/4 teaspoon browning sauce, optional

In a large Dutch oven or soup kettle, bring water to a boil. Add the potatoes, carrots, onion and seasonings;

return to a boil. Reduce heat; cover and simmer for 10 minutes.

Meanwhile, combine bread crumbs, egg and Worcestershire sauce. Crumble beef over mixture and mix well. Shape into 1-in. balls; add to Dutch oven along with the sweet potatoes and parsnips. Bring to a boil.

Reduce heat; cover and simmer for 15 minutes or until vegetables are tender.

Discard bay leaf. Stir in peas. Combine flour and cold water until smooth; stir into stew along with browning sauce if desired. Bring to a boil; cook and stir for 2 minutes or until thickened. **Yield:** 6 servings.

---

prize winning tips

✳✳✳✳✳

✳To prepare fried parsnips, trim roots and wash; do not peel. Slice thinly and fry in oil until tender and well browned. There's no need to season—the sweetness of the parsnips is flavor enough. Serve immediately.

Donna Christensen, Superior, Nebraska

✳Do you like scalloped potatoes but not the time it takes to make them? Try this: Combine frozen French fries with a homemade cheese sauce and bake until bubbly. You save all the time of peeling and slicing the potatoes.

Monna Buckley, McKinney, Texas

✳My husband has to have salt-free foods, so I substitute lemon-pepper seasoning for table salt in many of my potato dishes with delicious results.

Joyce Gelle, Rice, Minnesota

runners-up

parmesan potato soup

Tami Walters, Kingsport, Tennessee
Even my husband, who's not much of a soup eater, likes this. Our two boys do, too. With homemade bread and a salad, it's a satisfying meal.

      4 **medium baking potatoes (about 2 pounds)**
    3/4 **cup chopped onion**
    1/2 **cup butter**
    1/2 **cup all-purpose flour**
    1/2 **teaspoon dried basil**
    1/2 **teaspoon seasoned salt**
    1/4 **teaspoon celery salt**
    1/4 **teaspoon garlic powder**
    1/4 **teaspoon onion salt**
    1/4 **teaspoon pepper**
    1/4 **teaspoon rubbed sage**
    1/4 **teaspoon dried thyme**
  4-1/2 **cups chicken broth**
      6 **cups milk**
    3/4 **to 1 cup grated Parmesan cheese**
     10 **bacon strips, cooked and crumbled**

Pierce potatoes with a fork; bake at 375° for 40-60 minutes until tender. Cool, peel and cube; set aside.

In a large Dutch oven or soup kettle, saute onion in butter until tender. Stir in flour and seasonings until blended. Gradually add broth, stirring constantly. Bring to a boil; cook and stir for 2 minutes or until thickened. Add potatoes; return to a boil. Reduce heat; cover and simmer for 10 minutes.

Add milk and cheese; heat through. Stir in bacon.
Yield: 10-12 servings.

sunday boiled dinner

Arlene Oliver, Bothell, Washington
Generally, I start this dinner early in the morning or right before church. It originated with my Pennsylvania Dutch mother and grandmother. When I first served it to my husband, he enjoyed the hearty root vegetables so much that he asked me to make the dish more frequently, even during the summertime.

    1 **smoked boneless ham *or* pork shoulder**
       (about 2 pounds)
    1 **medium onion, quartered**
    2 **pounds carrots, halved**
    2 **pounds red potatoes, quartered**
    2 **pounds rutabagas, peeled and cut**
       into 1-1/2-inch cubes
    1 **teaspoon salt**
  1/2 **teaspoon pepper**
    1 **medium cabbage, halved**
Prepared horseradish, optional

In a large Dutch oven or soup kettle, place ham, onion, carrots, potatoes, rutabagas, salt and pepper. Add water just to cover; bring to a boil.

Place cabbage on top of vegetables. Reduce heat; cover and simmer for 1 hour or until the vegetables are tender.

Drain. Cut cabbage into wedges; remove core. Serve meat and vegetables with horseradish if desired. **Yield:** 8 servings.

runners-up

twice-baked sweet potatoes

Miriam Christophel, Battle Creek, Michigan
When I prepare these sweet potatoes, I like to serve them with ham. Those two different tastes always team well.

      6 large sweet potatoes (3-1/2 to 4 pounds)
  1/4 cup orange juice
      6 tablespoons cold butter, *divided*
  1/4 cup all-purpose flour
  1/4 cup packed brown sugar
  1/4 teaspoon ground cinnamon
  1/4 teaspoon ground ginger
  1/8 teaspoon ground mace
  1/4 cup chopped pecans

Pierce potatoes with a fork. Bake at 375° for 40-60 minutes or until tender. Let potatoes stand until cool enough to handle.

Cut them in half lengthwise; carefully scoop out pulp, leaving a 1/4-in. shell. Place pulp in a large bowl. Add orange juice. Melt 3 tablespoons butter; add to pulp and beat until smooth.

Stuff the potato shells; place in an ungreased 15-in. x 10-in. x 1-in. baking pan.

In a small bowl, combine flour, brown sugar, cinnamon, ginger and mace. Cut in remaining butter until crumbly. Stir in nuts. Sprinkle over potatoes. Bake at 350° for 20-25 minutes or until golden and heated through. **Yield:** 12 servings.

spiced baked beets

Margery Richmond, Lacombe, Alberta
Especially during fall and winter, this recipe is a favorite. With its red color, it looks great served at Christmastime. It's nice for taking to potlucks as well.

      4 cups shredded peeled beets (about 4 to 5 medium)
      1 medium onion, shredded
      1 medium potato, shredded
      3 tablespoons brown sugar
      3 tablespoons vegetable oil
      2 tablespoons water
      1 tablespoon cider vinegar
  1/2 teaspoon salt
  1/4 teaspoon pepper
  1/4 teaspoon celery seed
  1/8 to 1/4 teaspoon ground cloves

In a large bowl, combine the beets, onion and potato; set aside.

In a small bowl, combine brown sugar, oil, water, vinegar and seasonings. Pour over vegetables; toss to coat. Pour into a greased 1-1/2-qt. baking dish.

Cover and bake at 350° for 45 minutes, stirring occasionally. Uncover and bake 15-25 minutes longer or until vegetables are tender. **Yield:** 8-10 servings.

runners-up

Prize Winning Recipes 163

SQUASH A to Z

#1

ZUCCHINI
CUPCAKES

zucchini cupcakes
GRAND PRIZE WINNER

Squash is an easy-to-grow crop that typically leads to an overabundance (and great prices at the grocery and farm stand in fall). Before you resort to leaving bagfuls of your garden squash bounty on neighbors' doorsteps, check out these award-winning recipes from our A to Z Squash contest.

> "These cupcakes are such a scrumptious dessert, you actually forget you're eating your vegetables, too!"

The top picks from nearly 3,000 recipes submitted include both summer and winter varieties in delectable soups, side dishes, desserts and more. You'll be so proud to prepare and serve this tempting lineup of recipes that you may want to put in more squash plants next year!

The recipe for Zucchini Cupcakes, shared by Virginia Breitmeyer of Craftsbury, Vermont, was selected the Grand Prize Winner. "I asked my grandmother for this recipe after trying these fluffy, irresistible spice cupcakes at her house," Virginia says. "I love their creamy caramel frosting. These cupcakes are such a scrumptious dessert, you actually forget you're eating your vegetables, too!"

3 eggs
1-1/3 cups sugar
1/2 cup vegetable oil
1/2 cup orange juice
1 teaspoon almond extract
2-1/2 cups all-purpose flour
2 teaspoons ground cinnamon
2 teaspoons baking powder
1 teaspoon baking soda
1 teaspoon salt
1/2 teaspoon ground cloves
1-1/2 cups shredded zucchini
CARAMEL FROSTING:
1 cup packed brown sugar
1/2 cup butter
1/4 cup milk
1 teaspoon vanilla extract
1-1/2 to 2 cups confectioners' sugar

In a mixing bowl, beat eggs, sugar, oil, orange juice and extract. Combine dry ingredients; add to the egg mixture and mix well. Add zucchini and mix well.

Fill greased or paper-lined muffin cups two-thirds full. Bake at 350° for 20-25 minutes or until toothpick comes out clean. Cool for 10 minutes before removing from pans to wire racks.

For frosting, combine brown sugar, butter and milk in a saucepan. Bring to a boil over medium heat; cook and stir for 2 minutes or until thickened. Remove from the heat; stir in vanilla. Cool to lukewarm.

Gradually beat in confectioners' sugar until frosting reaches spreading consistency. Frost cupcakes. **Yield:** 1-1/2 to 2 dozen.

zucchini garden chowder

Nanette Jordan, Canton, Michigan

Years ago, when my husband and I put in our first garden, a neighbor suggested zucchini since it's easy to grow. Our kids were reluctant to try new things, so I used our squash in this cheesy chowder—it met with solid approval from all of us.

- 2 medium zucchini, chopped
- 1 medium onion, chopped
- 2 tablespoons minced fresh parsley
- 1 teaspoon dried basil
- 1/3 cup butter
- 1/3 cup all-purpose flour
- 1 teaspoon salt
- 1/4 teaspoon pepper
- 3 cups water
- 3 chicken bouillon cubes
- 1 teaspoon lemon juice
- 1 can (14-1/2 ounces) diced tomatoes, undrained
- 1 can (12 ounces) evaporated milk
- 1 package (10 ounces) frozen corn
- 1/4 cup grated Parmesan cheese
- 2 cups (8 ounces) shredded cheddar cheese

Pinch sugar, optional

Additional chopped parsley, optional

In a Dutch oven or soup kettle, saute the zucchini, onion, parsley and basil in butter until vegetables are tender. Stir in flour, salt and pepper. Gradually stir in water. Add the bouillon and lemon juice; mix well. Bring to a boil; cook and stir for 2 minutes or until thickened.

Add tomatoes, milk and corn; bring to a boil. Reduce heat; cover and simmer for 5 minutes or until corn is tender.

Just before serving, add cheeses; stir until melted. Add sugar and garnish with parsley if desired. **Yield:** 8-10 servings (about 2-1/2 quarts).

lemony acorn slices

Nell Fletcher, Sedalia, Colorado

I discovered this recipe a long time ago and have used it often. This is a nice change of pace from simple baked acorn squash. With the skin left on the slices and lemon sauce drizzled over them, this side dish looks as good as it tastes.

- 2 large acorn squash (about 2-1/4 pounds *each*)
- 1 cup plus 2 tablespoons water, *divided*
- 1/2 cup sugar
- 2 tablespoons lemon juice
- 1 tablespoon butter
- 1/4 teaspoon salt
- 1/8 teaspoon pepper

Lemon wedges and fresh mint, optional

Wash squash. Cut in half lengthwise; remove and discard the seeds and membrane. Cut each half crosswise into 1/2-in. slices; discard ends. Place slices in a large skillet. Add 1 cup water; bring to a boil. Reduce heat; cover and simmer for 20 minutes or until tender.

Meanwhile, in a heavy saucepan, combine sugar and remaining water. Cook over medium heat until sugar melts and syrup is golden, stirring occasionally. Remove from the heat; carefully add lemon juice, butter, salt and pepper. Cook and stir over low heat until butter melts.

Place the squash on a serving plate; top with the syrup. Garnish with lemon wedges and mint if desired. **Yield:** 6 servings.

zesty gazpacho salad

Teresa Fischer, Munster, Indiana
This refreshing salad is excellent for a summer cookout. Since you mix it ahead, the flavors have time to blend and there's no last-minute fussing. My friends ask me to bring it every time we get together for a meal.

- 2 medium zucchini, chopped
- 2 medium tomatoes, chopped
- 1 small ripe avocado, chopped
- 1 cup fresh *or* frozen corn, thawed
- 1/2 cup thinly sliced green onions
- 1/2 cup picante sauce
- 2 tablespoons minced fresh parsley
- 2 tablespoons lemon juice
- 1 tablespoon vegetable oil

> *Most winter squash can be substituted for pumpkin in most pie, bread or cookie recipes. Hubbard and banana squash work especially well.
>
> Mary Carroll, Fort Wayne, Indiana
>
> *Steaming is a great way to cook winter or summer squash—it preserves both nutrients and pretty color.
>
> Brenda Thompson, Chicora, Pennsylvania

- 3/4 teaspoon garlic salt
- 1/4 teaspoon ground cumin

In a bowl, combine the first five ingredients. In a small bowl, combine remaining ingredients; mix well.

Pour over zucchini mixture; toss to coat. Cover and refrigerate for at least 4 hours. **Yield:** 8-10 servings.

butternut sausage puff

Betty Humiston, Greenwich, New York
Any brunch is extra-special when this hearty souffle is included. The thyme and sausage are perfect complements to the delicately sweet butternut squash.

- 2 cups hot mashed butternut squash
- 3 eggs, *separated*
- 1/4 cup all-purpose flour
- 1/4 cup minced fresh parsley
- 2 tablespoons butter
- 2 teaspoons finely chopped onion
- 2 teaspoons lemon juice
- 1/2 teaspoon dried thyme
- 1/4 teaspoon salt
- 1/2 pound bulk pork sausage, cooked and drained

Fresh thyme, optional

In a bowl, combine squash, egg yolks, flour, parsley, butter, onion, lemon juice, thyme and salt; mix until well blended. Stir in the sausage. Cool for 10 minutes.

In a small mixing bowl, beat egg whites until stiff peaks form; fold into squash mixture. Pour into a greased and floured 2-qt. baking dish.

Bake, uncovered, at 375° for 45-50 minutes or until a knife inserted near the center comes out clean. Garnish with thyme if desired. **Yield:** 4-6 servings.

buttercup squash coffee cake

Mary Jones, Cumberland, Maine

My father grows a large squash patch, so each fall, I get an ample amount of his harvest. I make this treat to share with my co-workers. They rave about the moist cake, the crunchy streusel and the applesauce between the layers.

STREUSEL:
1/4 cup packed brown sugar
1/4 cup sugar
1/4 cup all-purpose flour
1/4 cup quick-cooking oats
1/4 cup chopped nuts
1-1/2 teaspoons ground cinnamon
   3 tablespoons cold butter

CAKE:
1/2 cup butter-flavored shortening
   1 cup sugar
   2 eggs
   1 cup mashed cooked buttercup squash
   1 teaspoon vanilla extract
   2 cups all-purpose flour
   2 teaspoons baking powder
1-1/2 teaspoons ground cinnamon
1/2 teaspoon baking soda
1/2 teaspoon salt
1/4 teaspoon ground ginger
1/4 teaspoon ground nutmeg
Pinch ground cloves
1/2 cup unsweetened applesauce

GLAZE:
1/2 cup confectioners' sugar
1/4 teaspoon vanilla extract
1-1/2 teaspoons hot water

Combine the first six ingredients. Cut in butter until crumbly; set aside. In a mixing bowl, cream shortening and sugar. Beat in eggs, one at a time. Beat in squash and vanilla. Combine dry ingredients; gradually add to creamed mixture. Spoon half into a greased 9-in. spring-form pan.

Spread applesauce over batter. Sprinkle with half of the streusel. Spoon remaining batter evenly over streusel. Top with remaining streusel.

Bake at 350° for 50-55 minutes or until a toothpick inserted near the center comes out clean. Cool for 10 minutes before removing sides of pan.

Combine glaze ingredients; drizzle over coffee cake. **Yield:** 10-12 servings.

toasted zucchini snacks

Jane Bone, Cape Coral, Florida

I added green pepper to this recipe I got years ago from a friend. I prepare this rich snack for company when zucchini is plentiful. Everyone seems to enjoy it—even those who say they don't care for zucchini.

   2 cups shredded zucchini
   1 teaspoon salt
1/2 cup mayonnaise
1/2 cup plain yogurt
1/4 cup grated Parmesan cheese
1/4 cup finely chopped green pepper
   4 green onions, thinly sliced
   1 garlic clove, minced
   1 teaspoon Worcestershire sauce
1/4 teaspoon hot pepper sauce
  36 slices snack rye bread

In a bowl, toss the zucchini and salt; let stand for 1 hour. Rinse and drain, pressing out excess liquid.

Add the next eight ingredients; stir until combined. Spread a rounded teaspoonful on each slice of bread; place on a baking sheet.

Bake at 375° for 10-12 minutes or until bubbly. Serve immediately. **Yield:** 3 dozen.

calico squash casserole

Lucille Terry, Frankfort, Kentucky
I have a thriving country garden and try a lot of recipes using my squash. It's a pleasure to present this beautiful casserole as part of a holiday menu or anytime.

- 2 cups sliced yellow summer squash (1/4 inch thick)
- 1 cup sliced zucchini (1/4 inch thick)
- 1 medium onion, chopped
- 1/4 cup sliced green onions
- 1 cup water
- 1 teaspoon salt, *divided*
- 2 cups crushed butter-flavored crackers
- 1/2 cup butter, melted
- 1 can (10-3/4 ounces) condensed cream of chicken soup, undiluted
- 1 can (8 ounces) sliced water chestnuts, drained
- 1 large carrot, shredded
- 1/2 cup mayonnaise
- 1 jar (2 ounces) diced pimientos, drained
- 1 teaspoon rubbed sage
- 1/2 teaspoon white pepper
- 1 cup (4 ounces) shredded sharp cheddar cheese

In a saucepan, combine the first five ingredients; add 1/2 teaspoon salt. Cover and cook until squash is tender, about 6 minutes. Drain well; set aside.

Combine crumbs and butter; spoon half into a greased shallow 1-1/2-qt. baking dish. Combine soup, water chestnuts, carrot, mayonnaise, pimientos, sage, pepper and remaining salt; fold into squash mixture. Spoon over crumbs.

Sprinkle with cheese and the remaining crumb mixture. Bake, uncovered, at 350° for 30 minutes or until lightly browned. **Yield:** 8 servings.

---

prize winning tips

✳ When preparing my favorite Italian or Mexican recipes, I often substitute shredded zucchini for half of the ground beef or sausage. It reduces the fat and makes the recipe more economical, too.

Trudy Overlin, Rigby, Idaho

✳ Here's an easy and tasty way to make acorn squash on the grill. Generously sprinkle each half with brown sugar, cinnamon, nutmeg and pepper. Dot each with 2 tablespoons butter and wrap tightly in foil. Cook, covered over medium heat for 25-30 minutes or until tender.

Theresa Hoffmann, Hatley, Wisconsin

✳ Try placing crumpled aluminum foil around the sides of filled squash shells to keep them from tipping during baking. Lining the pans with foil before baking squash can also cut down on the cleanup time.

Jan Roberts, Grain Valley, Missouri

two-season squash medley

Mary Beth LaFlamme, Eagle Bridge, New York
Both winter and summer squash star in this fun, colorful vegetable stir-fry. I've cooked in several restaurants and for many guests in my home, and this dish has been well-received for years.

- 2 tablespoons butter
- 2 tablespoons olive oil
- 1 medium yellow summer squash, sliced
- 1 medium zucchini, sliced
- 3/4 pound butternut squash, peeled, seeded and julienned
- 1 medium onion, sliced
- 1 medium green pepper, julienned
- 1 medium sweet red pepper, julienned
- 3 to 4 garlic cloves, minced
- 1 tablespoon minced fresh thyme *or* 1 teaspoon dried thyme
- 1/4 teaspoon garlic salt
- 1/4 teaspoon pepper

In a large skillet, heat the butter and oil over medium heat. Add vegetables, garlic and thyme. Cook and stir until tender, about 15 minutes. Add garlic salt and pepper. **Yield:** 6-8 servings.

> *It's easy to remove winter squash seeds with an ice cream scoop.*
> Michek Decoteau, Millbury, Massachusetts

curried beef-stuffed squash

Edna Lee, Greeley, Colorado
My husband and I look forward to this dinner. The savory beef tucked inside tender acorn squash halves is a satisfying combination. Plus, it's light and flavorful.

- 3 medium acorn squash (about 1 pound *each*), halved and seeded
- 1 pound ground beef
- 1/2 cup chopped onion
- 2 garlic cloves, minced
- 1 teaspoon beef bouillon granules
- 1/2 cup hot water
- 1/2 cup cooked rice
- 2 tablespoons chopped fresh parsley
- 1 tablespoon orange juice concentrate
- 1 teaspoon brown sugar
- 1 teaspoon curry powder
- 1/2 teaspoon ground ginger
- 1/4 teaspoon salt

Invert squash in a greased 15-in. x 10-in. x 1-in. baking pan. Bake, uncovered, at 350° for 35-45 minutes or until almost tender.

Meanwhile, in a skillet, cook beef, onion and garlic over medium heat until meat is no longer pink and onion is tender; drain.

Dissolve bouillon in water; add to skillet. Stir in remaining ingredients; mix well. Turn squash cut side up in pan and fill with meat mixture.

Fill pan with hot water to a depth of 1/4 in.; cover loosely with foil. Bake at 350° for 20-30 minutes or until heated through. **Yield:** 6 servings.

spaghetti squash boats

Vickey Lorenger, Detroit, Michigan
Several fresh, tasty ingredients go together in this recipe to make a spectacular summer supper. Spaghetti squash has an interesting texture that's lots of fun. Try it—you'll love it!

- 1 medium spaghetti squash (2 to 2-1/2 pounds)
- 1/4 pound ground beef
- 1/2 cup chopped onion
- 1/2 cup chopped green pepper
- 1/2 cup sliced fresh mushrooms
- 1 garlic clove, minced
- 1/2 teaspoon dried basil
- 1/2 teaspoon dried oregano
- 1/4 teaspoon salt
- 1/8 teaspoon pepper
- 1 can (14-1/2 ounces) diced tomatoes, drained
- 1/3 cup shredded part-skim mozzarella cheese

Cut squash in half lengthwise; scoop out seeds. Place squash cut side down in a baking dish. Fill pan with hot water to a depth of 1/2 in. Bake, uncovered, at 375° for 30-40 minutes or until tender.

When cool enough to handle, scoop out squash, separating strands with a fork; set shells and squash aside.

In a skillet, cook beef, onion and green pepper over medium heat until meat is no longer pink and vegetables are tender; drain.

Add mushrooms, garlic, basil, oregano, salt and pepper; cook and stir for 2 minutes. Add tomatoes; cook and stir for 2 minutes. Add squash; mix well.

Cook, uncovered, until liquid has evaporated, about 10 minutes. Fill shells; place in a shallow baking dish.

Bake, uncovered, at 350° for 15 minutes. Sprinkle with cheese; bake 5 minutes longer or until cheese melts. **Yield:** 4-6 side-dish servings or 2 main-dish servings.

butternut bisque

Marion Tipton, Phoenix, Arizona
A delicious dinner is even more memorable when I start with this creamy soup. It has a bit of zip and super squash flavor. I like serving things that disappear like this soup does. I always get empty bowls back.

- 2 medium carrots, sliced
- 2 celery ribs with leaves, chopped
- 2 medium leeks (white portion only), sliced
- 1 jalapeno pepper, seeded and minced
- 1/4 cup butter
- 2 pounds butternut squash, peeled, seeded and cubed (about 6 cups)
- 2 cans (14-1/2 ounces *each*) chicken broth
- 1/2 teaspoon ground ginger
- 1/2 cup half-and-half cream
- 1/2 teaspoon salt
- 1/4 teaspoon white pepper
- 1/2 cup chopped pecans, toasted

In a large saucepan, saute carrots, celery, leeks and jalapeno in butter for 10 minutes. Add the squash, broth and ginger; bring to a boil. Reduce heat; cover and simmer until the squash is tender, about 25 minutes.

Cool until lukewarm. In a blender or food processor, puree squash mixture in small batches until smooth; return to pan.

Add the cream, salt and pepper; mix well. Heat through but do not boil. Garnish with the pecans. **Yield:** 8 servings (2 quarts).

Editor's Note: When cutting or seeding hot peppers, use rubber or plastic gloves to protect your hands. Avoid touching your face.

TEMPTING TOMATOES

#1

SPINACH-TOPPED TOMATOES

spinach-topped tomatoes

I f you're "seeing red," maybe that's a good thing when it comes to juicy, delicious tomatoes. That's what our readers thought who entered the Tempting Tomatoes recipe contest.

Our panel of judges narrowed bushels of entries down to the most promising recipes. Their prize-winning picks here and on

> "The perfect taste of summer, this colorful side dish is sure to please."

the following pages include appetizers, main dishes, side dishes, soups, salads and more that take advantage of the vine-ripened goodness of all sorts of tomatoes.

The Grand Prize Winner is Spinach-Topped Tomatoes, shared by Ila Alderman of Galax, Virginia. "The perfect taste of summer, this colorful side dish is sure to please," Ila says.

"The spinach and tomato combined with Parmesan cheese give it a fabulous, fresh flavor that goes well with any meat."

1 package (10 ounces) frozen chopped spinach
2 chicken bouillon cubes
Salt
3 large tomatoes, halved
1 cup soft bread crumbs
1/2 cup grated Parmesan cheese
1/2 cup chopped onion
1/2 cup butter, melted
1 egg, beaten
1 garlic clove, minced
1/4 teaspoon pepper
1/8 teaspoon cayenne pepper
Shredded Parmesan cheese, optional

In a saucepan, cook spinach according to package directions with bouillon; drain well. Cool slightly; press out excess liquid.

Lightly salt tomato halves; place with cut side down on a paper towel for 15 minutes to absorb excess moisture. Meanwhile, in a small bowl, combine spinach with bread crumbs, Parmesan cheese, onion, butter, egg, garlic, pepper and cayenne. Mix well.

Place tomato halves cut side up in a shallow baking dish. Divide the spinach mixture over tomatoes. Sprinkle with shredded Parmesan cheese if desired. Bake at 350° for about 15 minutes or until heated through. **Yield:** 6 servings.

cathy's tomato-bean salad

Cathy Meizel, Flanders, New York

As far back as I can recall, my mother and grandmother made this salad…with a few of the ingredients "missing." You see, one night, I was preparing dinner for my future husband—who just happened to be a chef. Naturally, I wanted to impress him with my cooking! But my cupboards were bare—except for one can of chickpeas and one of olives. Into the salad they went. That was nearly 7 years ago now…and I'm still serving it the same way today!

    1 can (15 ounces) garbanzo beans *or* chickpeas,
      rinsed and drained
    4 large ripe tomatoes, sliced thick
    1 cup thinly sliced red onion
    1 can (6 ounces) medium pitted ripe olives,
      drained and halved
  1/2 cup olive oil
    5 to 6 large fresh basil leaves, snipped *or* 1
      tablespoon dried basil
  1/2 teaspoon dried oregano
  1/4 teaspoon pepper
Salt to taste
  1/8 teaspoon garlic powder

In a large salad bowl, layer beans, tomatoes, onion and olives. Combine all remaining ingredients; pour over vegetables.

  Cover and chill at least 3 hours or overnight. Serve chilled or at room temperature. **Yield:** 8 servings.

tomato quiche

Heidi Ann Quinn, West Kingston, Rhode Island

I first tried this recipe at a family gathering and loved it! It is a great meatless lunch or dinner for a warm day, served hot or cold. This is my most-requested dish for parties and a fairly simple one to make. Enjoy!

    1 cup chopped onion
    2 tablespoons butter
    4 large tomatoes, peeled, seeded, chopped
      and drained
    1 teaspoon salt
  1/4 teaspoon pepper
  1/4 teaspoon dried thyme
    2 cups (8 ounces) shredded Monterey Jack
      cheese, *divided*
    1 unbaked pie pastry (10 inches)
    4 eggs
1-1/2 cups half-and-half cream

In a skillet, saute onion in butter until tender. Add tomatoes, salt, pepper and thyme. Cook over medium-high heat until liquid is almost evaporated, about 10-15 minutes. Remove from the heat.

  Sprinkle 1 cup cheese into bottom of pie shell. Cover with tomato mixture; sprinkle with remaining cheese. In a mixing bowl, beat eggs until foamy. Stir in cream; mix well. Pour into pie shell.

  Bake at 425° for 10 minutes. Reduce heat to 325°; bake 40 minutes longer or until top begins to brown and a knife inserted near center comes out clean. Let stand for 10 minutes before cutting. **Yield:** 6-8 servings.

creamy sliced tomatoes

Doris Smith, Woodbury, New Jersey
This is a family favorite that's also popular with friends. It's a pretty presentation and perfect as a side dish. The basil and cool creamy dressing make the dish tasty and refreshing.

- 1 cup mayonnaise
- 1/2 cup half-and-half cream
- 3/4 teaspoon dried basil *or* 1-1/2 teaspoons chopped fresh basil, *divided*
- Lettuce leaves
- 6 medium tomatoes, sliced
- 1 medium red onion, thinly sliced into rings

In a small bowl, combine mayonnaise, cream and half of the basil. Cover and refrigerate.

Just before serving, arrange lettuce, tomatoes and onions on individual salad plates. Drizzle dressing over. Sprinkle with remaining basil. **Yield:** 12 servings.

tomato dill bisque

Susan Breckbill, Lincoln University, Pennsylvania
My family really enjoys this soup when we make it from our garden tomatoes. When those tomatoes are plentiful, I make a big batch (without mayonnaise) and freeze it. Then we can enjoy it even after the garden is gone for the season.

- 2 medium onions, chopped
- 1 garlic clove, minced
- 2 tablespoons butter
- 2 pounds tomatoes, peeled and chopped
- 1/2 cup water
- 1 chicken bouillon cube
- 1 teaspoon sugar
- 1 teaspoon dill weed
- 1/2 teaspoon salt
- 1/4 teaspoon pepper
- 1/2 cup mayonnaise, optional

In a large saucepan, saute onions and garlic in butter until tender. Add tomatoes, water, bouillon, sugar and seasonings. Cover and simmer 10 minutes or until tomatoes are tender. Remove from the heat; cool.

Puree in a blender or food processor. Return to saucepan. If a creamy soup is desired, stir in mayonnaise. Cook and stir over low heat until heated through. Serve warm. **Yield:** 5 servings (5 cups).

tomato pizza

Lois McAtee, Oceanside, California

My children liked to eat pizza with a lot of toppings, so I developed this recipe. With fresh tomatoes available year-round here, we still make it often, even though the kids are grown. It's a delightful change from usual meat-topped pizza.

- 6 medium firm tomatoes, thinly sliced
- 1 large baked pizza crust (13 to 16 inches)
- 2 tablespoons olive oil
- 1 teaspoon salt
- 1 teaspoon pepper
- 1 can (2-1/4 ounces) sliced ripe olives, drained, optional
- 1/2 cup diced green pepper
- 1/2 cup diced onion
- 1 tablespoon chopped fresh basil
- 1 cup (4 ounces) shredded part-skim mozzarella cheese
- 1 cup (4 ounces) shredded cheddar cheese

Place tomato slices in a circle on crust, overlapping slightly until crust is completely covered. Drizzle with olive oil. Season with salt and pepper. Cover with olives if desired, green pepper and onion. Sprinkle with basil.

Cover with mozzarella and cheddar cheeses. Bake at 400° for 15 minutes or until cheese is melted. Serve immediately. **Yield:** 8 servings.

> *To balance the acid of tomatoes, I add a tablespoon of grape jelly to my spaghetti sauce.
> Shirley Prejean, Cut Off, Louisiana

vegetable beef casserole

Evangeline Rew, Manassas, Virginia

This easy one-dish recipe has been a family favorite ever since it was handed down to me over 35 years ago from my husband's aunt. Add whatever vegetables you have on hand. A simple salad goes nicely with this dish.

- 3 medium unpeeled potatoes, sliced
- 3 carrots, sliced
- 3 celery ribs, sliced
- 2 cups fresh *or* frozen green beans
- 1 medium onion, chopped
- 1 pound lean ground beef
- 1 teaspoon dried thyme
- 1 teaspoon salt
- 1 teaspoon pepper
- 4 medium tomatoes, peeled, seeded and chopped
- 1 cup (4 ounces) shredded cheddar cheese

In a 3-qt. casserole, layer half of the potatoes, carrots, celery, green beans and onion. Crumble half of the uncooked beef over vegetables. Sprinkle with 1/2 teaspoon each of thyme, salt and pepper. Repeat layers.

Top with tomatoes. Cover and bake at 400° for 15 minutes. Reduce heat to 350°; bake about 1 hour longer or until vegetables are tender and meat is done.

Sprinkle with cheese; cover and let stand until cheese is melted. **Yield:** 6-8 servings.

tomato dumplings

Lucille Tucker, Clinton, Illinois

The wonderful, fresh tomato taste of the sauce complements these light, savory dumplings. They make a perfect side dish for a meal with beef. My family enjoys them very much.

- 1/2 cup finely chopped onion
- 1/4 cup finely chopped green pepper
- 1/4 cup finely chopped celery
- 1/4 cup butter
- 1 bay leaf
- 1 can (28 ounces) diced tomatoes, undrained
- 1 tablespoon brown sugar
- 1/2 teaspoon dried basil
- 1/2 teaspoon salt
- 1/4 teaspoon pepper

DUMPLINGS:
- 1 cup all-purpose flour
- 1-1/2 teaspoons baking powder
- 1/2 teaspoon salt
- 1 tablespoon cold butter
- 1 tablespoon snipped fresh parsley
- 2/3 cup milk

In a medium skillet, saute onion, green pepper and celery in butter until tender. Add bay leaf, tomatoes, brown sugar, basil, salt and pepper; cover and simmer for 5-10 minutes.

Meanwhile, for dumplings, combine flour, baking powder and salt in a bowl. Cut in butter. Add parsley and milk; stir just until mixed.

Drop by tablespoonfuls into six mounds onto simmering tomato mixture; cover tightly and simmer for 12-15 minutes or until a toothpick inserted into dumpling comes out clean. Discard bay leaf. Serve immediately. **Yield:** 6 servings.

★ ★ ★ ★ ★ prize winning tips

★ To use up your bounty of cherry tomatoes, try this easy salad. Cut cherry tomatoes in half and arrange in a pretty dish or shallow bowl. Sprinkle with garlic powder, seasoned salt and dried basil. Chill several hours; serve.

Eulalie Haas, Swanton, Ohio

★ To preserve fresh garden tomatoes for use in future casseroles and soups, wash and remove stems. Place whole tomatoes in plastic freezer bags and freeze. After defrosting, skins will easily peel off and the tomatoes can be diced and added to your dishes.

Bev Graaff, Hull, Iowa

★ If you want a chunky spaghetti sauce, do not puree the green peppers or onions in a blender or food processor. Instead, add them directly to the sauce after the tomatoes and sauce have started to thicken. Then cook until the vegetables are tender.

Kathi Richards, Dundee, Ohio

tomato bread salad

Dodi Hardcastle, Harlingen, Texas
We look forward to tomato season each year so we can make this unique and tasty recipe. It's a super dish for lunch, especially on warm summer days, and a great way to use your garden produce like onions, cucumbers and tomatoes. It also makes a good appetizer.

> 3 large tomatoes, seeded and finely chopped
> 1 medium cucumber, seeded and finely chopped
> 1/2 large sweet onion, finely chopped
> 1 cup loosely packed fresh basil, minced
> 1/4 cup olive oil
> 1 tablespoon cider vinegar
> 1 garlic clove, minced
> 1/2 teaspoon salt
> 1/4 teaspoon pepper
> 1 large loaf white *or* French bread

In a large bowl, combine tomatoes, cucumber and onion. In a small bowl, combine basil, oil, vinegar, garlic, salt and pepper. Pour over tomatoes and toss. Refrigerate for at least 1 hour.

Before serving, allow salad to come to room temperature. Cut bread into thick slices; toast under broiler until lightly browned. Top with salad. Serve immediately. **Yield:** 18 servings.

> *For a quick but attractive salad, place thickly sliced tomatoes on shredded lettuce. Sprinkle with chopped green onions. Border tomato slices with cucumber and radish slices. Drizzle with your favorite salad dressing.
> Edna Havens, Wann, Oklahoma

blt bites

Kellie Remmen, Detroit Lakes, Minnesota
These quick hors d'oeuvres may be mini, but their bacon and tomato flavor is full-size. I serve them at parties, brunches and picnics, and they're always a hit. Even my kids love them.

> 16 to 20 cherry tomatoes
> 1 pound sliced bacon, cooked and crumbled
> 1/2 cup mayonnaise
> 1/3 cup chopped green onions
> 3 tablespoons grated Parmesan cheese
> 2 tablespoons snipped fresh parsley

Cut a thin slice off of each tomato top. Scoop out and discard pulp. Invert the tomatoes on a paper towel to drain.

In a small bowl, combine all remaining ingredients. Spoon into tomatoes. Refrigerate for several hours. **Yield:** 16-20 appetizer servings.

*runners-up

tomato zucchini stew

Helen Miller, Hickory Hills, Illinois
This recipe's famous with my friends and the younger friends of my grown daughter and granddaughter. I make it for potlucks and other get-togethers. The town where I live is now considered city. When my late husband and I moved here over 40 years ago, though, it was country. He was an ex-farm boy and always had a large vegetable garden. We were well supplied for winter!

1-1/4 pounds bulk Italian sausage
1-1/2 cups sliced celery (3/4-inch pieces)
    8 medium fresh tomatoes (about 4 pounds), peeled and cut into sixths
1-1/2 cups tomato juice
    4 small zucchini, sliced into 1/4-inch pieces
2-1/2 teaspoons Italian seasoning
1-1/2 to 2 teaspoons salt
    1 teaspoon sugar
  1/2 teaspoon garlic salt
  1/2 teaspoon pepper
    3 cups frozen corn
    2 medium green peppers, sliced into 1-inch pieces
  1/4 cup cornstarch
  1/4 cup water
Shredded part-skim mozzarella cheese

In a 4-qt. Dutch oven, cook and crumble sausage over medium heat until no longer pink. Add celery and cook for 15 minutes; drain. Add tomatoes, tomato juice, zucchini and seasonings; bring to a boil. Reduce heat; cover and simmer for 20 minutes. Add corn and peppers; cover and simmer for 15 minutes.

Combine cornstarch and water until smooth; stir into stew. Bring to a boil; cook and stir for 2 minutes or until thickened. Sprinkle with cheese. **Yield:** 6-8 servings.

Editor's Note: Three 28-ounce cans of undrained diced tomatoes may be substituted for the fresh tomatoes and tomato juice.

spicy tomato steak

Anne Landers, Louisville, Kentucky
My family loves this spicy tomato dish. I came up with the recipe about 25 years ago after eating a similar dish on vacation in New Mexico. I came home and tried to duplicate it from memory. The results were delicious!

    2 tablespoons cider vinegar
    1 teaspoon salt
    1 teaspoon pepper
    1 pound boneless beef round steak, trimmed and cut into 1/4-inch strips
  1/4 cup all-purpose flour
    2 tablespoons olive oil
    3 medium tomatoes, peeled, seeded and cut into wedges
    2 medium potatoes, peeled and thinly sliced
    2 cans (4 ounces *each*) chopped green chilies
    1 garlic clove, minced
    1 teaspoon dried basil

In a mixing bowl, combine vinegar, salt and pepper; toss with beef. Cover and refrigerate for 30 minutes; drain.

Place flour in a bowl; add beef and toss to coat. In a skillet, cook beef in oil over medium heat for 15-20 minutes or until tender.

Add remaining ingredients. Cover and simmer for 20-30 minutes or until the potatoes are tender, stirring occasionally. **Yield:** 6 servings.

SUPER SALADS

#1

ORANGE
AVOCADO SALAD

orange avocado salad
GRAND PRIZE WINNER

Summer meals taste so good when a satisfying salad is part of the menu. Garden-fresh mixtures look inviting on the table and really hit the spot when warmer weather calls for lighter fare.

For our Super Salads contest, salad-loving subscribers shared luscious leafy salads, colorful fruit combinations, tasty taco salads, pleasing pasta salads, marinated medleys of vegetables and more. We received 4,600 recipes in all!

"For a beautiful salad with an unbeatable combination of flavors, you can't miss with this recipe."

After much shredding, tossing and topping fresh ingredients with delightful dressings, our Test Kitchen staff presented our taste panel with salad bowls full of refreshing creations. Orange Avocado Salad, from Latressa Allen of Fort Worth, Texas, was selected as the Grand Prize Winner.

"For a beautiful salad with an unbeatable combination of flavors, you can't miss with this recipe," says Latressa. "We love the mellow avocado together with sweet mandarin oranges and crisp cucumber. The tangy dressing makes this dish special."

DRESSING:
- 1/2 cup orange juice
- 1/4 cup vegetable oil
- 2 tablespoons red wine vinegar
- 1 tablespoon sugar
- 1 teaspoon grated orange peel
- 1/4 teaspoon salt

SALAD:
- 1 medium head iceberg lettuce, torn
- 2 cups torn red leaf lettuce
- 1 medium ripe avocado, peeled and sliced
- 1/4 cup orange juice
- 1 cucumber, sliced
- 1/2 medium red onion, thinly sliced into rings
- 1 can (11 ounces) mandarin oranges, drained

In a jar with tight-fitting lid, combine dressing ingredients; shake well. Chill.

Just before serving, toss greens in a large salad bowl. Dip the avocado slices into orange juice; arrange over greens (discard remaining juice). Add cucumber, onion and oranges. Serve with dressing. **Yield:** 6-8 servings.

layered chicken salad

Joanne Trentadue, Racine, Wisconsin
I prepare this satisfying salad Saturday evening and serve it to my husband and sons on Sunday after a round of golf. It's a winner on warm days—with a unique mix of vegetables like bean sprouts, green onions, water chestnuts and pea pods. It's lovely in a glass bowl.

- 4 to 5 cups shredded iceberg lettuce
- 1 medium cucumber, thinly sliced
- 1 cup canned bean sprouts
- 1 can (8 ounces) sliced water chestnuts, drained
- 1/2 cup thinly sliced green onions
- 1 pound canned pea pods, halved
- 4 cups cubed cooked chicken
- 2 cups mayonnaise
- 1 tablespoon sugar
- 2 teaspoons curry powder
- 1/2 teaspoon ground ginger

Cherry tomatoes and fresh parsley sprigs, optional

Place lettuce in the bottom of a 4-qt. glass salad bowl. Layer with cucumber, bean sprouts, water chestnuts, onions, pea pods and chicken.

In a small bowl, combine mayonnaise, sugar, curry and ginger. Spread over top of salad. Garnish with cherry tomatoes and parsley if desired. Cover and chill several hours or overnight. **Yield:** 8-10 servings.

fruit salad supreme

Lois Rutherford, St. Augustine, Florida
For a delightful fruit salad that's a snap to prepare, give this recipe a try. The sweet combination of pineapple, orange and cantaloupe, topped with onion and a tangy lime dressing, is one family and friends ask for often. It's also one of my favorites to serve in place of the usual tossed green salad topped with croutons.

- 2 cups watercress, stems removed
- 8 fresh *or* canned pineapple rings, halved
- 2 oranges, peeled and sliced crosswise
- 1-1/2 cups cantaloupe chunks
- 1/4 cup sliced green onions *or* 1 small sweet onion, chopped

LIME DRESSING:

- 1/4 cup vegetable oil
- 2 tablespoons lime juice
- 1 tablespoon sugar
- 1/4 teaspoon hot pepper sauce
- 1 tablespoon sour cream

On individual salad plates, arrange the watercress, pineapple and oranges. Top with the cantaloupe and onions.

In a small bowl, whisk oil, lime juice, sugar and hot pepper sauce until sugar is dissolved. Stir in sour cream. Serve with salads. **Yield:** 4 servings.

runners-up

cajun potato salad

Margaret Scott, Murfreesboro, Tennessee
I have been making this mouth-watering potato salad for about 20 years. My family likes spicy foods, and thanks to a son living in New Orleans, we have a constant supply of Cajun sausage for this recipe. Made with extra sausage, it's a filling one-dish meal.

- 2 pounds small red potatoes
- 1/2 cup chopped red onion
- 1/2 cup sliced green onions
- 1/4 cup minced fresh parsley
- 6 tablespoons cider vinegar, *divided*
- 1/2 pound fully cooked kielbasa *or* Cajun sausage, sliced
- 6 tablespoons olive oil
- 1 tablespoon Dijon mustard
- 2 garlic cloves, minced
- 1/2 teaspoon pepper
- 1/4 to 1/2 teaspoon cayenne pepper

Cook the potatoes in boiling salted water for 20-30 minutes or until tender; drain. Rinse with cold water; cool completely. Cut into 1/4-in. slices; place in a large bowl. Add the onions, parsley and 3 tablespoons vinegar; toss.

In a medium skillet, cook sausage in oil for 5-10 minutes or until it begins to brown. Remove with slotted spoon and add to potato mixture.

To drippings in skillet, add mustard, garlic, pepper, cayenne pepper and remaining vinegar; bring to a boil, whisking constantly. Pour over salad; toss gently. Serve immediately. **Yield:** 6 servings.

---

prize winning tips

★ Wash and dry salad greens the day before serving. I don't have a salad spinner, so I use this simple method instead: Shake excess water off greens and put them in a clean plastic bag with a sheet or two of paper toweling. Close the bag and whirl it around like a big windmill. This works just great!

Barbara McCalley, Allison Park, Pennsylvania

★ For crunchy coleslaw, cut a cabbage in half and soak it in salted water for 1 hour. Drain and proceed with the recipe.

Cheryl Maczko, Arthurdale, West Virginia

★ I add a handful of fresh cilantro with the lettuce and spinach when I make tossed salad. Cilantro's bold taste stands out against the milder greens.

Beth Walker, Round Rock, Texas

fruited wild rice salad

Larren Wood, Nevis, Minnesota

I created this salad recipe to feature wild rice, a delicious state crop, plus other harvest ingredients like apples and pecans. I make bushels of it each August when the small nearby village of Dorset hosts several thousand visitors at the Taste of Dorset festival.

DRESSING:
- 1/4 cup olive oil
- 1/3 cup orange juice
- 2 tablespoons honey

SALAD:
- 1 cup uncooked wild rice
- 2 Golden Delicious apples, chopped

Juice of 1 lemon
- 1 cup golden raisins
- 1 cup seedless red grapes, halved
- 2 tablespoons *each* minced fresh mint, parsley and chives

Salt and pepper to taste
- 1 cup pecan halves

Combine dressing ingredients; set aside. Cook rice according to package directions; drain if needed and allow to cool.

In a large bowl, toss the apples with lemon juice. Add raisins, grapes, mint, parsley, chives and rice. Add dressing and toss. Season with salt and pepper.

Cover and chill salad several hours or overnight. Just before serving, add the pecans and toss lightly. **Yield:** 8-10 servings.

spectacular overnight slaw

Ruth Lovett, Bay City, Texas

To come up with this dish, I used a number of different recipes plus some ideas of my own. It's great for potlucks because it's made the night before and the flavor keeps getting better. Whenever I serve it, I'm inundated with recipe requests.

- 1 medium head cabbage (2-1/2 pounds), shredded
- 1 medium red onion, thinly sliced
- 1/2 cup chopped green pepper
- 1/2 cup chopped sweet red pepper
- 1/2 cup sliced stuffed olives
- 1/2 cup white wine vinegar
- 1/2 cup vegetable oil
- 1/2 cup sugar
- 2 teaspoons Dijon mustard
- 1 teaspoon *each* salt, celery seed and mustard seed

In a 4-qt. bowl, combine the cabbage, onion, peppers and olives.

In a saucepan, combine remaining ingredients; bring to a boil. Cook and stir for 1 minute. Pour over vegetables and stir gently. Cover and refrigerate overnight. Mix well before serving. **Yield:** 12-16 servings.

*runners-up

parmesan vegetable toss

Judy Barbato, North Easton, Massachusetts
The first time I made this salad, it was with two others for a Fourth of July party years ago. This one disappeared long before the other two! It's great for feeding a hungry crowd. At our house, there's never any left over. I hope you enjoy it as much as we do.

    2 cups mayonnaise
  1/2 cup grated Parmesan cheese
  1/4 cup sugar
  1/2 teaspoon dried basil
  1/2 teaspoon salt
    4 cups fresh broccoli florets (about 3/4 pound)
    4 cups fresh cauliflowerets (about 3/4 pound)
    1 medium red onion, sliced
    1 can (8 ounces) sliced water chestnuts, drained
    1 large head iceberg lettuce, torn
    1 pound sliced bacon, cooked and crumbled
    2 cups croutons, optional

In a large bowl, combine mayonnaise, Parmesan cheese, sugar, basil and salt. Add broccoli, cauliflower, onion and water chestnuts; toss. Cover and refrigerate for several hours or overnight.

Just before serving, place lettuce in a salad bowl and top with vegetable mixture. Sprinkle with bacon. Top with croutons if desired. **Yield:** 16-18 servings.

southwestern bean salad

Lila Jean Allen, Portland, Oregon
My daughter gave me the recipe for this hearty, zippy salad. I've used it many times since and have received compliments on it. When it comes to bean salad, most people think of the sweet three-bean variety, so this slightly zesty version is a nice surprise.

    1 can (15-1/2 ounces) kidney beans, rinsed and drained
    1 can (15 ounces) black beans, rinsed and drained
    1 can (15-1/2 ounces) garbanzo beans, rinsed and drained
    2 celery ribs, sliced
    1 medium red onion, diced
    1 medium tomato, diced
    1 cup frozen corn, thawed
DRESSING:
  3/4 cup thick and chunky salsa
  1/4 cup vegetable oil
  1/4 cup lime juice
1-1/2 teaspoons chili powder
    1 teaspoon salt
  1/2 teaspoon ground cumin

In a bowl, combine the beans, celery, onion, tomato and corn. In a small bowl, combine all of the dressing ingredients; mix well. Pour over the bean mixture and toss to coat. Cover and chill for at least 2 hours. **Yield:** 10 servings.

SENSATIONAL SOUPS

#1

NEIGHBORHOOD
BEAN SOUP

neighborhood bean soup
GRAND PRIZE WINNER

C ooking can't get much more "country" than hearty, homemade soups. And soups can't get much more satisfying than the flavorful and filling fare simmered up in our Sensational Soups contest!

"Several neighbor ladies really enjoy this soup, and I love sharing it with them."

As they spooned their bowls clean to the bottom, our judges jotted down their impressions. Later, when notes were compared, one standout stood at the top of everyone's list—Neighborhood Bean Soup from Cheryl Trowbridge of Windsor, Ontario.

Says Cheryl about her Grand Prize Winner, "Several neighbor ladies really enjoy this soup, and I love sharing it with them. In fact, each leaves her own personal container in my pantry so I can ladle it full when I make a batch. After that's done, there are just a couple of servings left for me and my father."

Prepare a pot of her soup soon and you'll know why it's in demand. Better be sure, though, to make a big batch—in case the neighbors catch a whiff!

2 cups dried great northern beans
5 cups chicken broth
3 cups water
1 large meaty ham bone
2 to 3 tablespoons chicken bouillon granules
1 teaspoon dried thyme
1/2 teaspoon dried marjoram
1/2 teaspoon pepper
1/4 teaspoon rubbed sage
1/4 teaspoon dried savory
2 medium onions, chopped
3 medium carrots, chopped
3 celery ribs, chopped
1 tablespoon vegetable oil

Place beans in a Dutch oven or soup kettle; add water to cover by 2 in. Bring to a boil; boil for 2 minutes. Remove from the heat; cover and let stand for 1 hour.

Drain. Add broth, water, ham bone, bouillon and seasonings; bring to a boil. Reduce heat; cover and simmer for 2 hours.

Saute onions, carrots and celery in oil; add to soup. Cover and simmer 1 hour longer. Debone ham and cut into chunks; return to the soup. Skim fat. **Yield:** 10 servings (2-3/4 quarts).

chunky beef noodle soup

Lil Morris, Emerald Park, Saskatchewan
My husband and I lived for 11 years in the Arctic, where there was very little fresh produce and I had to order nonperishable groceries for a year ahead of time. This hearty soup—a meal in itself served with warm rolls— became a staple in our diet because it requires ingredients I could easily find.

- 1 pound boneless round steak, cut into 1/2-inch cubes
- 1 medium onion, chopped
- 2 garlic cloves, minced
- 1 tablespoon vegetable oil
- 2 cups water
- 1 can (14-1/2 ounces) diced tomatoes, undrained
- 1 can (10-1/2 ounces) condensed beef consomme, undiluted
- 1 to 2 teaspoons chili powder
- 1 teaspoon salt
- 1/2 teaspoon dried oregano
- 1 cup uncooked spiral pasta
- 1 medium green pepper, chopped
- 1/4 cup minced fresh parsley

In a large saucepan, cook round steak, onion and garlic in oil until the meat is browned and the onion is tender, about 5 minutes. Stir in water, tomatoes, consomme and seasonings; bring to a boil.

Reduce heat; cover and simmer until meat is tender, about 1-1/2 hours. Stir in pasta and green pepper. Simmer, uncovered, until noodles are tender, about 8 minutes. Add parsley. **Yield:** 8 servings (2 quarts).

marvelous mushroom soup

Beverly Rafferty, Winston, Oregon
Soup is tops on the list of things I love to cook. I've used this one as the beginning course to a meal…and as a Sunday supper with hot rolls and butter. When we had a small restaurant in Arizona, I made my mushroom soup every day. We never had any left over. It got raves at a deli I worked at, too.

- 1/2 pound fresh mushrooms, sliced
- 1 large onion, finely chopped
- 1 garlic clove, minced
- 1/2 teaspoon dried tarragon
- 1/4 teaspoon ground nutmeg
- 3 tablespoons butter
- 1/4 cup all-purpose flour
- 2 cans (14-1/2 ounces *each*) beef broth
- 1 cup (8 ounces) sour cream
- 1/2 cup half-and-half cream
- 1/2 cup evaporated milk
- 1 teaspoon lemon juice

Dash hot pepper sauce
Salt and pepper to taste

In a Dutch oven or soup kettle, saute the mushrooms, onion, garlic, tarragon and nutmeg in butter until vegetables are tender. Stir in flour until smooth. Gradually add broth; bring to a boil, stirring constantly.

Reduce heat to low; slowly add sour cream. Cook and stir until smooth. Stir in cream and milk. Add lemon juice, hot pepper sauce, salt and pepper. Heat through but do not boil. **Yield:** 6 servings.

stir-fried pork soup

Louise Johnson, Harriman, Tennessee
Especially to guests who enjoy the variety of Chinese cooking, this is a treat. I like serving it with fried noodles or rice as a side dish.

 2/3 pound boneless pork loin, cut into thin strips
 1 cup sliced fresh mushrooms
 1 cup chopped celery
 1/2 cup diced carrots
 2 tablespoons vegetable oil
 6 cups chicken broth
 1/2 cup chopped fresh spinach
 2 tablespoons cornstarch
 3 tablespoons cold water
 1 egg, lightly beaten
Pepper to taste

In a 3-qt. saucepan, stir-fry pork, mushrooms, celery and carrots in oil until pork is no longer pink and vegetables are tender. Add broth and spinach. Combine cornstarch and water to make a thin paste; stir into soup. Return to a boil; boil for 1 minute. Quickly stir in egg. Add pepper. Serve immediately. **Yield:** 4-6 servings.

> *To make a creamy potato soup extra special, top it with crumbled cooked bacon, shredded cheese and/or herbed croutons.
>
> Kelly Parsons, Seale, Alabama

swedish meatball soup

Debora Taylor, Inkom, Idaho
To me, this is a very comforting, filling, homey soup. I especially like cooking it during winter months and serving it with hot rolls, bread or muffins.

 1 egg
 2 cups half-and-half cream, *divided*
 1 cup soft bread crumbs
 1 small onion, finely chopped
 1-3/4 teaspoons salt, *divided*
 1-1/2 pounds ground beef
 1 tablespoon butter
 3 tablespoons all-purpose flour
 3/4 teaspoon beef bouillon granules
 1/2 teaspoon pepper
 1/8 to 1/4 teaspoon garlic salt
 3 cups water
 1 pound red potatoes, cubed
 1 package (10 ounces) frozen peas, thawed

In a bowl, beat egg; add 1/3 cup cream, bread crumbs, onion and 1 teaspoon of salt. Add beef; mix well. Shape into 1/2-in. balls. In a Dutch oven or soup kettle, brown meatballs in butter, half at a time. Remove from the pan; set aside. Drain fat.

To pan, add flour, bouillon, pepper, garlic salt and remaining salt; stir until smooth. Gradually stir in water; bring to a boil, stirring often. Add potatoes and meatballs.

Reduce heat; cover and simmer for 25 minutes or until the potatoes are tender. Stir in the peas and remaining cream; heat through. **Yield:** 8 servings (about 2 quarts).

cream of cabbage soup

Helen Riesterer, Kiel, Wisconsin
I've given this soup recipe to friends, who have varied it a little. One substituted summer squash and zucchini for the rutabaga. She said it tasted just great that way, too.

    4 cups water
    2 tablespoons chicken bouillon granules
    3 cups diced peeled potatoes
    1 cup finely chopped onion
    1 cup diced peeled rutabaga
  1/2 cup diced carrots
    6 cups chopped cabbage
    1 cup chopped celery
  1/2 cup chopped green pepper
    1 garlic clove, minced
    1 teaspoon salt
    1 teaspoon dill weed
    1 cup butter
    1 cup all-purpose flour
    2 cups milk
    2 cups chicken broth
  1/2 pound process cheese (Velveeta), cubed
  1/2 teaspoon dried thyme
Pepper to taste
Additional milk, optional

In a Dutch oven or soup kettle, bring water and bouillon to a boil. Add potatoes, onion, rutabaga and carrots. Reduce heat; cover and simmer for 5 minutes. Add cabbage, celery and green pepper; simmer, uncovered, for 5 minutes or until vegetables are crisp-tender. Add garlic, salt and dill.

In a saucepan, melt butter. Stir in flour; cook and stir over medium heat until golden. Gradually add milk and broth, stirring until smooth. Add cheese, thyme and pepper; cook on low until cheese is melted. Stir into vegetable mixture; simmer for 5 minutes. Thin with milk if needed. **Yield:** 12-14 servings (about 3-1/2 quarts).

monterey jack cheese soup

Susan Salenski, Copemish, Michigan
Main-meal soups are something I'm always on the lookout for. Since I love cheese and our kids like anything with Mexican flavor, I knew this one would be popular at our house. I've served it with tacos, nachos or a loaf of bread.

    1 cup chicken broth
    1 large tomato, peeled, seeded and diced
  1/2 cup finely chopped onion
    2 tablespoons chopped green chilies
    1 garlic clove, minced
    2 tablespoons butter
    2 tablespoons all-purpose flour
Salt and pepper to taste
    3 cups milk, *divided*
1-1/2 cups (6 ounces) shredded Monterey Jack cheese

In a 3-qt. saucepan, combine the first five ingredients; bring to a boil. Reduce heat; cover and simmer for 10 minutes or until vegetables are tender. Remove from the heat and set aside.

In another saucepan, melt butter. Stir in flour, salt and pepper. Cook and stir over medium heat until smooth. Gradually stir in 1-1/2 cups milk; bring to a boil. Boil for 1 minute, stirring constantly. Slowly stir into vegetable mixture. Add cheese and remaining milk. Cook and stir over low heat until cheese is melted. Serve immediately. **Yield:** 5 servings.

chicken 'n' dumpling soup

Rachel Hinz, St. James, Minnesota

This recipe's one I had to learn to marry into my husband's family! It is the traditional Hinz Christmas Eve meal, served before going to church. My father was a pastor who was always too keyed up from preaching to enjoy a big Sunday dinner. So I learned to make soup early on.

- 1 broiler/fryer chicken (3 to 3-1/2 pounds)
- 3 quarts water
- 1/4 cup chicken bouillon granules
- 1 bay leaf
- 1 teaspoon whole peppercorns
- 1/8 teaspoon ground allspice
- 6 cups uncooked wide noodles
- 4 cups sliced carrots
- 1 package (10 ounces) frozen mixed vegetables
- 3/4 cup sliced celery
- 1/2 cup chopped onion
- 1/4 cup uncooked long grain rice
- 2 tablespoons minced fresh parsley

DUMPLINGS:

- 1-1/3 cups all-purpose flour
- 2 teaspoons baking powder
- 1 teaspoon dried thyme
- 1/2 teaspoon salt
- 2/3 cup milk
- 2 tablespoons vegetable oil

In a Dutch oven or soup kettle, combine the first six ingredients; bring to a boil. Reduce heat; cover and simmer for 1-1/2 hours. Remove chicken; allow to cool.

Strain broth; discard bay leaf and peppercorns. Skim fat. Debone chicken and cut into chunks; return chicken and broth to pan. Add noodles, vegetables, rice and parsley; bring to a simmer.

For dumplings, combine flour, baking powder, thyme and salt in a bowl. Combine milk and oil; stir into dry ingredients. Drop by teaspoonfuls onto simmering soup. Reduce heat; cover and simmer for 15 minutes (do not lift the cover). **Yield:** 20 servings (5 quarts).

***** prize winning **tips**

* I make and freeze several batches of basic chicken soup in two-serving and four-serving containers. Then for a quick supper, I simply reheat the soup, add rice or pasta and cook for 20 to 30 minutes.

Coral Smith, Mt. Ayr, Iowa

* Homemade tomato soup provides a wonderful base for spaghetti or vegetable soup, as well as a tasty addition to meat loaf.

Juanita Pardue, Heath Springs, South Carolina

* Crushed red pepper flakes add extra zing to minestrone soup.

Nancy Solberg, Madison, Wisconsin

runners-up

best chicken noodle soup

Cheryl Rogers, Ames, Iowa
For years, I worked at making a chicken soup that tasted just like my mother's. When I realized I couldn't, I decided to come up with my own recipe. It was an immediate hit!

- 1 tablespoon dried rosemary, crushed
- 2 teaspoons garlic powder
- 2 teaspoons pepper
- 2 teaspoons seasoned salt
- 2 broiler/fryer chickens (3 to 3-1/2 pounds *each*)
- 1-1/2 quarts chicken broth
- 2-1/4 cups sliced fresh mushrooms
- 1/2 cup *each* chopped celery and onion
- 1/2 cup sliced carrots
- 1/4 teaspoon pepper

NOODLES:
- 2-1/2 cups all-purpose flour, *divided*
- 1 teaspoon salt
- 2 eggs
- 1 can (5 ounces) evaporated milk
- 1 tablespoon olive oil

Combine first four ingredients; rub over chickens. Place in an ungreased 13-in. x 9-in. x 2-in. baking pan. Cover and bake at 350° for 1-1/4 hours or until tender. Drain and reserve drippings. Skim fat. Cool chicken; debone and cut into chunks. Cover and refrigerate chicken.

In a Dutch oven or soup kettle, bring chicken broth and reserved drippings to a boil. Add mushrooms, celery, onion, carrots and pepper; simmer for 30 minutes.

Meanwhile, for noodles, set aside 1/3 cup of flour. Combine salt and remaining flour in a bowl. Beat eggs, milk and oil; stir into the dry ingredients. Sprinkle kneading surface with reserved flour; knead dough until smooth. Divide into thirds. Roll out each portion to 1/8-in. thickness; cut to desired width.

Freeze two portions to use at another time. Bring soup to a boil. Add one portion of noodles; cook for 7-9 minutes or until almost tender. Add chicken; heat through. **Yield:** 10 servings (2-3/4 quarts).

lentil barley soup

Anita Warner, Mt. Crawford, Virginia
Soups are one of my favorite things to prepare—they're so easy, and nothing is better on a chilly evening with some homemade bread or biscuits. I don't consider myself an "experienced" cook, but I do love to try new recipes with a country flair.

- 1 medium onion, chopped
- 1/2 cup chopped green pepper
- 3 garlic cloves, minced
- 1 tablespoon butter
- 1 can (49-1/2 ounces) chicken broth
- 3 medium carrots, chopped
- 1/2 cup dry lentils
- 1-1/2 teaspoons Italian seasoning
- 1 teaspoon salt
- 1/4 teaspoon pepper
- 1 cup cubed cooked chicken *or* turkey
- 1/2 cup quick-cooking barley
- 2 medium fresh mushrooms, chopped
- 1 can (28 ounces) crushed tomatoes, undrained

In a Dutch oven or soup kettle, saute the onion, green pepper and garlic in butter until tender. Add the broth, carrots, lentils, Italian seasoning, salt and pepper; bring to a boil. Reduce heat; cover and simmer for 25 minutes.

Add the chicken, barley and mushrooms; return to a boil. Reduce heat; cover and simmer for 10-15 minutes or until the lentils, barley and carrots are tender. Add the tomatoes and heat through. **Yield:** 8-10 servings (about 2-1/2 quarts).

split pea sausage soup

Donna Mae Young, Menomonie, Wisconsin
When my husband and I eat out and enjoy a dish, I go home and try to duplicate it. That's how I came up with this recipe. While it's good at any time, we like it full and hearty over the winter.

- 1 pound smoked kielbasa
- 1 pound dried split peas
- 6 cups water
- 1 cup chopped carrots
- 1 cup chopped onion
- 1 cup chopped celery
- 1 tablespoon minced fresh parsley
- 1 teaspoon salt
- 1/2 teaspoon coarse black pepper
- 2 bay leaves

Cut sausage in half lengthwise; cut into 1/4-in. pieces. Place in a Dutch oven or soup kettle; add remaining ingredients. Bring to a boil.

Reduce heat; cover and simmer for 1-1/4 to 1-1/2 hours or until peas are tender. Remove bay leaves. **Yield:** 8 servings (2 quarts).

> *The night before I prepare a big kettle of soup, I chop and measure all the veggies and refrigerate them in resealable plastic bags or in covered bowls. Next day, assembling the soup is a breeze!
> Rose Boudreaux, Bourg, Louisiana

savory tomato beef soup

Edna Tilley, Morganton, North Carolina
This soup's one my mother taught me to make. It's good all year but especially when the weather's cold. In winter, I serve it with grilled cheese sandwiches. It would also be a nice lunch with a side salad or homemade corn bread. Even our grandchildren—we have four—like it. It's a good way of getting them to eat their vegetables.

- 1 pound beef stew meat, cut into 1/2-inch cubes
- 1 small meaty beef soup bone
- 2 tablespoons vegetable oil
- 4 cups water
- 1 can (28 ounces) diced tomatoes, undrained
- 1 cup chopped carrots
- 1 cup chopped celery
- 1/4 cup chopped celery leaves
- 1 tablespoon salt
- 1/2 teaspoon dried marjoram
- 1/2 teaspoon dried basil
- 1/4 teaspoon dried savory
- 1/4 teaspoon dried thyme
- 1/8 teaspoon ground mace
- 1/8 teaspoon hot pepper sauce

In a Dutch oven or soup kettle, brown the stew meat and soup bone in oil. Add the remaining ingredients; bring to a boil. Reduce heat; cover and simmer for 4-5 hours or until meat is tender.

Skim fat. Remove meat from bone; cut into 1/2-in. cubes. Return to the soup and heat through. **Yield:** 6-8 servings (about 2 quarts).

CHILI COOK-OFF

\#1

MEATY THREE-BEAN
CHILI

meaty three-bean chili
GRAND PRIZE WINNER

Variety's not only the spice of life…it's also what seasons these winning entries in our Chili Cook-Off recipe contest. The savory creations here and on the pages that follow have it all— ground beef, pork, beef stew meat, sausage, chicken and an inventive assortment of beans as well. There is zesty chili, mild chili, traditional chili…plus some surprises, too. For filling fare, you're in the right place.

" **My chili's always been a winner with family and friends.** "

Be sure to check out Meaty Three-Bean Chili, the Grand Prize Winner. "I had never thought about entering a recipe until I saw the announcement for this chili contest," says Sandra Miller of Lees Summit, Missouri. "Then I couldn't resist. My chili's always been a winner with family and friends."

Easily doubled or tripled, Sandra's recipe is a crowd-pleaser, too. "I've made this chili for as many as 50 people," she says.

3/4 **pound Italian sausage links, cut into 1/2-inch chunks**
3/4 **pound ground beef**
1 **large onion, chopped**
1 **medium green pepper, chopped**
1 **jalapeno pepper, seeded and minced**
2 **garlic cloves, minced**
1 **cup beef broth**
1/2 **cup Worcestershire sauce**
1-1/2 **teaspoons chili powder**
1 **teaspoon pepper**
1 **teaspoon ground mustard**
1/2 **teaspoon celery seed**
1/2 **teaspoon salt**
6 **cups chopped fresh plum tomatoes (about 2 pounds)**
6 **bacon strips, cooked and crumbled**
1 **can (15-1/2 ounces) kidney beans, rinsed and drained**
1 **can (15 ounces) pinto beans, rinsed and drained**
1 **can (15 ounces) garbanzo beans, rinsed and drained**
Additional chopped onion, optional

In a 4-qt. kettle or Dutch oven, cook the sausage and beef over medium heat, until the meat is no longer pink; drain, reserving 1 tablespoon drippings. Set meat aside. Saute onion, peppers and garlic in the reserved drippings for 3 minutes. Add the broth, Worcestershire sauce and seasonings; bring to a boil over medium heat. Reduce heat; cover and simmer for 10 minutes.

Add tomatoes, bacon and browned sausage and beef; return to a boil. Reduce heat; cover and simmer for 30 minutes.

Add all of the beans. Simmer for 1 hour, stirring occasionally. Garnish with chopped onion if desired. **Yield:** 10-12 servings (3 quarts).

Editor's Note: When cutting or seeding hot peppers, use rubber or plastic gloves to protect your hands. Avoid touching your face.

santa fe chicken chili

Sonia Gallant, St. Thomas, Ontario
Stir up this chili on Sunday and you'll be set for a couple weekday meals. Although we're currently living in the city, my husband and I hope to return to the country someday.

- 2 pounds boneless skinless chicken breasts, cut into 1/2-inch cubes
- 4 medium sweet red peppers, diced
- 4 garlic cloves, minced
- 2 large onions, chopped
- 1/4 cup olive oil
- 3 tablespoons chili powder
- 2 teaspoons ground cumin
- 1/4 teaspoon cayenne pepper
- 1 can (28 ounces) diced tomatoes, undrained
- 2 cans (14-1/2 ounces *each*) chicken broth
- 2 cans (15-1/2 ounces *each*) kidney beans, rinsed and drained
- 1 jar (12 ounces) salsa
- 1 package (10 ounces) frozen corn
- 1/2 teaspoon salt
- 1/2 teaspoon pepper

In a 5-qt. kettle or Dutch oven over medium heat, saute chicken, peppers, garlic and onions in oil until the chicken is no longer pink and vegetables are tender, about 5-7 minutes.

Add chili powder, cumin and cayenne; cook and stir for 1 minute.

Add the tomatoes and broth; bring to a boil. Reduce heat; simmer, uncovered, for 15 minutes.

Stir in remaining ingredients; bring to a boil. Reduce heat; cover and simmer for 10-15 minutes or until the chicken is tender. **Yield:** 14-16 servings (4 quarts).

black bean sausage chili

Nanci Keatley, Salem, Oregon
My entire family urged me to send in this recipe! I came up with it one day when I wasn't sure what to do with a can of black beans I had. I just threw a bunch of stuff together, and out came a new chili that's become our favorite. My husband always tells me that I'm the world's best cook. That's nice, since he's the best husband in the world!

- 1 pound bulk Italian sausage
- 3 garlic cloves, minced
- 1/2 cup chopped green pepper
- 1/2 cup chopped onion
- 1 can (15 ounces) black beans, rinsed and drained
- 1 can (14-1/2 ounces) diced tomatoes, undrained
- 1 can (11 ounces) whole kernel corn, drained
- 1 can (8 ounces) tomato sauce
- 1 can (6 ounces) tomato paste
- 1/2 cup water
- 1 tablespoon chili powder
- 1 teaspoon dried oregano
- 3/4 teaspoon salt
- 1/2 teaspoon dried basil
- 1/4 teaspoon pepper
Shredded cheddar cheese, optional

In a 3-qt. saucepan, cook sausage and garlic over medium heat until sausage is no longer pink.

Add green pepper and onion. Cook and stir until onion is tender; drain. Add beans, tomatoes, corn, tomato sauce and paste, water, chili powder, oregano, salt, basil and pepper; bring to a boil. Reduce heat; cover and simmer for 30 minutes. Garnish with the cheese if desired. **Yield:** 6 servings (1-3/4 quarts).

chili for a crowd

Lisa Humphreys, Wasilla, Alaska

The basis for this recipe was handed down to me by my aunt, who said she got it from a "grizzled Montana mountain man." I added some zesty ingredients to come up with the final version. Spicy food is something that my husband's family isn't accustomed to, so I adjust the spices for them. In fact, with a few simple alterations to the "heat" index, I can serve this chili to anyone.

    3 pounds ground beef
    2 cans (28 ounces *each*) diced tomatoes,
       undrained
    4 cans (15 to 16 ounces *each*) kidney, pinto
       and/or black beans, rinsed and drained
    1 pound smoked kielbasa, sliced and halved
    2 large onions, halved and thinly sliced
    2 cans (8 ounces *each*) tomato sauce
  2/3 cup hickory-flavored barbecue sauce
1-1/2 cups water
  1/2 cup packed brown sugar
    5 fresh banana peppers, seeded and sliced
    2 tablespoons chili powder
    2 teaspoons ground mustard
    2 teaspoons instant coffee granules
    1 teaspoon *each* dried oregano, thyme and sage
  1/2 to 1 teaspoon cayenne pepper
  1/2 to 1 teaspoon crushed red pepper flakes
    2 garlic cloves, minced

In an 8-qt. kettle or Dutch oven, cook beef over medium heat until beef is no longer pink; drain.

Add remaining ingredients; bring to a boil. Reduce heat; cover and simmer for 1 hour, stirring occasionally. **Yield:** 20-24 servings (6 quarts).

chili with tortilla dumplings

Shirley Logan, Houston, Texas

Down here in Texas, we've always enjoyed the bold flavor of Southwestern cooking. This chili is a special favorite—I've prepared it for a crowd and just the two of us, too. The simple tortilla dumplings are a fun twist.

    2 pounds ground beef
    1 medium onion, chopped
    2 garlic cloves, minced
    2 cans (15-1/2 ounces *each*) kidney beans,
       rinsed and drained
    1 can (28 ounces) diced tomatoes, undrained
    1 can (14-1/2 ounces) chicken broth
    2 to 3 tablespoons chili powder
    1 teaspoon ground cumin
    1 teaspoon dried oregano
  1/2 teaspoon salt
    4 flour tortillas (7 inches)

In a 3-qt. saucepan, cook beef, onion and garlic over medium heat until beef is no longer pink; drain. Add the next seven ingredients; bring to a boil. Reduce heat; cover and simmer for 50 minutes. Halve each tortilla and cut into 1/4-in. strips.

Gently stir into soup; cover and simmer for 8-10 minutes or until the tortillas are softened. Serve immediately. **Yield:** 6-8 servings (2-1/4 quarts).

vegetable bean chili

Rene Fry, Hampstead, Maryland
Because it is so hearty, no one misses the meat in this chili. Both family—my husband and I have three daughters and one grandchild—and friends ask for it.

- 1 medium zucchini, sliced 1/4 inch thick
- 1 medium green pepper, chopped
- 1 cup chopped onion
- 1 cup shredded carrots
- 1/2 cup finely chopped celery
- 2 garlic cloves, minced
- 1/4 cup olive oil
- 1 can (28 ounces) diced tomatoes, undrained
- 1 jar (8 ounces) picante sauce
- 1 teaspoon beef bouillon granules
- 1-1/2 teaspoons ground cumin
- 1 can (15 ounces) garbanzo beans, rinsed and drained
- 1 can (15-1/2 ounces) chili beans, undrained
- 1 can (2-1/4 ounces) sliced ripe olives, drained
- 1 cup (4 ounces) shredded cheddar cheese

In a 4-qt. kettle or Dutch oven, saute zucchini, green pepper, onion, carrots, celery and garlic in oil until tender. Stir in tomatoes, picante sauce, bouillon and cumin; bring to a boil. Reduce heat; simmer, uncovered, for 30 minutes, stirring occasionally.

Add beans and olives; heat through. Garnish with cheese. **Yield:** 9 servings (2-1/4 quarts).

> ✳For convenience, I simmer my chili on low all day in my slow cooker after first browning the meat. I like to add a cup of shredded zucchini to my chili for additional bulk, nutrition and flavor.
> Linda Sinclair, Congress, Saskatchewan

zesty colorado chili

Beverly Bowman, Conifer, Colorado
Chili, like this meaty version, is a hearty winter staple up here in the mountains—especially for outdoor lovers like the two of us!

- 1 pound Italian sausage links
- 1 pound pork shoulder
- 2 pounds ground beef
- 2 medium onions, chopped
- 1 large green pepper, chopped
- 1 tablespoon minced garlic
- 1 can (29 ounces) tomato puree
- 1 can (28 ounces) diced tomatoes, undrained
- 1 cup beef broth
- 1 jalapeno pepper, seeded and minced
- 2 tablespoons brown sugar
- 1 tablespoon cider vinegar
- 2 teaspoons chili powder
- 2 teaspoons ground cumin
- 1 to 2 teaspoons crushed red pepper flakes
- 1 teaspoon dried basil
- 1 teaspoon dried oregano
- 1/2 teaspoon hot pepper sauce
- 2 cans (15-1/2 ounces *each*) kidney beans, rinsed and drained

Cut sausage into 1/2-in. pieces. Trim pork and cut into 1/2-in. pieces. In a 5-qt. kettle or Dutch oven, cook sausage, pork and beef over medium heat, until sausage and beef are no longer pink and the pork juices run clear; drain, reserving 1 tablespoon drippings. Set meat aside.

Saute onions, green pepper and garlic in reserved drippings until tender. Add the next 12 ingredients. Return meat to the pan; bring to a boil. Reduce heat; cover and simmer for 1 hour.

Add the beans and heat through. **Yield:** 12-14 servings (3-1/2 quarts).

tangy oven chili

Sue O'Connor, Lucan, Ontario

Frankly, I never cared much for chili. But my husband, Pat, likes it. So I just played around with ingredients until I came up with one I enjoyed—this one!

- 1 pound dried red kidney beans
- 2 pounds ground beef
- 2 medium onions, chopped
- 1 medium green pepper, chopped
- 2 envelopes chili seasoning mix
- 1-1/2 teaspoons salt
- 1-1/2 teaspoons pepper
- 1 teaspoon sugar
- 2 cans (28 ounces *each*) diced tomatoes, undrained
- 1 can (12 ounces) tomato paste
- 2 cans (8 ounces *each*) crushed pineapple, undrained
- 2 jars (4-1/2 ounces *each*) sliced mushrooms, drained
- 3 to 5 fresh jalapeno peppers, seeded and minced
- 3 cans (11-1/2 ounces *each*) V8 juice

Rinse beans and place in a large kettle or Dutch oven; cover with water. Bring to a boil; boil for 2 minutes. Remove from the heat; let stand for 1 to 4 hours or until softened. Drain, discarding liquid; set beans aside.

In a skillet, cook beef, onions and green pepper over medium heat until beef is no longer pink; drain. Stir in seasoning mixes, salt and pepper. Pour into an ovenproof 8-qt. Dutch oven. Add beans and remaining ingredients; mix well. Cover and bake at 350° for 1 hour.

Reduce heat to 325°; bake for 4-5 hours or until beans are tender, stirring every 30 minutes. **Yield:** 18-20 servings (5 quarts).

prize winning tips

✳✳✳✳✳

✳ I warm up leftover chili the next morning and fill everyone's thermoses with it so my family can have hot lunches. In addition, I pack little bags of shredded cheese and chopped onion to top each serving.

Earline Campbell, Pensacola, Florida

✳ Often, I make my chili so thick it can be served on hamburger buns as a sandwich or over chunks of corn bread.

Eleanor Steg, Stuartburn, Manitoba

✳ As a mother of five, I need a chili with child appeal! I stir in 1/4 cup of chocolate syrup per 8-cup batch for a little sweetener.

Sandra Murray, Marble Hill, Missouri

✳ I always add a tablespoon or two of molasses and the grated peel of an orange to my deluxe chili recipe.

Martha Creech, Kinston, North Carolina

chunky beef chili

Vicki Flowers, Knoxville, Tennessee
When I first tasted this chili that originated with my brother, I couldn't wait to share it.

- 1/2 cup all-purpose flour
- 1-1/2 teaspoons *each* dried thyme and rosemary, crushed
- 1-1/2 pounds beef stew meat, cut into 1-inch cubes
- 1/2 pound ground beef
- 1 can (14-1/2 ounces) beef broth
- 1 large onion, finely chopped
- 1/2 cup chopped green pepper
- 1 garlic clove, minced
- 1 can (4 ounces) chopped green chilies
- 1 to 2 jalapeno peppers, seeded and minced
- 1 can (15 ounces) crushed tomatoes
- 2 cans (15-1/2 ounces *each*) chili beans, undrained
- 1 can (15-1/2 ounces) pinto beans, rinsed and drained
- 1 can (15 ounces) white *or* red kidney beans, rinsed and drained
- 1 can (6 ounces) tomato paste
- 2 tablespoons ground cumin
- 1 teaspoon dried oregano
- 1/2 teaspoon *each* pepper, white pepper and cayenne pepper
- 3 to 4 drops hot pepper sauce
Shredded cheddar cheese, optional

In a plastic bag, combine flour, thyme and rosemary; add beef cubes, a few at a time and shake to coat. In a 4-qt. kettle or Dutch oven, cook ground beef and the beef cubes over medium heat until beef is no longer pink; drain.

Add remaining ingredients except cheese. Cover and simmer for 5 hours. Garnish with cheese if desired. **Yield:** 10-12 servings (3 quarts).

Editor's Note: When cutting or seeding hot peppers, use rubber or plastic gloves to protect your hands. Avoid touching your face.

hearty italian chili

Chloe Buckner, Edinburg, Pennsylvania
Beginning when I was just 5 years old, I was my grandmother's constant helper in the kitchen. And, like her, I can't seem to follow a recipe without changing it! That's how this one came about when I got bored with plain chili. The first time I served it at a potluck, people passed around copies of the recipe.

- 1 pound ground beef
- 1/2 pound bulk Italian sausage
- 1 medium onion, chopped
- 1/2 cup chopped green pepper
- 1 can *or* jar (26-1/2 to 30 ounces) spaghetti sauce
- 1 can (16 ounces) kidney beans, rinsed and drained
- 1 can (14-1/2 ounces) diced tomatoes, undrained
- 1 jar (4-1/2 ounces) sliced mushrooms, drained
- 1 cup water
- 1/3 cup halved sliced pepperoni
- 5 teaspoons chili powder
- 1/2 teaspoon salt
Pinch pepper

In a 3-qt. saucepan, cook beef, sausage, onion and green pepper over medium heat until the meat is no longer pink; drain.

Add remaining ingredients; bring to a boil. Reduce heat; simmer, uncovered, for 30 minutes. **Yield:** 6-8 servings (2-1/4 quarts).

garden harvest chili

Debbi Cosford, Bayfield, Ontario
Any time you're looking for a way to use up your garden bounty of zucchini and squash, this recipe gives a different taste sensation. My husband really enjoys it. This meatless chili looks as good as it tastes.

- 1 medium sweet red pepper, chopped
- 1 medium onion, chopped
- 4 garlic cloves, minced
- 2 tablespoons vegetable oil
- 1 tablespoon chili powder
- 1 teaspoon ground cumin
- 1 teaspoon dried oregano
- 2 cups cubed peeled butternut squash
- 1 can (28 ounces) diced tomatoes, undrained
- 2 cups diced zucchini
- 1 can (15 ounces) black beans, rinsed and drained
- 1 can (8-3/4 ounces) whole kernel corn, drained
- 1/4 cup minced fresh parsley

In a 3-qt. saucepan, saute red pepper, onion and garlic in oil until tender. Stir in chili powder, cumin, oregano, butternut squash and tomatoes; bring to a boil. Reduce heat; cover and simmer for 10-15 minutes or until squash is almost tender.

Stir in remaining ingredients; cover and simmer 10 minutes longer. **Yield:** 7 servings (1-3/4 quarts).

spicy white chili

Carlene Bailey, Brandenton, Florida
As far as I was concerned, the original version of this dish was fine. But, with a son who can't get enough spice, I added green chilies and other seasonings until I created this quick and easy chili that he's wild about.

- 2 medium onions, chopped
- 1 tablespoon vegetable oil
- 4 garlic cloves, minced
- 2 cans (4 ounces *each*) chopped green chilies
- 2 teaspoons ground cumin
- 1 teaspoon dried oregano
- 1/4 teaspoon cayenne pepper
- 1/4 teaspoon ground cloves
- 2 cans (14-1/2 ounces *each*) chicken broth
- 4 cups cubed cooked chicken
- 3 cans (15-1/2 ounces *each*) great northern beans, rinsed and drained
- 2 cups (8 ounces) shredded Monterey Jack cheese

Sour cream and sliced jalapeno peppers, optional

In a 3-qt. saucepan, saute onions in oil until tender. Stir in garlic, chilies, cumin, oregano, cayenne and cloves; cook and stir 2-3 minutes longer.

Add broth, chicken and beans; simmer, uncovered, for 15 minutes.

Remove from the heat. Add cheese; stir until melted. Garnish with sour cream and jalapeno peppers if desired. **Yield:** 6-8 servings (2-1/4 quarts).

BEST OF BEANS

#1

SPICY BEAN AND
BEEF PIE

spicy bean and beef pie
GRAND PRIZE WINNER

If you've been searching for new ways to add variety to your menus, the answer is in the bag (or can)—of beans!

The hearty mix of recipes from our Best of Beans contest is sure to please. The collection was selected from nearly 6,000 entries using kidney, navy, pinto, great northern, lima, garbanzo, black beans and more.

> "...a one-dish meal **that is something other than a casserole.**"

When you prepare some of these delicious recipes, there are sure to be compliments on your cooking, especially when you prepare the Grand Prize Winner, Spicy Bean and Beef Pie.

"My daughter helped me create this recipe one day when we wanted a one-dish meal that is something other than a casserole," says Debra Dohy of Massillon, Ohio. "This pie slices nicely and is a fun and filling dish."

1 pound ground beef
2 to 3 garlic cloves, minced
1 can (11-1/2 ounces) condensed bean with bacon soup, undiluted
1 jar (16 ounces) thick and chunky picante sauce, *divided*
1/4 cup cornstarch
1 tablespoon chopped fresh parsley
1 teaspoon paprika
1 teaspoon salt
1/4 teaspoon pepper
1 can (16 ounces) kidney beans, rinsed and drained
1 can (15 ounces) black beans, rinsed and drained
2 cups (8 ounces) shredded cheddar cheese, *divided*
3/4 cup sliced green onions, *divided*
Pastry for double-crust pie (10 inches)
1 cup (8 ounces) sour cream
1 can (2-1/4 ounces) sliced ripe olives, drained

In a skillet, cook beef and garlic over medium heat until beef is no longer pink; drain. In a large bowl, combine soup, 1 cup of picante sauce, cornstarch, parsley, paprika, salt and pepper; mix well. Fold in beans, 1-1/4 cups of cheese, 1/2 cup onions and the beef mixture.

Line pie plate with bottom pastry; fill with bean mixture. Top with remaining pastry; seal and flute edges. Cut slits in the top crust.

Bake at 425° for 30-35 minutes or until lightly browned. Let stand for 5 minutes before cutting. Garnish with sour cream, olives and remaining picante sauce, cheese and onions. **Yield:** 8 servings.

chicken provencale

Barbara Zeilinger, Columbus, Indiana
When I serve this entree at a dinner party, people always comment on the tender chicken and flavorfully seasoned beans. I sometimes fix it a day ahead—it's as good as it is the first day it's made.

1 broiler/fryer chicken (3 to 4 pounds), cut up
1 tablespoon vegetable oil
1-1/2 cups chopped onion
3 garlic cloves, minced
2 cans (15-1/2 ounces *each*) great northern beans, rinsed and drained
1 can (29 ounces) diced tomatoes, undrained
3 medium carrots, sliced 1/4 inch thick
1 tablespoon chicken bouillon granules
1 teaspoon dried thyme
1/2 teaspoon dried oregano
1/2 teaspoon pepper

In a skillet, brown the chicken in oil; remove and set aside.

Saute onion and garlic in drippings until tender. Stir in remaining ingredients.

Spoon into a 3-qt. baking dish; arrange chicken pieces on top. Cover and bake at 350° for 65-75 minutes or until chicken juices run clear. **Yield:** 4 servings.

hot five-bean salad

Angela Leinenbach, Newport News, Virginia
This crowd-pleaser is like a German potato salad made with colorful beans. My mom's been preparing this salad for years—it's so simple to create and great to take to church suppers.

8 bacon strips, diced
2/3 cup sugar
2 tablespoons cornstarch
1-1/2 teaspoons salt
Pinch pepper
3/4 cup vinegar
1/2 cup water
1 can (16 ounces) kidney beans, rinsed and drained
1 can (15-1/4 ounces) lima beans, rinsed and drained
1 can (15 ounces) garbanzo beans *or* chickpeas, rinsed and drained
1 can (14-1/2 ounces) cut green beans, drained
1 can (14-1/2 ounces) cut wax beans, drained

In a skillet, cook bacon over medium heat until crisp. Remove to paper towels to drain, reserving 1/4 cup drippings. Add sugar, cornstarch, salt and pepper to drippings. Stir in vinegar and water; bring to a boil, stirring constantly. Cook and stir for 2 minutes.

Add the beans; reduce heat. Cover and simmer for 15 minutes or until beans are heated through.

Place in a serving bowl; top with bacon. **Yield:** 10-12 servings.

cranberry baked beans

Wendie Osipowicz, New Britain, Connecticut
I knew I'd found a winner when I got the idea to simmer beans in cranberry juice. The tartness of the juice is a nice subtle contrast to the sweet brown sugar and molasses in these baked beans. They're wonderful warm or cold.

> 3 cups dried navy beans
> 5 cups cranberry juice
> 1/2 pound lean salt pork, diced
> 3/4 cup chopped onion
> 1/2 cup ketchup
> 1/4 cup molasses
> 5 teaspoons dark brown sugar
> 1-1/2 teaspoons ground mustard
> 1-1/2 teaspoons salt
> 1/8 teaspoon ground ginger

Place beans in a Dutch oven or soup kettle; add water to cover by 2 in. Bring to a boil; boil for 2 minutes. Remove from the heat; cover and let stand for 1 to 4 hours, or until softened.

Drain beans and discard liquid. Return beans to Dutch oven. Add cranberry juice; bring to a boil. Reduce heat; cover and simmer for 1 hour or until the beans are almost tender.

Drain, reserving cranberry liquid. Place beans in a 2-1/2-qt. casserole or bean pot; add remaining ingredients and 1-1/2 cups of cranberry liquid. Cover and bake at 350° for 3 hours or until beans are tender and of desired consistency, stirring every 30 minutes. Add reserved cranberry liquid as needed. **Yield:** 10-12 servings.

lima bean soup

Kathleen Olsack, North Cape May, New Jersey
Every year, there's a Lima Bean Festival in nearby West Cape May to honor the many growers there and showcase different recipes using their crop. This comforting chowder was a festival recipe contest winner years ago.

> 3 cans (14-1/2 ounces *each*) chicken broth
> 2 cans (15-1/4 ounces *each*) lima beans, rinsed and drained
> 3 medium carrots, thinly sliced
> 2 medium potatoes, peeled and diced
> 2 small sweet red peppers, chopped
> 2 small onions, chopped
> 2 celery ribs, thinly sliced
> 1/4 cup butter
> 1-1/2 teaspoons dried marjoram
> 1/2 teaspoon salt
> 1/2 teaspoon pepper
> 1/2 teaspoon dried oregano
> 1 cup half-and-half cream
> 3 bacon strips, cooked and crumbled

In a Dutch oven or soup kettle, combine the first 12 ingredients; bring to a boil over medium heat. Reduce heat; cover and simmer for 25-35 minutes or until vegetables are tender.

Add cream; heat through but do not boil. Sprinkle with bacon just before serving. **Yield:** 10-12 servings (3 quarts).

best-ever beans and sausage

Robert Saulnier, Clarksburg, Massachusetts
My wife devised this dish, which is extremely popular with our friends and family. When she asks, "What can I share?" the reply is always, "Bring your beans and sausage…and a couple copies of the recipe."

1-1/2	pounds bulk hot pork sausage
1	medium green pepper, chopped
1	medium onion, chopped
1	can (31 ounces) pork and beans
1	can (16 ounces) kidney beans, rinsed and drained
1	can (15-1/2 ounces) great northern beans, rinsed and drained
1	can (15-1/2 ounces) black-eyed peas, rinsed and drained
1	can (15 ounces) pinto beans, rinsed and drained
1	can (15 ounces) garbanzo beans *or* chickpeas, rinsed and drained
1-1/2	cups ketchup
3/4	cup packed brown sugar
2	teaspoons ground mustard

In a skillet, cook sausage over medium heat until no longer pink; drain. Add green pepper and onion; saute until tender.

Drain. Add remaining ingredients; mix well. Pour into a greased 13-in. x 9-in. x 2-in. baking dish. Cover and bake at 325° for 1 hour.

Uncover and bake 20-30 minutes longer or until bubbly. **Yield:** 12-16 servings.

pinto bean dip

Claire Rademacher, Whittier, California
Whenever there's a gathering, friends tell me, "Be sure to bring your bean dip!" With several delightful layers, this is more than a snack—some guests practically make a meal out of it. You'll need big chips to pick up all the scrumptious ingredients.

1	can (29 ounces) pinto beans, rinsed and drained
1-1/4	teaspoons salt, *divided*
1/4	teaspoon pepper
1/8 to 1/4	teaspoon hot pepper sauce
3	ripe avocados, peeled and pitted
4	teaspoons lemon juice
1	cup (8 ounces) sour cream
1/2	cup mayonnaise
1	envelope taco seasoning mix
1	cup sliced green onions
2	medium tomatoes, chopped
1-1/2	cups (6 ounces) shredded cheddar cheese
1	can (2-1/4 ounces) sliced ripe olives, drained

Tortilla chips

In a bowl, mash the beans with a fork; stir in 3/4 teaspoon salt, pepper and hot pepper sauce. Spread onto a 12-in. serving plate.

Mash avocados with lemon juice and remaining salt; spread over bean mixture.

Combine sour cream, mayonnaise and taco seasoning; spread over avocado layer. Sprinkle with onions, tomatoes, cheese and olives. Serve with tortilla chips. **Yield:** 25-30 servings.

hearty red beans and rice

Kathy Jacques, Chesterfield, Michigan

I picked up this recipe while working for the Navy in New Orleans. It's a mouth-watering combination of meats, beans and seasonings. I take this dish to many potlucks and never fail to bring home an empty pot.

- 1 pound dried red kidney beans
- 2 teaspoons garlic salt
- 1 teaspoon Worcestershire sauce
- 1/4 teaspoon hot pepper sauce
- 1 quart water
- 1/2 pound fully cooked ham, diced
- 1/2 pound fully cooked smoked sausage, diced
- 1 cup chopped onion
- 1/2 cup chopped celery
- 3 garlic cloves, minced
- 1 can (8 ounces) tomato sauce
- 2 bay leaves
- 1/4 cup minced fresh parsley
- 1/2 teaspoon salt
- 1/2 teaspoon pepper

Hot cooked rice

Place beans in a Dutch oven or kettle; add water to cover by 2 in. Bring to a boil; boil for 2 minutes. Remove from the heat; cover and let stand for 1 to 4 hours or until softened.

Drain beans and discard liquid. Add garlic salt, Worcestershire sauce, hot pepper sauce and water; bring to a boil. Reduce heat; cover and simmer for 1-1/2 hours.

Meanwhile, in a skillet, saute ham and sausage until lightly browned. Remove with a slotted spoon to bean mixture. Saute onion, celery and garlic in drippings until tender; add to the bean mixture. Stir in tomato sauce and bay leaves. Cover and simmer for 30 minutes or until beans are tender.

Discard bay leaves. Measure 2 cups of beans; mash and return to the bean mixture. Stir in parsley, salt and pepper. Serve over rice. **Yield:** 8-10 servings.

prize winning tips

★ If a recipe calls for tomato, lemon juice or vinegar, add it after the beans are tender. Otherwise, the acid in those ingredients will delay softening of the beans.

Georgia Hennings, Alliance, Nebraska

★ To quick-soak beans, put 1 lb. of dry beans in a kettle and cover with 6 to 8 cups of hot water. Bring to a boil and cook for 2 minutes; cover and remove from heat. Allow to stand for 1 hour. Drain, rinse and cook beans in fresh water. If you want to soak beans overnight, add 6 cups of cold water to 1 lb. of beans. Let stand at room temperature at least 6-8 hours. Drain in morning; rinse and cook beans in fresh water. Whichever method of soaking you use, simmer the beans afterward for about 2 hours or until tender, adding more water if necessary.

Cheryl Miller, Ft. Collins, Colorado

★ Cooked beans may be kept in the refrigerator for 4-5 days and in the freezer for up to 6 months.

Kathy Smith, Bar Harbor, Maine

vegetable chili

Charlene Martorana, Madison, Ohio

This chili, packed with beans and vegetables, has an appealing red color and fabulous flavor. I always make a large batch so that everyone can have seconds.

2 large onions, chopped
1 medium green pepper, chopped
3 garlic cloves, minced
1 tablespoon vegetable oil
1/2 cup water
2 medium carrots, cut into chunks
2 medium potatoes, peeled and cubed
1 can (14-1/2 ounces) chicken broth
1 to 2 tablespoons chili powder
2 tablespoons sugar
1 teaspoon ground cumin
3/4 teaspoon dried oregano
1 small zucchini, sliced 1/4 inch thick
1 small yellow squash, sliced 1/4 inch thick
2 cans (28 ounces *each*) crushed tomatoes
1/3 cup ketchup
1 can (16 ounces) kidney beans, rinsed and drained
1 can (15 ounces) garbanzo beans *or* chickpeas, rinsed and drained
1 can (15 ounces) black beans, rinsed and drained
1 can (15-1/2 ounces) black-eyed peas, rinsed and drained

In a Dutch oven or soup kettle, saute onions, green pepper and garlic in oil until tender. Add water and carrots; cover and cook over medium-low heat for 5 minutes.

Add potatoes, broth, chili powder, sugar, cumin and oregano; cover and cook for 10 minutes.

Add zucchini, squash, tomatoes and ketchup; bring to a boil. Reduce heat; cover and simmer for 15 minutes. Stir in beans and peas; simmer for 10 minutes. **Yield:** 12-16 servings.

bean 'n' burger pockets

Gwen Parsons, Boring, Oregon

This recipe started out as an alternative to baked beans— just for a change of taste. One day I decided to add ground beef and other ingredients, and now it's a main dish we enjoy often.

1-1/4 pounds ground beef
1 can (14-1/2 ounces) diced tomatoes, undrained
1 can (8 ounces) tomato sauce
1/2 cup chopped onion
1 garlic clove, minced
1 tablespoon brown sugar
1 teaspoon seasoned salt
1 teaspoon chili powder
1/2 teaspoon ground cumin
1/8 teaspoon *each* dried thyme, savory, marjoram, oregano and parsley flakes
1 can (8-3/4 ounces) navy beans, rinsed and drained
1 can (8-3/4 ounces) kidney beans, rinsed and drained
1 can (8-3/4 ounces) lima beans, rinsed and drained
5 pita breads, halved
1/2 cup shredded cheddar cheese, optional

In a heavy saucepan or Dutch oven, cook beef over medium heat until no longer pink; drain.

Add tomatoes, tomato sauce, onion, garlic, brown sugar and seasonings. Cover and simmer for 1 hour, stirring occasionally.

Stir in the beans; heat through. Spoon about 1/2 cup into each pita half. Top with the cheese if desired. **Yield:** 5 servings.

crazy quilt salad

Roseanne Martyniuk, Red Deer, Alberta

This sensational bean salad started out with my mother's recipe, which I changed a bit to suit our tastes. The thyme and mustard give it such zest. It's a staple menu item every time our family gets together.

- 1 can (16 ounces) kidney beans, rinsed and drained
- 1 can (15-1/4 ounces) lima beans, rinsed and drained
- 1 can (14-1/2 ounces) cut green beans, drained
- 1 can (14-1/2 ounces) cut wax beans, drained
- 1 cup thinly sliced celery
- 1 large green pepper, chopped
- 1/2 cup thinly sliced onion

DRESSING:
- 1/3 cup cider vinegar
- 1/4 cup vegetable oil
- 1-1/2 teaspoons ground mustard
- 1 teaspoon dried thyme
- 1/2 teaspoon salt
- 1/4 teaspoon pepper
- 1/4 teaspoon garlic powder

Place the first seven ingredients in a large bowl. Combine dressing ingredients; mix well. Pour over bean mixture; toss gently.

Cover and refrigerate for 6 hours or overnight, stirring occasionally. **Yield:** 10-12 servings.

chicken and black bean salad

Cindie Ekstrand, Duarte, California

Here in California, we cook out year-round. I grill extra chicken specifically for this quick meal. It's so colorful and fresh-tasting that even our kids love it.

- 1/3 cup olive oil
- 2 tablespoons lime juice
- 2 tablespoons chopped fresh cilantro
- 1-1/2 teaspoons sugar
- 1 garlic clove, minced
- 1/2 teaspoon chili powder
- 1/2 teaspoon salt, optional
- 1/4 teaspoon pepper
- 1 can (15 ounces) black beans, rinsed and drained
- 1 can (11 ounces) Mexicorn, drained
- 1 medium sweet red pepper, julienned
- 1/3 cup sliced green onions
- 6 cups torn romaine
- 1-1/2 cups cooked chicken strips

Additional cilantro, optional

In a jar with tight-fitting lid, combine the first eight ingredients; shake well and set aside.

In a bowl, toss beans, corn, red pepper and onions; set aside.

Arrange romaine on individual plates; top with bean mixture and chicken. Drizzle with dressing; garnish with cilantro if desired. **Yield:** 6 servings.

OODLES OF NOODLES

#1

PASTA WITH CHICKEN AND SQUASH

pasta with chicken and squash
GRAND PRIZE WINNER

There is no time for doodling or dawdling when noodles are on the menu. Wholesome and hearty, pasta is a palate-pleaser that gets eaten up fast.

An awesome combination of salads, soups, main dishes and desserts make up the winning recipes in our Oodles of Noodles

" It looks and tastes
extra special. "

contest. The collection was selected from nearly 4,500 entries calling for all kinds of pasta.

Trying these delicious recipes, including Grand Prize Winner Pasta with Chicken and Squash, means you'll hardly have to use your noodle to create wonderful meals.

"This is a scrumptious dish we enjoy often," says Pam Hall of Elizabeth City, North Carolina, who shares the recipe. "A bed of pasta is covered with a creamy cheese sauce, tender squash and strips of chicken that have been stir-fried with flavorful herbs. It looks and tastes extra special."

1 package (16 ounces) spiral pasta
2 cups heavy whipping cream
1 tablespoon butter
2 cups (8 ounces) shredded Mexican cheese blend *or* cheddar cheese
1 small onion, chopped
1 garlic clove, minced
5 tablespoons olive oil, *divided*
2 medium zucchini, julienned
2 medium yellow summer squash, julienned
1-1/4 teaspoons salt, *divided*
1/8 teaspoon pepper
1 pound boneless skinless chicken breasts, sliced
1/4 teaspoon *each* dried basil, marjoram and savory
1/4 teaspoon dried rosemary, crushed
1/8 teaspoon rubbed sage

Cook pasta according to package directions. Meanwhile, heat cream and butter in a large saucepan until butter melts. Add cheese; stir until cheese is melted. Rinse and drain pasta; add to cheese mixture. Cover and keep warm.

In a skillet, saute onion and garlic in 3 tablespoons oil until onion is tender. Add squash; cook until tender. Add 1 teaspoon of salt and pepper; remove and keep warm.

Add remaining oil to skillet; cook chicken with herbs and remaining salt until juices run clear. Place pasta on a serving platter; top with chicken and squash. **Yield:** 8 servings.

homemade manicotti

SueAnn Bunt, Painted Post, New York

These tender manicotti are much easier to stuff than the purchased variety. People are always amazed when I say I made my own noodles. My son fixed this recipe for friends, and they were extremely impressed with his cooking skills.

CREPE NOODLES:
1-1/2 cups all-purpose flour
   1 cup milk
   3 eggs
  1/2 teaspoon salt
FILLING:
1-1/2 pounds ricotta cheese
  1/4 cup grated Romano cheese
   1 egg
   1 tablespoon minced fresh parsley *or* 1 teaspoon dried parsley flakes
   1 jar (28 ounces) spaghetti sauce
Shredded Romano cheese, optional

Place flour in a bowl; whisk in milk, eggs and salt until smooth. Heat a lightly greased 8-in. skillet; pour about 2 tablespoons batter into center of skillet. Spread into a 5-in. circle. Cook over medium heat until set; do not brown or turn. Repeat with remaining batter, making 18 crepes. Stack crepes with waxed paper in between; set aside.

For filling, combine cheeses, egg and parsley. Spoon 3-4 tablespoons down the center of each crepe; roll up. Pour half of the spaghetti sauce into an ungreased 13-in. x 9-in. x 2-in. baking dish. Place the crepes seam side down over sauce; pour remaining sauce over top. Cover and bake at 350° for 20 minutes.

Uncover and bake 20 minutes longer or until heated through. Sprinkle with Romano cheese if desired. **Yield:** 6 servings.

spaghetti fruit salad

Carolyn Shepherd, O'Neill, Nebraska

My great-aunt gave me the recipe for this rich, fruity salad, which goes especially well with a ham dinner. Before I ever tasted it, I knew it would be good. I've never left her kitchen disappointed.

   1 cup confectioners' sugar
   2 eggs
  1/2 cup lemon juice
  1/2 teaspoon salt
  1/2 pound spaghetti, broken into 2-inch pieces
   1 can (20 ounces) pineapple tidbits
   3 medium tart apples, diced
   1 carton (8 ounces) frozen whipped topping, thawed
  1/4 cup chopped walnuts
Maraschino cherries, halved

In a saucepan, combine sugar, eggs, lemon juice and salt; cook and stir over medium heat until temperature reaches 160° and mixture is thickened, about 4 minutes. Cool completely.

Cook spaghetti according to package directions; drain and rinse in cold water. Place in a large bowl.

Drain pineapple, reserving juice. Pour juice over the spaghetti; stir in apples. Toss gently; drain. Stir in the egg mixture and pineapple. Cover and refrigerate overnight. Fold in whipped topping just before serving. Garnish with walnuts and cherries. **Yield:** 12-14 servings.

german hot noodle salad

Gordon Kremer, Sacramento, California
Here's a tasty take-off on German potato salad. It tastes like the traditional side dish but uses noodles in place of potatoes. Once my mother served this noodle salad, I was hooked.

- 2 cups wide egg noodles
- 3 bacon strips
- 1/4 cup chopped onion
- 1 tablespoon sugar
- 1 tablespoon all-purpose flour
- 1/4 teaspoon salt
- 1/8 teaspoon ground mustard
- 1/2 cup water
- 1/4 cup cider vinegar
- 1 cup sliced celery
- 2 tablespoons chopped fresh parsley

Cook noodles according to package directions. Meanwhile, in a skillet, cook the bacon over medium heat until crisp. Remove bacon to paper towels to drain, reserving 1 tablespoon drippings. Crumble and set aside.

In the skillet; saute onion in reserved drippings until tender. Stir in sugar, flour, salt and mustard; add water and vinegar. Cook and stir until thickened and bubbly, about 2-3 minutes.

Rinse and drain noodles; add to skillet. Stir in celery and parsley; heat through. Transfer to a serving bowl; sprinkle with bacon. **Yield**: 4 servings.

apricot cheese kugel

Florence Palermo, Melrose Park, Illinois
This sweet noodle kugel is a fun dessert and a super addition to any brunch buffet. My family and friends scrape the pan clean.

- 1 package (16 ounces) wide egg noodles
- 1 package (8 ounces) cream cheese, softened
- 1 cup butter, softened
- 1-1/2 cups sugar
- 1/2 cup lemon juice
- 12 eggs
- 1 jar (18 ounces) apricot preserves
- 1/2 teaspoon ground cinnamon, *divided*

Cook noodles according to package directions. Meanwhile, in a mixing bowl, beat cream cheese, butter and sugar until smooth; add lemon juice and mix well. Beat in eggs, one at a time. Drain and rinse noodles; add to egg mixture.

Spoon half into an ungreased 13-in. x 9-in. x 2-in. baking dish. Top with half of the preserves; sprinkle with half of the cinnamon. Repeat layers.

Bake, uncovered, at 325° for 45 minutes or until golden brown and a knife inserted near the center comes out clean. Serve warm. **Yield:** 12-16 servings.

Editor's Note: Kugel may be reheated in the oven or microwave.

ham and vegetable linguine

Kerry Kerr McAvoy, Rockford, Michigan
I've been pleasing dinner guests with this delicious pasta dish for years. The delicate cream sauce blends well with the colorful and hearty mix of vegetables. I chop the vegetables ahead and later prepare this dish in a snap.

- 1 package (8 ounces) linguine
- 1/2 pound fresh asparagus, cut into 1-inch pieces
- 1/2 pound fresh mushrooms, sliced
- 1 medium carrot, thinly sliced
- 1 medium zucchini, diced
- 2 cups julienned fully cooked ham
- 1/4 cup butter
- 1 cup heavy whipping cream
- 1/2 cup frozen peas
- 3 green onions, sliced
- 1/4 cup grated Parmesan cheese
- 1 teaspoon dried basil
- 3/4 teaspoon salt

Dash each pepper and ground nutmeg
Additional Parmesan cheese, optional

Cook linguine according to package directions. Meanwhile, in a large skillet, saute asparagus, mushrooms, carrot, zucchini and ham in butter until the vegetables are tender.

Add cream, peas, onions, Parmesan, basil, salt, pepper and nutmeg; bring to a boil. Reduce heat; simmer for 3 minutes, stirring frequently.

Rinse and drain linguine; add to vegetable mixture and toss to coat. Sprinkle with Parmesan cheese if desired. **Yield:** 4 servings.

tuna-stuffed jumbo shells

Phy Bresse, Lumberton, North Carolina
These light, fresh-tasting stuffed shells really star as part of a luncheon menu. I came up with this distinctive combination of ingredients by accident one day using leftovers from other recipes. It's a cool summer main dish.

- 10 jumbo pasta shells
- 1/2 cup mayonnaise
- 2 tablespoons sugar
- 1 can (12 ounces) tuna, drained
- 1 cup diced celery
- 1/2 cup diced green onions
- 1/2 cup diced green pepper
- 1/2 cup shredded carrot
- 2 tablespoons minced fresh parsley

CREAMY CELERY DRESSING:
- 1/4 cup sour cream
- 1/4 cup sugar
- 1/4 cup cider vinegar
- 2 tablespoons mayonnaise
- 1 teaspoon celery seed
- 1 teaspoon onion powder

Lettuce leaves and red onion rings, optional

Cook pasta according to package directions; rinse in cold water and drain. In a bowl, combine mayonnaise and sugar. Stir in tuna, celery, onions, green pepper, carrot and parsley. Spoon into pasta shells; cover and refrigerate.

For the dressing, combine sour cream, sugar, vinegar, mayonnaise, celery seed and onion powder.

Arrange lettuce, onion rings and shells on a serving platter; drizzle with dressing. **Yield:** 5 servings.

classic lasagna

Suzanne Barker, Bellingham, Washington

A definite crowd-pleaser, this classic lasagna is thick and meaty with lots of cheese—just the way I like it. Even though my parents were Hungarian, I have a weakness for savory Italian foods like this.

- 1/2 pound bulk Italian sausage
- 1/2 pound ground beef
- 1-1/2 cups diced onion
- 1 cup diced carrot
- 3 garlic cloves, minced
- 1/4 teaspoon crushed red pepper flakes
- 2 cans (28 ounces *each*) whole tomatoes, undrained
- 2 tablespoons tomato paste
- 1 teaspoon *each* sugar, dried oregano and basil
- 1 teaspoon salt
- 1 teaspoon pepper, *divided*
- 2 cartons (15 ounces *each*) ricotta cheese
- 3/4 cup grated Parmesan cheese, *divided*
- 1 egg
- 1/3 cup minced fresh parsley
- 1 package (12 ounces) lasagna noodles, cooked, rinsed and drained
- 2 cups (8 ounces) shredded part-skim mozzarella cheese

In a large saucepan, cook sausage, beef, onion, carrot, garlic and pepper flakes over medium heat, until meat is no longer pink and vegetables are tender; drain.

Add tomatoes, tomato paste, sugar, oregano, basil, salt and 1/2 teaspoon pepper; bring to a boil. Reduce heat; simmer, uncovered, for 45 minutes or until thick, stirring occasionally.

Combine ricotta, 1/2 cup Parmesan cheese, egg, parsley and remaining pepper.

In a greased 13-in. x 9-in. x 2-in. baking dish, layer a fourth of the noodles, a third of the ricotta mixture, a fourth of the meat sauce and 1/2 cup mozzarella cheese. Repeat layers twice. Top with the remaining noodles, sauce and Parmesan.

Cover and bake at 400° for 45 minutes. Sprinkle with remaining mozzarella; bake, uncovered, 10 minutes more. Let stand for 15 minutes before serving. **Yield:** 12 servings.

---

prize winning tips

✳ I make my family's favorite pasta salad with any noodles I have on hand, including spaghetti. But I think it turns out so pretty with tricolored spiral pasta.

Nancy Warren, Baltimore, Maryland

✳ To create a quick chow mein dinner from leftover meat and gravy, cut the meat into bite-size pieces. Cook chopped onion and celery until crisp-tender. Add meat and gravy and heat through.

Thicken with cornstarch, if necessary, then serve over noodles. Let everyone season with soy sauce to suit their own tastes.

Doris Guhr, Hillsboro, Kansas

✳ To give noodles a flavor boost, add a little chicken bouillon to the cooking water.

Angie Becker and Gracie Cargill, Thorndale, Texas

deli-style pasta salad

Joyce McLennan, Algonac, Michigan
Pasta provides a base for this tongue-tingling, make-ahead salad. It has lots of fresh and satisfying ingredients topped with a flavorful dressing. It's terrific to serve to company or take to a potluck.

- 1 package (7 ounces) tricolor spiral pasta
- 6 ounces thinly sliced hard salami, julienned
- 6 ounces provolone cheese, cubed
- 1 can (2-1/4 ounces) sliced ripe olives, drained
- 1 small red onion, thinly sliced
- 1 small zucchini, halved and thinly sliced
- 1/2 cup chopped green pepper
- 1/2 cup chopped sweet red pepper
- 1/4 cup minced fresh parsley
- 1/4 cup grated Parmesan cheese
- 1/2 cup olive oil
- 1/4 cup red wine vinegar
- 1 garlic clove, minced
- 1-1/2 teaspoons ground mustard
- 1 teaspoon dried basil
- 1 teaspoon dried oregano
- 1/4 teaspoon salt
Dash pepper
- 2 medium tomatoes, cut into wedges

Cook the pasta according to package directions; rinse in cold water and drain. Place in a large bowl; add the next nine ingredients.

In a jar with tight-fitting lid, combine the oil, vinegar, garlic, mustard, basil, oregano, salt and pepper; shake well.

Pour over salad; toss to coat. Cover and chill for 8 hours or overnight. Toss before serving. Garnish with tomatoes. **Yield:** 10-12 servings.

never-fail egg noodles

Kathryn Roach, Greers Ferry, Arkansas
Some 30 years ago, the small church I attended held a chicken and noodle fund-raiser supper. I was put in charge of noodles for 200 people! A dear lady shared this recipe and said it had been tried and tested by countless cooks. These noodles are just plain good eating!

- 1 egg plus 3 egg yolks
- 3 tablespoons cold water
- 1 teaspoon salt
- 2 cups all-purpose flour
Chopped fresh parsley, optional

In a mixing bowl, beat egg and yolks until light and fluffy. Add water and salt; mix well. Stir in flour. Turn onto a floured surface; knead until smooth. Divide into thirds. Roll out each portion to 1/8-in. thickness.

Cut noodles to desired width (noodles shown in the photo were cut 2 in. x 1/2 in.). Cook immediately in boiling salted water or chicken broth for 7-9 minutes or until tender.

Drain; sprinkle with parsley if desired. **Yield:** about 5-1/2 cups.

Editor's Note: Uncooked noodles may be stored in the refrigerator for 2-3 days or frozen for up to 1 month.

hearty chicken noodle soup

Cindy Renfrow, Sussex, New Jersey
These wonderful old-fashioned noodles give chicken soup a delightful down-home flavor.

- 1 stewing chicken (about 6 pounds), cut up
- 2 quarts water
- 1 large onion, quartered
- 1 cup chopped fresh parsley
- 1 celery rib, sliced
- 5 chicken bouillon cubes
- 5 whole peppercorns
- 4 whole cloves
- 1 bay leaf
- 2 teaspoons salt
- 1/2 teaspoon pepper
- Dash dried thyme
- 2 medium carrots, thinly sliced

NOODLES:
- 1-1/4 cups all-purpose flour
- 1/2 teaspoon salt
- 1 egg
- 2 tablespoons milk

In a large kettle, combine the first 12 ingredients; slowly bring to a boil. Reduce heat; cover and simmer for 2-1/2 hours or until the chicken is tender.

Remove chicken from broth; cool. Debone chicken; cut into chunks. Strain broth and skim fat; return to kettle. Add chicken and carrots.

For noodles, mix flour and salt in a medium bowl. Make a well in the center. Beat egg and milk; pour into the well. Stir together, forming a dough. Turn dough onto a floured surface; knead 8-10 times.

Roll into a 12-in. x 9-in. rectangle. Cut into 1/2-in. strips; cut strips into 1-in. pieces. Bring soup to a simmer; add noodles. Cover; cook for 12-15 minutes or until noodles are tender. **Yield:** 10-12 servings.

garden spaghetti salad

Gloria O'Bryan, Boulder, Colorado
This refreshing salad is very popular with my family, especially in summer when crisp sweet corn is fresh. It is particularly good alongside a grilled meat entree.

- 8 ounces spaghetti, broken into 2-inch pieces
- 1 tablespoon olive oil
- 2 cups cooked fresh *or* frozen corn
- 2 cups cooked fresh *or* frozen lima beans
- 2 medium tomatoes, peeled, seeded and chopped
- 3/4 cup thinly sliced green onions
- 1/3 cup minced fresh parsley
- 6 bacon strips, cooked and crumbled, *divided*

DRESSING:
- 1/3 cup olive oil
- 3 tablespoons red wine vinegar
- 2 tablespoons lemon juice
- 1 teaspoon sugar
- 1 teaspoon salt
- 1/4 teaspoon paprika
- Dash pepper

Cook spaghetti according to package directions; rinse in cold water and drain. Place in a large bowl; toss with oil. Add the next five ingredients; stir in three-fourths of the bacon.

In a small bowl, whisk all dressing ingredients. Pour over spaghetti mixture; toss gently. Garnish with remaining bacon. Serve immediately or chill. **Yield:** 10-12 servings.

JUST RIGHT RICE

#1

**APRICOT RICE
CUSTARD**

apricot rice custard
GRAND PRIZE WINNER

There's more than a grain of truth to the fact that rice is a key ingredient in many delicious dishes. It can star in bright breakfasts, super salads and side dishes, meaty main dishes and even delightful desserts.

That's just the kind of variety we saw in the more than 3,000 entries we received in the Just Right Rice recipe contest, which featured rice—long-grain, quick-cooking, brown, wild or combinations of these.

> " ...it's simple **and absolutely scrumptious.** "

The judges' tempting choices will convince your family and friends that a meal served with rice is twice as nice. The Grand Prize Winner is Apricot Rice Custard, shared by Elizabeth Montgomery of Taylorville, Illinois. "Creamy rice custard drizzled with apricot sauce makes a comforting dessert or a refreshingly different breakfast," Elizabeth says.

"Even people who haven't been cooking all that long will find it's easy to impress family and guests with this recipe since it's simple and absolutely scrumptious."

1 cup uncooked long grain rice
3 cups milk
1/2 cup sugar
1/2 teaspoon salt
2 eggs, lightly beaten
1/2 teaspoon vanilla extract
1/4 teaspoon almond extract
Dash ground cinnamon
SAUCE:
1 can (8-1/2 ounces) apricot halves
1 can (8 ounces) crushed pineapple, undrained
1/3 cup packed brown sugar
2 tablespoons lemon juice
1 tablespoon cornstarch

In a large saucepan, cook rice according to package directions. Stir in milk, sugar and salt; bring to a boil. Reduce heat to low. Stir 1/2 cup into eggs; return all to the pan, stirring constantly. Cook and stir for 15 minutes or until mixture reaches 160° or coats the back of a metal spoon (do not boil). Remove from the heat; stir in extracts and cinnamon.

For sauce, drain apricot syrup into a saucepan. Chop apricots; add to syrup. Stir in remaining sauce ingredients; bring to a boil. Boil for 2 minutes, stirring occasionally. Serve sauce and custard warm or chilled. **Yield:** 8-10 servings.

sizzling rice soup

Mary Woodke, Gardiner, New York
My family enjoys food with flair like this unique Asian soup. Whenever I serve it, it's such a hit that no one has much room for the main course. The children get a real kick out of watching the fried rice sizzle when it is added to the simmering soup.

1 cup uncooked long grain rice
8 cups chicken broth
2 cups cubed cooked chicken
2 cups sliced fresh mushrooms
1/4 cup chopped green onions
1 can (8 ounces) bamboo shoots, drained
1 can (8 ounces) sliced water chestnuts, drained
4 chicken bouillon cubes
1/2 teaspoon garlic powder
1 package (10 ounces) frozen peas
1/4 cup vegetable oil

Cook rice according to package directions. Spread on a greased 15-in. x 10-in. x 1-in. baking pan. Bake at 325° for 2 hours or until dried and browned, stirring occasionally; set aside.

In a large soup kettle or Dutch oven, combine the broth, chicken, mushrooms, onions, bamboo shoots, water chestnuts, bouillon and garlic powder. Cover and simmer for 1 hour.

Add peas; cook for 15 minutes more. Just before serving, heat oil in a skillet. Fry rice in hot oil until it is slightly puffed. Ladle soup into individual serving bowls. Immediately spoon some of the hot rice into each bowl. **Yield:** 10-12 servings (3 quarts).

> ✳If I have extra cooked long grain or wild rice after preparing a meal, I use the leftovers the next morning stirred into a batch of scrambled eggs. It really perks up breakfast.
>
> Sylvia Wiczek, Cushing, Minnesota

cranberry wild rice pilaf

Pat Gardetta, Osage Beach, Missouri
This wonderful, moist side dish is perfect for the holidays or anytime a meal requires a special touch. Dried cranberries, currants and almonds add color and texture. The ladies I work with all enjoy making this dish.

3/4 cup uncooked wild rice
3 cups chicken broth
1/2 cup pearl barley
1/4 cup dried cranberries
1/4 cup dried currants
1 tablespoon butter
1/3 cup sliced almonds, toasted

Rinse and drain rice; place in a saucepan. Add broth and bring to a boil. Reduce heat; cover and simmer for 10 minutes.

Remove from the heat; stir in the barley, cranberries, currants and butter. Spoon into a greased 1-1/2-qt. baking dish.

Cover and bake at 325° for 55 minutes or until liquid is absorbed and rice is tender. Add almonds and fluff with a fork. **Yield:** 6-8 servings.

three-rice pilaf

Ricki Bingham, Ogden, Utah
My family's favorite rice dish is this tempting medley of white, brown and wild rice. I prepare it as a side dish or a stuffing. In fall I add chopped dried apricots, and for the holidays I mix in dried cranberries. My guests always ask for seconds.

- 1/2 cup uncooked brown rice
- 1/2 cup finely chopped carrots
- 1/2 cup chopped onion
- 1/2 cup sliced fresh mushrooms
- 2 tablespoons vegetable oil
- 1/2 cup uncooked wild rice
- 3 cups chicken broth
- 1/4 teaspoon dried thyme
- 1/4 teaspoon dried rosemary, crushed
- 1/2 cup uncooked long grain rice
- 1/3 cup chopped dried apricots
- 2 tablespoons minced green onions
- 1/4 teaspoon salt
- 1/8 teaspoon pepper
- 1/2 cup chopped pecans, toasted

In a large saucepan, saute the brown rice, carrots, onion and mushrooms in oil for 10 minutes or until the rice is golden.

Add wild rice, broth, thyme and rosemary; bring to a boil. Reduce heat; cover and simmer for 25 minutes.

Stir in long grain rice; cover and simmer for 25 minutes or until liquid is absorbed and wild rice is tender. Remove from the heat; stir in apricots, green onions, salt and pepper. Cover and let stand for 5 minutes. Sprinkle with pecans just before serving. **Yield:** 8-10 servings.

curried rice ham rolls

Pamela Witte, Hastings, Nebraska
My mother gave me this recipe, which had been handed down to her. She prepared these hearty, flavorful ham rolls often for church luncheons, and they were a huge success every time. I find that even people who have never tried curry rave about the flavor.

- 1/2 cup chopped onion
- 2 tablespoons butter
- 4 cups cooked brown *or* long grain rice
- 1 tablespoon dried parsley flakes
- 1 teaspoon salt
- 1/2 teaspoon curry powder
- 12 slices deli ham (1/8 inch thick)
- 4 hard-cooked eggs, sliced

CURRY SAUCE:
- 1/4 cup butter
- 2 tablespoons cornstarch
- 1/4 teaspoon curry powder
- 1/4 teaspoon salt
- 2 cups milk

In a skillet, saute onion in butter until tender, about 3 minutes. In a large bowl, combine rice, parsley, salt, curry powder and onion.

Spoon about 1/3 cup down the center of each ham slice; roll up. Secure with toothpicks if desired. Place seam side down in a greased 13-in. x 9-in. x 2-in. baking pan. Arrange eggs on top.

For sauce, melt butter in a saucepan. Stir cornstarch, curry powder and salt until smooth. Gradually stir in milk. Bring to a boil; cook and stir for 2 minutes or until thickened.

Pour over the ham rolls. Cover and bake at 375° for 25 minutes. Uncover and bake for 10 minutes longer. **Yield:** 6 servings.

rice-stuffed peppers

Lisa Easley, Longview, Texas
Mother fixed this dish when we had company. The cheese sauce sets these stuffed peppers apart from others.

- 2 pounds ground beef
- 1 medium onion, chopped
- 1 small green pepper, chopped
- 2 garlic cloves, minced
- 1-1/2 teaspoons salt
- 1/2 teaspoon pepper
- 3-3/4 cups water
- 1 can (14-1/2 ounces) diced tomatoes, undrained
- 1 can (10 ounces) diced tomatoes and green chilies, undrained
- 1 can (15 ounces) tomato sauce
- 1 tablespoon ground cumin
- 3 cups uncooked instant rice
- 4 medium green peppers

CHEESE SAUCE:
- 1-1/2 pounds process American cheese, cubed
- 1 can (10 ounces) diced tomatoes and green chilies, undrained

In a Dutch oven, cook beef, onion, green pepper, garlic, salt and pepper over medium heat until beef is no longer pink; drain. Add the water, tomatoes, tomato sauce and cumin. Bring to a boil. Reduce heat; simmer, uncovered, for 10 minutes.

Stir in the rice; simmer, uncovered, for 5 minutes. Remove from the heat; cover and let stand for 5 minutes. Remove tops and seeds from the peppers; cut in half widthwise. Place in a large pan of boiling water; boil for 4 minutes.

Drain peppers and stuff with meat mixture. Place remaining meat mixture in an ungreased 13-in. x 9-in. x

2-in. baking dish; top with stuffed peppers, pressing down gently.

Cover and bake at 350° for 1 hour. In a saucepan, heat sauce ingredients until cheese is melted. Serve over peppers. **Yield:** 8 servings.

rice croquettes

Lucia Edwards, Cotati, California
As a newlywed, I used to agonize over meal preparation. Now I enjoy trying new recipes, and some—like this tasty side dish—turn out to be very popular with my family. These croquettes are crisp and golden and add some fun to a simple dinner like roast chicken and salad.

- 1/2 cup chopped onion
- 2 tablespoons butter
- 1 cup uncooked long grain rice
- 2-1/4 cups chicken broth
- 2 tablespoons chopped fresh parsley
- 1 egg, lightly beaten
- 1/2 cup grated Parmesan cheese
- 1 teaspoon dried basil
- 1/4 teaspoon pepper
- 1/2 cup dry bread crumbs

Cooking oil
Additional fresh parsley, optional

In a large saucepan, saute onion in butter until tender. Add rice; saute 3 minutes. Stir in broth and parsley; bring to a boil. Reduce heat; cover and simmer for 20 minutes. Cool for 30 minutes.

Stir in egg, cheese, basil and pepper. Moisten hands with water and shape 1/4 cupfuls into logs. Roll in crumbs.

In an electric skillet, heat 1/4 in. of oil to 365°. Fry croquettes, a few at time, for 3-4 minutes or until crisp and golden, turning often. Drain on paper towels. Garnish with parsley if desired. **Yield:** 16 croquettes.

creole skillet dinner

Bonnie Brann, Pasco, Washington

While living in Canada, I sampled this colorful dish at a neighbor's. The following Christmas, I served it instead of my traditional turkey, and I received numerous compliments on it. I frequently substitute shrimp or sausage for the chicken...or add all three.

- 4 cups chicken broth
- 2-1/2 cups uncooked long grain rice
- 1 cup chopped red onion
- 3 garlic cloves, minced, *divided*
- 1-1/4 teaspoons chili powder
- 1 teaspoon salt
- 1/2 teaspoon ground turmeric
- 1/4 teaspoon pepper
- 1 bay leaf
- 1 medium sweet red pepper, julienned
- 1 medium green pepper, julienned
- 2 green onions, sliced
- 1 teaspoon chopped fresh parsley
- 1/2 teaspoon dried basil
- 1/2 teaspoon dried thyme
- 1/4 teaspoon hot pepper sauce
- 2 tablespoons butter
- 1 cup sliced fresh mushrooms
- 1 medium tomato, chopped
- 1 cup frozen peas
- 1 pound boneless skinless chicken breasts, thinly sliced
- 2 tablespoons lemon juice
- 1/3 cup sliced almonds, toasted

In a saucepan, bring the broth, rice, onion, 1 teaspoon garlic, chili powder, salt, turmeric, pepper and bay leaf to a boil. Reduce heat; cover and simmer for 20 minutes or until rice is tender. Discard bay leaf.

In a skillet over medium-high heat, saute the next seven ingredients and remaining garlic in butter for 2 minutes. Add mushrooms; cook until peppers are crisp-tender. Add the tomato and peas; heat through. Remove from the heat. Add rice; keep warm.

In a skillet, cook and stir chicken in lemon juice over medium-high heat until no longer pink. Add to rice mixture; toss. Top with the almonds. **Yield:** 6 servings.

prize winning tips

★ I like to garnish my wild rice soup with toasted almonds. To toast 1/2 cup slivered almonds, in a skillet, saute almonds in 1/2 teaspoon melted butter over medium heat until almonds are golden brown. Watch carefully, since the nuts will go quickly from golden to burnt.

Donna Pfeilsticker, Shoreview, Minnesota

★ I give a little zip to my chicken and rice bake by adding garlic powder and Parmesan cheese to the recipe.

Karen Alexander, Gorrie, Ontario

★ Instead of the usual oatmeal or bread crumbs in my meat loaf, I use leftover cooked rice. It makes a tasty main dish we all look forward to.

Kathryn Lillie, Bothell, Washington

wild rice meat loaf

Genie Lang, Jamestown, North Dakota

I've shared this recipe with many friends. The unique, hearty meat loaf is full of surprises—tangy wild rice and pockets of cheddar cheese make it extra special. Even so, it's not that tricky to prepare…try it and see!

   2 eggs, beaten
   4 cups cooked wild rice
   2 cups (8 ounces) shredded cheddar cheese
   1 cup dry bread crumbs
   1 cup finely chopped onion
1/2 cup all-purpose flour
1-1/4 teaspoons salt
   1 teaspoon rubbed sage
3/4 teaspoon pepper
   1 pound uncooked lean ground beef

In a large bowl, combine the first nine ingredients. Crumble beef over mixture and mix well.

Firmly press into a greased 9-in. x 5-in. x 3-in. loaf pan. Bake, uncovered, at 350° for 70 minutes. Cover with foil during the last 15 minutes if the top is browning too quickly. **Yield:** 4-6 servings.

lemon rice salad

Margery Richmond, Lacombe, Alberta

This refreshing salad is wonderful served year-round. I have taken it to potluck suppers and made it for family barbecues, picnics and dinner parties. People seem to take to the combination of flavors in this dish. I like that it can be made ahead and still taste like I really fussed.

   1 cup olive oil
1/3 cup white wine vinegar
   1 garlic clove, minced
   1 to 2 teaspoons grated lemon peel
   2 teaspoons sugar
   1 teaspoon Dijon mustard
1/2 teaspoon salt
   6 cups cooked long grain rice
   2 cups cooked wild rice
   2 cups diced seeded cucumbers
2/3 cup thinly sliced green onions
1/4 cup minced fresh parsley
1/4 cup minced fresh basil *or* 1 tablespoon dried basil
1/2 teaspoon pepper
1/2 cup chopped pecans, toasted

In a jar with tight-fitting lid, combine the first seven ingredients; shake well.

In a large bowl, combine long grain and wild rice; add dressing and toss. Cover and refrigerate overnight.

Add the cucumbers, green onions, parsley, basil and pepper; mix well. Chill for 2 hours. Fold in pecans just before serving. **Yield:** 16-18 servings.

chicken rice burritos

Suzanne Adams, Laguna Niguel, California
For a nice alternative to beef and bean burritos, I use this recipe, which I discovered several years back. If I fix the chicken mixture the night before, the next day's dinner is a real snap.

  1/3 cup sliced green onions
    1 garlic clove, minced
    2 tablespoons butter
    7 cups shredded cooked chicken
    1 tablespoon chili powder
2-1/2 cups chicken broth, *divided*
    1 jar (16 ounces) picante sauce, *divided*
    1 cup uncooked long grain rice
  1/2 cup sliced ripe olives
    3 cups (12 ounces) shredded cheddar cheese, *divided*
  12 flour tortillas (10 inches), warmed
Additional picante sauce and cheddar cheese

In a skillet, saute onions and garlic in butter until tender. Stir in chicken, chili powder, 1/4 cup broth and 3/4 cup of picante sauce. Heat through; set aside.

In a medium saucepan, bring rice and remaining broth to a boil. Reduce heat; cover and simmer 20 minutes. Stir in remaining picante sauce; cover and simmer 5-10 minutes or until rice is tender. Stir into chicken mixture. Add olives and 2 cups cheese.

Spoon 1 cup filling, off center, on each tortilla. Fold sides and ends over filling, then roll up. Arrange burritos in two ungreased 13-in. x 9-in. x 2-in. baking dishes.

Sprinkle with the remaining cheese. Cover and bake at 375° for 10-15 minutes or until heated through. Garnish with picante sauce and cheese. **Yield:** 6 servings.

better than potato salad

Susan McCurdy, Elmhurst, Illinois
As soon as our family tried this delicious salad, it became a favorite, especially during the warmer months. It's a flavorful change of pace from traditional potato salad and it's easy to prepare. Everyone enjoys it.

    4 cups cooked long grain rice
    8 radishes, sliced
    4 hard-cooked eggs, chopped
    1 medium cucumber, seeded and chopped
    2 cups thinly sliced celery
  1/2 cup chopped onion
1-1/2 cups mayonnaise
    3 tablespoons prepared mustard
  3/4 teaspoon salt

In a large bowl, combine rice, radishes, eggs, cucumber, celery and onion. Combine mayonnaise, mustard and salt; mix well.

Pour over rice mixture and toss. Cover and refrigerate at least 1 hour. **Yield:** 12-14 servings.

"SAY CHEESE!"

#1

SAVORY
CHEESE SOUP

savory cheese soup

Cheese has a wonderful way of making everything you cook taste better. It adds appeal to many vegetables, builds creamy richness into snacks, soups and desserts, brings tang to dressings and sauces and makes hearty main dishes even more satisfying.

Our "Say Cheese!" contest proved the popularity of this "dairy" good ingredient—cooks from across the country entered nearly 3,000 recipes featuring many of their favorite cheeses such as flavorful cheddar, mozzarella, Parmesan and Swiss.

"Its big cheese taste blends wonderfully with the flavor of the vegetables."

The cheesy choices our judges selected as the winners are sure to bring satisfied smiles to the faces of family and friends when you prepare the recipes in your kitchen, too. Grand Prize Winner Savory Cheese Soup especially so.

"This delicious soup recipe was shared by a friend and instantly became a hit with my husband," says Dee Falk of Stromsburg, Nebraska. "Its big cheese taste blends wonderfully with the flavor of the vegetables."

1/4 cup chopped onion
3 tablespoons butter
1/4 cup all-purpose flour
1/4 teaspoon salt
1/8 teaspoon pepper
1/8 teaspoon garlic powder
2 cups milk
1 can (14-1/2 ounces) chicken broth
1/2 cup shredded carrots
1/2 cup finely chopped celery
1-1/2 cups (6 ounces) shredded cheddar cheese
3/4 cup shredded part-skim mozzarella cheese
Fresh *or* dried chives, optional

In a large saucepan, saute onion in butter until tender. Add the flour, salt, pepper and garlic powder; stir until smooth. Gradually add the milk; cook and stir over medium heat until thickened and bubbly.

Meanwhile, bring chicken broth to a boil in a small saucepan. Add carrots and celery; simmer for 5 minutes or until vegetables are tender. Add to milk mixture and stir until blended. Add cheeses. Cook and stir until melted (do not boil). Garnish with chives if desired.
Yield: about 4 servings.

muenster bread

Melanie Mero, Ida, Michigan
My sister and I won blue ribbons in 4-H with this bread many years ago. The recipe makes a beautiful round loaf with a layer of cheese peeking out of every slice.

   2 packages (1/4 ounce *each*) active dry yeast
   1 cup warm milk (110° to 115°)
 1/2 cup butter, softened
   2 tablespoons sugar
   1 teaspoon salt
3-1/4 to 3-3/4 cups all-purpose flour
   1 egg plus 1 egg yolk
   4 cups (1 pound) shredded Muenster cheese
   1 egg white, beaten

In a large mixing bowl, dissolve yeast in milk. Add butter, sugar, salt and 2 cups flour; beat until smooth. Stir in enough remaining flour to form a soft dough.

Turn onto a floured surface; knead until smooth and elastic, about 6-8 minutes. Place in a greased bowl, turning once to grease top. Cover and let rise in a warm place until doubled, about 1 hour. In a large bowl, beat egg and yolk; stir in cheese.

Punch dough down; roll into a 16-in. circle. Place in a greased 9-in. round baking pan, letting dough drape over the edges. Spoon the cheese mixture into center of dough. Gather dough up over filling in 1-1/2-in. pleats. Gently squeeze pleats together at top and twist to make a top knot. Allow to rise 10-15 minutes.

Brush loaf with egg white. Bake at 375° for 45-50 minutes. Cool on a wire rack for 20 minutes. Serve warm. **Yield:** 1 loaf.

cheese-stuffed shells

Lori Mecca, Grants Pass, Oregon
I tasted this rich, cheesy pasta dish at an Italian restaurant. I got the recipe and made a few changes to it.

   1 pound bulk Italian sausage
   1 large onion, chopped
   1 package (10 ounces) frozen chopped spinach, cooked and well drained
   1 package (8 ounces) cream cheese, softened
   1 egg, beaten
   2 cups (8 ounces) shredded part-skim mozzarella cheese, *divided*
   2 cups (8 ounces) shredded cheddar cheese
   1 cup cottage cheese
 1/4 cup grated Parmesan cheese
 1/4 teaspoon *each* salt and pepper
 1/8 teaspoon ground cinnamon, optional
  20 jumbo shell noodles, cooked and drained
SAUCE:
   1 can (29 ounces) tomato sauce
   1 tablespoon dried minced onion
1-1/2 teaspoons *each* dried basil and parsley flakes
   2 garlic cloves, minced
   1 teaspoon *each* sugar and dried oregano
 1/2 teaspoon salt
 1/4 teaspoon pepper

In a skillet, cook sausage and onion until meat is no longer pink; drain. Transfer to a large bowl. Stir in spinach, cream cheese and egg. Add 1 cup mozzarella, cheddar, cottage cheese, Parmesan and seasonings; mix well.

Stuff shells and arrange in a greased 13-in. x 9-in. x 2-in. baking dish. Combine sauce ingredients. Spoon over shells. Cover and bake at 350° for 40 minutes. Uncover; sprinkle with remaining mozzarella. Return to oven for 5 minutes or until cheese melts. **Yield:** 8-10 servings.

crustless swiss quiche

Marlene Kole, Highland Heights, Ohio

I received this recipe from my mother-in-law, an all-around great cook. Everyone raves about her quiche when she serves it at card parties. I love to cook, and turn to this staple when company vists.

- 1/2 cup butter
- 1/2 cup all-purpose flour
- 1-1/2 cups milk
- 2-1/2 cups cottage cheese
- 1 teaspoon baking powder
- 1 teaspoon salt
- 1 teaspoon Dijon mustard
- 9 eggs
- 2 packages (one 8 ounces, one 3 ounces) cream cheese, softened
- 3 cups (12 ounces) shredded Swiss cheese
- 1/3 cup grated Parmesan cheese

Melt butter in a medium saucepan. Stir in flour; cook and stir until bubbly. Gradually add milk; cook over medium heat, stirring occasionally, until sauce thickens. Remove from the heat; set aside to cool, about 15-20 minutes.

Meanwhile, combine cottage cheese, baking powder, salt and mustard; set aside. In a large mixing bowl, beat the eggs. Slowly add cream cheese, cottage cheese mixture and cream sauce. Fold in Swiss and Parmesan cheeses.

Pour into two greased 10-in. pie plates. Bake at 350° for 40 minutes or until puffed and lightly browned. Serve immediately. **Yield:** 16-20 servings.

mozzarella sticks

Mary Merchant, Barre, Vermont

I'm particularly fond of these tasty snacks because they're baked, not fried. Cheese is one of my family's favorite foods. Being of Italian descent, I cook often with ricotta and mozzarella cheeses.

- 2 eggs
- 1 tablespoon water
- 1 cup dry bread crumbs
- 2-1/2 teaspoons Italian seasoning
- 1/2 teaspoon garlic powder
- 1/8 teaspoon pepper
- 12 sticks string cheese
- 3 tablespoons all-purpose flour
- 1 tablespoon butter, melted
- 1 cup marinara *or* spaghetti sauce, heated

In a small bowl, beat eggs and water. In a plastic bag, combine bread crumbs, Italian seasoning, garlic powder and pepper. Coat cheese sticks in flour, then dip in egg mixture and bread crumb mixture. Repeat egg and bread crumb coatings. Cover and chill for at least 4 hours or overnight.

Place on an ungreased baking sheet; drizzle with butter. Bake, uncovered, at 400° for 6-8 minutes or until heated through. Allow to stand for 3-5 minutes before serving. Use marinara or spaghetti sauce for dipping. **Yield:** 4-6 servings.

Editor's Note: Regular mozzarella cheese, cut into 4-in. x 1/2-in. sticks, can be substituted for the string cheese.

lasagna in a bun

Cindy Morelock, Afton, Tennessee

Here's an interesting and delicious way to serve a great main dish and enjoy several different cheeses. My family loves the meat sauce and cheese tucked into the buns.

 8 sub *or* hoagie buns (8 inches)
 1 pound ground beef
 1 cup spaghetti sauce
 1 tablespoon garlic powder
 1 tablespoon dried Italian seasoning
 1 cup ricotta cheese
 1/4 cup grated Parmesan cheese
 1 cup (4 ounces) shredded cheddar cheese, *divided*
 1 cup (4 ounces) shredded part-skim mozzarella cheese, *divided*

Cut thin slices off the tops of the buns. Hollow out centers, leaving 1/4-in.-thick shells; discard tops and center or save for another use. In a skillet, cook ground beef over medium heat until no longer pink; drain. Add spaghetti sauce, garlic powder and Italian seasoning. Cook 4-5 minutes or until heated through.

Meanwhile, combine ricotta, Parmesan and half of cheddar and mozzarella cheeses; mix well. Spoon meat sauce into buns; top with cheese mixture. Place on a baking sheet. Cover loosely with foil.

Bake at 350° for 20-25 minutes. Uncover; sprinkle with remaining cheddar and mozzarella. Return to the oven for 2-3 minutes or until the cheese melts. **Yield:** 8 servings.

hot pizza dip

Karen Riordan, Fern Creek, Kentucky

I'm a busy stay-at-home mom. I love this recipe because it's easy to prepare in advance and keep refrigerated. I simply put it in the oven when guests arrive, and by the time I've poured beverages, the dip is ready to serve. It gets gobbled up quickly!

 1 package (8 ounces) cream cheese, softened
 1 teaspoon Italian seasoning
 1/4 teaspoon garlic powder
 2 cups (8 ounces) shredded part-skim mozzarella cheese
 1 cup (4 ounces) shredded cheddar cheese
 1/2 cup pizza sauce
 1/2 cup finely chopped green pepper
 1/2 cup finely chopped sweet red pepper
Tortilla chips *or* breadsticks

In a bowl, combine the cream cheese, Italian seasoning and garlic powder; spread on the bottom of a greased 9-in. pie plate. Combine the mozzarella and cheddar cheeses; sprinkle half over the cream cheese layer. Top with the pizza sauce and peppers. Sprinkle with the remaining cheeses.

Bake at 350° for 20 minutes. Serve warm with tortilla chips or breadsticks. **Yield:** about 3-1/2 cups.

runners-up

luscious almond cheesecake

Brenda Clifford, Overland Park, Kansas

I received this recipe along with a set of springform pans from a cousin at my wedding shower. It makes a heavenly cheesecake. My son Tommy often requests it in place of a birthday cake.

CRUST:
1-1/4 cups crushed vanilla wafers
3/4 cup finely chopped almonds
1/4 cup sugar
1/3 cup butter, melted

FILLING:
4 packages (8 ounces *each*) cream cheese, softened
1-1/4 cups sugar
4 eggs
1-1/2 teaspoons almond extract
1 teaspoon vanilla extract

TOPPING:
2 cups (16 ounces) sour cream
1/4 cup sugar
1 teaspoon vanilla extract
1/8 cup toasted sliced almonds

In a bowl, combine wafers, almonds and sugar; add the butter and mix well. Press into the bottom of an ungreased 10-in. springform pan; set aside.

In a large mixing bowl, beat cream cheese and sugar until creamy. Add the eggs, one at a time, beating well after each addition. Add extracts; beat just until blended.

Pour into crust. Bake at 350° for 55 minutes or until center is almost set. Remove from the oven; let stand for 5 minutes.

Combine sour cream, sugar and vanilla; spread over filling. Return to the oven for 5 minutes. Cool on a wire rack; chill overnight. Just before serving, sprinkle with almonds and remove sides of pan. Store in the refrigerator. **Yield:** 14-16 servings.

---

prize winning tips

* * * * *

*For maximum flavor, I let platters of sliced cheese sit out at room temperature for 30 minutes before serving.

Beth Thompson, Spokane, Washington

*My family loves cheese-stuffed manicotti, but stuffing the shells is no fun. A friend told me that she uses wonton wrappers instead of noodles. Simply place the filling on each wrapper and roll up. Then place the rolls in a pan seam side down and proceed with your regular recipe. After trying this method once, it is the only way I make manicotti.

Beverly Norris, Evanston, Wyoming

*Cheese reacts quickly to heat, so it's best to cook it slowly over low heat. To prevent cheese from curdling when I'm making a sauce or fondue, I toss the shredded cheese with a little flour or cornstarch first.

Gale Narlock, Wausau, Wisconsin

APPLE LADDER LOAF

apple ladder loaf
GRAND PRIZE WINNER

There is no greater simple pleasure than biting into a crunchy apple right off the tree. Now you and your family can enjoy that terrific taste anytime.

Apples are the shining stars of our Apple-a-Day recipe contest which brought in an assortment of appetizing dishes that rivals the numerous varieties of the flavorful fruit itself. With the best-of-the-best recipes here and on the following pages demonstrating how deliciously adaptable apples can be, how can you resist? Go ahead...take your pick.

> "Brimming with apples, the golden loaf is as versatile as it is attractive."

You may want to start with Apple Ladder Loaf, the Grand Prize Winner shared by Norma Foster of Compton, Illinois. "I first served my family this tender, tasty bread years ago," Norma says. "From the very first bite, it was a hit with everyone.

"Now I bake it often for church groups, potluck dinners and parties with friends. Brimming with apples, the golden loaf is as versatile as it is attractive. It works as a nice breakfast pastry or with a scoop of ice cream as a lovely dessert."

2 packages (1/4 ounce *each*) active dry yeast
1/4 cup warm water (110° to 115°)
1/2 cup warm milk (110° to 115°)
1/2 cup butter, softened
1/3 cup sugar
4 eggs
1 teaspoon salt
4-1/2 to 4-3/4 cups all-purpose flour
FILLING:
1/3 cup packed brown sugar
2 tablespoons all-purpose flour
1-1/4 teaspoons ground cinnamon
1/2 teaspoon ground nutmeg
1/8 teaspoon ground allspice
4 cups thinly sliced peeled tart apples
1/4 cup butter, softened
ICING:
1 cup confectioners' sugar
1 to 2 tablespoons orange juice
1/4 teaspoon vanilla extract

In a mixing bowl, dissolve yeast in water. Add milk, butter, sugar, salt, eggs and 2 cups flour. Beat on low speed for 3 minutes. Stir in enough remaining flour to form a soft dough. Knead on a floured surface until smooth and elastic, about 6-8 minutes. Place in a greased bowl, turning once to grease top. Cover and refrigerate overnight; punch down after 1-2 hours.

For filling, combine sugar, flour, cinnamon, nutmeg and allspice in a small bowl. Add apples; toss to coat. Set aside.

Punch dough down; divide in half. Roll each half into a 12-in. x 9-in. rectangle. Place each rectangle on a greased baking sheet. Spread with butter. Spread filling down center third of each rectangle.

On each long side, cut 1-in.-wide strips 3 in. into center. Starting at one end, fold alternating strips at an angle across filling; seal ends. Cover and let rise for 45-60 minutes or until nearly doubled.

Bake at 350° for 30-40 minutes or until golden brown. Combine icing ingredients until smooth; drizzle over warm loaves. Serve warm or at room temperature. **Yield:** 2 loaves.

apple snack squares

Julia Quintrell, Sumerco, West Virginia
As soon as I was old enough to stand on a chair, I started cooking. This recipe came from my sister-in-law. It's a favorite at our large family gatherings.

- 2 cups sugar
- 2 eggs
- 3/4 cup vegetable oil
- 2-1/2 cups self-rising flour
- 1 teaspoon ground cinnamon
- 3 cups diced peeled tart apples
- 1 cup chopped walnuts
- 3/4 cup butterscotch chips

In a bowl, combine sugar, eggs and oil. Stir in flour and cinnamon (batter will be thick). Stir in apples and nuts. Spread into a greased 13-in. x 9-in. x 2-in. baking pan. Sprinkle with chips.

Bake at 350° for 35-40 minutes or until golden and a toothpick inserted near the center comes out clean. Cool before cutting. **Yield:** 2 dozen.

Editor's Note: As a substitute for each cup of self-rising flour, place 1-1/2 teaspoons of baking powder and 1/2 teaspoon of salt in a measuring cup. Add all-purpose flour to equal 1 cup.

pork roast with apple topping

Paula Neal, Dolores, Colorado
Since I was in 4-H, I've been an avid cook. This recipe's one my mother-in-law and I developed together. The topping also goes great with pork chops, lean sausage balls or patties and ham.

- 1 boneless pork loin roast (3 to 3-1/2 pounds), trimmed
- 1/2 teaspoon poultry seasoning
- 1 jar (10 ounces) apple jelly
- 1 cup apple juice
- 1/2 teaspoon ground cardamom
- 1 cup chopped peeled tart fresh *or* dried apples
- 3 tablespoons chopped fresh *or* dried cranberries
- 5 teaspoons cornstarch
- 2 tablespoons water

Place roast on a rack in a shallow roasting pan and rub with poultry seasoning. Bake, uncovered, at 325° for 2-1/2 hours or until a meat thermometer reads 160°.

For topping, combine the apple jelly, juice and cardamom in a saucepan. Cook and stir over low heat until smooth. Add apples and cranberries; cook until tender, about 5-10 minutes.

Combine cornstarch and water until smooth; stir into apple mixture. Bring to a boil; cook and stir for 1-2 minutes or until thickened.

Remove roast from oven and let stand for 10 minutes before slicing. Serve with apple topping. **Yield:** 8-10 servings (about 2 cups topping).

caramel apple cream pie

Lisa Dinuccio, Boxford, Massachusetts
When I first made this pie for my family, the reactions weren't real words—they were more "Ooh!" and "Mmm!" I created it to enter in a local fair. My goal was an apple pie like no other, and it ended up winning third prize. "That was very interesting!" one judge said.

      1 pastry shell (9 inches)
  1/4 cup butter
  1/2 cup packed brown sugar
      4 medium tart apples, peeled and cut into
          1/2-inch chunks
  1-1/2 teaspoons pumpkin pie spice, *divided*
      1 to 2 tablespoons all-purpose flour
  1/2 cup caramel ice cream topping
  1/2 cup chopped pecans
      1 package (8 ounces) cream cheese, softened
  1/4 cup sugar
      1 egg
      1 tablespoon lemon juice
      1 teaspoon vanilla extract
Whipped topping

Bake pastry shell but do not prick. Cool. In a large skillet over medium heat, melt butter and brown sugar. Stir in apples and 1 teaspoon pumpkin pie spice; simmer for 12-15 minutes, stirring frequently, or until tender.

Stir in flour; cook and stir for 1 minute. Drizzle caramel topping over pastry shell; sprinkle with pecans. Spoon apple mixture over pecans; set aside.

In a mixing bowl, combine cream cheese, sugar, egg, lemon juice and vanilla; beat until smooth. Pour over apples. Bake at 350° for 35-45 minutes or until a knife inserted into the cream cheese layer comes out clean.

Cool on a wire rack. Chill thoroughly. To serve, top with dollops of whipped topping; sprinkle with remaining pumpkin pie spice. **Yield:** 8 servings.

honey apple salad

Mary Lou Hawkins, Brook Park, Ohio
All my favorite recipes are quick, simple and tasty. I came across this salad while looking for something to make with honey. Substituting several of the ingredients, I served it to my husband and two daughters. It was a hit!

  3-1/2 cups diced red apples
      2 tablespoons lemon juice
      2 cups green grapes
      1 cup thinly sliced celery
  1/2 cup chopped dates
  1/2 cup mayonnaise
  1/4 cup honey
      2 tablespoons sour cream
  1/2 teaspoon salt
  1/2 cup chopped walnuts

In a large bowl, toss apples with lemon juice. Add grapes, celery and dates.

In a small bowl, combine mayonnaise, honey, sour cream and salt; mix well.

Pour over apple mixture and toss to coat. Stir in the nuts. Serve immediately. **Yield:** 6-8 servings.

apple dumpling dessert

Janet Weaver, Wooster, Ohio
The credit for this goes to one of our three grown daughters. My husband loves apple dumplings, but they take so long to make. So Kathy created a quick-to-fix variation with a nice bonus: no bites of dry crust without filling since it's all mixed throughout!

PASTRY:
- 4 cups all-purpose flour
- 2 teaspoons salt
- 1-1/3 cups shortening
- 8 to 9 tablespoons cold water

FILLING:
- 8 cups chopped peeled tart apples
- 1/4 cup sugar
- 3/4 teaspoon ground cinnamon

SYRUP:
- 2 cups water
- 1 cup packed brown sugar

Whipped topping *or* vanilla ice cream, optional
Mint leaves, optional

In a bowl, combine the flour and salt; cut in shortening until the mixture resembles coarse crumbs. Sprinkle with water, 1 tablespoon at a time, and toss with a fork until dough can be formed into a ball. Divide the dough into four parts.

On a lightly floured surface, roll one part to fit the bottom of an ungreased 13-in. x 9-in. x 2-in. baking dish. Place in dish; top with a third of the apples. Combine sugar and cinnamon; sprinkle a third over apples.

Repeat layers of pastry, apples and cinnamon-sugar twice. Roll out remaining dough to fit top of dish and place on top. Using a sharp knife, cut 2-in. slits through all layers at once.

For syrup, bring water and sugar to a boil. Cook and stir until sugar is dissolved. Pour over top crust. Bake at 400° for 35-40 minutes or until browned and bubbly.

Serve warm with whipped topping or ice cream if desired. Garnish with mint if desired. **Yield:** 12 servings.

dutch apple cake

Elizabeth Peters, Martintown, Ontario
My husband and I came to Canada many years ago from Holland. This recipe, a family favorite, is one I found in a Dutch cookbook. It frequently goes along with me to potluck suppers.

- 3 medium peeled tart apples, sliced 1/4 inch thick (3 cups)
- 3 tablespoons plus 1 cup sugar, *divided*
- 1 teaspoon ground cinnamon
- 2/3 cup butter, softened
- 4 eggs
- 1 teaspoon vanilla extract
- 2 cups all-purpose flour
- 1/8 teaspoon salt

In a bowl, combine the apples, 3 tablespoons sugar and cinnamon; let stand for 1 hour.

In a mixing bowl, cream butter and remaining sugar. Add eggs, one at a time, beating well after each. Add vanilla. Combine flour and salt; gradually add to creamed mixture and beat until smooth.

Pour into a greased 9-in. x 5-in. x 3-in. loaf pan. Push apple slices vertically into batter, placing them close together.

Bake at 325° for 1-1/4 to 1-1/2 hours or until a toothpick inserted near the center comes out clean. Cover loosely with foil if top browns too quickly. Cool for 10 minutes on a wire rack. Remove from pan. Serve warm. **Yield:** 10-12 servings.

apple salsa with cinnamon chips

Carolyn Brinkmeyer, Aurora, Colorado

Both my husband and I were raised on farms, and we prefer home cooking to eating out. That works out fine since I love trying new recipes! I've served this treat as an appetizer and a snack. Plus, it's sweet enough to be a dessert. It's easy to transport besides.

SALSA:
- 2 medium tart apples, chopped
- 1 cup chopped strawberries
- 2 medium kiwifruit, peeled and chopped
- 1 small orange
- 2 tablespoons brown sugar
- 2 tablespoons apple jelly, melted

CHIPS:
- 8 flour tortillas (7 *or* 8 inches)
- 1 tablespoon water
- 1/4 cup sugar
- 2 teaspoons ground cinnamon

In a bowl, combine apples, strawberries and kiwi. Grate orange peel to measure 1-1/2 teaspoons; squeeze juice from orange. Add peel and juice to apple mixture. Stir in brown sugar and jelly.

For chips, brush tortillas lightly with water. Combine sugar and cinnamon; sprinkle over tortillas. Cut each tortilla into 8 wedges. Place in a single layer on ungreased baking sheets.

Bake at 400° for 6-8 minutes or until lightly browned. Cool. Serve with salsa. **Yield:** 4 cups salsa.

prize winning tips

★ ★ ★ ★ ★

★For my applesauce cupcakes, I use cream cheese frosting—but add 2 tablespoons of apple juice concentrate for flavor. My friends say the treats are rich and tasty.

Lupe Mirabal, Las Cruces, New Mexico

★I core and slice apples and dip each wedge into a mixture of 2 tablespoons sugar and 2 teaspoons ground cinnamon for a delicious snack.

Maisie Van Doren, Wenatchee, Washington

★To keep apples from absorbing strong odors in the refrigerator, store them in a plastic bag. They'll stay fresh longer and won't speed the ripening of other produce.

Tonya Farmer, Iowa City, Iowa

★When I want a nice, thick apple pie, I add an extra 1/2 cup of apple slices to the filling mixture.

Julie Ann Tucker, Columbus, Nebraska

PECAN PIE
MINI MUFFINS

pecan pie mini muffins
GRAND PRIZE WINNER

Nuts are scrumptious as snacks, but they can simplify meal planning for you, as we can see by the tempting winners of our Nuttiest Nuts recipe contest. Here, and on the following pages, you will find a variety of nuts used in a number of appetizingly inventive ways. Many of them take no longer than 30 minutes to prepare—making it easy for you to get cracking in the kitchen.

"They've become a never-fail favorite at potlucks, receptions and teas."

Even though selecting the Grand Prize Winner was a tough nut to crack, Pecan Pie Mini Muffins, shared by Pat Schrand of Enterprise, Alabama, took the top honors.

She and her husband Greg harvest hundreds of pounds of pecans on their farm. "We sell most of them wholesale," Pat says. "Of course, I always crack and freeze enough for us."

Pecans are one of her most often used recipe ingredients. "I knew I discovered a winner when I first tasted Pecan Pie Mini Muffins at a church coffee function a few years ago," she says. "They've become a never-fail favorite at potlucks, receptions and teas. Plus, Greg and I like them for breakfast or as a snack anytime."

1 cup packed brown sugar
1/2 cup all-purpose flour
1 cup chopped pecans
2/3 cup butter, melted
2 eggs, beaten

In a bowl, combine the brown sugar, flour and pecans; set aside. Combine the butter and eggs; mix well. Stir into the flour mixture.

Fill greased and floured miniature muffin cups two-thirds full. Bake at 350° for 22-25 minutes or until a toothpick comes out clean. Remove immediately to cool on wire racks. **Yield:** about 2-1/2 dozen.

honey pecan cheesecake

Tish Frish, Hampden, Maine

Birthdays and holidays are great times for cheesecake, and Thanksgiving's ideal for this particular one. In our annual church bake-off, it won first place.

- 1 cup crushed vanilla wafers (about 29 wafers)
- 5 tablespoons butter, melted
- 2 tablespoons sugar
- 1/4 cup ground pecans

FILLING:
- 3 packages (8 ounces *each*) cream cheese, softened
- 3/4 cup packed dark brown sugar
- 3 eggs
- 2 tablespoons all-purpose flour
- 1 tablespoon maple flavoring
- 1 teaspoon vanilla extract
- 1/2 cup chopped pecans

TOPPING:
- 1/4 cup honey
- 1 tablespoon butter
- 1 tablespoon water
- 1/2 cup chopped pecans

Combine the first four ingredients; press onto the bottom only of a greased 9-in. springform pan. Refrigerate.

In a mixing bowl, beat cream cheese and sugar. Add eggs; beat until smooth. Add flour, maple flavoring and vanilla; mix well. Stir in pecans. Pour into crust. Bake at 350° for 40-45 minutes or until center is nearly set. Cool on a wire rack for 10 minutes. Carefully run a knife around edge of pan to loosen; cool 1 hour longer. Refrigerate overnight.

For topping, combine the honey, butter and water in a small saucepan; cook and stir over medium heat for 2 minutes. Add nuts; cook 2 minutes longer (mixture will be thin). Spoon over cheesecake. Carefully remove sides of pan before serving. Refrigerate leftovers. **Yield:** 12 servings.

four-nut brittle

Kelly-Ann Gibbons, Prince George, British Columbia

We delight in being hospitable—it's the true mark of a country home...even if it is in the city. This recipe's one I created myself. I enjoy various kinds of nuts and wanted a candy that has a different crunch in every bite.

- 2 cups sugar
- 1 cup light corn syrup
- 1/2 cup water
- 1/2 cup salted peanuts
- 1/2 cup *each* coarsely chopped almonds, pecans and walnuts
- 1/4 cup butter
- 2 teaspoons baking soda
- 1-1/2 teaspoons vanilla extract

Butter the sides of a large heavy saucepan. Add sugar, corn syrup and water; bring to a boil, stirring constantly. Cook and stir over medium-low heat until a candy thermometer reads 238° (soft-ball stage). Stir in nuts and butter. Cook over medium heat to 300° (hard-crack stage).

Remove from the heat; vigorously stir in baking soda and vanilla until blended.

Quickly pour onto two greased baking sheets, spreading as thinly as possible with a metal spatula. Cool completely; break into pieces. Store in an airtight container with waxed paper between layers. **Yield:** 1-3/4 pounds.

Editor's Note: We recommend you test your candy thermometer before each use by bringing water to a boil; the thermometer should read 212°. Adjust your recipe temperature up or down based on your test.

macadamia fudge cake

Maguerite Gough, Salida, Colorado

Our daughter and her husband operate a cookie factory in Hawaii. After she sent a big supply of macadamia nuts, I came up with this cake I make for church dinners and ladies lunches.

- 1/2 cup butter, softened
- 3/4 cup sugar
- 1 egg
- 3/4 cup sour cream
- 1/2 teaspoon vanilla extract
- 1 cup all-purpose flour
- 1/4 cup baking cocoa
- 1-1/2 teaspoons instant coffee granules
- 1/2 teaspoon baking powder
- 1/2 teaspoon baking soda
- 1/4 teaspoon salt

TOPPING:

- 1 cup (6 ounces) semisweet chocolate chips
- 2/3 cup heavy whipping cream
- 1/2 cup sugar
- 2 tablespoons butter
- 2 tablespoons corn syrup
- 1 teaspoon vanilla extract
- 1-1/2 cups coarsely chopped macadamia nuts *or* almonds

In a mixing bowl, cream butter and sugar until fluffy. Beat in egg, sour cream and vanilla. Combine flour, cocoa, coffee, baking powder, baking soda and salt; add to creamed mixture and mix well.

Pour into a greased 9-in. round baking pan. Bake at 350° for 30 minutes or until a toothpick comes out clean. Cool for 10 minutes before removing from pan to a wire rack to cool completely.

For topping, combine chocolate chips, cream, sugar, butter and corn syrup in a saucepan; bring to a boil, stirring constantly. Reduce heat to medium; cook and stir for 7 minutes.

Remove from the heat; stir in vanilla. Cool for 10-15 minutes. Beat with a wooden spoon until slightly thickened, about 4-5 minutes. Stir in nuts. Place cake on a serving plate; pour topping over cake. **Yield:** 8-10 servings.

---

prize winning tips

✱ ✱ ✱ ✱ ✱

✱ I buy nuts in bulk around the holidays when the price is lower, then put 1-cup portions in small bags and store them in the freezer.

Esther Emmerick, Murrysville, Pennsylvania

✱ Pecans will stay fresh in an airtight container stored in the refrigerator for as long as 9 months and in the freezer for 2 years.

Elizabeth James, Brunswick, Missouri

✱ For added nutty flavor in cakes, try sprinkling finely chopped pecans on greased and floured cake pans before pouring in the batter.

Carol Ostrander, Marianna, Florida

✱ To keep chopped nuts from sinking to the bottom of cakes and quick breads, shake them in flour before adding to the batter.

Dorothy Vanis, Ulysses, Nebraska

butter pecan cake

Becky Miller, Tallahassee, Florida

Especially at Thanksgiving and Christmas, this cake is one that my family's enjoyed for many years. We love the tall slices, nutty flavor and buttery frosting.

2-2/3 cups chopped pecans
1-1/4 cups butter, softened, *divided*
    2 cups sugar
    4 eggs
    3 cups all-purpose flour
    2 teaspoons baking powder
1/2 teaspoon salt
    1 cup milk
    2 teaspoons vanilla extract
FROSTING:
    1 cup butter, softened
    8 to 8-1/2 cups confectioners' sugar
    1 can (5 ounces) evaporated milk
    2 teaspoons vanilla extract

Place pecans and 1/4 cup of butter in a baking pan. Bake at 350° for 20-25 minutes or until toasted, stirring frequently; set aside.

In a mixing bowl, cream sugar and remaining butter. Add eggs, one at a time, beating well after each addition. Combine flour, baking powder and salt; add to the creamed mixture alternately with milk. Stir in vanilla and 1-1/3 cups of toasted pecans.

Pour into three greased and floured 9-in. round baking pans. Bake at 350° for 25-30 minutes or until a toothpick comes out clean. Cool for 10 minutes before removing from pans to wire racks to cool completely.

For frosting, cream butter and sugar in a mixing bowl. Add the milk and vanilla; beat until smooth. Stir in the remaining toasted pecans. Spread the frosting between layers and over top and sides of cake. **Yield:** 12-16 servings.

walnut tart

Rovena Wallace, Trafford, Pennsylvania

The first time my husband tried this, he said there ought to be a law against anything tasting so good! I've served it at picnics and family occasions…and even once at a bridal shower. It's fine either as a dessert or for breakfast.

1/3 cup butter, softened
1/4 cup sugar
    1 egg yolk
    1 cup all-purpose flour
FILLING:
    2 cups coarsely chopped walnuts
2/3 cup packed brown sugar
1/4 cup butter
1/4 cup dark corn syrup
1/2 cup heavy whipping cream, *divided*

In a mixing bowl, cream butter and sugar until fluffy. Add egg yolk; mix well. Add flour just until blended (mixture will be crumbly).

Press onto the bottom and up the sides of an ungreased 9-in. tart pan with removable bottom. Bake at 375° for 12-14 minutes. Cool in the pan on a wire rack. Sprinkle nuts over crust.

In a heavy saucepan, combine sugar, butter, corn syrup and 2 tablespoons of cream. Boil and stir over medium heat for 1 minute. Pour over walnuts.

Bake at 375° for 10-12 minutes or until bubbly. Cool. Beat remaining cream until stiff. Serve tart at room temperature with whipped cream. **Yield:** 10-12 servings.

Editor's Note: An 11-in. x 7-in. x 2-in. baking pan may be used instead of a tart pan.

popcorn nut crunch

Midge Stolte, Blackfalds, Alberta

Our five children say it's not Christmas here until I make this. I usually double the recipe so I can put some in tins or baskets for hostess gifts when we're invited out. As long as it's kept in a dry place, Popcorn Nut Crunch will last—up to 3 weeks if you seal it in a tin.

2 quarts popped popcorn
1 cup blanched whole almonds, toasted
1 cup *each* pecan halves, cashews, Brazil nuts and hazelnuts, toasted
1-1/2 cups sugar
1 cup dark corn syrup
1/2 cup butter
1 teaspoon vanilla extract
1/2 teaspoon ground cinnamon

Place the popcorn and nuts in a lightly greased 5-qt. Dutch oven. Bake at 250° for 20 minutes.

Meanwhile, in a medium saucepan, combine sugar, corn syrup and butter; bring to a boil over medium heat, stirring constantly. Cook, without stirring, until a candy thermometer reads 290° (soft-crack stage).

Remove from the heat; stir in vanilla and cinnamon. Pour a small amount at a time over popcorn mixture, stirring constantly until the mixture is well coated. Immediately spread on greased baking sheets. Cool; break into pieces. Store in airtight containers. **Yield:** about 4 quarts.

Editor's Note: We recommend you test your candy thermometer before each use by bringing water to a boil; the thermometer should read 212°. Adjust your recipe temperature up or down based on your test.

bite-size fruitcakes

Alma Stearns, Lansing, Michigan

Because I didn't normally care for fruitcake, I had to have the recipe for this after I found out what it was I'd been enjoying at the office over the holidays!

1/2 cup butter, softened
1 cup packed brown sugar
3 eggs
2 cups all-purpose flour
1 teaspoon baking soda
1 cup (8 ounces) sour cream
2 packages (8 ounces *each*) chopped dates
1 pound Brazil nuts, coarsely chopped
1 pound pecans, coarsely chopped
3/4 pound chopped candied pineapple
3/4 pound candied cherries, halved
1 cup raisins
GLAZE:
1 egg, beaten
1/2 cup evaporated milk
1/4 cup water
Additional candied cherries, optional

In a large mixing bowl, cream the butter and sugar. Add eggs and mix well. Combine the flour and baking soda; add alternately to the creamed mixture with sour cream. Stir in the dates, nuts, pineapple, cherries and raisins.

Fill paper-lined miniature muffin cups three-fourths full. Bake at 300° for 40-50 minutes or until lightly browned and set.

For glaze, combine egg, milk and water; mix well. Brush over fruitcakes. Bake 10 minutes longer. Decorate with candied cherries if desired. Cool on wire racks. **Yield:** about 10 dozen.

PEAR PLEASURE

PEAR CUSTARD BARS

pear custard bars

Subtle sweetness and delightful juiciness make pears perfect for snacking and cooking. With a little imagination, creative cooks have found ways to include pears in recipes ranging from entrees to desserts.

That's the case with our Pear Pleasure contest. Cooks from coast to coast submitted over 1,800 recipes that put pears in breakfast dishes, salads and sandwiches, paired them with a variety of meats and featured them in breads, pies and pastries.

"When I take this crowd-pleasing treat to a potluck, I come home with an empty pan..."

Jeannette Nord's change-of-pace Pear Custard Bars were our judges' top pick for the Grand Prize. After just one bite, you'll understand why.

Says Jeannette from her home in San Juan Capistrano, California, "When I take this crowd-pleasing treat to a potluck, I come home with an empty pan every time. Cooking and baking come naturally to me—as a farm girl, I helped my mother feed my 10 siblings."

1/2 cup butter, softened
1/3 cup sugar
3/4 cup all-purpose flour
1/4 teaspoon vanilla extract
2/3 cup chopped macadamia nuts
FILLING/TOPPING:
1 package (8 ounces) cream cheese, softened
1/2 cup sugar
1 egg
1/2 teaspoon vanilla extract
1 can (15-1/4 ounces) pear halves, drained
1/2 teaspoon sugar
1/2 teaspoon ground cinnamon

In a mixing bowl, cream butter and sugar. Beat in the flour and vanilla until combined. Stir in the nuts. Press into a greased 8-in. square baking pan. Bake at 350° for 20 minutes or until lightly browned. Cool on a wire rack.

Increase heat to 375°. In a mixing bowl, beat cream cheese until smooth. Add sugar, egg and vanilla; mix until combined. Pour over crust. Cut pears into 1/8-in. slices; arrange in a single layer over filling. Combine sugar and cinnamon; sprinkle over pears.

Bake at 375° for 28-30 minutes (center will be soft set and will become firmer upon cooling). Cool on a wire rack for 45 minutes. Cover and refrigerate for at least 2 hours before cutting. Store in the refrigerator. **Yield:** 16 bars.

pork and pear stir-fry

Betty Phillips, French Creek, West Virginia
I've served this full-flavored stir-fry for years, always to rave reviews. Tender pork and ripe pears make a sweet combination, and a spicy sauce adds zip.

      1/2 **cup plum preserves**
        3 **tablespoons soy sauce**
        2 **tablespoons lemon juice**
        1 **tablespoon prepared horseradish**
        2 **teaspoons cornstarch**
      1/4 **teaspoon crushed red pepper flakes**
        1 **medium sweet yellow *or* green pepper, julienned**
  1/2 to 1 **teaspoon minced fresh gingerroot**
        1 **tablespoon vegetable oil**
        3 **medium ripe pears, peeled and sliced**
        1 **pound pork tenderloin, cut into 1/4-inch strips**
        1 **can (8 ounces) sliced water chestnuts, drained**
    1-1/2 **cups fresh *or* frozen snow peas**
        1 **tablespoon sliced almonds, toasted**
Hot cooked rice

In a bowl, combine the first six ingredients; set aside. In a skillet or wok, stir-fry yellow pepper and ginger in oil for 2 minutes. Add pears; stir-fry for 1 minute or until pepper is crisp-tender. Remove and keep warm. Stir-fry half of the pork at a time for 1-2 minutes or until meat is no longer pink.

Return pear mixture and all of the pork to pan. Add water chestnuts and reserved sauce. Bring to a boil; cook and stir for 2 minutes. Add peas; heat through. Sprinkle with almonds. Serve over rice. **Yield:** 4 servings.

pecan-pear tossed salad

Marjean Claassen, Sedgwick, Kansas
This salad has become a star at family gatherings. Once, when I forgot to bring it, dinner was postponed so I could go home and get it! To save time, I prepare the ingredients and dressing the day before, then combine them just before serving.

        2 **tablespoons fresh raspberries**
      3/4 **cup olive oil**
        3 **tablespoons cider vinegar**
        2 **tablespoons plus 1 teaspoon sugar**
  1/4 to 1/2 **teaspoon pepper**
SALAD:
        4 **medium ripe pears, thinly sliced**
        2 **teaspoons lemon juice**
        8 **cups torn salad greens**
      2/3 **cup pecan halves, toasted**
      1/2 **cup fresh raspberries**
      1/3 **cup (2 ounces) crumbled feta cheese**

Press the raspberries through a sieve, reserving the juice. Discard the seeds. In a jar with a tight-fitting lid, combine the oil, vinegar, sugar, pepper and reserved raspberry juice; shake well. Toss the pear slices with lemon juice; drain.

In a salad bowl, combine the salad greens, pears, pecans and raspberries. Sprinkle with cheese. Drizzle with dressing. **Yield:** 8 servings.

cinnamon-swirl pear bread

Joan Anderson, Winnipeg, Manitoba
Pears add moisture to this delightful bread. Try slices toasted to go along with Sunday brunch.

    3 cups chopped peeled ripe pears (about 3
      medium)
  1/2 cup water
1-1/4 cups plus 1 teaspoon sugar, *divided*
    3 packages (1/4 ounce *each*) active dry yeast
  1/2 cup warm water (110° to 115°)
    4 eggs, lightly beaten
  1/2 cup butter, softened
  1/2 cup honey
    2 teaspoons salt
    1 teaspoon almond extract
   10 to 11 cups all-purpose flour
    1 tablespoon ground cinnamon

In a saucepan, combine pears, water and 1/2 cup sugar. Simmer, uncovered, for 10-12 minutes or until tender. Drain well, reserving syrup. Add cold water if necessary to syrup to measure 1 cup; set aside.

In a mixing bowl, dissolve yeast in warm water. Add 1 teaspoon sugar; let stand for 10 minutes. Add eggs, butter, honey, salt, extract, 4 cups flour and reserved pears and syrup. Beat until smooth. Add enough remaining flour to form a soft dough.

Turn onto a floured surface; knead until smooth and elastic, about 6-8 minutes. Place in a greased bowl, turning once to grease top. Cover and let rise in a warm place until doubled, about 1-1/4 hours.

Punch dough down; divide into thirds. Roll each portion into a 16-in. x 8-in. rectangle. Combine cinnamon and remaining 3/4 cup sugar; sprinkle over dough to within 1/2 in. of edges. Roll up jelly-roll style, starting with a short side; pinch seams to seal. Place, seam side down, in three greased 9-in. x 5-in. x 3-in. loaf pans. Cover and let rise until doubled, about 45 minutes.

Bake at 375° for 20 minutes. Cover loosely with foil. Bake 15-20 minutes longer or until bread tests done. Remove from pans to wire racks to cool. **Yield:** 3 loaves.

pear waldorf pitas

Roxann Parker, Dover, Delaware
Here's a guaranteed table-brightener for a shower, luncheon or party. Just stand back and watch these sandwiches vanish. For an eye-catching presentation, I tuck each one into a colorful folded napkin.

    2 medium ripe pears, diced
  1/2 cup thinly sliced celery
  1/2 cup halved seedless red grapes
    2 tablespoons finely chopped walnuts
    2 tablespoons lemon yogurt
    2 tablespoons mayonnaise
  1/8 teaspoon poppy seeds
   10 miniature pita pockets, halved
Lettuce leaves

In a bowl, combine pears, celery, grapes and walnuts. In another bowl, combine yogurt, mayonnaise and poppy seeds; mix well. Add to pear mixture; toss to coat. Refrigerate for 1 hour or overnight.

To serve, line pita halves with lettuce and add 2 tablespoons pear mixture. **Yield:** 10 servings.

pear-stuffed tenderloin

Aloma Hawkins, Bixby, Missouri

This succulent entree is a classic you'll be proud to serve your family. There's very little fuss to making this main dish, and the meat always turns out extremely tender.

- 1 cup chopped peeled ripe pears
- 1/4 cup chopped hazelnuts *or* almonds, toasted
- 1/4 cup soft bread crumbs
- 1/4 cup finely shredded carrot
- 2 tablespoons chopped onion
- 1/2 teaspoon minced fresh gingerroot
- 1/4 teaspoon salt
- 1/4 teaspoon pepper
- 1 pork tenderloin (3/4 to 1 pound)

Vegetable oil

- 2 tablespoons orange marmalade

In a bowl, combine the first eight ingredients; set aside. Make a lengthwise cut three-quarters of the way through the tenderloin; open and flatten to 1/4-in. thickness. Spread pear mixture over tenderloin. Roll up from a long side; tuck in ends. Secure with toothpicks.

Place tenderloin on a rack in a shallow roasting pan. Brush lightly with oil. Bake, uncovered, at 425° for 20-25 minutes or until a meat thermometer inserted into pork reads 155°.

Brush with marmalade. Bake for 5-10 minutes longer or until thermometer reads 160°-170°. Let stand for 5 minutes. Discard the toothpicks and slice. **Yield:** 2-3 servings.

pear sundae french toast

Carol Schumacher, Menoken, North Dakota

Coming upon this creation in a potluck line, I left with a full plate and the recipe. Now my family oohs and aahs as soon as I bring out this fruit-topped favorite. It's great for brunch or as a fanciful finish to a meal.

- 1/4 cup plus 3 tablespoons packed brown sugar, *divided*
- 6 tablespoons butter, *divided*
- 1-1/4 teaspoons ground cinnamon, *divided*
- 3 medium ripe pears, peeled and sliced (about 2-1/2 cups)
- 3 eggs, lightly beaten
- 3/4 cup milk
- 1 teaspoon vanilla extract
- 1/4 teaspoon ground nutmeg
- 6 slices French bread (1 inch thick)

Ice cream

In a skillet, combine 1/4 cup brown sugar, 2 tablespoons butter and 1/4 teaspoon cinnamon; cook and stir until sugar is dissolved. Add pears; cook until tender.

In a bowl, combine the eggs, milk, vanilla, nutmeg, and remaining brown sugar and cinnamon. Dip bread in egg mixture to coat each side. Melt remaining butter in a skillet. Fry bread over medium heat for 2 minutes on each side or until golden brown. Top with ice cream and pear mixture. **Yield:** 6 servings.

poached pear surprise

Barbara Smith, Cannon Falls, Minnesota

Pears are my husband's favorite fruit, so he immediately declared this dessert "a keeper." It's elegant but easy, satisfying yet light. Plus, it's fun to watch the looks on the faces of our grandkids and great-grandkids when they discover the surprise filling inside.

- 4 **medium ripe pears**
- 1 **cup water**
- 1/2 **cup sugar**
- 1 **teaspoon vanilla extract**
- 1/3 **cup finely chopped walnuts**
- 2 **tablespoons confectioners' sugar**
- 1 **teaspoon milk**

CHOCOLATE SAUCE:

- 1/3 **cup water**
- 1/3 **cup sugar**
- 1/4 **cup butter**
- 1-1/3 **cups semisweet chocolate chips**

Fresh mint, optional

Core pears from bottom, leaving stems intact. Peel pears. Cut 1/4 in. from bottom to level if necessary. In a saucepan, bring water and sugar to a boil. Add pears; reduce heat. Cover and simmer for 10-15 minutes or until tender. Remove from the heat; stir vanilla into sugar syrup. Spoon over pears. Cover and refrigerate until chilled.

Meanwhile, combine walnuts, confectioners' sugar and milk; set aside. For chocolate sauce, combine water, sugar and butter in a small saucepan; bring to a boil. Remove from the heat; stir in chocolate chips until melted.

To serve, drain pears well; spoon nut mixture into cavities. Place on dessert plates; top with some of the chocolate sauce. Insert a mint leaf near stem if desired. Serve with the remaining chocolate sauce. **Yield:** 4 servings.

★ ★ ★ ★ ★ prize. winning **tips**

* I ripen pears at room temperature by placing them in a paper bag with an apple. I pierce the bag in several places with the tip of a knife. Unlike most fruit, pears are ripe when they're still fairly firm.

Becky Hague, South Jordan, Utah

---

* If you're eating a pear out of hand, there's no need to peel it. Just wash it thoroughly and enjoy! The skin should always be removed, though, for cooked dishes because it will darken and toughen when heated. Use a vegetable peeler or paring knife to remove it.

Tina Corrao, Waterford, Wisconsin

---

* When peaches are out of season, I substitute pears in my favorite cobbler recipe. If your cobbler lasts more than a day, try reheating a piece in the microwave. It'll taste like it's just warm from the oven!

Betty Brown, Paisley, Ontario

chicken in pear sauce

Andrea Lunsford, Spokane, Washington
Pairing poultry with pears brought applause from my husband and four growing children. Simple enough for everyday meals and ideal for company, this dish is a year-round standout.

      4 boneless skinless chicken breast halves
  1/2 teaspoon salt
  1/8 teaspoon white pepper
      2 tablespoons vegetable oil
      5 thick-cut bacon strips, diced
      1 can (14-1/2 ounces) chicken broth
      2 to 3 medium ripe pears, peeled and diced
      2 tablespoons cornstarch
      2 tablespoons cold water
  1/4 cup minced chives

Sprinkle chicken with salt and pepper. In a skillet over medium heat, cook chicken in oil on both sides for about 10 minutes or until juices run clear.

Meanwhile, in a saucepan, cook bacon until crisp. Drain, reserving 1 tablespoon drippings; set bacon aside. Gradually stir broth into the drippings, scraping pan to loosen browned bits. Bring to a boil. Boil, uncovered, for 5 minutes.

Add pears; return to a boil. Boil, uncovered, for 5 minutes or until pears are tender. Combine cornstarch and water until smooth; add the chives. Gradually stir into pear sauce; bring to a boil. Cook and stir for 2 minutes or until thickened and bubbly. Stir in bacon. Serve over the chicken. **Yield:** 4 servings.

blue cheese pear salad

Sherry Duval, Baltimore, Maryland
Guests at a barbecue we hosted one summer brought this cool, refreshing salad. Now it's a mainstay at most all our cookouts. The mingling of zesty tastes and textures instantly wakes up the taste buds.

     10 cups torn salad greens
       3 large ripe pears, peeled and cut into large pieces
   1/2 cup thinly sliced green onions
       4 ounces crumbled blue cheese
   1/4 cup slivered almonds, toasted
MUSTARD VINAIGRETTE:
   1/3 cup olive oil
       3 tablespoons red wine vinegar
1-1/2 teaspoons sugar
1-1/2 teaspoons Dijon mustard
       1 garlic clove, minced
   1/2 teaspoon salt
Pepper to taste

In a large bowl, combine the salad greens, pears, onions, cheese and almonds. In a jar with a tight-fitting lid, combine the vinaigrette ingredients; shake well. Pour over salad; toss to coat. Serve immediately. **Yield:** 8-10 servings.

caramel pear pie

Mary Kaehler, Lodi, California
A dear friend shared the recipe for this attractive pie. The caramel drizzle and streusel topping make it almost too pretty to eat. Knowing this dessert is waiting is great motivation for our children to eat all their vegetables.

    6 cups sliced peeled ripe pears (about 6
      medium)
    1 tablespoon lemon juice
  1/2 cup plus 3 tablespoons sugar, *divided*
    2 tablespoons quick-cooking tapioca
  3/4 teaspoon ground cinnamon
  1/4 teaspoon salt
  1/4 teaspoon ground nutmeg
    1 unbaked pastry shell (9 inches)
  3/4 cup old-fashioned oats
    1 tablespoon all-purpose flour
  1/4 cup cold butter
   18 caramels
    5 tablespoons milk
  1/4 cup chopped pecans

In a large bowl, combine pears and lemon juice. In another bowl, combine 1/2 cup sugar, tapioca, cinnamon, salt and nutmeg. Add to pears; stir gently. Let stand for 15 minutes. Pour into pastry shell. In a bowl, combine oats, flour and remaining sugar. Cut in butter until crumbly. Sprinkle over pears. Bake at 400° for 45 minutes.

Meanwhile, in a saucepan over low heat, melt caramels with milk. Stir until smooth; add pecans. Drizzle over pie. Bake 8-10 minutes longer or until crust is golden brown and filling is bubbly. Cool on a wire rack. **Yield:** 6-8 servings.

almond pear tartlets

Marie Rizzio, Traverse City, Michigan
Although they're quick to fix, you'll want to savor these pretty pastries slowly. Delicately spiced pears are complemented by an almond sauce and a crispy crust. Be prepared to share the recipe.

    1 egg, lightly beaten
  1/2 cup plus 6 tablespoons sugar, *divided*
  3/4 cup heavy whipping cream
    2 tablespoons butter, melted
  1/2 teaspoon almond extract
    1 package (10 ounces) frozen puff pastry shells,
      thawed
    2 small ripe pears, peeled and thinly sliced
  1/2 teaspoon ground cinnamon
  1/8 teaspoon ground ginger
  1/2 cup slivered almonds, toasted, optional

In a saucepan, combine the egg, 1/2 cup sugar, cream and butter. Cook and stir until the sauce is thickened and a thermometer reads 160°. Remove from the heat; stir in extract. Cover and refrigerate.

On an unfloured surface, roll each pastry into a 4-in. circle. Place in an ungreased 15-in. x 10-in. x 1-in. baking pan. Top each with pear slices. Combine cinnamon, ginger and remaining sugar; sprinkle over the pears.

Bake at 400° for 20 minutes or until the pastry is golden brown. Sprinkle with almonds if desired. Serve warm with the chilled cream sauce. **Yield:** 6 servings.

ROSY RHUBARB #1

STRAWBERRY RHUBARB
COFFEE CAKE

strawberry rhubarb coffee cake
GRAND PRIZE WINNER

I t's best known to some of us by its long-standing country nickname of "pieplant." Whatever you call it, though, there are few foods as delicious—fresh or frozen—as versatile rhubarb.

You and your waiting recipe file will see exactly what we mean as you get acquainted here and on the

" Most everyone who tastes this coffee cake asks for the recipe. "

following pages with the top prize winners from our Rosy Rhubarb recipe contest.

The Grand Prize Winner is Strawberry Rhubarb Coffee Cake shared by Dorothy Morehouse of Massena, New York. This moist, sweet-tangy coffee cake is an eye-opening breakfast or refreshing snack anytime. "Most everyone who tastes this coffee cake asks for the recipe," says Dorothy. "Whether you use fresh or frozen rhubarb, it always turns out nice.

"Lots of my friends grow rhubarb and they're glad to share their overabundance with me. Of course, when I use their 'garden gifts' in my baking, I always treat those friends to generous samples."

FILLING:
- 3 cups sliced fresh *or* frozen rhubarb (1-inch pieces)
- 1 quart fresh strawberries, mashed
- 2 tablespoons lemon juice
- 1 cup sugar
- 1/3 cup cornstarch

CAKE:
- 3 cups all-purpose flour
- 1 cup sugar
- 1 teaspoon baking powder
- 1 teaspoon baking soda
- 1/2 teaspoon salt
- 1 cup butter, cut into pieces
- 1-1/2 cups buttermilk
- 2 eggs
- 1 teaspoon vanilla extract

TOPPING:
- 1/4 cup butter
- 3/4 cup all-purpose flour
- 3/4 cup sugar

In a large saucepan, combine rhubarb, strawberries and lemon juice. Cover and cook over medium heat about 5 minutes. Combine sugar and cornstarch; stir into saucepan. Bring to a boil, cook and stir for 2 minutes or until thickened. Remove from heat and set aside.

In a large bowl, combine flour, sugar, baking powder, baking soda and salt. Cut in butter until mixture resembles coarse crumbs. Beat buttermilk, eggs and vanilla; stir into crumb mixture. Spread half of the batter evenly into a greased 13-in. x 9-in. x 2-in. baking dish. Carefully spread filling on top. Drop remaining batter by tablespoonfuls over filling.

For topping, melt butter in a saucepan over low heat. Remove from heat; stir in flour and sugar until mixture resembles coarse crumbs. Sprinkle over batter. Lay foil on lower rack to catch any juicy fruit spillovers. Place coffee cake on middle rack; bake at 350° for 40-45 minutes. Cool in pan. Cut into squares. **Yield:** 16-20 servings.

rhubarb cherry pie

Eunice Hurt, Murfreesboro, Tennessee
This easy pie is a special treat. It combines two mouth-watering tastes—rhubarb and cherries.

> 3 cups sliced fresh *or* frozen rhubarb (1/2-inch pieces)
> 1 can (16 ounces) pitted tart red cherries, drained
>
> 1-1/4 cups sugar
> 1/4 cup quick-cooking tapioca
> 4 to 5 drops red food coloring, optional

Pastry for double-crust pie (9 inches)

In a mixing bowl, combine first five ingredients; let stand for 15 minutes. Line a 9-in. pie plate with pastry; add filling. Top with a lattice crust; flute the edges.

Bake at 400° for 40-50 minutes or until the crust is golden and filling is bubbling. **Yield:** 8 servings.

berry rhubarb fool

Cheryl Miller, Fort Collins, Colorado
A "fool" is a British dessert that's usually made with custard. This is a quicker version I created. Rhubarb is a subtle flavor in these pretty, layered parfaits.

> 3 cups sliced fresh *or* frozen rhubarb (1-inch pieces)
> 1/3 cup sugar
> 1/4 cup orange juice

Pinch salt

> 1 cup heavy whipping cream
> 1 pint fresh strawberries, halved

Fresh mint leaves

In a saucepan, combine rhubarb, sugar, orange juice and salt. Bring to a boil. Reduce heat; cover and simmer for 6-8 minutes or until rhubarb is tender. Cool slightly. Pour into a blender container; cover and blend until smooth. Chill.

Just before serving, whip cream until stiff peaks form. Fold into rhubarb mixture until lightly streaked. In chilled parfait glasses, alternate layers of cream mixture and strawberries. Garnish each serving with a strawberry and a sprig of mint. **Yield:** 6 servings.

cherry rhubarb cobbler

Mary Ann Earnest, Effingham, Illinois

One day, I wanted to use up a leftover can of cherry pie filling that I had in the refrigerator. I added some diced rhubarb, then I turned to a cobbler recipe that I liked for the rest. It became a favorite—fast! This is such a simple way to enjoy the taste of spring that is hearty and comforting as well.

FILLING:

- 1 can (21 ounces) cherry pie filling
- 3 cups chopped rhubarb
- 1 cup sugar
- 4 tablespoons butter

CRUST:

- 1/2 cup shortening
- 1 cup sugar
- 1 egg
- 1 cup all-purpose flour
- 1 teaspoon baking powder
- 1/2 cup milk

Spread fruit in a 13-in. x 9-in. x 2-in. baking dish. Sprinkle with sugar and dot with butter.

For crust, cream shortening and sugar in a mixing bowl. Add egg and beat well. Combine flour and baking powder; add alternately with milk to creamed mixture.

Pour over fruit; bake at 350° for 50-60 minutes. **Yield:** about 12 servings.

rhubarb crumble

Linda Enslen, Schuler, Alberta

To tell you the truth, I'm not sure how well my crumble keeps...we usually eat it all in a day! You can make this with all rhubarb, but the apples and strawberries make this dessert extra good.

- 3 cups sliced fresh *or* frozen rhubarb (1/2-inch pieces)
- 1 cup cubed peeled apples
- 1/2 to 1 cup sliced strawberries
- 1/3 cup sugar
- 1/2 teaspoon ground cinnamon
- 1/2 cup all-purpose flour
- 1 teaspoon baking powder
- 1/4 teaspoon salt
- 4 tablespoons cold butter
- 2/3 cup packed brown sugar
- 2/3 cup quick-cooking oats

Vanilla ice cream, optional

Combine rhubarb, apples and strawberries; spoon into a greased 8-in. square baking dish. Combine sugar and cinnamon; sprinkle over rhubarb mixture. Set aside.

In a bowl, combine flour, baking powder and salt. Cut in butter until mixture resembles coarse crumbs. Stir in brown sugar and oats. Sprinkle over rhubarb mixture.

Bake at 350° for 40-50 minutes or until lightly browned. Serve warm or cold with a scoop of ice cream if desired. **Yield:** 6-8 servings.

almond rhubarb pastry

Lois Dyck, Coaldale, Alberta

One thing is certain, each time I serve this someone will ask for the recipe. I love to pull stalks from my big rhubarb plant for this yummy treat.

PASTRY:
- 3 cups all-purpose flour
- 1 tablespoon baking powder
- 1 teaspoon salt
- 1 cup shortening
- 2 eggs, beaten
- 1/4 to 1/3 cup milk, *divided*

FILLING:
- 1-1/2 cups sugar
- 1/4 cup quick-cooking tapioca
- 6 cups chopped fresh *or* frozen rhubarb

TOPPING:
- 1/2 cup butter
- 3/4 cup sugar
- 2 tablespoons milk
- 1/2 teaspoon vanilla extract
- 1 cup slivered almonds

Combine the flour, baking powder and salt; cut in shortening until the mixture resembles coarse crumbs. Mix the eggs and 1/4 cup milk; add to the dry ingredients and stir with a fork just until dough clings together. Add some or all of the remaining milk if necessary. Shape into a ball. Divide in half.

On a floured surface, roll half of dough into a 17-in. x 12-in. rectangle. Transfer to a greased 15-in. x 10-in. x 1-in. baking pan. Combine filling ingredients; let stand for 15 minutes. Sprinkle over dough in pan. Roll out remaining dough into a 15-in. x 10-in. rectangle. Place over filling. Fold bottom edge of dough over top layer of dough; press edges together to seal.

For topping, in a saucepan, melt butter; add sugar and milk. Bring to a gentle boil; boil 2-3 minutes, stirring constantly. Remove from heat; stir in vanilla. Spread over pastry. Sprinkle almonds on top.

Bake at 400° for 20 minutes; reduce heat to 300°. Bake 30-40 minutes longer or until golden brown. Serve warm or cold. **Yield:** 16-20 servings.

rhubarb pork chop casserole

Jeanie Castor, Decatur, Illinois

The usual reaction to this casserole is that it's a nice mix of sweet and tart and quite an unusual use of rhubarb. I enjoy rhubarb but I'm not a dessert person. So I like to use it for more than pies and cobblers.

- 4 pork loin chops (3/4 inch thick)
- 1 tablespoon vegetable oil
- Salt and pepper to taste
- 2-1/2 to 3 cups soft bread crumbs
- 3 cups sliced fresh *or* frozen rhubarb (1-inch pieces)
- 1/2 cup packed brown sugar
- 1/4 cup all-purpose flour
- 1 teaspoon ground cinnamon

In a large skillet, brown pork chops in oil and season with salt and pepper. Remove to a warm platter. Mix 1/4 cup pan drippings with bread crumbs. Reserve 1/2 cup; sprinkle remaining crumbs into a 13-in. x 9-in. x 2-in. baking dish.

Combine rhubarb, sugar, flour and cinnamon; spoon half over the bread crumbs. Arrange pork chops on top. Spoon remaining rhubarb mixture over chops. Cover with foil and bake at 350° for 30-45 minutes.

Remove foil. Sprinkle with reserved bread crumbs. Bake 10-15 minutes longer or until chops test done. **Yield:** 4 servings.

rhubarb dumplings

Elsie Shell, Topeka, Kansas

When I served these delectable dumplings at a recent gathering, I got lots of compliments.

SAUCE:

1-1/2 cups sugar
   1 tablespoon all-purpose flour
  1/2 teaspoon ground cinnamon
  1/4 teaspoon salt
1-1/2 cups water
  1/3 cup butter
   1 teaspoon vanilla extract
Red food coloring, optional

DOUGH:

   2 cups all-purpose flour
   2 tablespoons sugar
   2 teaspoons baking powder
  1/4 teaspoon salt
2-1/2 tablespoons cold butter
  3/4 cup milk

FILLING:

   2 tablespoons butter, softened
   2 cups finely chopped fresh *or* frozen rhubarb
  1/2 cup sugar
  1/2 teaspoon ground cinnamon

In a saucepan, combine sugar, flour, cinnamon and salt. Stir in water; add butter. Bring to a boil; cook and stir 1 minute. Remove from heat. Add vanilla and, if desired, enough food coloring to tint sauce a deep pink; set aside.

For dough, in a medium bowl, combine flour, sugar, baking powder and salt. Cut in butter until mixture resembles coarse crumbs. Add milk and mix quickly. Do not overmix. Gather dough into a ball and roll out on a floured surface into a 12-in. x 9-in. rectangle. Spread with softened butter; arrange rhubarb on top.

Combine sugar and cinnamon; sprinkle over rhubarb. Roll up from the long side and place seam side down. Cut roll into 12 slices. Arrange slices cut side up in a greased 13-in. x 9-in. x 2-in. baking dish. Pour sauce over. Bake at 350° for 35-40 minutes or until golden brown. **Yield:** 12 servings.

***** prize winning tips

* Once when my mother was making a strawberry-rhubarb pie and discovered she didn't have enough strawberries and rhubarb for the filling, she used diced apples to make up the difference. It tasted so good, she uses apples every time she makes this pie.

Tanya Person, Anchorage, Alaska

* Don't forget that rhubarb leaves are poisonous. Eat only the stems. Pick stalks when they are as thick as your thumb by twisting (not cutting) them off near the base of the plant. A pound of rhubarb equals 3-4 cups of sliced or 2 cups of cooked and pureed rhubarb.

Priscilla Weaver, Hagerstown, Maryland

* To take out any bitter taste in rhubarb before using it, cover it with boiling water, put lid on pan and let stand about 30 minutes.

Jeanie Castor, Decatur, Illinois

spiced rhubarb

Paula Pelis, Rocky Point, New York
This recipe has been in my family for years. It was handed down to me from my mother, who got it many decades ago from her mother. It's good hot or cold. I even like it spread on toast.

    10 cups diced fresh *or* frozen rhubarb
 4-1/2 cups sugar
     1 cup cider vinegar
     2 teaspoons ground cinnamon
 1/2 to 1 teaspoon ground cloves
 1/2 to 1 teaspoon ground allspice

In a large Dutch oven or kettle, combine all ingredients. Bring to a rapid boil; reduce heat and simmer for 60-70 minutes.

Pour into pint jars and refrigerate. Serve as a glaze for ham or spread on biscuits. **Yield:** about 4 pints.

cream cheese rhubarb pie

Beverly Kuhn, Orwell, Ohio
Whenever my mom and I have a "rhubarb attack," we make this pie! It's a tempting, tangy and creamy treat.

    1/4 cup cornstarch
     1 cup sugar
 Pinch salt
    1/2 cup water
     3 cups sliced fresh *or* frozen rhubarb
         (1/2-inch pieces)
     1 unbaked pie shell (9 inches)
 TOPPING:
     1 package (8 ounces) cream cheese, softened
     2 eggs
    1/2 cup sugar
 Whipped cream
 Sliced almonds

In a saucepan, combine the cornstarch, sugar and salt. Add water; stir until smooth. Add rhubarb. Bring to a boil; cook and stir for 2 minutes or until thickened. Pour into the pie shell; bake at 425° for 10 minutes.

Meanwhile, for topping, beat cream cheese, eggs and sugar until smooth. Pour over pie. Reduce heat to 325°. Bake for 35 minutes or until set. Cool. Chill several hours or overnight. Garnish with whipped cream and sliced almonds. **Yield:** 8 servings.

rhubarb pecan muffins

Mary Kubik, Lethbridge, Alberta
I usually make these for breakfast and as a coffee-time snack. It's a great use of a bounty of rhubarb.

    2 cups all-purpose flour
  3/4 cup sugar
1-1/2 teaspoons baking powder
  1/2 teaspoon baking soda
    1 teaspoon salt
  3/4 cup chopped pecans
    1 egg
  1/4 cup vegetable oil
    2 teaspoons grated orange peel
  3/4 cup orange juice
1-1/4 cups finely chopped rhubarb

In a large mixing bowl, combine the flour, sugar, baking powder, baking soda, salt and nuts. In another bowl, combine the egg, oil, orange peel and orange juice. Add to dry ingredients all at once and stir just until moistened. Stir in the rhubarb.

Fill 12 lightly greased muffin cups almost to the top. Bake at 375° for 25-30 minutes or until a toothpick comes out clean. Cool for 5 minutes before removing from pan to a wire rack. **Yield:** 1 dozen.

---

*It's easiest to freeze pieces of rhubarb in the amount you're likely to use most often—in quart containers, for instance.
Jane Nadler, Wright City, Missouri*

---

*Sprinkle nutmeg over the filling when making a rhubarb pie for a delightful dessert.
Dorothy Borchert, Knoxville, Iowa*

rosy rhubarb salad

Wanda Rader, Greeneville, Tennessee
At the holidays, this deliciously different salad is a great alternative to cranberry sauce. It goes well with pork or poultry. Its tartness rounds out a rich meal.

    3 cups sliced fresh *or* frozen rhubarb
      (1-inch pieces)
    1 tablespoon sugar
    1 package (3 ounces) raspberry gelatin
    1 cup unsweetened pineapple juice
    1 teaspoon lemon juice
    1 cup diced peeled apples
    1 cup diced celery
  1/4 cup chopped pecans

In a medium saucepan, cook and stir the rhubarb and sugar over medium-low heat until rhubarb is soft and tender. Remove from the heat; add the gelatin and stir until dissolved. Stir in the pineapple and lemon juices. Chill until partially set.

Stir in the apples, celery and pecans. Pour into a 4-1/2-cup mold coated with nonstick cooking spray or a glass bowl. Chill for several hours or overnight. **Yield:** 8 servings.

COOKIE COLLECTION

#1

CHOCOLATE MALTED
COOKIES

chocolate malted cookies
GRAND PRIZE WINNER

The only thing more comforting than a cookie warm from the oven is two cookies (or more)! And speaking of more, no recipe contest has ever stirred up more excitement than our Cookie Collection contest—13,000 entries made it the biggest in the history of Reiman Publications' magazines.

Cookie lovers shared favorite recipes for crisp and chewy cookies and bars of all kinds. Our food editors spent weeks sorting through the mountain of entries to select the most promising ones, then our Test Kitchen staff began measuring, mixing and baking. Our panel of judges had the tasty job of picking the winners.

At the top of the cookie jar is Grand Prize Winner Chocolate Malted Cookies from Teri Rasey-Bolf of Cadillac, Michigan. Says Teri, "These cookies are the next best thing to a good old-fashioned malted milk. With malted milk powder, chocolate syrup plus chocolate chips and chunks, these are the best cookies I've ever tasted!"

> "These cookies are the next best thing to a good old-fashioned malted milk."

1 cup butter-flavored shortening
1-1/4 cups packed brown sugar
1/2 cup malted milk powder
2 tablespoons chocolate syrup
1 tablespoon vanilla extract
1 egg
2 cups all-purpose flour
1 teaspoon baking soda
1/2 teaspoon salt
1-1/2 cups semisweet chocolate chunks
1 cup (6 ounces) milk chocolate chips

In a mixing bowl, combine the first five ingredients; beat for 2 minutes. Add egg. Combine the flour, baking soda and salt; gradually add to the creamed mixture, mixing well after each addition. Stir in chocolate chunks and chips.

Shape into 2-in. balls; place 3 in. apart on ungreased baking sheets. Bake at 375° for 12-14 minutes or until golden brown. Cool for 2 minutes before removing to a wire rack. **Yield:** about 1-1/2 dozen.

spice cookies
with pumpkin dip

Kelly McNeal, Derby, Kansas
My husband and kids eat the first dozen of these cookies, warm from the oven, before the next tray is even done.

1-1/2 cups butter, softened
    2 cups sugar
    2 eggs
  1/2 cup molasses
    4 cups all-purpose flour
    4 teaspoons baking soda
    2 teaspoons ground cinnamon
    1 teaspoon *each* ground ginger and cloves
    1 teaspoon salt
Additional sugar
PUMPKIN DIP:
    1 package (8 ounces) cream cheese, softened
    1 can (18 ounces) pumpkin pie mix
    2 cups confectioners' sugar
  1/2 to 1 teaspoon ground cinnamon
  1/4 to 1/2 teaspoon ground ginger

In a mixing bowl, cream butter and sugar. Add eggs, one at a time, beating well after each addition. Add molasses; mix well. Combine the flour, baking soda, cinnamon, ginger, cloves and salt; add to creamed mixture and mix well. Chill overnight.

Shape into 1/2-in. balls; roll in sugar. Place 2 in. apart on ungreased baking sheets. Bake at 375° for 6 minutes or until edges begin to brown. Cool for 2 minutes before removing to a wire rack.

For dip, beat cream cheese in a mixing bowl until smooth. Add pumpkin pie mix; beat well. Add sugar, cinnamon and ginger; beat until smooth. Serve with cookies. Store leftover dip in the refrigerator. **Yield:** about 20 dozen cookies (3 cups dip).

coconut washboards

Tommie Sue Shaw, McAlester, Oklahoma
I've been making my husband these cookies most of the years we've been married. Our great-grandchildren like to come over to munch on the chewy treats, too.

  1/2 cup butter, softened
  1/2 cup shortening
    2 cups packed brown sugar
    2 eggs
  1/4 cup water
    1 teaspoon vanilla extract
    4 cups all-purpose flour
1-1/2 teaspoons baking powder
  1/2 teaspoon baking soda
  1/4 teaspoon salt
    1 cup flaked coconut

In a mixing bowl, cream the butter, shortening and sugar for 2 minutes or until fluffy. Add eggs; mix well. Gradually add water and vanilla; mix well. Combine flour, baking powder, baking soda and salt; add to the creamed mixture. Fold in coconut. Cover and refrigerate for 2-4 hours.

Shape into 1-in. balls. Place 2 in. apart on greased baking sheets; flatten with fingers into 2-1/2-in. x 1-in. oblong shapes. Press lengthwise with a floured fork. Bake at 400° for 8-10 minutes or until lightly browned. Cool 2 minutes before removing to a wire rack. **Yield:** about 9 dozen.

lemon butter cookies

Judy McCreight, Springfield, Illinois
These tender cutout cookies have a slight lemon flavor that makes them stand out from the rest. They're very easy to roll out compared to other sugar cookies I've worked with. I know you'll enjoy them as much as we do.

- **1 cup butter, softened**
- **2 cups sugar**
- **2 eggs, beaten**
- **1/4 cup milk**
- **2 teaspoons lemon extract**
- **1/2 teaspoon salt**
- **4-1/2 cups all-purpose flour**
- **2 teaspoons baking powder**
- **1/4 teaspoon baking soda**

Colored sugar, optional

In a mixing bowl, cream the butter and sugar. Add the eggs, milk and lemon extract. Combine dry ingredients; gradually add to creamed mixture. Cover and chill for 2 hours.

Roll out on a lightly floured surface to 1/8-in. thickness. Cut with a 2-in. cookie cutter dipped in flour. Place 2 in. apart on ungreased baking sheets. Sprinkle with colored sugar if desired.

Bake at 350° for 8-9 minutes or until the edges just begin to brown. Remove to wire racks to cool. **Yield:** about 13 dozen.

rolled oat cookies

Kathi Peters, Chilliwack, British Columbia
I like to keep some of this dough in the freezer at all times since it's so handy to slice, bake and serve at a moment's notice. So they're the perfect cookie to serve drop-in guests or to take to bake sales or potluck suppers. These wholesome cookies are also super with a cup of coffee—in fact, we occasionally grab a few for breakfast when we're in a hurry.

- **1 cup butter**
- **1 cup packed brown sugar**
- **1/4 cup water**
- **1 teaspoon vanilla extract**
- **3 cups quick-cooking oats**
- **1-1/4 cups all-purpose flour**
- **1 teaspoon salt**
- **1/4 teaspoon baking soda**

In a mixing bowl, cream the butter and sugar. Add the water and vanilla; mix well. Combine the dry ingredients; add to creamed mixture and mix well. Chill for 30 minutes.

Shape dough into two 1-1/2-in. rolls; wrap tightly in waxed paper. Chill for 2 hours or until firm. Cut into 1/2-in. slices and place 2 in. apart on greased baking sheets. Bake at 375° for 12 minutes or until lightly browned. Remove cookies to wire racks to cool. **Yield:** about 3-1/2 dozen.

chocolate thumbprints

Laura Bryant German, West Warren, Massachusetts
A group of friends had a weekly "movie night" during winters on Martha's Vineyard, and we'd take turns making a chocolate treat to share. These terrific cookies were an instant success. Once they made their debut, I had to make them many more times.

- 1/2 cup butter, softened
- 2/3 cup sugar
- 1 egg, *separated*
- 2 tablespoons milk
- 1 teaspoon vanilla extract
- 1 cup all-purpose flour
- 1/3 cup baking cocoa
- 1/4 teaspoon salt
- 1 cup finely chopped walnuts

FILLING:
- 1/2 cup confectioners' sugar
- 1 tablespoon butter, softened
- 2 teaspoons milk
- 1/4 teaspoon vanilla extract
- 26 milk chocolate kisses

In a mixing bowl, beat butter, sugar, egg yolk, milk and vanilla until light and fluffy. Combine flour, cocoa and salt; gradually add to creamed mixture. Cover and chill 1 hour or until firm enough to roll into balls.

Meanwhile, in a small bowl, lightly beat egg white. Shape dough into 1-in. balls; dip in egg white, then roll in nuts. Place on greased baking sheets. Make an indentation with thumb in center of each cookie. Bake at 350° for 10-12 minutes or until center is set.

Combine the first four filling ingredients in a small bowl; mix until smooth. Spoon 1/4 teaspoon into each warm cookie; gently press a chocolate kiss in the center. Carefully remove from baking sheet to wire racks to cool. **Yield:** about 2 dozen.

chocolaty double crunchers

Cheryl Johnson, Upper Marlboro, Maryland
I first tried these fun crispy cookies at a family picnic when I was a child. Packed with oats, cornflakes and coconut, they quickly became a "regular" at our house.

- 1/2 cup butter, softened
- 1/2 cup sugar
- 1/2 cup packed brown sugar
- 1 egg
- 1/2 teaspoon vanilla extract
- 1 cup all-purpose flour
- 1/2 teaspoon baking soda
- 1/4 teaspoon salt
- 1 cup quick-cooking oats
- 1 cup crushed cornflakes
- 1/2 cup flaked coconut

FILLING:
- 2 packages (3 ounces *each*) cream cheese, softened
- 1-1/2 cups confectioners' sugar
- 2 cups (12 ounces) semisweet chocolate chips, melted

In a mixing bowl, cream butter and sugars. Add egg and vanilla; mix well. Combine flour, baking soda and salt; add to creamed mixture and mix well. Add oats, cornflakes and coconut.

Shape into 1-in. balls and place 2 in. apart on greased baking sheets. Flatten with a glass dipped lightly in flour. Bake at 350° for 8-10 minutes or until lightly browned. Remove to wire racks to cool.

For filling, beat cream cheese and sugar until smooth. Add the chocolate; mix well. Spread about 1 tablespoon on the bottom of half of the cookies and top each with another cookie. Store in the refrigerator. **Yield:** about 2 dozen.

*runners-up

frosted ginger cookies

Jeanne Matteson, South Dayton, New York

My husband and I just built a new house in a small rural community in western New York. I work all day in an office, and I enjoy baking in the evening to relax. The wonderful aroma of these soft, delicious cookies in our oven has made our new house smell like home.

1-1/2 cups butter
   1 cup sugar
   1 cup packed brown sugar
   2 eggs
 1/2 cup molasses
   2 teaspoons vanilla extract
4-1/2 cups all-purpose flour
   1 tablespoon ground ginger
   2 teaspoons baking soda
   2 teaspoons ground cinnamon
 1/2 teaspoon salt
 1/2 teaspoon ground cloves

FROSTING:
 1/3 cup packed brown sugar
 1/4 cup milk
   2 tablespoons butter
   2 cups confectioners' sugar
 1/2 teaspoon vanilla extract *or* caramel flavoring
Pinch salt

In a mixing bowl, cream butter and sugars. Add the eggs, one at a time, beating well after each addition. Stir in molasses and vanilla; mix well. Combine dry ingredients; gradually add to creamed mixture. Drop by tablespoonfuls 2 in. apart onto ungreased baking sheets. Bake at 325° for 12-15 minutes or until cookies spring back when touched lightly (do not overbake). Remove to wire racks.

For frosting, in a medium saucepan, bring brown sugar, milk and butter to a boil; boil for 1 minute, stirring constantly. Remove from the heat (mixture will look curdled at first). Cool for 3 minutes. Add confectioners' sugar, vanilla and salt; mix well. Frost warm cookies. **Yield:** about 6 dozen.

---

prize winning **tips**

★ ★ ★ ★ ★

★As a special treat for my family, I'll wrap some of my chocolate chip cookie dough around miniature Snickers bars before baking. My family searches the cookie jar for these hidden treasures!

Hazel Staley, Gaithersburg, Maryland

★To make my sugar cookies more festive, I dip the bottom of a glass in colored sugar rather than plain sugar before flattening the cookies.

Donna Harvey, Tunkhannock, Pennsylvania

★Try crumbling old-fashioned sugar cookies on top of ice cream for a yummy topping.

Judy Swartz, Lancaster, California

VERY CHOCOLATE
BROWNIES

very chocolate brownies
GRAND PRIZE WINNER

Rich, chewy and oh-so-chocolaty, brownies are an irresistible treat savored by kids of all ages.

Whether old-fashioned classics or new varieties topped with fluffy frostings, brownies never fail to satisfy. For our Brownies Can't Be Beat! contest, readers entered more than 5,500 of their all-time favorites.

> "The fluffy melt-in-your-mouth top layer is absolutely heavenly."

Since any of the winning scrumptious squares will get eaten up fast, you may consider them a "flash in the pan." But they'll have real staying power as part of your recipe collection. We're sure Very Chocolate Brownies, the Grand Prize Winner, will soon become a family favorite.

Arlene Butler of Ogden, Utah shared the recipe, saying, "I've spent years trying different recipes in search of the perfect brownie...and this scrumptious version might be it. The fluffy melt-in-your-mouth top layer is absolutely heavenly. It's impossible to eat just one!"

4 squares (1 ounce *each*) unsweetened chocolate
3/4 cup butter
2 cups sugar
3 eggs
1 teaspoon vanilla extract
1 cup all-purpose flour
1 cup coarsely chopped walnuts

TOPPING:
1 cup (6 ounces) semisweet chocolate chips
1/4 cup water
2 tablespoons butter
1 cup heavy whipping cream, whipped

In a microwave or double boiler, melt the chocolate and butter; cool for 10 minutes. Add the sugar; mix well. Stir in the eggs and vanilla. Add the flour; mix well. Stir in the walnuts.

Line a 13-in. x 9-in. x 2-in. baking pan with foil and grease the foil. Pour batter into pan. Bake at 350° for 25-30 minutes or until a toothpick inserted near the center comes out with moist crumbs (do not overbake). Cool completely.

For topping, melt chocolate chips, water and butter in a microwave or double boiler; stir until smooth. Cool to room temperature. Fold in whipped cream. Spread over brownies. Chill before cutting. Store leftovers in the refrigerator. **Yield:** 3 dozen.

chunky blond brownies

Rosemary Dreiske, Keldron, South Dakota
Every bite of these chewy brownies is packed with chunks of white and semisweet chocolate and macadamia nuts. We have lots of excellent cooks in this rural community, so it's a challenge coming up with a potluck offering that stands out. These usually do—and they're snapped up almost immediately.

```
1/2  cup butter, softened
3/4  cup sugar
3/4  cup packed brown sugar
  2  eggs
  2  teaspoons vanilla extract
1-1/2 cups all-purpose flour
  1  teaspoon baking powder
1/2  teaspoon salt
  1  cup vanilla or white chips
  1  cup semisweet chocolate chunks
  1  jar (3-1/2 ounces) macadamia nuts or 3/4 cup
     blanched almonds, chopped, divided
```

In a mixing bowl, cream the butter and sugars. Add the eggs and vanilla; mix well. Combine flour, baking powder and salt; add to creamed mixture and mix well. Stir in vanilla chips, chocolate chunks and 1/2 cup nuts.

Spoon into a greased 13-in. x 9-in. x 2-in. baking pan; spread to evenly cover bottom of pan. Sprinkle with remaining nuts. Bake at 350° for 25-30 minutes or until golden brown. Cool on a wire rack. **Yield:** 2 dozen.

brownie pie a la mode

Beverly Thornton, Cortlandt Manor, New York
Cutting brownies into wedges and topping them with fudge sauce dresses them up quickly and easily.

```
1/2  cup sugar
  2  tablespoons butter
  2  tablespoons water
1-1/2 cups semisweet chocolate chips
  2  eggs
  1  teaspoon vanilla extract
2/3  cup all-purpose flour
1/4  teaspoon baking soda
1/4  teaspoon salt
3/4  cup chopped walnuts
FUDGE SAUCE:
  1  cup (6 ounces) semisweet chocolate chips
1/2  cup evaporated milk
1/4  cup sugar
  1  tablespoon butter
Vanilla ice cream
```

In a small saucepan over medium heat, bring sugar, butter and water to a boil. Remove from the heat; stir in chocolate chips until melted. In a mixing bowl, beat eggs and vanilla. Add chocolate mixture; mix well. Combine flour, baking soda and salt; add to chocolate mixture. Stir in walnuts. Pour into a greased 9-in. pie plate. Bake at 350° for 28-30 minutes or until a toothpick inserted near the center comes out clean. Cool on a wire rack.

For fudge sauce, heat chocolate chips, milk, sugar and butter in a microwave or double boiler until chocolate and butter are melted; stir until smooth. Drizzle some over pie. Cut into wedges; serve with ice cream and additional sauce. **Yield:** 6-8 servings.

runners-up

volcano brownie cups

Kellie Durazo, Merced, California

I cherish recipes like this—without fuss or extra time, I can turn out an elegant, irresistible dessert that looks like I've been baking all day. I enjoy entertaining, and these treats always elicit oohs and aahs from guests.

    1 cup butter, softened
  1/2 cup sugar
    3 eggs
    3 egg yolks
    1 teaspoon vanilla extract
    2 cups (12 ounces) semisweet chocolate chips, melted
    1 cup all-purpose flour
  1/4 teaspoon salt
    1 cup ground toasted pecans
    6 squares (1 ounce *each*) white baking chocolate
Confectioners' sugar

In a mixing bowl, cream butter and sugar. Add eggs, yolks and vanilla; mix well. Add melted chocolate. Combine flour and salt; add to creamed mixture. Stir in nuts. Spoon into six greased 10-oz. custard cups; place on a baking sheet. Bake at 350° for 10 minutes.

Push one square of chocolate into center of each brownie. Bake 18-20 minutes longer or until a toothpick inserted in the brownie comes out clean. Remove from the oven and let stand for 5 minutes. Run a knife around edge of custard cups; invert onto serving plates. Dust with confectioners' sugar. Serve warm. **Yield:** 6 servings.

Editor's Note: To reheat, return brownie to custard cup and bake at 350° for 10 minutes.

triple layer brownie cake

Barbara Dean, Littleton, Colorado

This cake is a sure way to satisfy true chocolate lovers and is perfect for any occasion.

  1-1/2 cups butter
      6 squares (1 ounce *each*) unsweetened chocolate
      3 cups sugar
      5 eggs
  1-1/2 teaspoons vanilla extract
  1-1/2 cups all-purpose flour
    3/4 teaspoon salt
FROSTING:
      2 packages (8 ounces *each*) semisweet baking chocolate
      3 cups heavy whipping cream
    1/2 cup sugar, optional
      2 milk chocolate candy bars (1.55 ounces *each*), shaved

In a microwave or double boiler, melt butter and chocolate. Stir in sugar. Add eggs, one at a time, beating well after each. Stir in vanilla, flour and salt; mix well. Pour into three greased and floured 9-in. round cake pans. Bake at 350° for 23-25 minutes or until a toothpick inserted near the center comes out clean. Cool for 10 minutes; remove from pan to a wire rack to cool completely.

For frosting, melt chocolate in a heavy saucepan over medium heat. Gradually stir in cream and sugar if desired until well blended. Heat to a gentle boil; boil and stir for 1 minute. Remove from heat; transfer to a mixing bowl. Refrigerate for 2-3 hours or until mixture reaches a pudding-like consistency, stirring a few times. Beat until soft peaks form. Immediately spread between layers and over top and sides of cake. Sprinkle with shaved chocolate. Store in refrigerator. **Yield:** 16-20 servings.

moist cake brownies

Louise Stacey, Dane, Wisconsin

These brownies have been in my recipe collection since I was 9 years old. I've added to and altered the recipe over the years, and now I think it has the perfect amount of everything, including semisweet and milk chocolate chips and pecans. They are my husband's and son's favorite.

- 2/3 cup butter
- 3/4 cup baking cocoa
- 1/4 cup vegetable oil
- 2 cups sugar
- 4 eggs
- 2 teaspoons vanilla extract
- 1-1/2 cups all-purpose flour
- 1 teaspoon baking powder
- 1 teaspoon salt
- 2/3 cup semisweet chocolate chips
- 1/2 cup milk chocolate chips
- 1 cup coarsely chopped pecans
- Confectioners' sugar
- Pecan halves, toasted, optional

Melt butter in a large saucepan. Whisk in cocoa and oil until smooth. Cook and stir over low heat until cocoa is blended. Remove from the heat; stir in sugar. Add eggs, one at a time, stirring well after each addition. Stir in vanilla. Combine flour, baking powder and salt; add to cocoa mixture. Stir in chocolate chips and nuts.

Spread into a greased 13-in. x 9-in. x 2-in. baking pan. Bake at 350° for 25-30 minutes or until a toothpick inserted near the center comes out clean. Cool. Dust with confectioners' sugar. Garnish with pecan halves if desired. **Yield:** 2 dozen.

cookies 'n' cream brownies

Darlene Markel, Sublimity, Oregon

You won't want to frost these brownies, since the marbled top is too pretty to cover up. Besides, the tasty cream cheese layer makes them taste like they're already frosted. The crushed cookies add extra chocolate flavor and a fun crunch.

CREAM CHEESE LAYER:
- 1 package (8 ounces) cream cheese, softened
- 1/4 cup sugar
- 1 egg
- 1/2 teaspoon vanilla extract

BROWNIE LAYER:
- 1/2 cup butter, melted
- 1/2 cup sugar
- 1/2 cup packed brown sugar
- 1/2 cup baking cocoa
- 2 eggs
- 1/2 cup all-purpose flour
- 1 teaspoon baking powder
- 1 teaspoon vanilla extract
- 12 cream-filled chocolate sandwich cookies, crushed

In a small mixing bowl, beat the cream cheese, sugar, egg and vanilla until smooth; set aside. For brownie layer, combine butter, sugars and cocoa in a large mixing bowl; blend well. Add eggs, one at a time, beating well after each addition. Combine flour and baking powder; stir into the cocoa mixture. Stir in vanilla and cookie crumbs.

Pour into a greased 11-in. x 7-in. x 2-in. baking pan. Spoon cream cheese mixture over batter; cut through batter with a knife to swirl. Bake at 350° for 25-30 minutes or until a toothpick inserted near the center comes out with moist crumbs. Cool completely. **Yield:** 2 dozen.

runners-up

fudge-topped brownies

Judy Olson, Whitecourt, Alberta

If you love brownies and fudge, why not combine the two? Mix up a pan of these exquisite brownies for any holiday or special gathering...or just when you want to treat yourself to the ultimate chocolate dessert.

  1 cup butter
  4 squares (1 ounce *each*) unsweetened chocolate
  2 cups sugar
  2 teaspoons vanilla extract
  4 eggs
1-1/2 cups all-purpose flour
  1 teaspoon baking powder
1/2 teaspoon salt
  1 cup chopped walnuts

TOPPING:
4-1/2 cups sugar
  1 can (12 ounces) evaporated milk
1/2 cup butter
  1 package (12 ounces) semisweet chocolate chips
  1 package (11-1/2 ounces) milk chocolate chips
  1 jar (7 ounces) marshmallow creme
  2 teaspoons vanilla extract
  2 cups chopped walnuts

In a saucepan over low heat, melt butter and chocolate. Remove from heat. Blend in sugar and vanilla. Beat in eggs. Combine flour, baking powder and salt; add to chocolate mixture. Stir in nuts. Pour into a greased 13-in. x 9-in. x 2-in. baking pan. Bake at 350° for 25-30 minutes or until top springs back when lightly touched.

In a heavy saucepan, combine sugar, milk and butter; bring to a boil over medium heat. Reduce heat; simmer 5 minutes, stirring constantly. Remove from heat. Stir in chips, creme and vanilla; beat until smooth. Add nuts. Spread over warm brownies. Freeze until firm. Cut into 1-in. squares. Store in the refrigerator. **Yield:** about 10 dozen.

---

prize winning tips

★ ★ ★ ★ ★

★ To add a glossy look to your iced brownies, frost them while they are still warm.
> Juanita Thompson, Grand Rapids, Michigan

★ I like to dress up my brownies for birthdays and other special occasions by garnishing them with whole strawberries and chocolate curls.
> Gertrude Sawatzky, MacGregor, Manitoba

★ As a flavorful alternative, I will sometimes substitute mint extract for vanilla in my brownies.
> Andrea Hiebert, Dallas, Oregon

runners-up

ICE CREAM SOCIAL

#1

ROCKY ROAD
FREEZE

S ummertime offers all sorts of delights—and none of them is more eagerly anticipated than ice cream! That dairy-good dessert was the refreshingly cool focus of our Ice Cream Social contest.

There was lots of lip smacking as our taste panel dug into homemade ice creams, sherbets and freezes, poured on delectable sauces and munched tasty toppings. After the last spoon had been licked clean came the difficult part—selecting the Grand Prize Winner.

" ...Rocky Road Freeze is ideal for anyone making ice cream for the first time. "

That honor went to Sheila Berry of Carrying Place, Ontario for her chocolaty Rocky Road Freeze. "The first time I served it at a dinner party, it was a big hit," says Sheila. "Everyone raved about the rich taste. Still, they hesitated before asking for my recipe. They figured homemade ice cream would be just too complicated. So they were pleasantly surprised to learn how easy it is. In fact, my Rocky Road Freeze is ideal for anyone making ice cream for the first time."

1 can (14 ounces) sweetened condensed milk
1/2 cup chocolate syrup
2 cups heavy whipping cream
1 cup miniature marshmallows
1/2 cup miniature chocolate chips
1/2 cup chopped salted peanuts

In a small bowl, combine the milk and chocolate syrup; set aside. In a mixing bowl, beat cream until stiff peaks form. Fold in chocolate mixture, marshmallows, chocolate chips and peanuts.

Transfer to a freezer-proof container; cover and freeze for 5 hours or until firm. Remove from freezer 10 minutes before serving. **Yield:** about 1-1/2 quarts.

peach melba ice cream pie

Judy Vaske, Bancroft, Iowa

On a hot night, this pie makes a very refreshing dessert. Like most wonderful recipes, it came from a friend. As the third oldest among nine children, I've been cooking for a crowd as long as I can remember! This pie has long been a favorite.

1-1/2 cups flaked coconut
  1/3 cup chopped pecans
    3 tablespoons butter, melted
    1 quart frozen peach yogurt, softened
    1 pint vanilla ice cream, softened
    1 tablespoon cornstarch
    1 tablespoon sugar
    1 package (10 ounces) frozen raspberries in syrup, thawed
    1 cup sliced fresh *or* frozen peaches, thawed

Combine coconut, pecans and butter; press onto the bottom and up the sides of an ungreased 9-in. pie plate. Bake at 350° for 12 minutes or until crust begins to brown around edges. Cool completely.

Spoon frozen yogurt into crust; smooth the top. Spread ice cream over yogurt. Cover and freeze for 2 hours or until firm.

In a small saucepan, combine cornstarch and sugar; drain raspberry juice into pan. Bring to a boil; cook and stir for 2 minutes. Remove from the heat; add raspberries. Cover and chill.

Remove the pie from the freezer 10 minutes before serving. Arrange the peaches on top of the pie; drizzle with a little of the sauce. Pass the remaining sauce around with slices of the pie. **Yield:** 6-8 servings.

sunshine sherbet

Barbara Looney, Fort Knox, Kentucky

Together, my mother and I "invented" this recipe. Warm, humid evenings in Georgia, where I grew up, were all the inspiration we needed! It became a regular part of gatherings with family and friends. After I got married, my boys and their pals would all be there when the sherbet left the freezer. Today my grandkids love to dig into bowls of it as well.

    2 cups sugar
1-1/2 cups water
    2 cups milk
    2 cups heavy whipping cream
1-1/2 cups orange juice
    1 can (12 ounces) evaporated milk
  1/3 cup lemon juice
    2 teaspoons grated orange peel
    8 drops red food coloring, optional
  1/2 teaspoon yellow food coloring, optional

In a saucepan over medium heat, bring sugar and water to a boil; boil for 5 minutes. Cool completely. Add remaining ingredients; mix well.

Pour into the cylinder of an ice cream freezer and freeze according to the manufacturer's directions. Remove from the freezer 10 minutes before serving. **Yield:** about 2 quarts.

homemade ice cream sandwiches

Kea Fisher, Bridger, Montana

My mom sent me this recipe. We love it, and so does the company I serve it to. I inherited my love of cooking from my mother. She's a former home economics teacher. When we were growing up, each of us kids had one night a week when we prepared supper for the rest of the family.

    1 package (18-1/4 ounces) chocolate cake mix
  1/4 cup shortening
  1/4 cup butter, softened
    1 egg
    1 tablespoon water
    1 teaspoon vanilla extract
  1/2 gallon ice cream

In a mixing bowl, combine cake mix, shortening, butter, egg, water and vanilla; beat until well blended. Divide into four equal parts. Between waxed paper, roll one part into a 10-in. x 6-in. rectangle. Remove one piece of waxed paper and flip dough onto an ungreased baking sheet. Score the dough into eight pieces, each 3 in. x 2-1/2 in. Repeat with remaining dough. Bake at 350° for 8-10 minutes or until puffed.

Immediately cut along the scored lines and prick holes in each piece with a fork; cool on baking sheets. Cut ice cream into 16 slices, each 3 in. x 2-1/2 in. x 1 in. Place ice cream between two chocolate cookies; wrap in plastic wrap. Freeze on a baking sheet overnight. Store in an airtight container. **Yield:** 16 servings.

Editor's Note: Purchase a rectangular-shaped package of ice cream in the flavor of your choice for the easiest cutting.

caramel fried ice cream

Darlene Markel, Sublimity, Oregon

At times, I substitute strawberry or Neapolitan for the vanilla ice cream. Our children used to love eating out at Mexican restaurants just so they could order fried ice cream for dessert. When I came upon this recipe, I copied it down quickly!

    1 quart vanilla ice cream
  1/4 cup heavy whipping cream
    2 teaspoons vanilla extract
    2 cups flaked coconut, finely chopped
    2 cups finely crushed cornflakes
  1/2 teaspoon ground cinnamon
CARAMEL SAUCE:
    1 cup sugar
  1/2 cup butter
  1/2 cup evaporated milk
Oil for deep-fat frying

Using a 1/2-cup ice cream scoop, place eight scoops of ice cream on a baking sheet. Cover and freeze for 2 hours or until firm. In a bowl, combine cream and vanilla. In another bowl, combine coconut, cornflakes and cinnamon. Remove ice cream from freezer; wearing plastic gloves, shape the ice cream into balls. Dip balls into cream mixture, then roll in coconut mixture, making sure to coat entire surface. Place coated balls on a baking sheet. Cover and freeze 3 hours or until firm.

For caramel sauce, heat sugar in a heavy saucepan over medium heat until partially melted and golden, stirring occasionally. Add butter. Gradually add milk, stirring constantly. Cook and stir for 8 minutes or until sauce is thick and golden; keep warm.

Heat oil in an electric skillet or deep-fat fryer to 375°. Fry ice cream balls until golden, about 30 seconds. Drain on paper towels. Serve immediately with caramel sauce. **Yield:** 8 servings.

brownie ice cream cones

Marlene Rhodes, Panama City, Florida

Often, I'll find a recipe that sounds interesting, copy it down and put my own twist on it. That's just what I did with these. I make them for our children when they have friends over. They love the combination of a brownie and ice cream in a cone.

  1 package (4 ounces) German sweet chocolate
1/4 cup butter
3/4 cup sugar
  2 eggs
1/2 cup all-purpose flour
1/2 cup chopped walnuts, optional
  1 teaspoon vanilla extract
24 cake ice cream cones (about 3 inches tall)
24 scoops ice cream
Colored *or* chocolate sprinkles

In a saucepan over low heat, melt the chocolate and butter, stirring frequently. Cool slightly; pour into a bowl. Add sugar and eggs; mix well. Stir in flour, walnuts if desired and vanilla.

Place the ice cream cones in muffin cups; fill half full with batter. Bake at 350° for 20-22 minutes or until brownies are set on top and a toothpick inserted near the center comes out with moist crumbs (do not overbake). Cool completely.

Just before serving, top each with a scoop of ice cream and garnish with sprinkles. **Yield:** 2 dozen.

frosty lemon pie

Judith Wilke, Dousman, Wisconsin

This pie is a nice light and refreshing finish to a summer picnic or patio supper. I like that it can be made ahead and kept in the freezer until you're ready to serve.

3/4 cup sugar
1/3 cup lemon juice
1/4 cup butter
Dash salt
  3 eggs, beaten
  2 pints vanilla ice cream, softened, *divided*
  1 graham cracker crust (9 inches)
Whipped topping, fresh mint and lemon peel, optional

In a saucepan, combine sugar, lemon juice, butter and salt; cook and stir over medium heat until sugar is dissolved and the butter is melted. Add a small amount to eggs; return all to the pan. Cook and stir over medium heat until thickened (do not boil). Refrigerate until completely cooled.

Spread half of the ice cream into the crust; freeze for 1 hour or until firm. Cover with half of the lemon mixture; freeze for 1 hour or until firm. Repeat layers. Cover and freeze for several hours or overnight.

Remove from the freezer 10 minutes before serving. If desired, garnish with whipped topping, mint and lemon peel. **Yield:** 8 servings.

strawberry brownie bombe

Joanne Watts, Kitchener, Ontario

A friend and I dreamed up this recipe. We use it to entertain and for special family dinners. For an extra touch, you can dip the strawberries in chocolate.

- 1 package (21-1/2 ounces) fudge brownie mix
- 1/2 cup chopped walnuts
- 1/2 cup strawberry preserves
- 1 quart strawberry ice cream, softened
- 2 cups heavy whipping cream
- 3 drops red food coloring, optional
- 1/4 cup confectioners' sugar

Pastry bag *or* heavy-duty resealable plastic bag
Star pastry tip #8B *or* #20
Fresh strawberries and mint, optional

Prepare brownie mix according to package directions for cake-like brownies. Stir in walnuts. Pour the batter into two greased and waxed paper-lined 8-in. round baking pans. Bake at 350° for 30 minutes or until a toothpick inserted near the center comes out clean. Cool completely in pans.

Line a 1-1/2-qt. metal bowl with foil. Cut and fit one brownie layer to evenly line the inside of the bowl (brownie may crack). Spread preserves over brownie layer. Freeze for 15 minutes. Fill brownie-lined bowl with ice cream; smooth top. Cover and freeze for 3 hours or until ice cream is firm.

Place remaining brownie layer on a serving plate. Remove bowl from freezer; uncover. Invert onto brownie layer; remove bowl and foil. Return to freezer.

In a mixing bowl, beat cream and food coloring until soft peaks form. Add sugar and beat until stiff peaks form; set aside 1-1/2 cups. Spread remaining whipped cream over top and sides of bombe.

Cut a small hole in the corner of a pastry or plastic bag and insert star tip. Fill with reserved whipped cream; pipe border at base of bombe. Holding the bag straight up and down, form stars on top. Garnish with strawberries and mint if desired. **Yield:** 16 servings.

Editor's Note: Unfrosted bombe may be frozen for up to 3 days.

★ ★ ★ ★ ★ prize winning tips

★ A popular dessert at our house is one part angel food cake chunks combined with two parts softened ice cream. Serve with the topping of your choice.

Mary McCreery, Boynton Beach, Florida

★ To soften ice cream topping that has been refrigerated, I place the can or jar in hot water until it's pourable. You can also put the topping in a microwave-safe dish and heat it in the microwave for just a few seconds.

Nancy Newton, Greendale, Wisconsin

★ If you'd like to prevent a sticky coating, put plastic wrap directly on top of ice cream in the container when you freeze it.

Beverly Matheson, Taylorsville, Utah

runners-up

RICH TRUFFLE
WEDGES

rich truffle wedges

Chocolate—the very word turns heads and sparks smiles. Mouths water at the mere thought of all the sweet and satisfying delicacies that call for chocolate as a main ingredient.

For our Celebrate Chocolate recipe contest, more than 6,500 devoted chocolate fans submitted their favorite chocolate concoctions—brownies, cookies, cakes, candies, beverages and more.

> " I've made this decadent dessert many times—to the delight of family and guests. "

Whether it's to impress holiday guests or satisfy a craving, each of the winning recipes here is an irresistible way to celebrate chocolate—bar none.

You'll certainly want to start with our Grand Prize Winner, Rich Truffle Wedges. The recipe comes from Patricia Vatta of Norwood, Ontario. "I've made this decadent dessert many times— to the delight of family and guests," says Patricia. "It has a scrumptious, fudgy consistency and big chocolate taste. The tart raspberry sauce complements the flavor and looks lovely spooned over each serving."

1/2 cup butter
6 squares (1 ounce *each*) semisweet chocolate, chopped
3 eggs
2/3 cup sugar
1 teaspoon vanilla extract
1/4 teaspoon salt
2/3 cup all-purpose flour
GLAZE:
1/4 cup butter
2 squares (1 ounce *each*) semisweet chocolate
2 squares (1 ounce *each*) unsweetened chocolate
2 teaspoons honey
SAUCE:
2 cups fresh *or* frozen unsweetened raspberries
2 tablespoons sugar
Whipped cream, fresh raspberries and mint, optional

In a microwave or double boiler, melt butter and chocolate; stir until smooth. Cool for 10 minutes. In a mixing bowl, beat eggs, sugar, vanilla and salt until thick, about 4 minutes. Blend in chocolate mixture. Stir in the flour; mix well.

Pour into a greased and floured 9-in. springform pan. Bake at 350° for 25-30 minutes or until a toothpick inserted near the center comes out clean. Cool completely on a wire rack.

Combine glaze ingredients in a small saucepan; cook and stir over low heat until melted and smooth. Cool slightly. Run a knife around the edge of springform pan to loosen; remove cake to serving plate. Spread glaze over the top and sides; set aside.

For sauce, puree the raspberries in a blender or food processor. Press through a sieve if desired; discard seeds. Stir in sugar; chill until serving.

Spoon sauce over individual servings. Garnish with whipped cream, raspberries and mint if desired. **Yield:** 12 servings.

chocolate caramel candy

Jane Meek, Pahrump, Nevada
This dazzling treat tastes like a Snickers bar but has homemade flavor beyond compare.

   2 tablespoons butter
   1 cup (6 ounces) milk chocolate chips
   1/4 cup butterscotch chips
   1/4 cup creamy peanut butter
FILLING:
   1/4 cup butter
   1 cup sugar
   1/4 cup evaporated milk
1-1/2 cups marshmallow creme
   1/4 cup creamy peanut butter
   1 teaspoon vanilla extract
1-1/2 cups chopped salted peanuts
CARAMEL LAYER:
   1 package (14 ounces) caramels
   1/4 cup heavy whipping cream
ICING:
   1 cup (6 ounces) milk chocolate chips
   1/4 cup butterscotch chips
   1/4 cup creamy peanut butter

Line a 13-in. x 9-in. x 2-in. pan with foil; butter the foil with 2 teaspoons butter; set aside.

In a small saucepan, combine chips and peanut butter; stir over low heat until melted and smooth. Spread into the foil-lined pan. Refrigerate until set.

For filling, in a small heavy saucepan, melt the butter over medium heat. Add the sugar and milk; bring to a gentle boil. Reduce heat to medium-low; boil and stir for 5 minutes.

Remove from the heat; stir in the marshmallow creme, peanut butter and vanilla. Add peanuts. Spread over first layer. Refrigerate until set.

For caramel layer, in a small heavy saucepan, combine the caramels and cream; stir over low heat until melted and smooth. Cook and stir 4 minutes longer. Spread over the filling. Refrigerate until set.

For icing, in another saucepan, combine chips and peanut butter; stir over low heat until melted and smooth. Pour over caramel layer. Refrigerate for at least 4 hours or overnight.

Remove from the refrigerator 20 minutes before cutting. Remove from pan and cut into 1-in. squares. Store in an airtight container. **Yield:** about 8 dozen.

orange chocolate meltaways

Lori Kostecki, Wausau, Wisconsin
The terrific combination of chocolate and orange makes these some of the best truffles I've ever had. As holiday gifts, they're showstoppers.

   1 package (11-1/2 ounces) milk chocolate chips
   1 cup (6 ounces) semisweet chocolate chips
3/4 cup heavy whipping cream
   1 teaspoon grated orange peel
2-1/2 teaspoons orange extract
1-1/2 cups finely chopped toasted pecans
COATING:
   1 cup (6 ounces) milk chocolate chips
   2 tablespoons shortening

Place chocolate chips in a mixing bowl; set aside. In a saucepan, bring cream and orange peel to a gentle boil; immediately pour over chips. Let stand for 1 minute; whisk until smooth. Add the extract. Cover and chill for 35 minutes or until mixture begins to thicken.

Beat for 10-15 seconds or just until mixture lightens in color (do not overbeat). Spoon rounded teaspoonfuls onto waxed paper-lined baking sheets. Cover and chill for 5 minutes.

Gently shape into balls; roll half in nuts. In a microwave or double boiler, melt chocolate and shortening; stir until smooth. Dip remaining balls in chocolate. Place on waxed paper to harden. Store in the refrigerator. **Yield:** 6 dozen.

runners-up

chocolate angel cake

Joyce Shiffler, Manitou Springs, Colorado

When I married in 1944, I could barely boil water. My dear mother-in-law taught me her specialty—making the lightest of angel food cakes ever. This chocolate version is an easy, impressive treat. For many years, it was our son's first choice for his birthday cake.

- 1-1/2 cups confectioners' sugar
- 1 cup cake flour
- 1/4 cup baking cocoa
- 1-1/2 cups egg whites (about 10 eggs)
- 1-1/2 teaspoons cream of tartar
- 1/2 teaspoon salt
- 1 cup sugar

FROSTING:

- 1-1/2 cups heavy whipping cream
- 1/2 cup sugar
- 1/4 cup baking cocoa
- 1/2 teaspoon salt
- 1/2 teaspoon vanilla extract
- Chocolate leaves, optional

Sift together confectioners' sugar, flour and cocoa three times; set aside.

In a mixing bowl, beat egg whites, cream of tartar and salt until soft peaks form. Add sugar, 2 tablespoons at a time, beating until stiff peaks form. Gradually fold in cocoa mixture, about a fourth at a time.

Spoon into an ungreased 10-in. tube pan. Carefully run a metal spatula or knife through batter to remove air pockets. Bake on lowest oven rack at 375° for 35-40 minutes or until the top springs back when lightly touched and cracks feel dry.

Immediately invert pan; cool completely. Run a knife around edges and center tube to loosen; remove cake.

In a mixing bowl, combine the first five frosting ingredients; cover and chill for 1 hour. Beat until stiff peaks form. Spread over top and sides of cake. Store in the refrigerator. Garnish with chocolate leaves if desired. **Yield:** 12-16 servings.

---

prize winning tips

* * * * *

*For chocolate cakes or cookies, dust baking pans and cookie sheets with unsweetened cocoa instead of flour to avoid a "floury" look and to add extra richness.

Candice Marie Curry, Hamilton, Ohio

*If a chocolate cake is difficult to remove from the pan, return it to a warm oven for 30-60 seconds. Then invert it onto a plate or cooling rack.

Marilyn Gift, Clive, Iowa

*Use a vegetable peeler to shave solid chocolate for garnishing. Also, when melting solid chocolate for use in recipes, grate it first so it will melt faster.

Gladys Earl, Menomonie, Wisconsin

*For great chocolate chip cookies, I add 1 teaspoon of cinnamon to the batter.

Kelly Lyn Rits, Austin, Texas

---

runners-up

chocolate dipped brownies

Jackie Archer, Clinton, Iowa
My family calls these bars "the world's chocolatiest brownies" and is more than happy to gobble up a batch whenever I make them. They're a deliciously jolly part of our Christmas cookie collection.

- 3/4 cup sugar
- 1/3 cup butter
- 2 tablespoons water
- 4 cups (24 ounces) semisweet chocolate chips, *divided*
- 1 teaspoon vanilla extract
- 2 eggs
- 3/4 cup all-purpose flour
- 1/2 teaspoon salt
- 1/4 teaspoon baking soda
- 2 tablespoons shortening
- 1/2 cup chopped pecans, toasted

In a saucepan over medium heat, bring sugar, butter and water to a boil; remove from the heat. Stir in 1 cup of chocolate chips and vanilla; stir until smooth. Cool for 5 minutes.

Beat in eggs, one at a time, until well mixed. Combine flour, salt and baking soda; stir into chocolate mixture. Stir in another cup of chips.

Pour into a greased 9-in. square baking pan. Bake at 325° for 35 minutes or until set. Cool completely. Place in the freezer for 30-40 minutes (do not freeze completely). Cut into bars.

In a microwave or heavy saucepan, melt remaining chips with shortening; stir until smooth. Using a small fork, dip brownies to completely coat; shake off excess. Place on waxed paper-lined baking sheets; immediately sprinkle with nuts.

Allow to set. Store in an airtight container in a cool place. **Yield:** 3 dozen.

neapolitan cheesecake

Sherri Regalbuto, Carp, Ontario
This rich, creamy cheesecake won first-place ribbons at many fairs and is my family's preferred dessert.

CRUST:
- 1 cup chocolate wafer crumbs (18 wafers)
- 3 tablespoons butter

FILLING:
- 3 packages (8 ounces *each*) cream cheese, softened
- 3/4 cup sugar
- 1/4 cup heavy whipping cream
- 3 eggs, lightly beaten
- 1 teaspoon vanilla extract
- 2 squares (1 ounce *each*) semisweet chocolate, melted and cooled
- 2 squares (1 ounce *each*) white baking chocolate, melted and cooled
- 1/3 cup mashed sweetened strawberries

Red liquid food coloring, optional

TOPPING:
- 3 squares (1 ounce *each*) semisweet chocolate, melted
- 2 tablespoons butter
- 2 teaspoons shortening, *divided*
- 1 square (1 ounce) white baking chocolate

In a small bowl, combine wafer crumbs and butter. Press onto the bottom of a greased 9-in. springform pan. Place pan on a baking sheet. Bake at 350° for 10 minutes. Cool on a wire rack. Reduce heat to 325°.

In a large mixing bowl, beat cream cheese until smooth. Gradually beat in sugar and cream. Add eggs and vanilla; beat on low just until combined. Divide batter into thirds. Add melted semisweet chocolate to a third. Spread over crust. Add melted white chocolate to another third. Spread over semisweet layer. Stir strawberries and a few drops of food coloring if desired into remaining portion. Spread over white chocolate layer. Place pan on a double-thickness of heavy-duty foil (about 16 in. x 16 in.). Securely wrap foil around pan.

Place springform pan in a large baking pan. Fill larger pan with hot water to a depth of 1 in. Bake at 325° for 70-75 minutes or until center is just set. Remove springform pan from water bath. Cool on a wire rack for 10 minutes. Carefully run a knife around the edge of pan to loosen; cool for 1 hour longer. Remove foil. Refrigerate overnight.

Melt semisweet chocolate, butter and 1 teaspoon shortening in a heavy saucepan or microwave; stir until smooth. Cool 5 minutes. Remove sides of pan. Pour melted chocolate mixture over cheesecake. Melt white chocolate and remaining shortening. Drizzle over cheesecake. Refrigerate until chocolate is firm. Refrigerate leftovers. **Yield:** 12-14 servings.

chocolate meringue stars

Edna Lee, Greeley, Colorado
These light, delicate and chewy cookies certainly make for merry munching.

- **3 egg whites**
- **3/4 teaspoon vanilla extract**
- **3/4 cup sugar**
- **1/4 cup baking cocoa**
GLAZE:
- **3 squares (1 ounce *each*) semisweet chocolate**
- **1 tablespoon shortening**

In a mixing bowl, beat the egg whites and vanilla until soft peaks form. Gradually add the sugar, about 2 tablespoons at a time, beating until stiff peaks form. Gently fold in the cocoa.

Place in a pastry bag with a large open star tip (#8b). Line baking sheets with ungreased parchment paper. Pipe stars, about 1-1/4-in. diameter, onto parchment paper, or drop by rounded teaspoonfuls. Bake at 300° for 30-35 minutes or until lightly browned. Remove from parchment paper; cool on wire racks.

In a microwave or heavy saucepan, melt chocolate and shortening; stir until smooth. Dip the cookies halfway into glaze; place on waxed paper to set. **Yield:** about 4 dozen.

chocolate truffle cookies

Dealine Fortenberry, McComb, Mississippi
Here's a snack for serious chocolate lovers. These enticing cookies are crisp on the outside and soft on the inside, somewhat bittersweet and very chocolaty. I usually make them to share at get-togethers otherwise, I'd eat them all myself! I'm always asked for the recipe.

- **4 squares (1 ounce *each*) unsweetened chocolate**
- **2 cups (12 ounces) semisweet chocolate chips, *divided***
- **1/3 cup butter**
- **1 cup sugar**
- **3 eggs**
- **1-1/2 teaspoons vanilla extract**
- **1/2 cup all-purpose flour**
- **2 tablespoons baking cocoa**
- **1/4 teaspoon baking powder**
- **1/4 teaspoon salt**
Confectioners' sugar

In a microwave or double boiler, melt unsweetened chocolate, 1 cup of chocolate chips and butter; cool for 10 minutes.

In a mixing bowl, beat sugar and eggs for 2 minutes. Beat in vanilla and the chocolate mixture.

Combine flour, cocoa, baking powder and salt; beat into chocolate mixture. Stir in remaining chocolate chips. Cover and chill for at least 3 hours.

Remove about 1 cup of dough. With lightly floured hands, roll into 1-in. balls. Place on ungreased baking sheets.

Bake at 350° for 10-12 minutes or until lightly puffed and set. Cool on pan 3-4 minutes before removing to a wire rack to cool completely.

Repeat with remaining dough. Dust with confectioners' sugar. **Yield:** about 4 dozen.

PIE POTPOURRI

#1

CHEDDAR PEAR PIE

cheddar pear pie

Any way you slice it, pie is a terrific treat. Old-fashioned and traditional or unusual and deliciously different, the wonderful wedges delight senses and tempt taste buds.

The winners of our Pie Potpourri contest are no exception. Home cooks entered almost 5,000 pies with a vast variety of crusts and fillings.

> " I make sure to have copies of the recipe with me since people always ask for it. "

Try our taste panel's picks in your kitchen—you'll find that getting sincere compliments is easy as pie!

At the top of this luscious lineup is Cheddar Pear Pie, picked as the Grand Prize Winner. Cynthia LaBree of Elmer, New Jersey shared the scrumptious dessert.

"I take this pie to lots of different gatherings, and I make sure to have copies of the recipe with me since people always ask for it," says Cynthia. "It's amusing to see some folks puzzling over what's in the filling—they expect apples but love the subtle sweetness of the pears."

---

4 large ripe pears, peeled and thinly sliced
1/3 cup sugar
1 tablespoon cornstarch
1/8 teaspoon salt
1 unbaked pastry shell (9 inches)
TOPPING:
1/2 cup shredded cheddar cheese
1/2 cup all-purpose flour
1/4 cup butter, melted
1/4 cup sugar
1/4 teaspoon salt

In a bowl, combine pears, sugar, cornstarch and salt. Pour into pastry shell. Combine topping ingredients until crumbly; sprinkle over filling.

Bake at 425° for 25-35 minutes or until crust is golden and cheese is melted. Cool on a wire rack for 15-20 minutes. Serve warm. Store in the refrigerator. **Yield:** 6-8 servings.

chocolate raspberry pie

Ruth Bartel, Morris, Manitoba
After tasting this pie at my sister-in-law's house, I had to have the recipe. I love the chocolate and raspberry layers separated by a dreamy cream layer.

    1 unbaked pastry shell (9 inches)
    3 tablespoons sugar
    1 tablespoon cornstarch
    2 cups fresh *or* frozen unsweetened raspberries, thawed
FILLING:
    1 package (8 ounces) cream cheese, softened
    1/3 cup sugar
    1/2 teaspoon vanilla extract
    1/2 cup heavy whipping cream, whipped
TOPPING:
    2 squares (1 ounce *each*) semisweet chocolate
    3 tablespoons butter

Line unpricked pastry shell with a double thickness of heavy-duty foil. Bake at 450° for 8 minutes. Remove foil; bake 5 minutes longer. Cool on a wire rack.

In a saucepan, combine sugar and cornstarch. Stir in the raspberries; bring to a boil over medium heat. Boil and stir for 2 minutes. Remove from the heat; cool for 15 minutes. Spread into shell; refrigerate.

In a mixing bowl, beat cream cheese, sugar and vanilla until fluffy. Fold in whipped cream. Carefully spread over raspberry layer. Cover and refrigerate for at least 1 hour.

Melt chocolate and butter; cool for 4-5 minutes. Pour over filling. Cover and chill for at least 2 hours. Store in the refrigerator. **Yield:** 6-8 servings.

fluffy caramel pie

Ginger Hendricksen, Wisconsin Rapids, Wisconsin
I bake a variety of pies, but this is the one my husband likes best. The gingersnap crumb crust is a tangy contrast to the sweet, lighter-than-air caramel filling.

1-1/2 cups crushed gingersnaps (about 30 cookies)
    1/4 cup butter, melted
FILLING:
    1/4 cup cold water
      1 envelope unflavored gelatin
     28 caramels
      1 cup milk
Dash salt
    1/2 cup chopped pecans
      1 teaspoon vanilla extract
      1 cup heavy whipping cream, whipped
Caramel ice cream topping and additional pecans, optional

Combine the cookie crumbs and butter; press onto the bottom and up the sides of a greased 9-in. pie plate. Cover and chill.

Meanwhile, place cold water in a heavy saucepan; sprinkle with gelatin. Let stand for 1 minute. Add caramels, milk and salt; cook and stir over low heat until gelatin is dissolved and caramels are melted. Refrigerate for 1-2 hours or until mixture mounds when stirred with a spoon.

Stir in pecans and vanilla. Fold in whipped cream. Pour into crust. Refrigerate for 6 hours or overnight. Garnish with ice cream topping and pecans if desired. Store in the refrigerator. **Yield:** 6-8 servings.

frosted orange pie

Delores Edgecomb, Atlanta, New York
With its fresh-tasting filling and fluffy frosting, this pretty pie is truly an elegant final course.

    3/4 cup sugar
    1/2 cup all-purpose flour
    1/4 teaspoon salt
1-1/4 cups water
      2 egg yolks, lightly beaten
      2 to 3 tablespoons grated orange peel
    1/2 teaspoon grated lemon peel
    1/2 cup orange juice
      2 tablespoons lemon juice
      1 pastry shell (9 inches), baked
FROSTING:
    1/2 cup sugar
      2 egg whites
      2 tablespoons water
    1/8 teaspoon *each* cream of tartar and salt
    1/2 cup flaked coconut, toasted

In a saucepan, combine sugar, flour and salt; gradually add water. Cook and stir over medium-high heat for 2-3 minutes or until thickened and bubbly. Remove from heat. Gradually stir 1/2 cup into egg yolks; return all to pan. Bring to a gentle boil; cook and stir for 2 minutes. Remove from the heat; stir in orange peel and lemon peel. Gently stir in juices. Pour into pastry shell. Cool on a wire rack for 1 hour. Chill at least 3 hours.

In a heavy saucepan or double boiler, combine sugar, egg whites, water, cream of tartar and salt. With a portable mixer, beat on low speed for 1 minute. Continue beating on low over low heat until frosting reaches 160°, about 8-10 minutes.

With a stand mixer, beat on high until frosting forms stiff peaks, about 7 minutes. Spread over chilled pie. Just before serving, sprinkle with coconut. Store in the refrigerator. **Yield:** 6-8 servings.

triple fruit pie

Jeanne Freybler, Grand Rapids, Michigan
My goal is to create pies as good as my mother's. I came up with this recipe to use up fruit in my freezer. The first time I made it, my family begged for seconds. If I continue making pies this good, maybe someday our two daughters will be striving to imitate mine!

1-1/4 cups *each* fresh blueberries, raspberries and chopped rhubarb
    1/2 teaspoon almond extract
1-1/4 cups sugar
    1/4 cup quick-cooking tapioca
    1/4 teaspoon ground nutmeg
    1/4 teaspoon salt
      1 tablespoon lemon juice
Pastry for double-crust pie (9 inches)

In a large bowl, combine fruits and extract; toss to coat. In another bowl, combine sugar, tapioca, nutmeg and salt. Add to fruit; stir gently. Let stand for 15 minutes.

Line a 9-in. pie plate with bottom crust; trim pastry even with edge. Stir lemon juice into fruit mixture; spoon into the crust. Roll out remaining pastry; make a lattice crust. Seal and flute edges.

Bake at 400° for 20 minutes. Reduce heat to 350°; bake 30 minutes longer or until the crust is golden brown and the filling is bubbly. **Yield:** 6-8 servings.

Editor's Note: Frozen berries and rhubarb may be substituted for fresh; thaw and drain before using.

fudgy pecan pie

Ellen Arndt, Cologne, Minnesota
*This started out as just a plain chocolate pie that I
"dressed up" for company. Now when I serve it, guests
often tell me, "Your pie looks too good to eat—but I won't
let that stop me!"*

- 1 **unbaked pastry shell (9 inches)**
- 1 **package (4 ounces) German sweet chocolate**
- 1/4 **cup butter**
- 1 **can (14 ounces) sweetened condensed milk**
- 1/2 **cup water**
- 2 **eggs, beaten**
- 1 **teaspoon vanilla extract**
- 1/4 **teaspoon salt**
- 1/2 **cup chopped pecans**

FILLING:
- 1 **cup cold milk**
- 1 **package (3.9 ounces) instant chocolate pudding mix**
- 1 **cup whipped topping**

TOPPING:
- 1 **cup heavy whipping cream**
- 1 **tablespoon confectioners' sugar**
- 1 **teaspoon vanilla extract**

Line unpricked pastry shell with a double thickness of
heavy-duty foil. Bake at 450° for 5 minutes. Remove foil
and set shell aside. Reduce heat to 375°.

In a heavy saucepan, melt chocolate and butter.
Remove from the heat; stir in milk and water. Add a small
amount of hot chocolate mixture to eggs; return all to the
pan. Stir in vanilla and salt. Pour into shell; sprinkle with
nuts. Cover edges with foil. Bake for 35 minutes or until
a knife inserted near the center comes out clean. Remove
to a wire rack to cool completely.

In a mixing bowl, beat milk and pudding mix until
smooth. Fold in whipped topping. Spread over nut layer;
cover and refrigerate. In a mixing bowl, beat cream
until soft peaks form. Add sugar and vanilla, beating
until stiff peaks form. Spread over pudding layer.
Refrigerate until set, about 4 hours. **Yield:** 6-8 servings.

peanutty ice cream pie

Donna Cline, Pensacola, Florida
*A friend gave me this recipe over 25 years ago.
The unique crust makes these cool slices extra nutty and
perfect for a party. I keep the recipe handy since it's great
for any occasion.*

- 1-1/3 **cups finely chopped peanuts**
- 3 **tablespoons butter, melted**
- 2 **tablespoons sugar**

FILLING:
- 1/4 **cup peanut butter**
- 1/4 **cup light corn syrup**
- 1/4 **cup flaked coconut**
- 3 **tablespoons chopped peanuts**
- 1 **quart vanilla ice cream, softened**

Miniature M&M's *or* semisweet chocolate chips

Combine the peanuts, butter and sugar; press onto the
bottom and up the sides of a greased 9-in. pie plate.
Cover and refrigerate for 15 minutes.

In a large bowl, combine peanut butter and corn syrup.
Add coconut and peanuts. Stir in ice cream just until
combined. Spoon into crust. Cover and freeze overnight
or until firm. Just before serving, sprinkle with M&M's
or chocolate chips. **Yield:** 6-8 servings.

farm apple pan pie

Dolores Skrout, Summerhill, Pennsylvania
Be prepared when you take this pie to a covered-dish supper—people always ask for a copy of the recipe!

EGG YOLK PASTRY:
   5 cups all-purpose flour
   4 teaspoons sugar
 1/2 teaspoon salt
 1/2 teaspoon baking powder
1-1/2 cups shortening
   2 egg yolks, lightly beaten
 3/4 cup cold water
FILLING:
   5 pounds tart baking apples, peeled and thinly sliced
   4 teaspoons lemon juice
 3/4 cup sugar
 3/4 cup packed brown sugar
   1 teaspoon ground cinnamon
 1/2 teaspoon ground nutmeg
 1/4 teaspoon salt
Milk
Additional sugar

In a bowl, combine flour, sugar, salt and baking powder; cut in shortening until the mixture resembles coarse crumbs. Combine yolks and cold water. Sprinkle over dry ingredients; toss with fork. If needed, add additional water, 1 tablespoon at a time, until the mixture can be formed into a ball. Divide dough in half. On a lightly floured surface, roll half of dough to fit a 15-in. x 10-in. x 1-in. baking pan. Sprinkle apples with lemon juice; arrange half of them over dough.

Combine the sugars, cinnamon, nutmeg and salt; sprinkle half over apples. Top with remaining apples; sprinkle with remaining sugar mixture.

Roll remaining pastry to fit pan; place on top of filling and seal edges. Brush with milk and sprinkle with sugar. Cut vents in top pastry.

Bake at 400° for 50 minutes or until crust is golden brown and filling is bubbly. **Yield:** 18-24 servings.

lemon supreme pie

Jana Beckman, Wamego, Kansas
The combination of the cream cheese and tart lemon in this recipe is wonderful.

   1 unbaked deep-dish pastry shell (9 inches)
LEMON FILLING:
1-1/4 cups sugar, *divided*
   6 tablespoons cornstarch
 1/2 teaspoon salt
1-1/4 cups water
   2 tablespoons butter
   2 teaspoons grated lemon peel
   4 to 5 drops yellow food coloring, optional
 1/2 cup fresh lemon juice
CREAM CHEESE FILLING:
   2 packages (one 8 ounces, one 3 ounces) cream cheese, softened
 3/4 cup confectioners' sugar
1-1/2 cups whipped topping
   1 tablespoon lemon juice

Line unpricked pastry shell with a double thickness of heavy-duty foil. Bake at 450° for 8 minutes. Remove foil; bake 5 minutes longer. Cool on a wire rack.

In a saucepan, combine 3/4 cup sugar, cornstarch and salt. Stir in water; bring to a boil over medium-high heat. Reduce heat; add the remaining sugar. Cook and stir for 2 minutes or until thickened and bubbly. Remove from the heat; stir in butter, lemon peel and food coloring if desired. Gently stir in lemon juice (do not overmix). Cool to room temperature, about 1 hour.

In a mixing bowl, beat cream cheese and sugar until smooth. Fold in whipped topping and lemon juice. Refrigerate 1/2 cup for garnish. Spread remaining cream cheese mixture into shell; top with lemon filling. Chill overnight.

Place reserved cream cheese mixture in a pastry bag with a #21 star tip; pipe stars onto pie. Store in the refrigerator. **Yield:** 6-8 servings.

potluck apple pie

Alma Lynne Gravel, Trappe, Pennsylvania
In charge of dessert for a fund-raising dinner at our church, I experimented and came up with this scrumptious pie made in a jelly roll pan.

2-1/4 cups all-purpose flour, *divided*
  1/4 cup water
Pinch salt
   1 cup shortening
FILLING:
  1/2 cup maple syrup, *divided*
   3 pounds tart apples (8 to 9 medium), peeled and thinly sliced
1-1/4 cups sugar
  1/4 cup lemon juice
   2 teaspoons ground cinnamon
   1 teaspoon vanilla extract
TOPPING:
   1 cup all-purpose flour
  1/2 cup packed brown sugar
  1/2 cup cold butter
   1 cup chopped pecans

In a small bowl, combine 1/4 cup flour and water until smooth; set aside. In a large bowl, combine salt and remaining flour; cut in shortening until mixture resembles coarse crumbs. Add reserved flour mixture; knead gently until dough forms a ball.

Press dough onto the bottom and up the sides of an ungreased 15-in. x 10-in. x 1-in. baking pan. Spread 1/4 cup syrup over crust. Arrange apples over syrup. Combine sugar, lemon juice, cinnamon, vanilla and remaining syrup; drizzle over apples.

For topping, combine flour and sugar in a bowl; cut in butter until the mixture resembles coarse crumbs. Stir in pecans. Sprinkle over filling. Bake at 350° for 1 hour or until apples are tender. **Yield:** 18-24 servings.

peach plum pie

Susan Osborne, Hatfield Point, New Brunswick
When I want to impress guests, this is the pie I prepare. Peaches, plums and a bit of lemon peel are a refreshing trio that wakes up taste buds. It's a family favorite that's requested often.

   2 cups sliced peeled fresh *or* frozen peaches, thawed and drained
   2 cups sliced peeled fresh purple plums
   1 tablespoon lemon juice
  1/4 teaspoon almond extract
1-1/2 cups sugar
  1/4 cup quick-cooking tapioca
  1/2 to 1 teaspoon grated lemon peel
  1/4 teaspoon salt
Pastry for double-crust pie (9 inches)
   2 tablespoons butter

In a large bowl, combine the peaches, plums, lemon juice and extract. In another bowl, combine sugar, tapioca, lemon peel and salt. Add to fruit mixture and stir gently; let stand for 15 minutes.

Line a 9-in. pie plate with bottom crust; add the filling. Dot with butter. Roll out remaining pastry to fit top of pie; cut slits in pastry. Place over filling. Trim, seal and flute edges. Cover the edges loosely with foil.

Bake at 450° for 10 minutes. Reduce heat to 350°. Remove foil; bake 35 minutes longer or until crust is golden brown and filling is bubbly. **Yield:** 6-8 servings.

maple apple cream pie

Christi Paulton, Phelps, Wisconsin
We think this deliciously different dessert is a nice change from a traditional apple pie. Who can resist its tender apples smothered in a silky maple-flavored cream? This pie is definitely worth a try.

    1 unbaked pastry shell (9 inches)
    2 tablespoons butter
    6 medium Golden Delicious apples (about 2
      pounds), peeled and cut into eighths
  1/2 cup packed brown sugar
  1/3 cup maple syrup
    2 tablespoons cornstarch
    1 can (12 ounces) evaporated milk
    1 egg yolk
    1 teaspoon vanilla extract
  1/2 cup heavy whipping cream
  1/4 teaspoon ground cinnamon
    1 tablespoon sugar

Line unpricked pastry shell with a double thickness of heavy-duty foil. Bake at 450° for 8 minutes. Remove foil; bake 5 minutes longer. Cool on a wire rack.

In a skillet, melt butter. Add apples and brown sugar; cook and stir until apples are tender and coated, 15-20 minutes. Cool to room temperature. Spread evenly into shell.

In a saucepan, combine syrup and cornstarch until smooth. Gradually add milk. Bring to a boil. Boil and stir for 2 minutes or until thickened and bubbly. Remove from heat. Gradually stir 1/4 cup into egg yolk; return all to pan. Cook over low heat for 2 minutes. Remove from heat; add vanilla. Cool to room temperature. Pour over apples. Chill until set, about 2 hours.

In a mixing bowl, beat cream until soft peaks form. Add cinnamon. Gradually add sugar, beating until stiff peaks form. Serve with pie. Store in the refrigerator. **Yield:** 6-8 servings.

ricotta nut pie

Renee Bennett, Manlius, New York
I'm proud to serve this full pie at special dinners for family and guests. Similar to a traditional Italian ricotta pie but with a few fun twists, it's a satisfying dessert that's not overly sweet. I can't resist the yummy combination of almonds, ricotta cheese, apricots and chocolate.

1-1/2 cups crushed vanilla wafers (about 45
      cookies)
  1/4 cup butter, softened
  1/3 cup apricot preserves
    1 carton (15 ounces) ricotta cheese
  1/2 cup sugar
    1 teaspoon vanilla extract
    3 squares (1 ounce *each*) semisweet baking
      chocolate, chopped
  1/2 cup finely chopped toasted almonds
  1/4 cup chopped dried apricots
    1 cup heavy whipping cream, whipped
  1/4 cup slivered almonds, toasted

Combine the wafer crumbs and butter; press onto the bottom and up the sides of an ungreased 9-in. pie plate. Bake at 375° for 6-8 minutes or until the crust is lightly browned; cool.

Spread preserves over crust. In a mixing bowl, beat the ricotta, sugar and vanilla until smooth. Stir in chocolate, chopped almonds and apricots. Fold in whipped cream. Spoon into the crust. Sprinkle with slivered almonds. Cover and refrigerate overnight. **Yield:** 6-8 servings.

coconut-banana cream pie

Tammy Olson, Bruce, South Dakota
After tasting it at a bake sale, I got the recipe for this pie from a friend, then adapted it. I make it for family gatherings—it's everyone's favorite treat—and also for when company comes by.

CRUST:
- 3 **cups flaked coconut**
- 7 **tablespoons butter**

FILLING:
- 3/4 **cup sugar**
- 1/4 **cup all-purpose flour**
- 3 **tablespoons cornstarch**
- 1/4 **teaspoon salt**
- 3 **cups half-and-half cream**
- 4 **egg yolks, lightly beaten**
- 2 **teaspoons vanilla extract**
- 2 **large firm bananas, sliced**

Whipped cream and sliced bananas, optional

In a skillet, saute coconut in butter until golden. Press all but 2 tablespoons into the bottom and up the sides of a greased 9-in. pie plate. Bake at 350° for 7 minutes.

In a saucepan, combine the sugar, flour, cornstarch and salt. Gradually add cream and bring to a boil. Cook and stir over medium-high heat until thickened and bubbly. Reduce heat; cook and stir 2 minutes longer. Remove from the heat; stir a small amount of milk mixture into egg yolks; return all to pan, stirring constantly. Bring to a gentle boil; cook and stir 2 minutes longer.

Remove from the heat, Gently stir in vanilla. Cool to room temperature without stirring. Place bananas in the crust. Cover with cream mixture. Chill until set, about 2 hours.

Sprinkle with reserved coconut. If desired, garnish with whipped cream and bananas. **Yield:** 6-8 servings.

apple cranberry pie

Janet Morgan-Cavallaro, Pincourt, Quebec
Although it's my husband who's the cook at our house, I enjoy baking. A good friend passed along this recipe to me. The pie was an instant hit, and I've been giving the recipe to other friends ever since.

- 2 **cups fresh *or* frozen cranberries**
- 1-3/4 **cups sugar**
- 1/3 **cup quick-cooking tapioca**
- 1/4 **cup water**
- 2 **teaspoons grated orange peel**
- 3 **cups sliced peeled baking apples**

Pastry for double-crust pie (9 inches)
- 1 **egg white, beaten**
- 1 **tablespoon water**

Additional sugar

In a saucepan, combine the cranberries, sugar, tapioca, water and orange peel. Bring to a boil, stirring occasionally. Remove from the heat and stir in apples. Set saucepan in a pan of cold water for 10 minutes, stirring occasionally.

Meanwhile, line pie plate with the bottom pastry. Pour filling into crust. Top with remaining pastry or a lattice crust. If using a full top crust, cut a few slits in it. Beat egg white and water until foamy; brush over top pastry. Sprinkle with sugar.

Bake at 375° for 45-55 minutes or until crust is golden brown and filling is bubbly. Cool completely. **Yield:** 6-8 servings.

german chocolate pie

Cheryl Jacobson, Chino Valley, Arizona
I'm known among family and friends for my desserts. This one is their most request. It's been a sweet standby of mine for more than 20 years now.

        1 package (4 ounces) German sweet chocolate
    1/4 cup butter
        1 can (12 ounces) evaporated milk
1-1/2 cups sugar
        3 tablespoons cornstarch
    1/8 teaspoon salt
        2 eggs, lightly beaten
        1 teaspoon vanilla extract
        1 unbaked deep-dish pastry shell (9 inches)
    1/2 cup chopped pecans
1-1/3 cups flaked coconut

In a saucepan, melt chocolate and butter over low heat, stirring to mix well. Remove from the heat and gradually blend in milk; set aside.

In a bowl, combine the sugar, cornstarch and salt. Stir in eggs and vanilla. Gradually stir in the chocolate mixture. Pour into pastry shell. Combine pecans and coconut; sprinkle over filling.

Bake at 375° for 45-50 minutes or until puffed and browned. Cool 4 hours. Chill (filling will become firm as it cools). **Yield:** 6-8 servings.

very raspberry pie

Kathy Jones, West Winfield, New York
We live along a 130-year-old railroad track (our house once was a train station) that is edged a couple weeks a year with wild raspberries that I pick for my pie.

RASPBERRY TOPPING:
        6 cups fresh raspberries, *divided*
        1 cup sugar
        3 tablespoons cornstarch
    1/2 cup water
CREAM FILLING:
        1 package (8 ounces) cream cheese, softened
        1 cup whipped topping
        1 cup confectioners' sugar
        1 graham cracker crust (9 inches)
Fresh mint, optional

Mash about 2 cups raspberries to measure 1 cup; place in a saucepan. Add sugar, cornstarch and water.

Bring to a boil, stirring constantly; cook and stir 2 minutes longer. Strain to remove berry seeds if desired. Cool to room temperature, about 20 minutes.

Meanwhile, for filling, beat cream cheese, whipped topping and confectioners' sugar in a mixing bowl. Spread in bottom of crust.

Top with remaining raspberries. Pour cooled raspberry sauce over top. Refrigerate until set, about 3 hours. Store in the refrigerator. Garnish with mint if desired. **Yield:** 6-8 servings.

old-fashioned custard pie

Maxine Linkenauger, Montverde, Florida
*This recipe came from the best cook in West Virginia—
my mother! I just added a little to her ingredients. I'm a
widow, and my grown children live in another state.
So mostly I make my custard pie for church and
club functions. It's the most different pie of all the ones
in my collection.*

Pastry for single- *or* double-crust pie (9 inches)
    4 eggs
2-1/2 cups milk
  1/2 cup sugar
    1 teaspoon vanilla extract
    1 teaspoon almond extract
  1/2 teaspoon salt
    1 teaspoon ground nutmeg

Line pie plate with bottom pastry; flute edges or prepare a braided crust (see Editor's Note). Bake at 400° for 10 minutes.

Meanwhile, beat the eggs in a large bowl. Add the remaining ingredients; mix well. Pour into crust. Cover the edges with foil.

Bake for 20-25 minutes or until a knife inserted near the center comes out clean. Cool completely. Store in the refrigerator. **Yield:** 6-8 servings.

Editor's Note: Pastry for a double crust is needed only if a braided crust is desired. To prepare braided crust: Trim pastry even with the edge of the pie plate; brush with water. From the top pastry, cut 12 strips, each 1/4 in. thick. Using three strips at a time, braid pastry on edge of crust, attaching ends together. Press down gently. Bake as directed.

cream puff pie

Holly Camozzi, Rohnert Park, California
*When I was a girl, my mother, sister and I made mini
cream puffs. Instead of making several small cream puffs,
I make one big pie for big appetites!*

CRUST:
  1/2 cup water
  1/4 cup butter
  1/2 teaspoon salt
  1/2 cup all-purpose flour
    2 eggs
FILLING:
  3/4 cup sugar
  1/3 cup all-purpose flour
  1/8 teaspoon salt
    2 eggs, lightly beaten
    2 cups milk
    1 teaspoon vanilla extract
    2 cups whipped cream, *divided*
Chocolate sauce *and/or* fresh raspberries, optional

In a large saucepan, bring water, butter and salt to a boil. Add flour all at once and stir until a smooth ball forms. Remove from the heat; let stand for 5 minutes. Add eggs, one at a time beating, well after each addition. Continue beating until the mixture is smooth and shiny.

Spread onto the bottom and halfway up the sides of a well-greased 9-in. pie plate. Bake at 400° for 35-40 minutes. Cool completely.

For filling, in a saucepan, combine sugar, flour and salt. Stir in milk until smooth. Cook and stir over medium-high heat until thickened and bubbly. Reduce heat, cook and stir 2 minutes more. Remove from the heat. Stir a small amount into eggs; return all to a saucepan, stirring constantly. Bring to a gentle boil. Cook and stir 2 minutes longer. Stir in vanilla. Cool. Fold in 1 cup of whipped cream. Pour into the crust. Top with remaining whipped cream. Chill for 2 hours. Garnish with chocolate sauce and/or raspberries if desired. **Yield:** 6-8 servings.

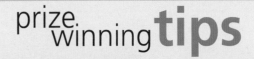

* To prevent your pie shell from shrinking as it bakes, put rolled pastry in a pie plate, then place an empty pie plate inside it. Bake 10 minutes. Remove the empty plate; continue baking until crust is golden.

Narcie Stahr, Laurelville, Ohio

* To decorate your pumpkin pie, roll out leftover pastry, use a knife or cookie cutter to cut out shapes. Brush cutouts with beaten egg or milk and sprinkle with cinnamon-sugar. Bake them on a baking sheet until golden; cool on a wire rack. Put shapes on pie as soon as it comes out of the oven.

Jeanne Smith, St. Stephen, New Brunswick

* Soggy crusts in fruit pies a problem? Try sprinkling the bottom crust with sugar before adding fruit fillings.

Susan Elliott, Bancroft, Ontario

* To cut a meringue pie neatly, dip a sharp knife into water; shake off excess drops. Cut a piece, then repeat the process.

Dolores Skrout, Summerhill, Pennsylvania

* I make cutouts for the top of my pies using cookie cutters and leftover pastry.

Jeanne Smith, St. Stephen, New Brunswick

* Use a plastic bowl rather than a glass one when mixing pie crust. The dough won't stick to the bowl and is much easier to handle.

Gill Morin, Methuen, Massachusetts

* When making a two crust pie, I brush a little water around the edge of my bottom crust before putting on the top crust. This creates a good seal once the two are crimped together. I never have any filling bubbling out between the crusts, ruining my pie's appearance.

Vistola Evans, West Point, Virginia

* When I make a peach pie, I squeeze half of a freshly cut orange over the filling. Eating a piece of this pie makes me feel like I'm standing in an orchard eating a peach just off the tree.

Marie Gonsalves, Sebastopol, California

* For an apple pie with a mouth-watering caramel apple taste, drizzle maple syrup over the apples before putting on the top crust.

Darlene Markel, Sublimity, Ohio

rhubarb meringue pie

Nancy Koopmann, Farley, Iowa
Each year, we grow quite a bit of rhubarb...so the main ingredient when I make this pie is homegrown! It's my favorite rhubarb dessert come spring.

- 3 **tablespoons butter**
- 3 **cups diced fresh *or* frozen rhubarb**
- 2 **cups sugar, *divided***
- 3 **tablespoons cornstarch**
- 1/4 **teaspoon salt**
- 1/2 **cup half-and-half cream**
- 3 **egg yolks, beaten**
- 1 **pastry shell (9 inches), baked**

MERINGUE:
- 3 **egg whites**
- 1/2 **teaspoon vanilla extract**
- 1/4 **teaspoon cream of tartar**
- 6 **tablespoons sugar**

In a saucepan, melt butter. Add rhubarb and 1-1/2 cups sugar; cook over medium heat until rhubarb is tender, about 10 minutes.

In a bowl, combine the cornstarch, salt and remaining sugar. Stir in cream until smooth. Stir into rhubarb mixture. Cook and stir over medium-high heat until thickened and bubbly. Reduce heat; cook and stir 2 minutes longer. Remove from the heat. Stir a small amount of hot filling into egg yolks; return all to pan, stirring constantly. Bring to a gentle boil; cook and stir 2 minutes longer. Remove from the heat. Pour into pastry shell.

For meringue, beat egg whites until foamy; add vanilla and cream of tartar. Gradually add sugar, beating until stiff peaks form. Immediately spread over pie, sealing to the edge of the pastry.

Bake at 350° for 12-15 minutes or until meringue is golden brown. Cool completely. Store in the refrigerator. **Yield:** 6-8 servings.

lemon sour cream pie

Nancy Beran, St. Peter, Minnesota
One bite and people marvel over this pie. Some even say it reminds them of cheesecake. The recipe was shared by a friend; now, I'm glad to do the same.

- 1 **cup sugar**
- 1/4 **cup cornstarch**
- 1/8 **teaspoon salt**
- 1 **cup milk**
- 3 **egg yolks, beaten**
- 1/4 **cup butter**
- 1/4 **cup fresh lemon juice**
- 1 **teaspoon grated lemon peel**
- 1 **cup (8 ounces) sour cream**
- 1 **pastry shell (9 inches), baked**

MERINGUE:
- 3 **egg whites**
- 1/2 **teaspoon vanilla extract**
- 1/4 **teaspoon cream of tartar**
- 6 **tablespoons sugar**

Lemon peel strips, optional

In a saucepan, combine the sugar, cornstarch and salt. Gradually stir in the milk until smooth. Bring to a boil over medium heat, stirring constantly. Cook and stir for 2 minutes.

Remove from the heat. Stir a small amount of hot filling into egg yolks; return all to the pan, stirring constantly. Bring to a gentle boil; cook and stir for 2 minutes. Remove from the heat; stir in butter, lemon juice and peel. Set aside.

For meringue, beat egg whites, vanilla and cream of tartar until soft peaks form. Add sugar, 1 tablespoon at a time, beating until stiff peaks form; set aside. Fold sour cream into the lemon mixture; pour into pastry shell. Cover with meringue, sealing to edges of pastry.

Bake at 350° for 12-15 minutes or until golden. Garnish with lemon peel strips if desired. Cool completely. Store in the refrigerator. **Yield:** 6-8 servings.

pumpkin pecan pie

Jean Lockwood, Bayfield, Colorado
I've yet to meet a person who doesn't have room for a piece of this dessert! Up here 8,000 feet in the Rockies, my husband and I enjoy retirement. We're active in our little church (where I try all my recipes on people who love to eat!).

    2 eggs
1/4 cup sugar
1/4 cup packed brown sugar
    1 teaspoon all-purpose flour
    1 teaspoon pumpkin pie spice
1/4 teaspoon salt
2/3 cup cooked pumpkin
2/3 cup milk
    1 unbaked deep-dish pastry shell (9 inches)
PECAN TOPPING:
    2 eggs
1/2 cup dark corn syrup
    2 tablespoons brown sugar
    2 tablespoons molasses
    1 tablespoon all-purpose flour
    1 teaspoon vanilla extract
1/2 teaspoon salt
1/2 cup chopped pecans
    1 cup pecan halves

In a mixing bowl, beat eggs, sugars, flour, pie spice and salt until smooth. Mix in pumpkin. Gradually beat in milk. Pour into pastry shell.

Bake at 425° for 10 minutes. Reduce the temperature to 350° and bake 15 minutes longer.

For pecan topping, beat eggs in a mixing bowl until foamy. Add corn syrup, brown sugar, molasses, flour, vanilla and salt. Pour over filling. Sprinkle with chopped pecans; cover with pecan halves.

Bake at 350° for 30-35 minutes or until set. Cool completely. Store in refrigerator. **Yield:** 6-8 servings.

peach blueberry pie

Sue Thumma, Shepherd, Michigan
"Boy…I never thought of putting these two ingredients together. What a flavor!" That's what I hear most often after folks try this pie that I invented one day when I was short of peaches for a full crust. As a family, we—my husband, our two boys and I—enjoy the fruity treat often.

    1 cup sugar
1/3 cup all-purpose flour
1/2 teaspoon ground cinnamon
1/8 teaspoon ground allspice
    3 cups sliced peeled fresh peaches
    1 cup fresh blueberries
    1 tablespoon butter
Pastry for double-crust pie (9 inches)
Milk
Cinnamon-sugar

In a bowl, combine the sugar, flour, cinnamon and allspice. Add the peaches and blueberries; toss gently.

Line pie plate with bottom crust; add the filling. Dot with butter. Top with a lattice crust. Brush crust with milk; sprinkle with cinnamon-sugar.

Bake at 400° for 40-45 minutes or until crust is golden brown and filling is bubbly. Cool completely. **Yield:** 6-8 servings.

Editor's Note: Frozen fruit may be used if it is thawed and well drained.

CARROT LAYER CAKE

carrot layer cake

Everyone has heard the expression "a piece of cake" used to describe an assignment that's easily accomplished. That catchy phrase was definitely not uttered during our Take the Cake contest!

Consider the challenge of baking dozens of different cakes in a single

> "The pecan filling is an unexpected treat that makes a lasting impression..."

day. Then ponder the daunting—if delicious—duty that faced our panel of judges, sampling all those tempting layer cakes, sheet cakes, bundt cakes, pound cakes, filled cakes and cupcakes...and eventually having to decide on a single favorite.

When the flour dust finally settled, the Grand Prize was awarded to Linda Van Holland of Innisfail, Alberta for her delightfully different Carrot Layer Cake.

"When people cut into my cake, they are pleasantly surprised," says Linda. "The pecan filling is an unexpected treat that makes a lasting impression on taste buds."

FILLING:
- 1 cup sugar
- 2 tablespoons all-purpose flour
- 1/4 teaspoon salt
- 1 cup heavy whipping cream
- 1/2 cup butter
- 1 cup chopped pecans
- 1 teaspoon vanilla extract

CAKE:
- 1-1/4 cups vegetable oil
- 2 cups sugar
- 2 cups all-purpose flour
- 2 teaspoons ground cinnamon
- 2 teaspoons baking powder
- 1 teaspoon baking soda
- 1 teaspoon salt
- 4 eggs
- 4 cups finely shredded carrots
- 1 cup raisins
- 1 cup chopped pecans

FROSTING:
- 3/4 cup butter, softened
- 2 packages (3 ounces *each*) cream cheese, softened
- 1 teaspoon vanilla extract
- 3 cups confectioners' sugar

In a heavy saucepan, combine sugar, flour and salt. Stir in cream; add butter. Cook and stir over medium heat until the butter is melted; bring to a boil. Reduce heat. Simmer, uncovered, for 30 minutes, stirring occasionally. Stir in nuts and vanilla. Set aside to cool.

In a mixing bowl, beat oil and sugar for 1 minute. Combine flour, cinnamon, baking powder, baking soda and salt; add to the creamed mixture alternately with eggs. Mix well. Stir in carrots, raisins and nuts. Pour into three greased and floured 9-in. round baking pans. Bake at 350° for 35-40 minutes or until a toothpick inserted near the center comes out clean. Cool in pans 10 minutes; remove to wire racks and cool completely.

For frosting, beat butter, cream cheese and vanilla until smooth. Gradually beat in sugar. Spread filling between cake layers. Frost sides and top of cake. Store in the refrigerator. **Yield:** 16-20 servings.

peanut butter chocolate cake

Dorcas Yoder, Weyers Cave, Virginia
In our chocolate-loving house, this snack cake disappears very quickly!

    2 cups all-purpose flour
    2 cups sugar
  2/3 cup baking cocoa
    2 teaspoons baking soda
    1 teaspoon baking powder
  1/2 teaspoon salt
    2 eggs
    1 cup milk
  2/3 cup vegetable oil
    1 teaspoon vanilla extract
    1 cup brewed coffee, room temperature
PEANUT BUTTER FROSTING:
    1 package (3 ounces) cream cheese, softened
  1/4 cup creamy peanut butter
    2 cups confectioners' sugar
    2 tablespoons milk
  1/2 teaspoon vanilla extract
Miniature semisweet chocolate chips, optional

In a mixing bowl, combine dry ingredients. Add eggs, milk, oil and vanilla; beat for 2 minutes. Stir in coffee (batter will be thin). Pour into a greased 13-in. x 9-in. x 2-in. baking pan. Bake at 350° for 35-40 minutes or until a toothpick inserted near the center comes out clean. Cool completely on a wire rack.

For frosting, beat cream cheese and peanut butter in a mixing bowl until smooth. Beat in sugar, milk and vanilla. Spread over cake. Sprinkle with chocolate chips if desired. Store in the refrigerator. **Yield:** 12-16 servings.

pumpkin pecan cake

Joyce Platfoot, Wapakoneta, Ohio
I'm a full-time wife and mother who enjoys baking. This cake is a favorite.

    2 cups crushed vanilla wafers (about 50)
    1 cup chopped pecans
  3/4 cup butter, softened
CAKE:
    1 package (18-1/4 ounces) spice cake mix
    1 can (16 ounces) solid-pack pumpkin
  1/4 cup butter, softened
    4 eggs
FILLING/TOPPING:
  2/3 cup butter, softened
    1 package (3 ounces) cream cheese, softened
    3 cups confectioners' sugar
    2 teaspoons vanilla extract
  1/2 cup caramel ice cream topping
Pecan halves

In a mixing bowl on medium speed, beat the wafers, pecans and butter until crumbly, about 1 minute. Press into three greased and floured 9-in. round baking pans.

In another mixing bowl, beat cake mix, pumpkin, butter and eggs for 3 minutes. Spread over crust in each pan. Bake at 350° for 30 minutes or until a toothpick inserted near center comes out clean. Cool in pans 10 minutes; remove to wire racks and cool completely.

For filling, combine butter and cream cheese in a small mixing bowl. Add sugar and vanilla; beat on medium until light and fluffy, about 3 minutes. Thinly spread between layers (crumb side down) and on the sides of cake. Spread caramel topping over top of cake, allowing some to drip down the sides. Garnish with pecans. Store in the refrigerator. **Yield:** 16-20 servings.

cranberry-orange pound cake

Sheree Swistun, Winnipeg, Manitoba
This pretty pound cake is a favorite at the summer resort my husband and I operate.

1-1/2 cups butter, softened
2-3/4 cups sugar
    6 eggs
    1 teaspoon vanilla extract
2-1/2 teaspoons grated orange peel
    3 cups all-purpose flour
    1 teaspoon baking powder
  1/2 teaspoon salt
    1 cup (8 ounces) sour cream
1-1/2 cups chopped fresh *or* frozen cranberries
VANILLA BUTTER SAUCE:
    1 cup sugar
    1 tablespoon all-purpose flour
  1/2 cup half-and-half cream
  1/2 cup butter, softened
  1/2 teaspoon vanilla extract

In a mixing bowl, cream butter. Gradually beat in sugar until light and fluffy, about 5-7 minutes. Add eggs, one at a time, beating well after each addition. Stir in vanilla and orange peel. Combine flour, baking powder and salt; add to the creamed mixture alternately with sour cream. Beat on low just until blended. Fold in cranberries. Pour into a greased and floured 10-in. fluted tube pan. Bake at 350° for 65-70 minutes or until a toothpick inserted near the center comes out clean. Cool in pan for 10 minutes; remove to a wire rack and cool completely.

In a small saucepan, combine sugar and flour. Stir in cream and butter; bring to a boil over medium heat, stirring constantly. Boil for 2 minutes. Remove from the heat and stir in vanilla. Serve warm over cake. **Yield:** 16 servings (1-1/2 cups sauce).

sunflower potluck cake

Lola Wiemer, Clarklake, Michigan
I wish I knew who to thank for the idea for my cake. I first saw it on the dessert table at a picnic. Later, for something different, I did my own variation.

  3/4 cup butter, softened
1-2/3 cups sugar
    3 eggs
    1 teaspoon vanilla extract
    2 cups all-purpose flour
  2/3 cup baking cocoa
1-1/4 teaspoons baking soda
    1 teaspoon salt
  1/4 teaspoon baking powder
1-1/3 cups water
    1 cup prepared chocolate frosting, *divided*
    1 cup (6 ounces) semisweet chocolate chips
   22 cream-filled sponge cakes
    1 teaspoon milk

In a mixing bowl, cream butter and sugar. Add eggs, one at a time, beating well after each addition. Add vanilla. Combine dry ingredients; add to the creamed mixture alternately with water. Pour into two greased and floured 9-in. round baking pans. Bake at 350° for 25-30 minutes or until a toothpick inserted near the center comes out clean. Cool in pans for 10 minutes; remove to wire racks and cool completely. Freeze one layer for future use.

Set aside 1 tablespoon frosting. Frost top and sides of remaining cake. Place cake in the center of a large round tray (about 18 in.). Arrange chocolate chips on top of cake. Place sponge cakes around cake. Mix reserved frosting with milk; drizzle over sponge cakes. **Yield:** 22 servings.

pumpkin cake
with caramel sauce

Roberta Peck, Fort Hill, Pennsylvania
If a recipe has pumpkin in it, it's likely I'll enjoy it! This one resulted when I added my favorite key ingredient to an old recipe for spice cake that I had.

     2 cups all-purpose flour
     2 cups sugar
     2 teaspoons baking soda
     2 teaspoons ground cinnamon
     1 teaspoon ground nutmeg
   1/2 teaspoon salt
     4 eggs
     1 can (16 ounces) solid-pack pumpkin
     1 cup vegetable oil
CARAMEL SAUCE:
1-1/2 cups packed brown sugar
     3 tablespoons all-purpose flour
Pinch salt
1-1/4 cups water
     2 tablespoons butter
   1/2 teaspoon vanilla extract

In a mixing bowl, combine the first six ingredients. In another bowl, beat eggs, pumpkin and oil until smooth; add to the dry ingredients. Mix until well blended, about 1 minute. Pour into a greased 13-in. x 9-in. x 2-in. baking pan. Bake at 350° for 35-40 minutes or until a toothpick inserted near the center comes out clean. Cool on a wire rack.

For sauce, combine brown sugar, flour and salt in a saucepan. Stir in water and butter; bring to a boil over medium heat. Boil for 3 minutes, stirring constantly. Remove from the heat; stir in vanilla. Cut cake into squares and serve with warm sauce. **Yield:** 12-15 servings.

chocolate sheet cake

Dianne Medwid, Dauphin, Manitoba
My son frequently requested this chocolaty cake for his birthday when he was growing up.

     2 cups sugar
     2 cups all-purpose flour
     1 teaspoon baking soda
   1/2 teaspoon salt
   1/2 cup butter
   1/4 cup baking cocoa
     1 cup water
     2 eggs
   1/2 cup buttermilk
     1 teaspoon vanilla extract
ICING:
   1/2 cup butter
   1/4 cup baking cocoa
   1/3 cup milk
     2 cups confectioners' sugar
     1 teaspoon vanilla extract
     1 cup chopped walnuts

In a mixing bowl, combine the first four ingredients; set aside. In a small saucepan, bring butter, cocoa and water to a boil. Add to dry ingredients and mix well. In a small mixing bowl, beat eggs. Add buttermilk and vanilla; mix well. Stir into cocoa mixture. Pour into a greased 15-in. x 10-in. x 1-in. baking pan. Bake at 375° for 20-22 minutes or until a toothpick inserted near the center comes out clean.

Meanwhile, in a saucepan, bring butter, cocoa and milk to a boil, stirring constantly. Remove from the heat; add sugar and vanilla. Mix well. Spread over hot cake; immediately sprinkle with nuts. Cool completely on a wire rack. **Yield:** 16-20 servings.

lemon meringue cake

Debra Blair, Glenwood, Minnesota
*My husband likes lemon meringue pie, so I figured
this would appeal to him. It's become his favorite cake.*

1/4 cup butter, softened
1/2 cup sugar
1 egg plus 2 egg yolks
1 cup all-purpose flour
1 teaspoon baking powder
1/3 cup milk
1/2 teaspoon vanilla extract

FILLING:
2 egg yolks
1 cup water
3/4 cup sugar
1/3 cup all-purpose flour
1/2 teaspoon grated lemon peel
1/4 cup fresh lemon juice
1 tablespoon butter

MERINGUE:
4 egg whites, room temperature
1/2 teaspoon cream of tartar
1/2 cup sugar

In a mixing bowl, cream butter and sugar. Add egg and yolks; mix well. Combine flour and baking powder; add to creamed mixture alternately with milk. Mix well. Add vanilla. Pour into a greased and floured 9-in. round baking pan. Bake at 350° for 25-30 minutes or until a toothpick inserted near the center comes out clean. Cool in pan 10 minutes; remove to a wire rack and cool completely.

In a heavy saucepan, combine egg yolks, water, sugar, flour and peel; bring to a gentle boil over medium heat, stirring constantly. Cook and stir for 2-3 minutes or until thickened. Stir in lemon juice and butter.

Place cake on a baking sheet; spoon filling on top of cake up to 1/2 in. from the edge. Beat egg whites until foamy. Add cream of tartar; beat on high for 1 minute. Add sugar, 1 tablespoon at a time, beating well after each addition. Beat until stiff peaks form, about 3 minutes. Carefully spread over filling, sealing to edges of cake. Bake at 350° for 12-15 minutes or until lightly browned. **Yield:** 6-8 servings.

---

prize winning tips

*****

*With my from-scratch recipe for angel food cake, I often add part of a package of my favorite Jell-O® flavor to the flour before it goes into the egg whites. It lends nice flavor and a pretty color.

Mrs. Mervin Eash, Burr Oak, Michigan

*What could be easier? I bake my lemon pound cake ahead and freeze it for last-minute get-togethers and family gatherings. To serve, I just thaw it and top with fresh fruit, ice cream or a dessert sauce.

Barbara Wellons, Charlotte, Tennessee

buttermilk banana cake

Arlene Grenz, Linton, North Dakota
When I was a girl, this was my family's favorite Sunday cake. Since I'm "nuts" about nuts, I added the pecans.

> 3/4 cup butter, softened
> 1 cup sugar
> 1/2 cup packed brown sugar
> 2 eggs
> 1 cup mashed ripe banana
> 1 teaspoon vanilla extract
> 2 cups cake flour
> 1 teaspoon *each* baking powder and soda
> 1/2 teaspoon salt
> 1/2 cup buttermilk

FILLING/FROSTING:

> 1/2 cup half-and-half cream
> 1/2 cup sugar
> 2 tablespoons butter
> 2 tablespoons all-purpose flour
> 1/4 teaspoon salt
> 1 teaspoon vanilla extract
> 1/2 cup chopped pecans
> 2 cups heavy whipping cream
> 1/4 cup confectioners' sugar

In a mixing bowl, cream butter and sugars until fluffy. Add eggs; beat for 2 minutes. Add banana and vanilla; beat for 2 minutes. Combine the flour, baking powder, baking soda and salt; add to creamed mixture alternately with buttermilk. Pour into two greased and floured 9-in. round baking pans. Bake at 375° for 25-30 minutes or until a toothpick inserted near the center comes out clean. Cool in pans 10 minutes; remove to wire racks and cool completely.

For filling, combine half-and-half, sugar, butter, flour and salt in a saucepan. Bring to a boil; cook and stir for 2 minutes. Remove from the heat; stir in vanilla and pecans. Cool. Spread between cake layers.

For frosting, beat whipping cream until soft peaks form. Gradually beat in the confectioners' sugar; beat until stiff peaks form. Spread over top and sides of cake. Store in the refrigerator. **Yield:** 12-16 servings.

mocha cupcakes

Lorna Smith, New Hazelton, British Columbia
This recipe is one that I have called on over the years for numerous occasions—birthdays, PTA meetings, for serving to company, etc. Everyone likes it.

> 1 cup boiling water
> 1 cup mayonnaise
> 1 teaspoon vanilla extract
> 2 cups all-purpose flour
> 1 cup sugar
> 1/2 cup baking cocoa
> 2 teaspoons baking soda

MOCHA FROSTING:

> 3/4 cup confectioners' sugar
> 1/4 cup baking cocoa
> 1/2 to 1 teaspoon instant coffee granules

Pinch salt

> 1-1/2 cups heavy whipping cream

In a mixing bowl, combine water, mayonnaise and vanilla. Combine flour, sugar, cocoa and baking soda; add to the mayonnaise mixture and beat until well mixed.

Fill greased or paper-lined muffin cups two-thirds full. Bake at 350° for 20-25 minutes or until a toothpick inserted near the center comes out clean. Cool in tins 10 minutes; remove to wire racks and cool completely.

Combine the first four frosting ingredients in a mixing bowl. Stir in cream; cover and chill with beaters for 30 minutes. Beat frosting until stiff peaks form. Frost the cupcakes. **Yield:** about 1-1/2 dozen.

Editor's Note: Do not substitute reduced-fat or fat-free mayonnaise for regular mayonnaise in this recipe.

caramel apple cake

Paulette Reyenga, Brantford, Ontario
A wonderful harvest of apples that we picked up at a local orchard one year inspired me to adjust a recipe I'd seen and come up with this moist cake.

- 1/2 cup chopped walnuts
- 1/3 cup packed brown sugar
- 1 cup flaked coconut
- 2-1/2 cups all-purpose flour
- 1-1/2 cups sugar
- 1-1/2 teaspoons baking soda
- 1 teaspoon salt
- 1/2 teaspoon baking powder
- 1/4 teaspoon ground cinnamon
- 2 eggs
- 1/2 cup evaporated milk
- 1/3 cup water
- 2 cups finely shredded peeled apples

CARAMEL TOPPING:
- 1/3 cup packed brown sugar
- 1/4 cup evaporated milk
- 2 tablespoons butter

Combine walnuts, brown sugar and coconut; set aside. In a mixing bowl, combine the next six ingredients. In a small bowl, combine eggs, milk, water and apples; add to flour mixture. Mix well. Pour into a greased 13-in. x 9-in. x 2-in. baking pan. Sprinkle with nut mixture. Bake at 325° for 45-50 minutes or until a toothpick inserted near the center comes out clean.

Meanwhile, in a heavy saucepan, combine the topping ingredients; cook over medium heat, stirring constantly, until the sugar is dissolved and the mixture has thickened slightly, about 8 minutes. Poke holes with a fork in top of the hot cake; immediately spoon topping over cake. Cool completely on a wire rack. **Yield:** 12-15 servings.

chocolate chiffon cake

Dorothy Haag, Mt. Horeb, Wisconsin
There were 11 of us to cook for when I was young. This was a recipe that my mother had. If there were cracked eggs from the laying hens she kept, it was always a good way of using them up! Like my parents, my husband and I have nine children, all of them grown.

- 2/3 cup baking cocoa
- 3/4 cup hot water
- 1-1/2 cups cake flour
- 1-3/4 cups sugar
- 1 teaspoon baking soda
- 1 teaspoon salt
- 1/2 cup vegetable oil
- 7 eggs, *separated*
- 1 teaspoon vanilla extract
- 1/2 teaspoon cream of tartar
- Confectioners' sugar

In a small bowl, stir cocoa and water until smooth; cool. In a large bowl, combine flour, sugar, baking soda and salt. Add oil, egg yolks, vanilla and cocoa mixture; stir until smooth. In a mixing bowl, beat the egg whites until foamy. Add cream of tartar; beat until stiff peaks form. Gradually fold in egg yolk mixture. Pour into an ungreased 10-in. tube pan.

Bake on lowest rack at 325° for 60-65 minutes or until the top springs back when lightly touched and cracks feel dry. Immediately invert pan on a bottle; cool completely. Loosen sides of cake from pan and remove. Dust with confectioners' sugar. **Yield:** 12-16 servings.

General Recipe Index

Alphabetical Recipe Index